Confronting the Occupation

Confronting the Occupation

Work, Education, and Political Activism of Palestinian Families in a Refugee Camp

MAYA ROSENFELD

Stanford University Press
Stanford, California
2004

Stanford University Press
Stanford, California

© 2004 by the Board of Trustees of the
Leland Stanford Junior University.
All rights reserved.

Printed in the United States of America
on acid-free, archival-quality paper

Library of Congress Cataloging-in-Publication Data

Rosenfeld, Maya.
  Confronting the occupation : work, education, and political
activism of Palestinian families in a refugee camp / Maya
Rosenfeld.
      p. cm.
  Presented as the author's Ph. D. thesis, University of California,
Berkeley.
  Includes bibliographical references and index.
  ISBN 0-8047-3751-7 (cloth : alk. paper)—
ISBN 0-8047-4987-6 (pbk. : alk. paper)
  1. Occupations—West Bank—Duhaysheh (Refugee camp)
  2. Education—West Bank—Duhaysheh (Refugee camp)
  3. Palestinian Arabs—West Bank—Duhayshah (Refugee camp)—
Political activity. 4. Palestinian Arabs—West Bank—Duhayshah
(Refugee camp)—Economic conditions. 5. Palestinian Arabs—
West Bank—Duhayshah (Refugee camp)—Social conditions.
I. Title.
  HF5382.5.W47C46 2004
  956.95'2—dc22   2003024658

Original Printing 2004
Last figure below indicates year of this printing:

13   12   11   10   09   08   07   06   05   04

Designed by Rob Ehle
Typeset by Classic Typography in 10.5/12 Bembo

For my parents, Shulamit Carmi and Henry Rosenfeld, who taught me to believe in socialism and international solidarity.

For the people of Dheisheh, whose steadfastness and struggle have been and continue to be a source of inspiration and hope.

"Men make their own history, but they do not do it as they please; they do not make it under self-selected circumstances, but under circumstances existing already, given and transmitted from the past."
—Karl Marx

Contents

14 pages of photographs follow page 166

MY PERSONAL ACQUAINTANCE with the people of Dheisheh camp began in the summer of 1987, nearly four decades after the inception of their refugee existence, and some twenty years into their experience under Israeli military occupation. Three distinct social generations were apparent in the camp at the time. Members of the older generation were born, raised, and spent part of their adult lives in dozens of villages that then existed in central Palestine. They were uprooted from their homes, lands, and peasant livelihood in the course of the 1948 war and, following long months of wandering, ended up in Dheisheh camp—a mere twenty-five kilometers from their destroyed villages of origin. The children born to them in the 1940s and early 1950s were brought up in the wretchedness of the early years of refugee reality, but nonetheless, were first in their families to acquire formal education in the schools set up by the United Nations Relief and Works Agency for Palestine Refugees in the Near East (UNRWA). This second, or intermediate, generation, came of age under Jordanian rule, against the backdrop of mounting radical Arab nationalism, a nascent Palestinian resistance, and later, the Arab defeat in the 1967 war. Men and women that were born in the camp between the late 1950s and the early 1970s to parents who by then had become day wage laborers, formed the third, or younger refugee, generation, the one that matured into the era of Israeli military occupation. With their representation in secondary schools, colleges, and universities ever on the increase, and as they faced escalating Israeli repression, many members of this generation were soon to be drawn into the ranks of the Palestinian national movement, by then a fully engaged entity.

Six months after my first encounter with the Dheishehians, I had the opportunity to witness all three generations as they participated in the making of the (first) Intifada, the Palestinian popular uprising that broke out in the Occupied Territories in December 1987. Men and women, old, young and very young, educated and illiterate, trained and inexperienced took to the camp streets and alleys. In line with the goals articulated by the Unified

National Leadership of the Uprising (UNLU), they demanded an end to the Israeli occupation, recognition of the Palestinian Liberation Organization (PLO) as the legitimate representative of the Palestinian people, and self-determination in their independent state. While Dheishehians adhered to unarmed resistance, the Israeli army responded with unprecedented levels of violence. Live ammunition was used against demonstrators leading to the killing and wounding of dozens, and the imprisonment of hundreds of men between the ages of fourteen and forty-five; homes were raided, people beaten and harassed, a curfew regime was imposed, schools were shut down, and all entrances to the camp were blocked.

Dheishehians mobilized all the social resources at their disposal to confront these measures and sustain the Intifada. With sons, brothers, and husbands in prison, and men laid off from their jobs in Israeli construction sites, many women—young and old, day laborers and professionals—became sole providers for entire households that often numbered ten and even fifteen persons. Families of prisoners, the dead, and the wounded formed networks of support and solidarity, popular clinics offered medical care free of charge, and voluntary committees provided emergency services. Indeed, the motto that decorated the biweekly leaflets of the UNLU echoed throughout the camp: "No voice shall rise above the voice of the Intifada."

Yet, as high as their voice rose, and as great as were the commitment and sacrifice, their impact was insufficient. In the wake of waning Arab support for the PLO following the Gulf War, the dismantling of the Soviet Union, and the expanding hegemony of the United States, prospects were grim for converting the achievements of the Intifada into concrete political gains. As one of my oldest friends in Dheisheh repeatedly said at the time (early 1990s), the Intifada created foundations for advancing a political solution but was far short of determining the conditions for its realization.

The limitations and shortcomings of the Declaration of Principles (signed between Israel and the PLO in September 1993) and the interim agreements that followed notwithstanding, after the establishment of the Palestinian National Authority (PNA) in parts of the West Bank and Gaza Strip, Dheisheh gradually entered a new era. Late in 1995 the towns of Bethlehem, Beit Sahour, and Beit Jala, along with the three adjacent refugee camps—Dheisheh, al-ʿAzza, and ʿAida, were incorporated into "zone A," that is, the areas transferred to Palestinian control. A far cry from territorial sovereignty, this implied, nevertheless, that more than twenty-seven years of constant Israeli military presence inside the camp were brought to an end. By the mid-1990s almost all political prisoners from Dheisheh had been released from Israeli jails. A substantial number of them were subsequently recruited into various branches of the Palestinian security and police forces, while others were absorbed in the nascent administration/state sector. Salaries were very low, but employment—a scarce resource in the impoverished economy of the Palestinian territories—was secure. In yet another sphere, expanding opportunities for acquiring postsecondary education enabled more camp youths to attend colleges, universities, and training centers.

While these incremental, positive developments were gaining ground, however, living standards of a significantly large number of family households in Dheisheh—those that for many years had depended on wage work in Israel for a living—continued to deteriorate. Confronted by an ongoing Israeli closure policy that sealed off access to former workplaces inside the green line, and by the absence of alternative employment opportunities in the local labor market, hundreds of laborers were doomed to long-term unemployment. Nor could those laid off without compensation by Israeli employers, or their families, rely on the newly formed Palestinian government agencies for relief provisions. Weakened constantly by the Israeli refusal to proceed with the implementation of the Oslo Accords and redeploy (withdraw) its forces in the West Bank, and itself dependent on the generosity of donors, the PNA was engaged with economic survival rather than with the building of a social welfare system.

Against this background, one salient change that marked the transitional "Oslo years" in Dheisheh was the gradual shift in the form and content of public activism. While Dheisheh remained a highly politicized community, the political organizations and parties that dominated the scene in the 1980s and early 1990s, and that focused primarily on mass mobilization and the education of cadres, slowly gave way to community-oriented institutions that accorded preference to the development of social services and cultural activities. The public figures who initiated and invigorated this shift were, mainly, veteran activists and former leaders of the—now by and large disintegrated—erstwhile influential political structures in the camp and the Bethlehem region. Their reevaluation of the past and search for new directions converged here with the pressing needs of an ever-expanding refugee population, whose expectations for major improvements in social, economic, and political conditions were frustrated.

An embodiment of this emergent tendency is to be found in the Ibdaᶜ (literally, creative ability, originality) Cultural Center, which began operating in Dheisheh in the early 1990s. From a modest recreation center for children it gradually developed into a full-blown institution that runs a complex network of facilities, projects, and activities, including a day care center and kindergarten, a computer center, a folklore dance group, a sports club, language and art courses for children and adults, training programs, and since 2000, a newly built guesthouse, restaurant, and film theater. Through its renowned folklore dance group (also called Ibdaᶜ) the center won local and, eventually, international publicity that enabled it to establish firm connections with a host of foreign institutions, promote fund-raising, and attract volunteers from Europe, North America, and Japan. Indeed, over the last decade Dheisheh became one of the most frequently toured places in the West Bank, a "must site" on the itinerary of delegations and solidarity groups from all over the world.

This same decade had also seen growing concerns among Dheishehians over their refugee status and identity. These were directly fed by the absence of any progress whatsoever in the Israeli-Palestinian negotiations on the refugee issue. While the Madrid Conference that preceded the Oslo process established a specialized multilateral work group for advancing a solution to the Palestinian refugee problem, the Declaration of Principles postponed this fundamental issue to the final-status negotiation stage. Given the Israeli reluctance to proceed with the transfer of territories to the PNA, however, this prospective stage was never embarked upon. Interrelated with the above, and contributing to additional unrest within the camp, were the uncertain future and dwindling resources of UNRWA—thus far the only agency that provided basic social services in the camp, the deteriorating situation of the Palestinian refugee community in Lebanon, and the incitement of successive Israeli governments against the "right of return."

In response to the crisis, community activists from Dheisheh joined local, regional, and across-borders campaigns that were started by camp and noncamp refugees in an attempt to bring their plight and struggle to the forefront of the Palestinian public agenda, and to put pressure on the PLO and the PNA. On the practical level of everyday activism in the camp this led to the establishment of various committees and the organization of conferences alongside less conventional activities such as organized trips of the camp elders to the sites of their destroyed villages, the initiation of oral-history documentation projects, and the establishment of on-line correspondence between Dheisheh youths and their counterparts from refugee camps in Lebanon. While initiatives such as these may have carried an embarrassing political message for the PNA, those who stood behind them were not affiliated with official opposition parties.

In retrospect, the above outlined trends that evolved in the Dheisheh camp of the 1990s may help us reconstruct the circumstances that prevailed there, and to varying extents in other locales in Palestine, at the eve of the second Intifada. Yet none of the developments can be identified as a direct cause leading to its outbreak at the end of September 2000, let alone provide an explanation for the unfolding of the events that took place since. This latter task lies beyond my current undertaking. In what follows I confine myself to a brief comment on this latest confrontation and the impact it has had on the people of Dheisheh.

At the time of writing these lines, Dheishehians, along with more than three million Palestinians in the West Bank and Gaza Strip, are two years into the Intifada. Over this period they have seen more death, destruction, and devastation than was witnessed throughout the decades of Israeli Occupation, including the first uprising (late 1987 through mid-1993). The escalation of Israeli military aggression was already apparent at the very early stage—marked by the mass demonstrations and clashes that took place mainly on the outskirts of Palestinian towns and municipalities, where minuscule zone A (then under Palestinian control) intersected with zones B and C (more than 75 percent of the West Bank—at the time still under Israeli military control). From their shielded posts and armored vehicles, snipers from the Israel Defense Forces (IDF) fired into crowds of Palestinian civilian demonstrators, resulting in the killing of hundreds and wounding of thousands within several weeks. In Dheisheh, Bethlehem, and the adjacent towns, camps, and villages, one funeral procession and memorial ceremony succeeded another, with most victims in their teens and early twenties; local hospitals and clinics operated at several times their regular capacity, and homes of mourning families turned into twenty-four-hour gathering places for the entire community.

None of this, however, prepared them for the ordeal that was yet to come following the aborted Israeli-Palestinian summit at Taba (convened in January 2001, still within the guidelines of what became known as "the Clinton ideas") and the subsequent downfall of Ehud Barak and his government in early February 2001. With Ariel Sharon in power (and George W. Bush in the White House) a full-scale war of destruction was soon to be waged against the PNA—now declared an enemy—targeting the political leadership, government institutions and symbols of national sovereignty, the institutions of civil society, economic activity and agricultural production, physical infrastructure, land and water resources, movement and transportation, in short, the entire population and its livelihood. A whole arsenal of "conventional" weapons of mass destruction, including tanks, attack helicopters, F-16s, guided missiles, and bulldozers were employed in this assault, which—by Sharon's second year in office—culminated in a series of bloody incursions into all Palestinian cities and towns and the subsequent subjection of their residents to martial law.

As the IDF tightened its grip with additional restrictive measures and collective punishments, and more so as one military operation followed another, Dheishehians saw their living space shrinking further and further and their lives becoming increasingly cheaper. At first it was the numerous checkpoints—enforcing the closure policy—that blocked their road to Jerusalem, Ramallah, and Nablus, cutting them off from work, medical treatment, central government institutions, markets, and contacts. Then, as siege (or "encirclement," in the military jargon) was imposed on locales within the Bethlehem district itself, access to local services, public facilities, businesses, as well as to kin and friends in the nearby sealed-off villages and towns became even more difficult. Finally, incursions followed by weeks and then months of reoccupation paralyzed social and economic activity, in fact movement as such, forcing a curfew regime that imprisoned people in their homes and backyards. Curfew was not the gravest of atrocities that the repeated military assaults carried in their wake, however. Neighborhoods were shelled, "curfew breakers"—including children, old people, medical teams, and ambulances—were fired upon, water and sewage infrastructures were smashed, houses demolished, homes and institutions raided, furniture and appliances ruined, valuables stolen.

In the wake of these devastating circumstances, members of the fourth refugee generation—once the children of the first Intifada and teenagers of the Oslo years—are coming of age in Dheisheh. Substantial collective efforts and resources were invested in the education and welfare of these young people, and high expectations and hopes were cultivated around their future. They were destined—so it was believed—to reap the fruits of long years of struggle and endurance. Now, as they confront an attempt to push them backward, to the margins of history, they have little choice but to join hands with their predecessors and continue the fight for freedom. To them, their parents, and grandparents this book is dedicated.

Acknowledgments

THIS BOOK IS THE product of long years and several stages of work, in the course of which I benefited from the assistance, effort, and support of many people and several institutions. I am indebted to the Wenner-Gren Foundation for Anthropological Research for supporting my field research, and to the Ford Foundation and the Harry S. Truman Research Institute for their generous grants. I especially thank Baruch Kimmerling of the Hebrew University of Jerusalem for his ongoing encouragement and friendship.

Conducting research in Dheisheh refugee camp, then under Israeli military occupation, would not have been possible without the cooperation, trust, hospitality, and commitment of numerous individuals, dozens of families, and major community institutions in the camp. The list of those who extended their help is literally in the hundreds, and here I must confine myself: My heartfelt thanks to all.

Isma'il Ramadan and Muhammad Laham, my oldest acquaintances and friends in Dheisheh, introduced me to the multifaceted reality of camp life in the summer of 1987, years before I began to do research there. Both were recently released political prisoners who had spent many years in Israeli jails, both were to be imprisoned again several months later, after the first Intifada broke out. The insightful observations and analyses they shared with me at the time and the warmth and kindness with which they and their families accepted me provided major incentive for my later work.

When I began doing fieldwork in Dheisheh in late spring of 1992, the residence of the Abu-'Aker family became my first "home base." It was from late breakfasts at their house that I would depart for my daily excursions in the camp, and to where I would return in the early evening to recount my adventures over sweet tea. Umm Nidal (Malika), Abu Nidal (Na'im) and their children, who had lost a son/brother in the Intifada less than two years earlier, spared no effort to make me feel welcome, grace that I will always treasure.

In the months and years that followed I alternated many home bases and spent countless hours with Dheishehian families. Many have come to treat me as a family member. The generous hospitality they provided during times of great economic hardship, often dire poverty, and the care and love they conveyed while they faced routine harassment under the Occupation, are beyond repayment. I am particularly grateful to the Abu-Ghalus family, especially Miriam and Ibrahim; the Abu-Laban family, especially Mufida and Youssef, the Laham family, especially Zohra and Muhammad, Umm ʿAdel and Abu ʿAdel; the Hajajra family, especially Yusra; the ʿAtallah family, especially Umm Akram, the al-Seifi family; the Ramadan family, especially Raja and Ismaʿil, Umm ʿAdel, Fatma, Ahlam, ʿAdnan and Muhammad; the ʿAdawi family, and the Shaheen family.

The input on the part of some of the individuals I interviewed over the years, or with whom I discussed ideas, in terms of time invested and willingness to share experiences and thoughts, deserves special notice. I am indebted to (the late) Mahmud al-Khatib (Abu Nabil), Noah Salame, Miriam Abu-Ghalus, Khaled al-Seifi, Ahmad Muhaisen, Saleh Abu-Laban, Nidal Abu-ʿAker, Nasser Laham, ʿAdnan Ramadan, Fatma Jaʿfari, and Yusra Abu-Laban.

Ziyad Farraj, ʿAdel ʿAdawi, Nathem ʿOdeh, and Khaled ʿAtta—at the time either university graduates or students of the social sciences—were my research assistants when I carried out surveys in Dheisheh. I thank them for their dedicated work. I am especially indebted to Ziyad Farraj for his invaluable advice throughout the first stage of my fieldwork and to ʿAdel ʿAdawi for his contribution to my survey on women and employment.

Hussein Shaheen, the Dheisheh camp officer on behalf of UNRWA, helped in facilitating my "entrance to the field" at the early stages of fieldwork, and has always treated me as a most welcome guest at both his office and home. Khaled al-Seifi, the founder and director of Ibdaʿ Cultural Center, followed my work with much enthusiasm and extended his moral support throughout.

I thank Daniel Boyarin of the University of California, Berkeley, for believing in this project and advancing the conversion of my dissertation into book form. I wish to thank Chaia Beckerman for her careful reading and professional editing of the final version of the manuscript.

Finally, no words of gratitude will suffice to express my appreciation for the contribution of my parents, Shulamit Carmi and Henry Rosenfeld. Both have accompanied my work from the initial stages of field research to the final ones, both have incorporated the world of the Dheishehians into their lives, and have read and reread various drafts of the manuscript, always furthering it with their invaluable (but not always easy-to-accept) criticism.

Confronting the Occupation

Introduction

THE 1948 WAR AND its aftermath—which saw Palestinians uprooted from their homes and land, dispersed, and scattered—shattered the social history of individuals and communities alike. In the decades that followed the war, the Palestinians in exile struggled with the ordeals of refugee existence.

The upheaval wrought major transformations in the areas of work, education, and political activism. Prior to 1948 an agrarian complex of kin, land, and community was central to the work lives of most Palestinians. After the 1948 war the majority of Palestinians were refugees or part of minority communities removed from agriculture. Relocated in and around urban settings, they were dependent on wage labor and international relief. In exile, mainly as day wage laborers, and as salaried professionals and semiprofessionals, their work lives became dependent on labor markets, local and distant.

In Mandatory Palestine schooling and standard education were mainly the privilege of limited strata among Palestinians, which were predominantly urban and male. In exile new levels of education—basic and later also secondary and tertiary—characterized many refugee communities. Acquiring education as refugees implied dependence on services and provisions of relief by nongovernmental agencies and heavy reliance on family support. Yet throughout the 1970s and well into the 1980s, the academic accomplishments of second- and third-generation refugees, men and women, surpassed those in all Arab countries and in quite a few Western ones as well.

The reemergence of the Palestinian national movement in the 1960s and the public recognition it gained, especially after the 1973 war, underline a third important change. Entering the Middle East political arena, the movement mobilized Palestinians throughout the Diaspora and Palestine.

In major respects the changes were rapid; the Palestinians who came of age in the 1960s already had "profiles" significantly different from those of their parents. Most had some years of education, some job experience, and some record of participation in the national liberation movement. Yet change, in part dependent on the type of the regime and on the political economies of the "host countries," took place under divergent conditions: varying degrees of military and political repression, social exclusion, and economic marginalization. Incorporation of Palestinians into the manual labor force took place mainly along the margins of national labor markets, which rarely offered steady employment. Academic achievements, skills, and expertise, while without doubt assets to their holders, only slightly benefited the development and well-being of Palestinian communities as such.

Meanwhile, the Palestinian national movement confronted recurring attempts to crush it or subjugate its leadership and political agenda. The military and political power of Israel was backed by the support of the United States; several Arab regimes sought to repress it as well. The incremental political and diplomatic victories that the national movement won over the years were almost overshadowed by the casualties, hardships, and destruction experienced by members of the movement and by Palestinian communities at large. In short, the "grand" sociopolitical transformation incorporated a strong element of survivalist struggle.[1]

Tensions and contradictions inhered in a gradual accumulation of new socioeconomic and political capacities by Palestinian refugees within antagonistic systemic conditions. Thus dissonance confronted me throughout my work with the people of Dheisheh refugee camp. In fact, it was my early acquaintance with the often surprising social gains in the refugee community that pressed me to formulate questions that would later occupy my field research and writing.

Dheisheh Refugee Camp: Progress Despite an Extremely Unequal Power Structure

Located south of Bethlehem on a hilly slope that stretches along the main road connecting Jerusalem and Hebron, densely populated Dheisheh (as of 2002 more than eleven thousand persons lived in an area of one-half a square kilometer) is home to four generations of refugees. It is one of fifty-nine Palestinian refugee camps that exist today in the West Bank, Gaza Strip, Jordan, Lebanon, and Syria, accommodating approximately 1.3 million people, or what amounts to about one-third of the registered refugee population.[2]

Spanning two major wars and four political regimes, the life histories of Dheisheh elders began under the British Mandate that terminated with the 1948 war and their becoming refugees. The annexation of the West Bank to the Hashemite kingdom in 1950 brought them under Jordanian rule, which came to an end in the 1967 war. In the twenty-eight years that followed, these elders and their descendants lived under Israeli military occupation. At the end of 1995, in the wake of the Oslo Accords, they saw the redeployment of the Israeli troops from the camp and subsequently its assignment to "zone A," the region that was transferred to the Palestinian National Authority (PNA) under highly restrictive conditions.

All Dheishehians are of peasant ancestry, originating from more than forty villages located within a fairly small region in central Palestine.[3] All of these villages were destroyed in the course of the 1948 war or shortly after. Uprooted from their homes and lands, the peasants-cum-refugees sought asylum in the villages and towns of the Hebron and Bethlehem region, the southern part of an area that would be known subsequent to the war as the West Bank. Some wandered for months, others for years, before settling in Dheisheh, with several temporary places of residence.[4] Israeli refusal to allow the return of the displaced Palestinians prolonged their refugee status indefinitely.

Through 1949 many settled in camps that were set up by the Red Cross and other charitable and relief societies and which eventually (starting from May 1950) came under the administrative custody of the United Nations Relief and Works Agency for Palestine Refugees in the Near East (UNRWA).[5] Many Dheishehians first arrived at the site of the camp during the spring and summer of 1949, though influx of families that resided temporarily in other camps and locations continued throughout the early 1950s. The camp's population did not stabilize until the second part of that decade.

Dheisheh, then, came into existence as a result of total disintegration of a way of life—the war brought displacement, separating and scattering kin and kin groupings. Loss of village homes, fields, and orchards preceded confinement to a refugee camp that had no agricultural or other economic resources. Individuals and families were now forced to depend on scarce jobs outside the camp and on assistance for food and shelter from UNRWA.

Less than two decades after having restarted their lives in Dheisheh, thousands of Dheishehians, including entire families, fled the camp to the East Bank of Jordan in fear of the outcome of the 1967 war. Israel's subsequent denial of their right to return rendered them refugees for the second time. The Dheishehians who remained entered a new era, that of life under Israeli Occupation.

My first introduction to Dheisheh came in the summer of 1987 on a one-time journalistic assignment. The outbreak of the Intifada in December of the same year brought my return. For several years I continued to visit the camp on a fairly regular basis, as a member of an Israeli protest movement and of a human rights organization, and by this time as a personal friend of not a few Dheishehians. It was only in the spring of 1992 that I returned to Dheisheh to do field research for a doctoral dissertation in the department of sociology and anthropology at the Hebrew University, an engagement that lasted through early 1996.

My recollections of early (pre-research) visits to Dheisheh are infused with impressions of the physical environment and living conditions. What was immediately evident was the absence of basic infrastructure in the camp. There was not a single decent road; the streets, mostly unpaved, had no sidewalks or streetlights and came right up to the walls of the houses on either side. Sewage flowed in open channels in the narrow alleys and passageways between the houses, draining into the camp's main street. Huge puddles collected from the first rain of the season in the middle of every street and, like the mud, remained throughout the winter. The supply of running water via the Israeli Civil Administration was irregular, and the camp suffered severe water shortages, especially during the summer.

In the late 1980s and early 1990s many Dheishehians still lived in dilapidated, cube-shaped shelters that were constructed in the late 1950s. The majority of the camp homes, however, had seen an ongoing process of renovation and expansion, often improvised, usually using cheap construction materials, and recognizable by poorly insulated walls, year-round dampness, and other shortcomings. In most homes the furniture, meager and basic, was worn out. Striking was the absence of items geared to the needs of children; the paucity of closets, tables, and desks; and the sight of old electrical appliances that had long since become outmoded in Israel. Houses and additions were often so haphazardly stuck together as to seem piled one on top of the other. Garbage and rubbish accumulated in the few remaining uninhabited areas.

The presence of the Israeli army was no less conspicuous than the material wretchedness. Dheisheh of the late 1980s and early 1990s was a congested dwelling zone under military siege. An army camp consisting of a number of tent encampments manned by dozens of soldiers had been set up alongside the camp, only a few meters away from homes. A high wire fence, with tin sheets along its strands, enclosed the entire western exposure of the camp. High concrete barriers blocked the main entrance and all the approach streets that linked up with the Jerusalem-Hebron road. Vehicular and foot patrols of armed soldiers moved up and down the streets and alleys twenty-four hours a day; demonstrations and stone throwing were put down by live gunfire, often causing casualties; and curfews and various collective punishments were frequently meted out.

Relatively few Dheishehians made their living inside the camp. Many of those whom I came to know, men and women, old and young, were familiar with West Jerusalem and the numerous settlements that surround it, and also with Beit Shemesh, Tel Aviv, and more distant towns and cities where they commuted daily for work. Their ranks included skilled and nonskilled laborers, veterans attached to one workplace since 1967, others who had worked and lost their jobs, and transient laborers who moved from one work place to another. The majority would face layoffs and prolonged unemployment in the wake of the closure policy that the Israeli authorities imposed in the early 1990s.

Surprising in light of the harsh conditions was the significant size of the camp's "student body," in particular secondary school pupils, and the large number of young Dheishehians who were then studying at universities or colleges in the West Bank and elsewhere, or who had recently graduated. I least expected the high percentage of female students, and especially the number of women teachers and nurses. From stories recounted by my hosts, I learned of the hundreds of migrant workers from Dheisheh, mainly teachers, engineers, accountants, and others who, in the course of the last decades, had found employment in the Gulf states and were sending home remittances.

I was most impressed by the intensity and articulation of political life in the camp. Via my introduction to released political prisoners and members of their families, I learned that almost every family in Dheisheh had a "representative" who had been incarcerated in an Israeli prison, and many had spent long years behind bars. Through them I became exposed to the manifold opinions, ideologies, and political organizations in the camp.

The outbreak of the Intifada provided a unique opportunity to witness the camp residents, adults and youth, female and male, veteran activists and passive or inexperienced "irregulars," as they were drawn into the eye of the storm that swept the West Bank and Gaza Strip. I met parents whose children were shot when participating in street actions, often opposite their homes, youths severely injured by dumdum bullets, mothers who traveled from one prison to another in search of a detained son, parents who became sworn supporters of the organizations with which their children were affiliated.

On yet another plane, these same encounters demonstrated the central place of the family and of familism in the social life of the camp. Many of the families that received me as a guest were especially large, with ten or more children. Among the younger generation the number of persons in the family was fewer, but they lived, for the most part, under the same roof with parents or brothers. Extended households were prevalent and often included parents, unmarried children, and two, three, and even four nuclear families of married sons, all of whom shared the same kitchen, bathroom, and living space. This multigenerational stage in the life cycle of the majority of families could last for two decades and more.

Considering the diversity of villages of origin among the Dheishehians, the relative preservation of patrilocal residence was striking. I came across sections of neighborhoods or streets populated by a number of generations of first-, second-, and third-degree relatives of the same patrilineage. At the same time, the custom of arranged, endogamous marriage was pervasive, even if not the rule. While these family-kin characteristics highlighted continuity with the past, other features marked differences, variations, and even innovations in family life. I met families in which almost all members were day wage earners who had worked or were working in Israel and others in which several of the sons and/or daughters were or had been migrant workers in the Gulf states and elsewhere. There were families in which not a single son or daughter had completed high school and others in which all had acquired a university or college degree. Some families still lived in old UN-RWA shelters, while others had built new homes, relatively comfortable and spacious. I met parents with fourteen and even sixteen children, and I met young couples who were planning to have only two or three. In some families the women had never worked outside the home, and in others women earned the main income. In several families I saw double standards: some daughters had acquired professions while their sisters entered arranged marriages at age sixteen or seventeen; some sons and daughters were married to close relatives, and others had met their spouses at university or in a political movement.

The educational achievements of a large number of men and women in Dheisheh, their professional skills and qualifications, and their capacity for sustaining an organized political struggle belied the existential conditions: a history beginning with dislocation and destruction, continuing with underdevelopment, and culminating in subjection to prolonged military occupation. It is no secret that prolonged socioeconomic deprivation and neglect impairs educational excellence, and that military and political oppression do not in themselves foster an organized resistance. Circumstances like these often promote such phenomena as crime, a high percentage of school dropouts, drug abuse, and an atmosphere of pessimism and despair, along with a massive return to religion. Hence the challenge of explaining the processes through which individuals as well as the collective in Dheisheh developed substantial social and political resources.

Preliminary observations clearly pointed to unambiguous (albeit nonuniform in spread and degree) development in central dimensions of the social and political constituency in Dheisheh, whereas the political economy as a totality (including conditions of occupation, family traditions, and refugee status) did not encourage such development, but rather placed numerous obstacles in its way. The challenge, in terms of research and theory, therefore, was to provide causal historical explanations for changes (specifically in the spheres of education, professional achievement, and political activism and organization) that were cumulative over three or four generations and that, it appeared to me, could not be explained away as "system"-determined, albeit they were system-related. I further sought to assess whether, in the final analysis, such changes were profound enough to alter some of the boundaries of the power system.

Since a number of scholars, Palestinians and others, working within the broad conceptual paradigm of dependency and modern world system theories, have approached similar problems, I first looked at their research and analyses, but questioned the sufficiency and fruitfulness of this paradigm for explanation of social and political developments that have taken place in the Occupied Territories in general, and in Dheisheh refugee camp in particular.

Applying the Paradigm of Dependency to the Occupied Territories

The socioeconomic conditions in the occupied Palestinian territories have been subject to analysis via dependency theory, modern world system theory, and the theory of unequal development, as formulated and elaborated by Frank (1971, 1969, 1975), Wallerstein (1974), and Amin (1974, 1976), their contemporaries and followers. These theoretical approaches, which constitute a reply and an alternative to modernization theory, offer comprehensive systemic explanation, grounded in extensive historical, economic, and political research, to the causes of underdevelopment. Whereas modernization models group nation-states into "sets" along a scale of relative development according to presumed criteria of modernity versus traditionalism, dependency and world system theories endorse the concept of one global (capitalist) system, wherein the growing prosperity of developed states and regions is made possible and sustained through the protracted underdevelopment of others. Underdevelopment is explained not as a stage that gives way eventually to increased development, or as an inherent sociocultural property, but rather as an outcome of an ongoing process, the origins of which can be traced to the early outward expansion of capitalism from the metropolis (Western Europe) and its modes of imperialist penetration into "satellite" regions.

Whereas the initial advantage enjoyed by the colonial states rested primarily in their military capacities, established trade, and centralized power, advanced capitalism based its advantage on control over the organization and distribution of production. The development of the core or center and the subsequent, interrelated underdevelopment of the periphery was no longer contingent upon direct colonial control of the former over the latter, but rather on a well-defined and structured division of labor. Former colonies were relegated the role of providing cheap labor power and producing agricultural goods and raw materials for the developed core, as well as becoming consumers of the core's industrial produce. The economic "specialization" of the periphery and the distorted class structures that supported its perpetuation became central fetters to the development of independent industrial infrastructures, reinforcing and ensuring prolonged dependency upon the core. Hence the development of underdevelopment.[6]

It may be that the case of the Occupied Territories diverges somewhat from the ideal type of the thesis of the development of underdevelopment because the expansionist propensities of the Israeli state were anchored in a political-militaristic orientation.[7] Nonetheless, in terms of the policies implemented by the occupier, the economic benefits conferred upon it, and the long-term detrimental consequences for the occupied, the terminology of dependency and underdevelopment could not have been more apt. Indeed, it would probably be fair to suggest that—leaving aside reports of Israeli state officials and functionaries, on the one hand,[8] and some of the prolific academic yield of the Oslo era, on the other[9]—most students of the socioeconomic transformation in the Palestinian Territories sought to integrate a specific analysis of the political economy of the Occupation into the general paradigm of dependency.

The history of underdevelopment in the West Bank and Gaza Strip did not start with the occupation of these areas by Israel in 1967. It can be traced, rather, to the interlocking of the direct consequences of the 1948 war—primarily the settlement in the Jordanian-ruled West Bank and the Egyptian-governed Gaza Strip of hundreds of thousands of refugees from the internal and coastline regions of Palestine, and the subsequent severance of these territories (and people) from what had previously been their economic, commercial, and urban centers and major agricultural hinterland. Absence or near absence of industrialization, low agricultural productivity, soaring rates of unemployment, and growing dependence on labor migration to the oil-rich Gulf countries, combined with highly coercive regime politics, were the underlying socioeconomic realities of both territories.[10] Extreme disparities between the economy of Israel, with its developed industrial, technological, and agricultural infrastructure and its fairly extensive welfare services, and the economies of the West Bank and the Gaza Strip predated the 1967 Occupation and should be viewed as one of the preexisting conditions that facilitated Israeli economic domination in the years to follow.

Israeli control over the Palestinian territories was military and political in origin, with both remaining ongoing features of Occupation. The control system rested on five "institutionalized pillars": (1) concentration of all authority, legislative, executive, and judiciary, in the hands of regional military commanders; (2) administration by military orders of all spheres of civilian affairs (by the late 1980s the military government had issued approximately twelve hundred such orders); (3) prohibition of Palestinian political-social institutions and activities; (4) full control over Palestinian land and water resources, including ongoing land confiscation (especially after 1977), the establishment of numerous civilian Jewish settlements and dozens of military bases, and the construction of a vast road infrastructure; and (5) the restructuring of the judicial system so as to invest military courts with overriding jurisdictional power that practically dispensed with the authority of preexisting civil courts.[11]

Jamil Hilal (1976) characterized Israeli colonial control as a coercive "unequal exchange" between occupier and occupied. The Occupation transformed the West Bank and Gaza Strip into a captive market for Israeli products, wherein 90 percent of the commodities originated in Israel; the share of Palestinian products amounted to 2 percent of Israeli imports. This was a direct consequence of an Israeli policy that prevented competing Palestinian agricultural goods from entering the country's borders; imposed heavy restrictions on export from the Territories to other markets, as well as high tariffs and taxes on imports (other than Israeli) to the Territories; systematically denied permits and licenses to Palestinian entrepreneurs; and closed the local banking system. In an ongoing process, hundreds of thousands of *dunums* (four *dunums* equal approximately one acre) of Palestinian agricultural land were confiscated and turned into Israeli state property for settlement, parks, roads, and enclosures.

The export of Palestinian labor from the Territories to Israel formed the other side of the unequal exchange. Within seven years of Occupation approximately one-third of all employed persons from the Occupied Territories had become day laborers in Israel, primarily in the construction and service sectors. However, the conditions of proletarianization—primarily, the dispersal rather than concentration of workers, the day wage basis of their employment, the repression of unionization, the absence of industrial centers inside the Territories, and the concomitant near-absence there of direct confrontation between labor and capital as well as of developed class-based organizations—inhibited or distorted the formation of class consciousness (Hilal 1976, 10–15).

Focusing on the proletarianization of West Bank peasantry, Salim Tamari developed Hilal's thesis by pointing to the contradiction-ridden process that ensnared peasants-cum-workers: While agricultural land became increasingly marginalized as a source of livelihood and status, work inside Israel, especially in the construction branch, did not create a sufficient basis for a full-blown class transformation. The casual and seasonal nature of employment, the reliance of employers on kin-based forms of recruitment, and the relegation of overseer jobs to Palestinian workers, which minimized friction between Jewish employer and Palestinian laborer on the work site, all militated against the consolidation of a genuine working-class identity and consciousness. At the same time, continued residence in the village, intermittent return to agricultural work in the wake of layoffs, and the regular maintenance of a farmstead by women and older family members contributed to the preservation of peasant identity and values (Tamari 1981, 39–62).

Tamari analyzed the development of the national movement in the Occupied Territories as a process that proceeded alongside underdevelopment.

Since, according to his scheme, the Palestinian working class—the quintessential social product of the "integration" of the Palestinian economy into that of Israel—was characterized by a distorted class consciousness, it did not carry a revolutionary potential (Tamari 1981, 60; 1991, 61). Correspondingly, the reservoir of potential carriers of resistance was significantly diminished, now encompassing elements from the bourgeoisie and petit bourgeoisie: specifically, the intelligentsia, professionals, merchants, and entrepreneurs—in other words, the relatively better-positioned strata whose upward mobility had been denied or severely hampered. Tamari's class analysis, drawing on the assumptions of the dependency model, pointed to a dead end, or at least to very limited openings.

An illuminating example of the application of the dependency paradigm is provided by Randa Siniora's study on female employment in West Bank–based Palestinian textile workshops that produced goods for Israeli companies (Siniora 1989). Drawing on the writings of Emmanuel (1972) and Amin (1976) on mechanisms of surplus extraction from the periphery and its transfer to the core, Siniora showed how a combination of the lack of initial capital, obsolete equipment, absence of government funding, and heavy restrictions on marketing pushed small textile producers from the West Bank into subcontracting for Israeli firms. Inherent instability, reflecting the ongoing fluctuations in the Israeli market, and underpaid employees, the overwhelming majority of whom were young unmarried women, became the most salient features of the textile branch.

Yusif Sayigh finds that the case of the Palestinian Territories can be only partially subsumed under the dependency paradigm. He defined the Israeli military occupation as a case of "internal colonialism," wherein the economic dependency of the Palestinians is a concomitant of their ongoing dispossession. Uprooting, land confiscation, deportation, denial of rights, harassment of institutions—all subsumed under "dispossession"—are an integral part of the infrastructure in which dependency is grounded, not a separate component; hence the conceptual incorporation of military repression into the analysis of dependency (Yusif Sayigh 1988, 264–72). Further, Sayigh saw protracted dependency in the Occupied Territories as having led to pauperization, that is, to relative economic decline (the basis for this assessment being an evaluation of the economic potential of the West Bank prior to the Occupation and a comparison with the relevant indicators of growth in neighboring Arab countries) (1988, 273–82).

Pauperization received central attention in Sara Roy's comprehensive research on the economy of the Gaza Strip (for example, 1986, 1990, 1994a, 1995a). Aware of the absence of a suitable theoretical paradigm to analyze the case of the Occupied Territories (1995a, 121), Roy developed an elaborate scheme, the leading concept of which was "de-development." The choice of this term, as distinct from "underdevelopment," aims to under-score an ongoing retrogression, the origins of which can be traced to three structural components of Israeli policy: dispossession of the Palestinian pop-ulation from land and water resources; externalization or "pumping out" of Palestinian labor, fed by the drying up of the local economic infrastructure; and deinstitutionalization, that is, the destruction or suffocation of Palestin-ian institutions.

The relationship between the political economy of the Occupation and political development posed a problem for the proponents of the depen-dency-underdevelopment paradigm. Sayigh's analysis, for example, led him to the conclusion that only an external force that would impose change from without could bring an end to the circular pattern by which depen-dency is reproduced (1988, 279–80). In this respect his prognosis echoed Meron Benvenisti's "irreversibility" thesis, which claimed that by the mid-1980s the institutionalization of the Israeli occupation had reached a "criti-cal mass," that is, a point of no return that nullified the chances for change from within (Benvenisti 1987, 66–80).

The growth of a popular, mass-based resistance movement in the Occu-pied Territories negated the predictions of the dependency-underdevelop-ment paradigm and highlighted the inadequacy of this approach. That this incompatibility between theory and empirical reality posed difficulty to scholars was manifest in the pervasive tendency among them to sever the analysis of political transformation in the Occupied Territories from that of the social and economic structure, examining political action as a separate, almost autonomous sphere.[12]

More than any preceding historical development, it was the eruption of the Intifada in 1987, and in particular its perseverance, that exposed the weak-nesses of the dependency approach. By all criteria a popular uprising, the Intifada mobilized most sectors of the Palestinian society. The mass partici-pation of youth, students, women, camp refugees, villagers, townspeople, workers, shopkeepers, and teachers in organized and spontaneous collective protest action were all related to the major "social and class transformation" that took place under the Occupation. Joost Hiltermann (1991a) has pointed to the interrelationship among socioeconomic structural preconditions to mass mobilization; the emergence of a developed infrastructure of popular, locally based organizations linked with the widely legitimized leadership of the Palestine Liberation Organization (PLO); and the successive stages that enabled them to transform mobilization into collective action. The implica-tions of his comprehensive research certainly went beyond the binding premises of the dependency approach.

The main shortcoming of the dependency paradigm for the Occupied Territories is its circularity: the system generates, reproduces, and reinforces the unequal power balance between occupier and occupied.[13] The account taken of the impact of change from within is negligible. Nonetheless, developments that succeeded the uprising—including the asymmetry inherent in the terms of the Oslo Accords, the political and economic weakness (fragility) of the PNA, and the absence of international guarantees for Palestinian sovereignty—make it hard to escape the notion that in the "competition" between structural determination and human agency, the former outweighs the latter, but does not erase it.

In the case of the Dheisheh refugee camp specifically, central economic, social, and political features certainly "fit" dependency theory. However, the theory does not explain other central features of social life in Dheisheh, especially those that could be traced to the cumulative effects of education and politicization on women's status, gender, and intergenerational relations, and the mobilization of the community. Moreover, education- and politicization-related changes tend to introduce a constant element of tension and conflict into the social formations and relationships within which they take place, rather than merely reproduce them. Indeed, my preliminary findings more than suggested the necessity of integrating "change from within" into the conceptual and methodological framework of analysis.

In Search of a Theory of Social Practice

Recent decades have witnessed a shift within anthropology—and in a tight interrelationship with developments outside the discipline—away from the influences of structuralism, structural Marxism, and political economy and toward a search after theories of practice (Ortner 1984).[14] Identifying with the trend, Ortner has portrayed the political economy approach in anthropology as deterministic "economism," criticizing its proponents for ascribing omnipotent powers to the expansion of the capitalist world system while reducing the history of peripheral societies to the consequences of capitalist penetration. The deeds and reflections of "real people on the ground"—the true agents of history-making and the raison d'être of anthropological fieldwork—are relegated to the margins (1984, 143, 144). The problem, then, is whether, given system-imposed constraints and barriers, people on the dominated side can act and by doing so effectively direct the course of their history toward more favorable outcomes.[15]

Preoccupation with the core problem of the interrelationship between system and praxis, structure and action, and determinism and voluntarism underscored the intellectual projects of both Anthony Giddens and Pierre Bourdieu. Giddens described his structuration theory as an attempt to break with the antinomy of structure and action that had long dichotomized sociological literature, and to substitute for it an analysis of the recursive process by which structure and agency, mutually dependent, condition and (re)produce each other (Giddens 1979, 49, 69). Along somewhat parallel lines, Bourdieu's conceptualization of habitus, which evolved out of his field research among the Kabyle Berbers of Algeria in 1959–60 (Bourdieu 1979, vii), is viewed as an attempt to bridge analyses of objective conditions and subjective behavior by tracing the mechanism through which structures are assimilated into routines of thought and behavior that govern people's everyday conduct.

In the discussion of refugees in Dheisheh, the key question is whether theoretical constructs such as structuration and habitus can transcend the central weakness of the dependency paradigm—the circular reproduction of a system of domination.

Bourdieu's research exposed him to colonial reality in general and to the then-expanding Algerian rural and urban subproletariat in particular. In *Algeria 1960* he charged that this class lacked the capacities for developing class consciousness and consequently could not become a revolutionary element (1979, 50–63). Rather, the limited and backward subjective expectations found among members of this class fit their objective positions within the system.[16] The fact that the supposedly unchanging "circularity" of the colonial system in Algeria was shattered by the victory of the Algerian revolution (in 1962) so shortly after Bourdieu completed his fieldwork there reveals the shortcomings of his analysis.[17]

The assumption of a correspondence between the subjective expectations of members of social groups and their system-determined "objective probabilities" is integral to the notion of habitus (Bourdieu and Passeron 1977). Reproduction of the system is as much dependent on adaptation from below as on efforts to legitimize it from above. Those on the bottom rungs of the ladder adjust their expectations, aspirations, preferences, and inclinations (partially subsumed under Bourdieu's "dispositions"); their acceptance of their limited objective prospects serves to guarantee the undisturbed perpetuation of the system.[18]

Notwithstanding his emphasis of human practice, therefore, Bourdieu's habitus is part of an essentially deterministic, ahistoric theory of social reproduction, not of social change. In the words of Richard Jenkins, "Structures produce the habitus, which generates practice, which reproduces the structures and so on" (Jenkins 1982, 273). And he comments elsewhere: "It remains difficult to understand, how, in Bourdieu's model of practice, actors and collectivities can intervene in their own history in any substantial fashion" (Jenkins 1992, 83).

Aware of the functionalist "trap" threatening a "structure-conditioned" theory of action, Giddens built on the general assumption that "every social actor knows a great deal about the conditions of reproduction of the society

of which he or she is a member" (Giddens 1979, 5). Along with the definition of structure in terms of "rules and resources" (66), this leading premise
of structuration is crucial to rendering it a "nonfunctionalist manifesto" (7).
Accordingly, and unlike Bourdieu's "enacted" subjects, Giddens's actors are
reflexive, endowed with both "practical" and "discursive" levels of consciousness through which they organize their knowledge and provide ratio-
nalizations for their actions and motives. At the same time, however, they are
not fully aware of the totality of conditions within which they act ("unac-
knowledged conditions of action") or of the totality of outcomes produced
("unintended consequences of action") (54–59).

The abstract (or what amounts to noncontextualized) nature of Giddens's structuration renders it vulnerable to criticism. Though his conceptualization of structure—as "both enabling and constraining . . . not a barrier
to action, but essentially involved in its production" (69)—appear highly
promising (Callinicos 1987, 84–86), he does not tell us why or how (knowledgeable) actors act in a fashion that challenges the power structure (Jenkins
1982, 273). Even more problematic is the definition of structure in terms of
"rules," since this does not differentiate between the structure of specific institutions and structure in the economic-social-political sense of the term
(John Thompson 1989). Social actors may know a great deal about the rules
of conduct within particular settings, such as their workplace, yet the structural fundamentals or "laws" of the socioeconomic system are by and large
invisible. Moreover, it is precisely these latter invisible fundamentals that determine, to a great extent, the differential access to resources of actors across
a spectrum of class, gender, race, and so on, and hence also determine their
abilities to act (Thompson 1989, 62–66).

It appears that the tour of the terrain of "habitus" and "structuration" has
led to an endpoint quite similar to that which closed the examination of the
dependency-underdevelopment paradigm. If the perpetual reproduction
that inheres in the latter approach can be attributed to a "system-centered-
ness" that denies the transformative capacities of social forces that come
from "within," then Giddens's and Bourdieu's actors—while indefatigably
exercising their agency, whether consciously or unwittingly—reproduce and
perpetuate the same system.

A Conceptual Framework for the Study of
Social Change in Dheisheh Refugee Camp

How then to benefit from the insights of the dependency–world system
paradigm while also exploring social agency? My approach focused on
analysis of the interrelationship between the determinants of the political

economic system of the Israeli Occupation (placed within a wider, regional context) on the one hand, and the actions of Dheishehian men and women over three successive generations on the other.

I looked at three central macrosocial spheres that affected people's daily lives: wage labor, education, and political organization. Each was studied in relation to the systemic and historic contexts within which they existed. To give *wage labor* concrete meaning I examined the position of Palestinian laborers with respect to accessible labor markets. The context here, first and foremost, is the segregated, restricted opening of the Israeli labor market to Palestinian female and male day laborers after the 1967 war and the concomitant nondevelopment of the local (Palestinian) industry, agriculture, and public service sectors.

Acquisition of education takes its concrete meaning from the institutional settings that either facilitated or obstructed access to elementary, secondary, and tertiary education by refugee descendents in Dheisheh. Crucial here are the roles played by UNRWA, the Israeli military government and Civil Administration, government-sponsored universities in the Arab world and the former Socialist bloc, and West Bank–based private universities. I also looked at the connection between education and upper mobility, within the context of the regional political economy of labor migration to the Persian Gulf vis-à-vis the underdevelopment of the public sector in the West Bank.

Finally, the power relations within which political resistance to the Occupation materialized gave concrete meaning to *political organization*. The context here is chiefly the peculiar course of development of the Palestinian national movement in the Occupied Territories in light of the repressive military and political means employed against it by the Israeli authorities.

On another level, work, education, and politics were studied as *channels* or *avenues of social transformation*. The breakdown of the research population into three generational groups (old, intermediate, and young) and the further breakdown of each generational category along gender lines enabled the tracing of change over time. Thus the empirical and conceptual building blocks of my research were the labor histories, education histories, and political activism histories (or, as it turned out in the case of men, imprisonment histories) of three successive generations of men and women in Dheisheh. I saw these histories as protracted "confrontational encounters" between my subjects—day workers, students, the professionally and semi-professionally employed, and political activists and prisoners—and the varied forms of inequality, discrimination, and repression emanating from the political-economic system to which they were subjected. At the same time, however, practices in each sphere yielded, to a lesser or greater extent (dependent often on gender and age), various resources in the forms of income, skill, expertise, experience, knowledge, consciousness, and political standing. Hence the potentiality that inheres in the work, schooling, and political activism histories of the subjects of this study.

The examination of the familial settings and relationships within which the three-tiered histories were embedded was as central to the analysis as was the study of the systemic contexts within which they unfolded. One of my guiding premises was that in the absence of state institutions, particularly the absence of state-sponsored social services, and under conditions that undermine economic development and when military rule holds sway, individuals are driven toward a heightened dependency on the support of family and kin. Moreover, political parties, trade unions, and voluntary associations were either prohibited or subject to constant military-political surveillance, leaving the family as one of the few groups not defined as an "illegal organization."

While there are circumstantial links between the centrality of the family in the Dheishehian community and the extreme conditions of refugee existence and military government, the roots of the former lie in history and culture. Sociocultural research on Arab societies—rural, urban, and tribal—has assigned a central place to the family and kinship ties and affiliations; social-economic-political-religious relations flow toward and evolve from these. Even researchers who distanced themselves from ahistorical generalizations about "the Arab family" as sui generis, emphasizing the variations in family types along lines of class, religious affiliation, urban-rural contrasts, and policy of the central government, characterized Arab societies as outstandingly familial.[19]

There is empirical-methodological justification for my use of families as research units. The focus on families allowed me to follow developments, changes, and continuity over a period of several generations. Dheisheh posed an additional advantage in its prevalence of especially large nuclear families that had close ties with the branches of their extended families. The diversity and the variation that in many instances can be found within a single Dheishehian family—in terms of age and gender composition and the varied histories of employment, education, and political activity—offer the researcher a kind of complete microcosm.

Drawing on my qualitative and quantitative findings pertaining to the labor, school, and political activism histories of the three generations, I reconstructed patterns of gender- and age-based divisions of labor that developed within families over time in all three spheres. Examined as key mechanisms through which families coped with and confronted the inferior and vulnerable statuses of their members, the patterns were further analyzed as grounds for the changing socioeconomic relationships within (multigenerational) families in the camp.

Among other findings this exploration discloses the fact that the persistence of a family division of labor, though it provides support and protection, relies to a great extent on the family's ability to exercise patriarchal control over the resources and behavior of its female and young male members. The inherent contradiction between familial support and protection and patriarchal demands and restrictions was investigated as a source of further tension and conflict in the lives of individuals; it also presented an opening for the emergence of transformed gender relations in household economies and among the younger generations.

In what instances and to what extent are family divisions of labor and responsibility successful in confronting the extreme structural inequalities that pervade the work, education, and political experiences of their members—and thus in promoting improvement in their chances in life, standards of living, and social statuses? Under what conditions can resources obtained through work, education, and political activism challenge patriarchal control and contribute to relative social and economic independence? These interrelated questions (among others) bear directly on the complex problem of social change in Dheisheh, as well as in other communities that share similar family characteristics. They are also, to paraphrase Levi-Strauss's formulation, "good to work with," or accessible to the researcher, as I endeavor to show in the following chapters.

Methodology

GENERATIONAL AND GENDER CATEGORIES

As mentioned, the empirical and conceptual building blocks of my research were the labor, school, and political activism histories of three successive generations of men and women in Dheisheh. The division of the research population into sociological generations was employed for this purpose: an older generation, encompassing men over sixty and women over fifty-five; an intermediate generation, encompassing men aged forty-four to fifty-five and women aged forty-one to fifty-four; and a young (sometimes referred to as "younger") generation, encompassing men aged twenty-five to forty and women aged twenty-one to forty.

The generation and gender categories are not absolutes. It may be argued, for example, that a fourth refugee generation, encompassing young men and women aged fifteen to twenty should have been incorporated into the analysis, that my definition of the "younger generation" encompasses too wide an age range, or that my age breakdown excludes several subgroups, such as men aged fifty-five to fifty-nine.

My choice of generation groups and age demarcations was preceded by lengthy preliminary research. My main guideline was the attempt to apply research categories that would best reflect discernible and meaningful differences among the adult Dheishehian female and male population in terms of central determinants that affected the "life–chances" of these refugees. Among these determinants were the impact of war and uprooting, the availability of wage work opportunities, the possibilities for acquiring basic and advanced education, the exposure to military and political repression, and the impact of political socialization. In the final analysis, however, the proof for the validity of the proposed generation and gender categories lies in their empirical fruitfulness, that is, in enabling me to underscore trends of change over time.

METHODS OF DATA COLLECTION

Data was collected through various methods, including comprehensive surveys of sample populations, numerous in-depth interviews with individuals, and ongoing home visits to families over substantial periods of time. All interviews and data collection were conducted in Arabic.

The core sample

One major data source comprised structured interviews conducted in 1993 among a sample of 120 Dheishehian married couples (heads of families). These included thirty-nine couples (seventy-eight respondents) from the older generation, forty-one couples (eighty-two respondents) from the intermediate generation, and forty couples (eighty respondents) from the younger generation. The 120 families in this sample represented approximately 8 percent of the family households in Dheisheh from UNRWA's 1991–92 population register.

The sample was designed—with the aid of UNRWA's register—so that Dheisheh refugees originating from all the main villages of origin are represented (although the relative shares in the sample of refugees originating from the various villages did not fully match the breakdown of the camp population along this line). The UNRWA register also enabled me to choose respondents and group them according to the generational criteria that I adopted. However, the (almost) even breakdown of the 120 couples in the sample into three generational groups (thirty-nine, forty-one, and forty couples in each), does not reflect the age composition of the camp population, wherein the young are heavily overrepresented and the elderly constitute a small fraction.

The 120 couples in the sample were interviewed during the summer of 1993 with the help of four young men from Dheisheh camp—Ziyad Farraj, a social worker; ʿAdel ʿAdawi, Nathem ʿOdeh, and Khaled ʿAtta, then third-year students in the social sciences department at Bethlehem University—whom I hired as research assistants. All interviews took place at the homes of the interviewees and lasted between two and three hours each, on average. Questionnaires included closed- and open-ended questions; slightly different questionnaires were prepared for each generational group. My assistants and I also drafted brief reports about the housing and living condition in each home.

We asked each respondent to answer detailed questions about her/his work history and current working life, education, involvement in political activism, and imprisonment history. Other questions included a range of topics: background on the respondent's family of origin before and after settling in Dheisheh; number of children born to the respondent; number of family members currently sharing the same household with the respondent; housing and living conditions; sources of income sustaining the household other than the respondent's own wage work; education of the respondent's children; and incidents of political imprisonment among the respondent's children.

The data on each of the six subgroups that constituted the sample population are referred to in the text as findings on, or results of, the *core sample*. Data collected through participants in the core sample about family members other than themselves—for example, information about the work histories and the education of fathers, mothers, and siblings of respondents—is referred to in the text as pertaining to an *additional sample* or a *larger sample*.

A survey on women and employment

A second major source of data was a survey on women and employment that I conducted in 1994 among the entire adult female population of one residential area (or neighborhood) in Dheisheh. The decision to supplement the findings from the core sample with additional data on women and work resulted from my attempt to "compensate" for the lower rate of participation by women in the labor force. The survey encompassed 446 women aged sixteen and older, who were grouped into three age categories: 318 women aged sixteen to forty, seventy-five women aged forty-one to fifty-four, and fifty-three women aged fifty-five and older—groupings that corresponded closely to my generational categories. Unlike the participants in the core sample, these surveyed women were not interviewed at length. Rather, I asked the subjects to provide key details on their employment histories (names and locations of current and previous workplaces, type of work, length of employment, and level of income), their education, and their marital status. The data thus collected is referred to in the text as results of the *survey on women and employment*.

Generational and gendered profiles

The findings gathered from the core sample of interviewees and the survey on women and employment facilitated the construction of prototypical "profiles" of Dheishehian laborers, students, professional, and semiprofessional employees, political activists, and political prisoners along the lines of generation and gender. Intra- and intergenerational comparison of these profiles underscores major trends of change over the time period between 1950 and 1996.

Long-term relationships with individuals and families

The central contribution of the core sample and survey notwithstanding, the sources that yielded information of utmost importance, in terms of both richness and depth, were the long-term, at times highly intense, relationships that I established with many dozens of individuals and with more than twenty families (some extended, others nuclear) in Dheisheh. Maintaining these relationships entailed, primarily, ongoing visits to family homes, where I spent time with my acquaintances. Much of this time was devoted to recurrent conversations with the same persons (often with several family members in each home)—at times in the form of in-depth interviews, at many other times in the form of open discussions or casual chats—on topics related directly and less directly to my research objectives. The visits also provided ample opportunity for me to follow routine, everyday family life closely, and to observe the interaction and relationships among family members on a regular basis. Some of my relationships with Dheishehian families lasted throughout my fieldwork (1992–96) and, in fact, continued for many years thereafter.

Unlike the participants in the core sample and in the survey on women, who were chosen randomly (except for the demands arising from the generation, gender, and village of origin criteria), the Dheishehians with whom long-term relationships were established and maintained were selected on the basis of personal acquaintance. I had already become friends with some of these individuals and families during my relatively long "pre-research" encounter with Dheisheh; I had become acquainted with others through their participation in the pilot interviews that I conducted at an early stage of my fieldwork, and still others following their participation in the core sample. I initiated contact with many through the recommendation and mediation of my "veteran" acquaintances in the camp.

The information collected through ongoing visits of families, extensive interviewing, and follow-up conversations, together with the large data base provided by the core sample and the survey, enabled me to reconstruct the age- and gender-based divisions of labor and roles that developed over time within Dheishehian families in the three spheres under investigation.

The Structure of the Book

The structure of the book mirrors, to a great extent, the conceptual framework presented above. It is divided into three parts corresponding to the three major spheres of the research: day wage labor and family life in Dheisheh; education, professional employment, and family life in Dheisheh; and political activism and family life in Dheisheh. Each part opens with a short introduction that outlines its main themes and objectives and provides a concise content description of the chapters that follow. The first chapter in each part is devoted to a discussion of the relevant systemic context—the political economy of the Israel Occupation, the institutional settings that facilitated or obstructed the acquisition of education by Dheishehian refugees, and the course of development of the Palestinian national movement in the Occupied Territories, respectively. These are followed, in each part, by a chapter or chapters that dwell on the life histories of Dheishehians from three generations, as day wage laborers, as students and salaried employees, and as political activists and prisoners, respectively. The remaining chapter or chapters in each part are devoted to the presentation and analysis of patterns of organization of family life that developed in response to the experiences endured and resources obtained by family members—in the labor markets (Israeli and local), in the course of acquiring an education, while being migrant workers in the Gulf, in the resistance movement, and in Israeli prisons.

An Israeli Researcher in a Palestinian Refugee Camp

Few anthropology students are unacquainted with Clifford Geertz's description of "entering the field" at the opening of his account of a cockfight in Bali (Geertz 1973a). Geertz relates that the attitude of Balinese villagers toward him and his wife changed dramatically in the course of an antigambling police raid on the local cockfight arena. The Geertzes, who until then had been ignored, Balinese fashion, by the locals, discovered that their flight from the police, right along with the native villagers, broke down all the barriers of distrust, winning them goodwill and respect.

If Geertz was trying to tell his readers that the plunge into the field is likely to expose the investigator to trials and assessments at the hands of the local population, his message is perhaps superfluous, but if in addition he was hinting at an instant recipe for rapport, one must take what he writes with a grain of salt. As in other settings of human relations, trust during fieldwork is not built in a moment or in the course of a single incident, but is repeatedly put to the test. Were I English or French or even a woman from the Palestinian Diaspora, gaining people's confidence and willingness to share their experiences and thoughts would have been an ongoing business.

But beyond this general requirement, my being an Israeli woman conducting academic research in a Palestinian refugee camp, like the circumstances under which the fieldwork took place, influenced in various ways the process of building relations and the nature of my day-to-day experience in the camp. In the Dheisheh that I came to know there was not one person, old or young, who was not acquainted with or had not met other Israelis before meeting me, and very few who had not visited or spent time in locations within the state of Israel. Thousands of men and hundreds of women in the camp had worked during various periods of their lives for Israeli contractors or employers in Jerusalem, Tel Aviv, Beersheva, and so on; hundreds of men had been confined in Israeli prisons, and hundreds more had been held in detention centers. There was no family whose home had not been invaded at least once by Israeli soldiers; no man or woman who had not been searched at the military roadblocks, no child who had not each and every day encountered a military patrol going past his or her home; and very few youths who had not been beaten by soldiers or sent scurrying for shelter by rifle fire or tear gas canisters aimed in their direction.

But this is only part of the picture, perhaps the more stereotypical part, since Dheishehians had encountered not only "the employer," "the soldier," and "the prison guard," but rather all sorts of employers and sometimes—though this was much less frequent—even soldiers and prison guards who treated them decently. Furthermore, very many Dheishehians took an interest in, and were familiar with, political life and the political forces in Israel, and some spent considerable time and effort in learning about them in depth. Very few of the people I met entertained a one-dimensional picture of "the Israeli." On the contrary, not an insignificant number among them distinguished between the Left and the Right, and between the different shades and varieties of Left and Right, with a precision worthy of Israeli scholars and reporters. Many were knowledgeable about activists in left-wing movements and human rights organizations in Israel as well as left-wing public figures, journalists, and attorneys, and several had even made personal contact with Israeli activists. Some remembered solidarity visits made years earlier and would recount them in detail.

There were also other dimensions to their acquaintance with Israel and Israelis, such as the fluency in Hebrew found among some of the day laborers and quite a few of the former prisoners, or the custom that had taken hold among many Dheisheh families of visiting the ruins of their villages of origin. These were situated at a distance of a half-hour or an hour's travel from the camp, near the Israeli moshavim and kibbutzim or even within the boundaries of those settlements. All this is to say that, even when

I was "entering the field," Dheishehians didn't treat me as "the Israeli woman" but rather very much wanted to hear and know what *kind* of an Israeli I was.

"What kind of an Israeli" had to do not only with my outlook and my political views—though these were certainly at the forefront of the Dheis-hehians' political and intellectual curiosity—but also with my personal history and that of my family, my lifestyle in Jerusalem, my work at the university, and my social life. This curiosity, informed by the facts that people were familiar with, or had heard about Israelis and Israel, and their thirst for non-mediated contacts with Israelis that may become meaningful and "different," made their mark on our acquaintanceships and on our mutually developing relations. Many of my interviewees, both men and women, made a habit of "interviewing" me in the course of our meetings. They were eager to find out what I had to say about the "green cards" that were issued at the time, preventing their carriers from entering Israel;[20] about decisions of Israel's High Court of Justice that permitted house demolitions and deportations and appeared never to disappoint the expectations of the military authorities; about the ongoing expansion of the settlement of Efrat, which was rapidly swallowing up what was left of the open land reserves in their vicinity; and about the near absence of reaction on the part of the Israeli public to what was happening to them, residents of the Occupied Territories.

Later, when they discovered that much of what infuriated, annoyed, or astounded them had a similar effect on me, they sought to learn more about my private life; how I could "manage" as an unmarried woman, why I lived apart from my parents, and also, whether I served in the army and could shoot a gun. And of course they wondered why on earth I chose them as the subject of my study, as well as what those at the university thought of that research, and whether or not it could damage my career.

There I was, spending entire afternoons "lecturing" to my hosts about the many advantages, alongside no few difficulties, of leading an independent life as an unmarried woman in the modern Israel of the 1990s; recounting reminiscences from the loneliest, most alienating, and most boring two years of my life when I was in a secretarial job in the IDF; and making painstaking efforts to provide coherent explanation for the shifts, twists, turns, and at times tormenting decisions that marked the course of my restless journey from the natural sciences, via philosophy of science, to the social sciences, the journey that finally brought me to them. Gradually enabling me to shed my strangeness, these "counterinterviews" had the cumulative effect of reconstructing me as a "whole" human being, real and exposed, who did not need to explain and justify each time where she was "coming from" and where she was going. To add that the counterinterviews also provided opportunity for me to rearticulate for myself where I was coming from and where I was going is probably superfluous.

The conditions and circumstances under which I worked also had a strong influence on building mutual understanding. Doing fieldwork in a refugee camp that was under military rule, especially during the Intifada years, meant being present where violent oppression and the struggle against it were the normal order of things. It meant getting to or staying in Dheisheh even during days of curfew, when Dheishehians were ordered to remain indoors, and where disobedience could endanger one's life; it meant sharing dishes of rice, lentils, and mostly lots of bread with families who had known long months of privation; it meant watching soldiers beating and abusing Dheishehians in the street before my eyes; witnessing the use of live bullets to break up demonstrations and stone throwing; visiting the homes of the wounded; and sitting with families mourning the dead. It also meant rejoicing with parents, relatives, and friends when a prisoner was released from jail or following news broadcasts about a prisoners' hunger strike with a mixed sense of anxiety and pride, knowing that some of my acquaintances from the camp were likely among the strikers. It meant, of course, to taste the pain, suffering, and rage, and both the resistance and the powerlessness of the men, women, and children about whom I was writing. Indeed, from the moment I became a participant, the question of "how to behave" in the extreme situations to which I was exposed did not confront me as such, nor did it often return to me in my reflections and afterthoughts.

Nonetheless, my presence during curfews, while tension was at its peak, or as part of condolence delegations, was not taken for granted. It was hard to avoid interaction or confrontation with IDF soldiers, since throughout the major part of my fieldwork Dheisheh was a terrain of extensive military activity, so to speak, with both foot and motorized patrols moving up and down its streets and alleyways morning, noon, evening, and night, and with soldiers stationed on "strategic" rooftops inside the camp. I opted for as little contact with them as possible, especially after I was informed in no uncertain terms by both soldiers and officers that I was not welcome to remain in an area that had been declared a "closed military zone," unless I possessed a permit from the district commander and was accompanied by a security guard. Keeping a low profile did not demand sophisticated logistics on my part, however, since most of my time was spent inside houses and since the camp neighborhoods offered plenty of narrow connecting alleyways that were seldom visited by soldiers, and also because the army units stationed in Dheisheh kept changing every few weeks.

The Dheishehians observed my evasion of soldiers with some amusement. What need had an Israeli woman to search for a hiding place from the IDF? The assumption that I had immunity where they did not was sound and justified, and I never pretended that my games of "cat and mouse" in any way resembled their daily confrontations with armed soldiers. Still, despite the knowing glances and the humor, the Dheishehians interpreted my persistence as additional testimony to my understanding, and yes, doggedness; on more than one occasion I overheard my hosts reporting to neighbors or friends about the "adventures" that I had experienced on my way to or from their homes.

The "immunity" I was thought to have was also linked to the more realistic or less realistic expectations of me that some of the people developed. The relatively few instances of stereotypical attitudes came mostly from the older generation in the camp. Some of them believed, or at least wanted to believe, that as an Israeli woman I must have connections with and access to the military government or the Civil Administration, the two branches of government that made their lives miserable, and that I could help them or their children get work permits or permits for "family reunification" and the like. Usually, it was the sons, daughters, or friends of these people with expectations, rather than I, who convinced them that they were wrong. Accurately and at considerable length, they explained my status, my limitations, and even my views about those functionaries with whom I had been asked to intervene.

Notwithstanding the importance I attach to the nature of the encounter, the process of becoming acquainted, and the circumstances in which my fieldwork took place, it seems to me that the most decisive component in building the mutual relations—the trust, the amity, and the cooperation between the people of Dheisheh and me—was their own active participation in a study that concerns itself with areas so central to their world. Each domain of the in-depth interviews—work, education, and politics—directly touched the lives of every family and every interviewee, albeit in different ways and to differing extents, and provided them an opportunity to illuminate these subjects for me from the vantage points that were important and significant for them.

Without a doubt, the most sensitive subject was political imprisonment, if only because at that time either the word of informers or an admission of political affiliation was likely to result in lengthy incarceration. The readiness to be interviewed, at times bordering on enthusiasm, and the openness that I encountered on the part of former prisoners deserves closer examination. In large part, I attribute it to the widespread recognition among these activists, as individuals and as a group, of the value and significance of their prison experience, and to the importance they themselves attached to the documentation of their sociopolitical history. Some had kept prison notes or diaries while in jail, and many others entertained the idea of writing and perhaps publishing their reminiscences. Their recognition of the potential value of my work also played a considerable role in facilitating its progress; it often happened that an interviewee would introduce me to friends, primarily former prison mates, whom he thought able to enhance my knowledge and understanding of one matter or another. If not for this advice and active mediation, I would have probably missed out on some of the most astute commentators who eventually ended up as key contributors to my research.

To a greater extent, the readiness of former prisoners to cooperate should be attributed to the fact that at the time many of them were grappling with their own positions on theoretical and practical problems similar to those they were asked to relate to in the interviews. Consequently, rather than follow the course of a structured questionnaire, many of our conversations took the form of an exchange of thoughts and ideas about such issues as the study programs that political prisoners developed inside Israeli jails or the relevance of Marxist thinking to the education of Palestinian activists. My interviewees and I were at first surprised to discover the many commonalties that united us in terms of general outlook and belief, despite obvious dissimilarities and disagreements. The literature they consulted, the writings that inspired them, the historical leaders they admired, so it turned out, mirrored my own inclinations and preferences. It also turned out that many of these men belonged to the same generation as me, and that some had entered Bethlehem University at the same time that I began my studies at the Hebrew University. A salient difference was that at about the same stage that I became active in the Jewish-Arab student group "Campus," they had been sent to serve time in Israeli prisons on charges of political activism.[21]

Finally, the enthusiasm of former prisoners should also be attributed to the inner conviction that motivated and engaged them at that time. It is quite reasonable to assume that if had I begun fieldwork two years later, when many of the hopes that accompanied and nurtured the Intifada had been shattered and some of its outstanding achievements had dissipated, I would have met with a different atmosphere in Dheisheh, and the fullness of the world of political prisoners that was revealed to me in 1992–93 would have been less accessible. Taken together, these lines of reasoning go a long way to explain what would at first appear to be a paradox: that precisely the most sensitive subject, one whose broaching might have been expected to elicit suspicion and hesitation, instead brought the highest level of response and cooperation on the part of interviewees who were, at once, most deeply involved and most vulnerable.

Notwithstanding the powerful effect of solidarity in creating and reinforcing understanding, it is not the same as sharing status, identity, or an ongoing existential fate. At no stage during fieldwork did I "go Dheishehian," whatever that might boil down to, or entertain myself with the illusion of becoming Dheishehian—though I must confess that, at the time, a taxi driver's remark concerning my Dheishehian-like pronunciation was enough to "make my day." And the recurring gesture on the part of my hosts to extend their family or *hamule* title to me: "But sure, by now you've become Maya Laham…" (or Abu-ᶜAker, or Abu-Laban), could not have been more flattering. If I did not "go Dheishehian," it was not because of formal academic advice or requirements concerning "detachment," for these are almost impossible to observe, and it was not so much because of the wide sociocultural gap that separated my upbringing, background, and style of living from that of the Dheishehians, for in times of great upheaval, and those were certainly such times, even the most marked differences appear to be bridgeable or at least manageable. Neither was it the national divide that stopped me, since the supposedly obliging rules and the comforting lures of nationalism had lost their biding power and appeal for me long before Dheisheh appeared upon my horizons. Rather, the barrier rested in the fact that no matter how close shared experiences could bring me with the Dheishehians, at the end of the day I returned to and remained a member of a world that was apart from theirs. The land of Occupation and military regime and the land of statehood, citizenship, and entitlements, it should be recalled, form a single geographical unit, the distances within which are ridiculously small. Indeed, it takes approximately twenty to twenty-five minutes to drive from my home in West Jerusalem to Dheisheh. It was this unbearable proximity of the "worlds apart" that overwhelmed me throughout my fieldwork (and long after that stage was over), ensuring that I carried both contrasting realities wherever I went, rather then dwelling comfortably in either.

PART ONE

Occupation, Day Wage Labor, and Family Life in Dheisheh

Introduction

THROUGHOUT MOST years of the Israeli Occupation the majority of workers from Dheisheh were day laborers who worked in Israel, particularly in West Jerusalem and the surrounding settlements. This fact was by no means unique to Dheisheh; it can be seen as a central characteristic of the occupational structure of the West Bank and Gaza Strip from the mid-1970s until the early 1990s. The cross-regional dependence on employment opportunities in the Israeli labor market that prevailed during those years is indicative of the homogenizing effects of the political economy of the Occupation on the various social constituencies of the Palestinian population—villagers, urbanites, noncamp refugees, and camp dwellers. At the same time this dependence found specific manifestations and expressions in the work and life histories of members of each community and social group.

Wage laborers from Dheisheh included men and women of three successive generations. In the first generation were the uprooted villagers of 1948 who had arrived in Dheisheh as adults and who were in their forties or fifties in 1967 when the Israeli Occupation started. In the intermediate generation were those who came to Dheisheh as children in 1948 or were born shortly after the war, and who were in their twenties or late teens in 1967. Those who belong to the younger generation and who came of age in the 1970s and 1980s lived all or most of their lives under the Occupation.

Most men of the older generation and a substantial number of those in the intermediate one had begun their working lives as laborers under Jordanian rule, and some, under British rule. Most women of the older and intermediate generation, some men of the intermediate generation, and all the younger women and men joined the labor force during the Occupation. Thus, the unfolding of the working lives of all the groups can be viewed as part of the process of the proletarianization of peasants and refugees over more than fifty years.

This part of the book addresses the interrelationships between military occupation, the working lives of male and female wage laborers, and central dimensions of family life in Dheisheh. Chapter 1 highlights components of the political economy of the Israeli Occupation, that is, the "systemic context" within which wage labor by the Dheishehians took place. Chapter 2 discusses the work histories of laborers from the perspectives of generation and gender. The breakdown into subgroups along these lines supplements statistical indicators and concepts, such as participation in the labor force, and rate of unemployment, with data concerning the work experiences and the standard of living held by individuals during given periods of their lives. One is thus able to trace the effects of the determinants of the Occupation at the microsocial level. The detailed examination of the subgroups facilitates a subsequent intergenerational comparison of the main characteristics of labor histories, forming the basis for generalizations with respect to the social process involved.

Chapter 3 looks at female and male wage laborers in the context of the life and work cycle of the multigenerational refugee family. I analyze family patterns of organization, particularly family divisions of labor, in their relation to the labor market, and the impact of wage labor on internal family relationships and statuses. This perspective enables a view of family organization as a form of confrontation with and joint struggle against systemic restrictions and impediments that emanate from the Israeli military control, on the one hand, while illuminating inequalities, tensions, and conflicts generated within in the family, on the other.

CHAPTER 1

Israeli Occupation

THE SYSTEMIC CONTEXT

The West Bank Within the Jordanian Economy Prior to 1967

THE 1948 WAR HAD disastrous consequences for economic development in what was to become the West Bank.[1] Formerly an integral part of Palestine, this area was now severed from the territory on which Israel was established, cut off from its main trading routes, ports, and commercial, urban, and cultural centers. Thousands lost their jobs who prior to the war had depended on waged employment away from their home locales, mainly in the port cities of Jaffa and Haifa or with the British army and police force. Landed property, cultivated fields, and orchards that remained within the new Israeli state were lost to their owners.

Hundreds of thousands of refugees fled to the West Bank in the course of the 1948 war and its aftermath, almost doubling the original population (465,800 in 1946 according to the British census) according to some sources. Estimates of the size of the refugee population vary; the UN economic mission gave the figures of as many as 431,500 refugees in the West Bank and 100,905 in the East Bank in 1950, while the United Nations Relief and Works Agency for Palestine Refugees in the Near East (UNRWA) estimated a total of 465,000 refugees in both locales.[2] Approximately one-third of the refugees, most of peasant origin, settled in some twenty refugee camps in the West Bank, including the Jordan Valley; others settled in towns and on their outskirts, and to a lesser extent in villages. However, the initial distribution of refugees on the two banks of the Jordan River changed rapidly, due to ongoing migration from the West Bank to the Amman region.

King Abdullah's annexation of the West Bank to Jordan in 1950 profoundly changed the sociodemographic composition of his kingdom. To the indigenous population of Transjordan, estimated at 450,000 in 1948—mainly nomadic, seminomadic, and sedentary Bedouin tribes; rural non-Bedouins; and a small urban population—were added some 800,000 to 900,000 persons, approximately half of them refugees, who were subsequently granted Jordanian citizenship. This large Palestinian population was relatively more advanced in terms of education and literacy, standards of health services, size of urban centers (including mixed Arab and Jewish cities), participation in the waged labor force, and spread of political organizations, trade unions, and newspapers. Some of the disparities between the Palestinian and indigenous Transjordanian populations had lasting sociopolitical consequences in the decades that followed (Mishal 1978, 3–5; Owen 1988).

Initially a creation of colonial interests and divisions on a sparsely populated, desert terrain, Jordan of the 1950s and 1960s was characterized by scarcity of water and cultivable land, absence of state infrastructure and services, exaggerated expenditure on defense, and reliance on military and other aid, mainly British. Jordan remained an agrarian country, with agriculture accounting for nearly 35 percent of the employed in the early 1960s, though no more than 13 percent of the land was cultivable. Less than 11 percent of the employed Jordanians were in (light) manufacturing in 1961, most in the processing of agricultural produce (soap, tobacco, canning), cement production, and the extraction of phosphates.

Government allocations for infrastructure, construction, industry, and transportation facilities were almost exclusively invested in the East Bank, and especially in the region of the capital, Amman. This preferential policy, along with joblessness in the West Bank, gave rise to accelerated migration to Amman and its vicinity, especially by refugees, and to a corresponding rapid process of urbanization in that region. Indeed, the population of the East Bank more than doubled between 1949 and 1961, with Amman growing from 43,000 in 1944 to 246,000 in 1961 and 350,000 in 1967; approximately two-thirds were Palestinians (Aruri 1972, 50–69).

In 1961 the labor force participation in Jordan was only 23 percent, indicating both the high proportion of the young (under fourteen) in the population and the underutilization of the employable population. The rate of unemployment among refugees in 1955 was as high as 50 percent, with the majority of the other half temporarily or seasonally employed (International Bank for Construction and Development 1957). Labor migration from Jordan (mainly to the Persian Gulf) reached more than one hundred thousand in 1967, with the majority of migrants being Palestinians. Starting in the 1960s, remittances from workers abroad began to acquire increasing weight in the Jordanian economy (Kanovsky 1989; Share 1987, 33–34; Seccombe 1987, 119). The expanding armed and police forces, largely maintained and subsidized through external aid, constituted another major branch of employment; together with the administration, this accounted for almost one-fifth of the labor force in the early 1960s.

The Jordanian economy had a very low absorptive capacity with respect to the overwhelming majority of the Palestinian refugees. Landless, propertyless, and dependent on the basic provisions and services of UNRWA, the refugee population was forced into labor migration for its livelihood. Labor migration took various forms: seasonal, as in grain harvesting and olive picking, with whole refugee families spending the summer months working as sharecroppers in the fields and orchards of large landowners; temporary, in construction and quarrying jobs throughout the country; and work stints of longer or shorter duration, as in the migration, via not yet established and sometimes illegal routes, of laborers to Kuwait and Saudi Arabia.

Acquisition of education by the second refugee generation would create, starting from the early 1960s, a new labor migrant, the skilled and professional. The Israeli occupation would then open up a new labor market for Palestinians.

Israeli Military and Political Control

Israel's occupation of the West Bank and Gaza Strip in June 1967 brought a population of approximately one million Palestinians under military control. An estimated 250,000 Palestinians, who fled or were displaced during the war, were not allowed to return to the West Bank (Zureik 1996, 21).

As of June 6, 1967, executive, legislative, and judicial power was vested in the military government. Some fifteen hundred military orders regulating all aspects of life, civilian, economic, and political, of the occupied population were enforced over the years between 1967 and 1993 (JMCC [Jerusalem Media and Communications Centre], April 1994). The four hundred "core orders" that were issued during the first four years (1967 to 1971) laid the foundation for the Occupation regime. These orders provided the military government full control over the use and allocation of land and water, including the power to expropriate land, all transactions in immovable property, export and imports of goods, operation of the banking system, administration of local and municipal councils, and the issuing of identity cards, licenses, travel, work, and professional permits. Military courts were established and given exclusive jurisdiction over "security offenses," political activity was banned, printed material was subject to censorship, and far-reaching restrictions were imposed on human rights (Shehadeh 1993, 104–5).

CONTROL OVER LAND AND WATER RESOURCES

Israel did not formally annex the Occupied Territories, but the enactment of military orders made possible the expropriation and confiscation of between 60 and 70 percent of the lands of the West Bank and at least 40 percent of the territory of the Gaza Strip (UNCTAD 1993, 26). Land seizure, which began in the first year of the Occupation, was accelerated in late 1970s, with the coming to power of the first Likud government (Benvenisti 1984; Shehadeh 1993), and it was vigorously continued into the second half of the 1990s; that is, long after the signing of the Declaration of Principles between Israel and the Palestine Liberation Organization (PLO) (Aronson 1996; JMCC 1997; B'tselem 2002). Expropriations, which included state-owned, public, and private lands, were carried out under a variety of pretexts and titles—such as "security needs," "public purposes," "nature reserves," and "absentee property"—facilitated by the adjustment of judicial procedures for that purpose.[3] Only 2 percent of the land was acquired through purchases or lease from Palestinians (UNCTAD 1993, 26).

Expropriated land served a range of Israeli military, economic, and political interests, primarily the establishment of more than 140 Jewish settlements, the rendering of large areas into closed military zones, the construction of a ramified road network that connected settlements and army camps with Israel proper, and the subsequent bisecting and "cantonization" of the Palestinian territory (Benvenisti 1984; Center for Policy Analysis on Palestine 1995; JMCC 1997). At the same time, Israel imposed heavy restrictions on the rights of Palestinians to build on, reclaim, and cultivate the land remaining in their hands. Nor were Palestinians served by the huge Israeli government investment in infrastructure, transport facilities, and service utilities, all of which bypassed Palestinian cities, towns, villages, and refugee camps (World Bank 1993, vol. 5, 7–8).

Israeli control over water and its allocation had two major consequences: severe restrictions on water supplies to Palestinian households and for agriculture, and extensive use of the water resources within Palestinian territory for the benefit of Israel and its settlements. Although the majority of Palestinian localities in the West Bank were connected to the Israeli water network, control over the allocation of water supply was vested entirely in the military government and its Civil Administration, which set quotas and prices. Data for the 1980s and 1990s shows that average per-capita water consumption in the West Bank was between one-fifth and one-fourth of that in Israel and the settlements, while costs for agriculture-related uses were higher by far (Elmusa 1994, 19–20; B'tselem 1998). Moreover, while military orders prevented Palestinians from drilling new wells or deepening existing ones and imposed a low ceiling on permissible water discharge, no similar restrictions were placed on Mekorot, the Israeli water company, which was permitted extensive drilling (Awartani 1988, 142–43).

As comprehensive as the aggressive and prolonged enforcement of military orders was, however, it does not fully explain the economic and social changes that took place under them.

Palestinian Workers and Wage Labor in Israel

Rising demand for labor in construction and agriculture led to the opening of the Israeli labor market, albeit under various restrictions, to Palestinian workers from the Occupied Territories, inducing significant changes in the composition of the labor force there within a short time period. Between 1968 and 1975 the number of Palestinians employed in Israel (and in Jewish settlements beyond the green line) increased sevenfold, from 9,000 to 66,300 (CBS [Central Bureau of Statistics] 1980, 969). These newcomers to the Israeli labor market can be roughly divided into three categories: workers who had lost their workplaces as a result of the war or who sought better employment opportunities (many of them laborers from refugee camps and poorer urban neighborhoods), as well as former employees of the Jordanian police and army; formerly self-employed workers (mainly peasants who had previously worked their land), artisans, and small merchants;[4] and new participants in the labor force, mainly young people who had reached working age in the postwar period (Hilal 1976).

The 66,300 Palestinian laborers who worked in Israel in 1975 constituted one-third of the employed and more than half of all wage workers from the Occupied Territories (CBS 1980, 696, 697), an indirect indicator of the scarcity of employment opportunities on the local markets. The twelve years that followed were marked by a more moderate annual increase in the number of those employed in Israel, who totaled 109,000 in 1987 (the eve of the Intifada), with only slight changes in their relative share of the Palestinian labor force. Thus, the 94,700 workers from the Occupied Territories who were employed in Israel in 1986 constituted 35.2 percent of the labor force and 57.7 percent of all wage workers (CBS 1988, 722, 727, 729). Data relating separately to the Gaza Strip reveal that workers in Israel constituted 45.4 percent and 67.5 percent of the labor force and wage laborers, respectively (CBS 1988, 722, 727, 729). The difference is to be attributed to the more rapid depletion of sources of livelihood inside the Gaza Strip, where agricultural land was much smaller in comparison with that in the West Bank, and where three-quarters of the population are refugees.

It should be borne in mind, however, that all above figures of the Israeli Central Bureau of Statistics (CBS) pertain to workers registered through the labor exchanges (that is, those bearing work permits). It is generally acknowledged that approximately 30 percent of the Palestinians who worked in Israel in the late 1980s and early 1990s were nonregistered. Thus, a reliable source estimated the actual number of Palestinians who worked in Israel in 1990 at 120,000 to 150,000 (Kav La'Oved, June 1992).

During the years 1975–87, the breakdown by economic branches of Palestinian laborers employed in Israel was more or less constant: between 45 and 55 percent worked in building and construction, between 12 and 16 percent in agriculture, and between 17 and 21 percent in (labor-intensive) industry, while between 13 and 20 percent were employed in various manual services such as kitchen work, catering, cleaning, and vehicle repair (CBS 1988, 781). Palestinians from the Occupied Territories were barred from employment in the state-owned government sector, as well as in all the registered professions inside Israel, a fact that partially accounts for the concentration of Palestinian workers in a few branches and solely in manual labor. It is worth mentioning that in 1987 only 3.4 percent of all employed Israeli Jews worked in the construction branch, whereas 30.4 percent were employed in public services (CBS 1993, 384–85). While Palestinians from the Occupied Territories constituted only some 7.2 percent of all employed in Israel (1987), their share among those employed in construction was as high as 40 percent (Zakai 1988, 14).

Unlike Israeli workers, however, Palestinians employed in Israel did not receive social benefits. According to an Israeli government decision dating from 1970, the wages of Palestinian workers who were registered with the labor exchanges were subject to deductions—the same percentages taken from Israeli workers—for National Insurance (social security), income tax, pension funds, and health insurance. Nonetheless, Palestinian workers were denied the principal rights provided by the National Insurance Institute, namely, unemployment benefits, pension, disability payment, and widow and dependent children allowances, in spite of the deductions from their wages to these ends; compensation was awarded only in the case of work-related injury (Kav La'Oved, June 1992). Under the title of "organization tax," Palestinian workers paid dues to the Histadrut—the General Federation of Israeli Trade Unions—despite the fact that residents of the Occupied Territories were denied membership in Israeli trade unions. Nor were West Bank or Gaza Strip trade unions recognized by the Histadrut, and they were in fact outlawed by the military government.

Moreover, workers from the Occupied Territories who were employed in Israel, registered and nonregistered alike, received their wages on a day-to-day basis, no matter how long they worked for the same employer, much to their detriment in terms of pay, seniority, and protection against layoff. Throughout the years of Israeli rule Palestinian workers from the Occupied Territories were prohibited from remaining overnight in Israel proper. Work in Israel was not accompanied, therefore, by the migration of laborers and their families to the locations of employment.

Complementary Dimensions of the System: Contraction and Underdevelopment of Local Economic Branches

Whereas ongoing demand for labor (albeit subject to fluctuations) in specific branches of the Israeli economy constituted the main "pull" factor that drew workers to seek employment in Israel, the economic policy of the occupation regime in the Territories provided the major "push" factor that discharged workers from the local market and forced them to seek work away from home. The components of this policy were, primarily, a total lack of governmental investment in the development of infrastructure and of industry; the flooding of the Palestinian market with (tax-exempted) Israeli industrial goods and agricultural produce, accompanied by heavy restrictions on Palestinian agricultural exports; extensive land confiscation and substandard allocation of water; denial of permits to Palestinian entrepreneurs; and the absence of state-sponsored incentives in the form of subsidies, tax concessions, and credit facilities. They all contributed to a process of underdevelopment of the local economy, and to the ongoing contraction of employment opportunities within its boundaries. Several trends loom large:

The marginalization of village-based agriculture as a source of subsistence and income. The consequences of this marginalization process are clearly manifest in the steep decline in the rate of those employed in local agriculture. Whereas in 1970 42.5 percent of the locally employed labor force in the West Bank and 31.6 percent in the Gaza Strip worked in agriculture, mainly on village farms, the rates in 1987 were 26 percent and 16 percent, respectively (CBS 1988, 727); the figures for the two areas in 1997 were as low as 10.8 percent and 10.1 percent, respectively (PCBS 1998). At the same time, approximately 60 percent of the West Bank population continued to reside in rural localities (more than four hundred villages) (Heiberg and Ovensen 1993, 42).

Nondevelopment of local industry and subcontracting for Israeli firms. According to a comprehensive report by the UN Conference on Trade and Development (UNCTAD), the manufacturing sector "was the weakest link in the Palestinian economy in the twenty-five years of occupation. . . . Its share in Gross Domestic Product (GDP) had remained as low as 5 to 6 percent, much of it linked to the Israeli economy through subcontracting arrangements with Israeli firms where the benefits of value added through higher pricing policies accrued to Israeli enterprises rather than to the Palestinian entrepreneurs" (UNCTAD 1993, 13). Simcha Bahiri noted that "the relative size of the combined West Bank and Gaza Strip industry was only an insignificant

1.4 percent of Israeli industry," and that the total value added by West Bank industry comprised a lower output than that of some of Israel's corporations (Bahiri 1987, 17). Thus, the relative share of persons employed in Occupied Territories–based "industry" remained almost unchanged between 1970 and 1987, accounting for between 14 and 16 percent of the locally employed labor force (CBS 1988, 727). In absolute numbers, it was a minor increase, from 21,000 to 28,500 employees over seventeen years.

"Industrial" establishments in the West Bank and Gaza Strip prior to and through the Occupation consisted predominantly of small-scale, labor-intensive workshops, wherein family labor and financing played a significant role. Of 2,497 establishments in the West Bank in 1985, only fifty-five employed more than twenty-one workers, and 2,300 employed fewer than eight workers, the average number of employees per enterprise being 4.3 (Bahiri 1987, 70). In 1987 approximately 1,900 establishments in the Gaza Strip employed a total of 9,000 workers, an average of four to five workers each (Roy 1995a, 234). Manufacturing firms were mainly engaged in processing foodstuffs, textiles and clothing, leather products, wood and wood products, rubber, plastics, metals and nonmetallic minerals, and olive oil soap, while services included electrical and vehicle repairs, printing shops, and so forth (Awartani 1979; UNCTAD 1993, 14).

The significantly lower costs of labor in the Occupied Territories encouraged Israeli firms, especially in the textile, clothing, and leather branches, to outsource production, or rather the finishing of manufactured goods, under subcontracting arrangements, to West Bank and Gaza Strip workshops. Lack of capital, machinery, subsidies, or credit facilities, along with adverse marketing conditions, forced local entrepreneurs to enter such arrangements, which, in general, were short-lived, marked by chronic instability due to fluctuations in demands, priorities, and marketing preferences of the Israeli owners.

Contraction of the public (government) sector.   Under Israeli rule all branches and affairs of the public (formerly government) sector were in the hands of the military government.[5] Beginning in 1981, and in the wake of an Israeli attempt to strengthen its hold over the Palestinian territories, the (military) administration of civilian departments was extended to the Civil Administration. While the population of the Occupied Territories almost tripled during the years of Occupation—from around one million in 1967 to 2.8 million in 1997 (PCBS 1998)—the public sector saw ongoing contraction and retrenchment, reflected in both the deteriorating standard of public services and facilities, especially in the spheres of education and health, and in the decrease in its relative share as an employer. In light of the absence of indigenous Palestinian government institutions, the negligible expenditures of the Israeli authorities on public services, and a corresponding very low rate of recruitment to jobs in the Civil Administration, the contribution of the public sector to the absorption of professional and semiprofessional labor power was marginal. Moreover, it showed a steady decrease over time. Thus, whereas in 1970 employees in the public sector accounted for 12.7 percent and 15.3 percent of the locally employed labor force in the West Bank and Gaza, respectively, the corresponding rates for 1992 were 11.3 and 9.7 percent (CBS 1993, 780).

Out-migration from the Occupied Territories as a demographic factor.   Restricted employment opportunities in the Israeli labor market and dwindling opportunities for work inside the West Bank and Gaza Strip were major reasons for the rising rate of out-migration, mainly labor migration. This phenomenon, which, as noted, was already of significant magnitude during the pre-Occupation era, acquired much wider scope starting from the mid-1970s and into the mid-1980s, corresponding to the growing demand for skilled and professional labor in the Gulf states. Between 1975 and 1982, 102,000 persons left the West Bank, a figure equal to 56.6 percent of the natural population increase during those years (179,900) (CBS 1985, 703). According to Eitan Sabatello, young men with secondary and postsecondary education were highly overrepresented in the migrant population. Indeed, he found that with respect to certain age cohorts, specifically those born in the 1950s and 1960s, the number of male migrants exceeded that of men who remained (Sabatello 1984, 4–7).

The Third Decade of Occupation: Closures and Drastic Decline in Employment

Since the eruption of the Intifada in December 1987, and increasingly from the early and mid-1990s, the scope of Palestinian employment in Israel has undergone a steep decline. Excessive use of curfew—the most common means of collective punishment—during the first three years of the uprising, prevented entire populations from leaving their homes for longer and shorter periods.[6] For many, layoff and then unemployment followed curfew-forced absence from work. Then, in January 1991, upon the outbreak of the Gulf War, Palestinians of the Occupied Territories were subjected to an extended curfew, and entrance into Israel was barred for more than two months. When they returned to their former workplaces, thousands of workers discovered that their employers had found replacements. Starting in 1992, Israel enforced a series of periodic closures on the Territories, which it justified as a reaction to Palestinian terrorist attacks against Israeli citizens.[7] Previous policy was replaced by new regulations that conditioned work in Israel on holding permits from the Civil Administration. Work permits were issued on a selective basis, according to (changing) criteria of age, marital and family status, and "security record."

According to the findings of the comprehensive survey conducted by the Fafo Institute for Applied Social Research in 1992, of the entire labor force in the Occupied Territories, the relative share of workers employed in Israel decreased from 35.4 percent in 1987 to 26 percent in 1991–92. The rate in the West Bank was at a low of 22 percent, while a breakdown along type of locales found the steepest decline among residents of refugee camps: only 15 percent of the labor force continued to work in Israel at the time. Less than 30 percent of the male labor force in the Gaza Strip was fully employed, as against a high of around 55 percent in the category of partially or part-time employed. The corresponding figures for the West Bank were 50 percent and 43 percent, respectively (Heiberg and Ovensen 1993, 188–93, 201–2). In the context of the Occupied Territories, the category of "part-time employed" referred to workers who were essentially jobless for a substantial part of the period surveyed.

While Palestinians were being forced out of their workplaces in Israel, no alternative employment opportunities were created in the Territories. Moreover, the mass expulsion of hundreds of thousands of Palestinians from Kuwait in the months that preceded the Gulf War meant that thousands of families in the Territories who were accustomed to receiving remittances lost a central source of income.

The enforcement of a comprehensive general closure in March 1993 marked a further step in the direction of tightening the borders of Israel— including annexed Arab Jerusalem—to Palestinians of the Occupied Territories in general, and to Palestinian workers in particular. Tens of thousands lost their jobs in the immediate wake of that closure, which has not been officially lifted since (as of 2003). Once again, eligibility for (short-term) work permits was contingent upon the worker's obtaining a series of additional documents from various departments of the Civil Administration, including a security clearance, and upon specific age and family status criteria.[8] In the wake of pressure from big contractors in the construction and agriculture branches, Israel began to import tens of thousands of migrant laborers from Romania, Thailand, Turkey, the Philippines, China, and elsewhere, replacing the "discharged" Palestinians at building sites, restaurants, and in agriculture. By May 1995 their number was estimated at approximately one hundred thousand.

The permit and quota policy continued into the second half of the 1990s, with the number of Palestinians working in Israel dropping to a low of a few thousand, and rising to a high of fifty to sixty thousand during months of more "relaxed" regulations, very far below the estimated 120,000 to 150,000 at the end of the previous decade. It is highly unlikely that a smooth mass "dismissal" of workers would have been possible had the right to unemployment benefits been recognized.

CHAPTER 2

Dheishehians and Day Wage Labor
in Israel and the West Bank

At a certain point in our conversation my interviewees,
members of the Mashni family, grew curious to learn
where I worked. I told them that I teach at the Hebrew
University. "Where?" they inquired about the exact location. "At Mount Scopus or at Givat Ram?" Five of the
Mashnis had worked at the Givat Ram campus; the father
as a gardener, the mother and three sons as cleaners. At the
time of my visit—July 1993, five months after the first
general closure was imposed—they had all been laid off.

The Older Refugee Generation: Male Wage Laborers

Members of the older refugee generation were born in the 1920s and early
1930s. Under British Mandate rule they worked on their lands as *fallahun*
(peasants) and shepherds. During World War II and until the British evacua-
tion of Palestine, many were employed for shorter or longer periods with
the Mandate's police force or as laborers in British army camps, ammunition
storehouses, and factories. After the uprooting from their villages, they wandered as displaced persons for many months, at times for as long as six or
seven years, from one place of refuge to another until finally settling in
Dheisheh. In the course of the Jordanian rule, the majority subsisted with
great difficulty on casual wage labor in construction and agriculture, and on
the meager relief rations that UNRWA provided. Some served for a number of years in the Jordanian army, others found more permanent employment with the UNRWA sanitation and maintenance departments or with
the municipality of Bethlehem, still others migrated to the East Bank in
search of work, and a few ran small grocery shops and bakeries in the camp.
They first lived in tents and later in the tiny shelters that were set up by
UNRWA, a room per family with outside toilet and kitchen.
    When the Occupation was imposed in June 1967, the younger members
of this generation were in their late thirties and the older in their forties and

early fifties. Some were already parents to adult sons and daughters who had started families of their own, some had children who completed college or university and had migrated in search of professional employment. Given their relatively advanced ages and the presence of younger candidates—more capable and fit for work—among their close kin, a low rate of participation in the post-1967 Dheishehian labor force might have been predicted for this generation. Yet members of this generation were among the first Dheishehians to be incorporated into the ranks of the employed in Israel and the Jewish settlements, and they endured as "daily migrant laborers" for longer years than many of their younger counterparts.

CHARACTERISTICS AND CONDITIONS OF EMPLOYMENT

Of the thirty-nine men who were included in my core sample, twenty-nine had worked in Israel for time periods that ranged from three to twenty-four years. Forty of eighty participants in a larger sample were reported to have spent most of their employment during the Occupation in Israel and/or the settlements.[1] The combined data make it plausible to assume that between 50 and 75 percent of the Dheishehian men who belong to the older generation had worked in Israel and/or the settlements for varying time periods. Employment with Israeli contractors among this age group was still rare in 1968–69, became prevalent in the early 1970s, and remained commonplace until the first year of the Intifada (1988), after which time it declined sharply, becoming negligible in the 1990s.

From the early 1970s onward, laborers from Dheisheh were hired by Israeli building contractors and contracting companies to work in West Jerusalem and in the mushrooming settlements that were expanding rapidly on expropriated Arab land on the outskirts of the city and the more distant surroundings. Interviewees usually responded with a long list of locations when asked to provide their work history. While shedding light on the nature of their working experiences, their answers also revealed something about the politics of Jerusalem's changing topography during the last few decades. A typical example, using names in Arabic and Hebrew alternately, is seen in Abu Mahmud's reply: "I worked in Bayit Vegan, in Deir Yasin, in Maliha, in Neve Yacov, then in Gilo, and then in Hizma." Bayit Vegan is a Jewish neighborhood in West Jerusalem; Deir Yasin and Maliha are the names of two Palestinian villages that ceased to exist in the aftermath of the 1948 war, on the land and ruins of which stand Jewish residential areas and industrial centers (Givat Shaul and Manhat); Neve Yacov and Gilo are two large "satellite" Jewish neighborhoods, to the north and south of Jerusalem, respectively, which were built on expropriated land that was annexed to the city's municipal boundaries shortly after the 1967 war; Hizma is a Palestinian village located between Jerusalem and Ramallah. In the context of Abu Mahmud's answer, however, it refers to the large Jewish settlement Pisgat Zeev, which was built on the land of Hizma proper and on that of nearby villages.

Most members of this generation worked on building and infrastructure projects as masons, plasterers, tilers, stonecutters, quarry workers, road builders, and so on, the majority with the status of what is known in colloquial Arabic and Hebrew as an "ordinary" laborer (ʿamil ʿadi in Arabic, poel pashut or poel ragil in Hebrew), a minority as overseers. Others were service workers and gardeners, mainly in public institutions such as hospitals, university campuses, and schools, but also in private institutions and homes. Several interviewees worked as nonskilled factory laborers in Jerusalem and the town of Beit Shemesh, in the clothing and textile industry and in food processing and packing, though this form of employment was less prevalent. Men over sixty, as well as men who suffered from disability or chronic illness, often worked as night watchmen at construction sites.

All twenty-nine who had worked with Israeli employers spent at least some part of their working lives in construction, where work is extremely demanding physically and at times dangerous. Abu Ahmad, a sixty-year-old stonecutter, more than forty years on the job, twenty of them under Israeli employers, described the grueling routine:

I am no longer the man I used to be. I can feel the tiredness coming over me. Each day I leave home around six in the morning and return after four in the afternoon. I operate a machine that chops the stones and then proceed with the cutting using a big hammer. Much of my work is done in the shade (under a roof) but on many occasions I spend the entire working day in the sun.

Particularly dangerous are the jobs that take place on scaffolding and others that involve the carrying and moving of heavy loads. Three of the twenty-nine men suffered severe head, arm, or leg injuries that left them permanently disabled. However, the need for income, especially in the absence of entitlement to social benefits, has given rise to an inclination to delay retirement and stretch the years of employment as far as possible.

All laborers who worked in Israel were hired on a day basis, and their wages were calculated by the hour. There was no distinction in this respect between "legal" workers who were registered with the local labor exchange and nonregistered ("illegal") workers, whose employment was not reported by employers to the tax authorities. Neither was there a distinction between laborers who worked for big construction corporations, others who were employed by medium and small contractors, and those who worked in factories. At the end of each month a registered laborer received a paycheck that specified the number of full workdays and partial days. Days or hours of absence due to illness or personal circumstances, or as a result of curfew, closure, and other means of collective punishment, were deducted. Nonregistered laborers were hired "per project," often indirectly, via a local subcontractor who paid "his" workers upon the completion of the task or part of it, according to the prevalent wages on the market. In 1986–87, the last two years of more-or-less regular employment in Israel among members of this age group, the average daily wage of an unskilled, "ordinary" construction laborer was around thirty shekels (NIS). In 1993–94 the average daily wages were sixty to seventy shekels for an unskilled construction laborer, forty to fifty shekels for a watchman, gardener, or cleaner, and NIS 100 to 120 for highly skilled laborers and overseers. The gap between the 1986–87 and 1993–94 pay scales reflects the devaluation of the shekel during this time period (one shekel equaled approximately $0.33 in 1993–94). In 1993 the average monthly wages of a Palestinian construction worker in Israel amounted to about one-third of an Israeli construction worker's.[2]

The twenty-nine participants in the sample who had worked in Israel were employed there for an average of 13.4 years. Since employment with Israeli contractors was rare before 1970, and since the majority were "discharged" shortly after the outbreak of the Intifada, the average is taken against a possible total of eighteen years. Indeed, apart from those who suffered severe injuries or became chronically ill, the majority of the respondents reported that they had been "attached" to Israeli employers for fifteen years or more. The total time of attachment to the Israeli labor market, however, is often more an indication of a worker's perseverance than of continuous employment. One has to distinguish between two categories of workers: the significantly smaller one includes those who were employed by one contractor or contracting company throughout most years of work, while the much larger group encompasses those workers who had circulated between many employers, at times dozens. The twenty-nine workers under review reported working for seven employers on average. Many found it hard to recall the names of all their former employers and workplaces.

Palestinians working in Israel and registered with the Labor Bureau were denied the principal rights to which Israeli citizens were entitled through the National Insurance Law, despite the required insurance reductions. Nonpayment of unemployment benefits was a salient consequence of this exclusionist policy.[3] Movement from one employer to another meant a search for alternative employment that could last many months without income. Many of the interviewees noted long interruptions between jobs, and some pointed out that the sum total of years of joblessness equaled the years of employment. Thus, the discontinuous or intermittent nature of employment in Israel often implied a large gap between the "gross" years of attachment to Israeli employers and the actual or net years of waged employment. Even highly skilled laborers who were fortunate to have spent most years of employment with a single contractor were not spared the plight of layoff, as in the case of Abu Mustafa, a highly esteemed veteran stonecutter:

I was working for the same company for over fifteen years. I was the most experienced person and the most exacting and professional at work. They used to call me the "engineer," and put me in charge of fifteen other laborers. Then one day the boss comes and tells me that he is sorry but there is no need for my work any longer. I sat at home for two years and waited. At my age, where could I go? Then one day the boss called and asked me to go back to work.

Most members of the older generation who worked in Israel stopped working during the first year of the Intifada. These were days of great turmoil in Dheisheh, marked by mass participation of camp residents in protest demonstrations and by massive measures of repression on the part of the Israeli army. Recurring curfews of long and short duration that were imposed on the camp every other week or so forced all residents to stay shut in inside their homes and resulted in frequent absences of laborers from their workplaces. In addition, most workers observed the calls of the Unified National Leadership of the Uprising (UNLU) for general strikes on specified dates and occasions. Israeli employers did not wait too long and recruited whatever alternative labor they could find. Although in the years that followed many members of this generation made attempts to rejoin the labor force despite their age, only a small number succeeded, and then not in construction proper. Of the few who continued to work in Israel in the early 1990s, the majority were employed as night watchmen at construction sites, working twelve-hour shifts for fifty to sixty shekels.

Another, concomitant consequence of employment on a day or hourly basis and exclusion from National Insurance benefits was the denial of the right to pension upon retirement or dismissal from work. Aging registered workers whose contracts were not renewed by the employers, like those who retired due to age or disability, were entitled to a one-time severance compensation payment that equaled average monthly income multiplied by the number of years of work with the last employer. Since the majority had changed workplaces many times, the duration of "last employment" rarely exceeded several years. In any case, the total sums were extremely low. Abu ʿAdnan, who had worked in Israel for twenty-four years, a record twenty-one with the same contracting company, and who retired in 1992 at the age of sixty-five, received the highest compensation sum of all workers in my sample: NIS 13,600 (approximately forty-five hundred dollars at the time), calculated on the basis of an average monthly income of NIS 620 multiplied by twenty-one years. Many workers, however, were not registered with the Labor Bureau and thus were not entitled even to this meager compensation.

Abu Fuad said that when he retired, close to age seventy, he received NIS 1,600 on the basis of his wage for the last two years: "In the ten years that preceded those two last years, I was not registered, but I worked for the same contractor, who finally laid me off without any compensation. I cannot imagine what it would be like if all my previous bosses would give me the compensations I deserve." Almost all the interviewees described themselves as "ordinary" laborers, a somewhat misleading term that often pertains more to the level of income and to status than to skill and competence at work. Many among those who so designated themselves had spent years as skilled stonecutters or masons, but enjoyed no form of promotion. The case of Nimer, a sixty-two-year-old skilled stonecutter with thirty-six years' experience on the job, is illuminating:

I've been working with the same contractor, Ben–Giat, for almost fourteen years now. They pay me by the hour; if I miss a day they take it off. I worked in Beit Hakerem, Gilo, and Kiryat Yovel, and also in Khalil (Hebron), at the place where Levinger lives.[4] The boss hardly remembers my name, sometimes calls me Omar, sometimes Nimer. He pays me fifty-three shekels per day [in 1992]. Whenever I ask for a raise he says that this is not the right time and that I should be patient.

Very few interviewees were promoted to the status of overseers. Among the exceptions was Abu Mustafa, Nimer's younger brother (two years' his junior), who was employed by the same contractor (Ben-Giat). In 1992 his daily wage of NIS 120 was more than twice that of his brother, and the highest among all interviewees in my sample. As seen above, however, Abu Mustafa's expertise and relatively elevated position did not stop his employer from laying him off without advance notice when there was no "need" for his work.

Temporariness, lack of job security, and absence of promotion were therefore intrinsic to working in the Israeli labor market. Employment on a day basis, along with the denial of basic entitlements to unemployment benefits and pension, were the fundamental condition that undermined the possibility for job stability and upward mobility.

ALTERNATIVES TO WORK IN ISRAEL AND THE SETTLEMENTS

A reasonable estimate is that 25 percent of the members of the older generation never worked in Israel or the settlements. Most were manual laborers who were employed with UNRWA, or by the Bethlehem municipality, while some were shopkeepers and owners of small bakeries in Dheisheh. The relative advantage of UNRWA employment was in job stability (most had been employed by the agency since the 1950s), regular income, and the pension fund, all of which held increasing importance as against the inherent instability that accompanied work in Israel. However, jobs in the relevant departments of the agency—distribution, sanitation, and maintenance—were few, since UNRWA did not expand the scope of these services over the years, and turnover was low. Although Dheisheh is an active, overpopulated dwelling area, it has never had a commercial center of any significance within its confines, nor are there industries inside the camp. People do basic shopping in the central markets of Bethlehem, which are within easy reach and where goods are cheaper; purchases in the local shops are mainly of bread, soft drinks, cigarettes, falafel, sweets, and snacks. Among shop owners of the older generation are some who started their tiny businesses in the 1950s with money they received for the sheep and goats they brought with them from their villages. Most such shops are located in the owner's homes or in an adjacent yard, are no larger than small kiosks, and are maintained by family members, particularly the elderly. None of the grocery and greengrocer shops that belong to members of this generation has expanded into a profitable business. In fact, few provide more than a meager subsistence, and frequently the goods are consumed mainly by the owner's extended family, as happened to Abu ʿAwni, who recently closed his grocery: "My family 'ate up' the shop; there was no point in keeping it going."

Rare were the members of the older generation who had spent their entire working lives as construction or factory laborers in the West Bank. Most of those who turned to the local labor market did so after years of work in Israel, and usually in the wake of deteriorating health, a work-related injury and/or prolonged unemployment. Opportunities were scarce, however, particularly so for aging members of this generation. They were limited to positions as watchmen or maintenance workers in small-scale building projects or in public institutions and to jobs in the small industrial enterprises in the region, such as a plastics factory in Beit Sahour, three small factories in Doha (bordering on Dheisheh and Beit Jala) that produced cement and cement blocks, and olive oil presses in Beit Jala. Moreover, daily wages in the West Bank were about one-third to one-half lower than the respective wages for work in Israel. Hence, we find wage labor in the Bethlehem region to have functioned as a last resort and often as the last "station" in the long trajectory that laborers of the old generation traversed in the course of their working lives.

The Older Refugee Generation: Female Wage Laborers

Women who belong to the older generation were born and raised in the villages of origin; the youngest among them were girls of ten or eleven at the time of the uprooting in 1948, while the oldest were in their late teens and twenties. Some had passed the first years of refugee existence with their parents, others who had been married in the villages arrived in Dheisheh with their husbands and husband's kin. In the course of Jordanian rule, the majority had six to seven children on average, a circumstance that did not stop many of them from taking part in seasonal work in agriculture, primarily in grain harvesting and olive picking in the fields and orchards of big landowners. Long-term wage employment was not prevalent among women during those decades, though camp women who worked as housemaids, laundresses, and cooks in private households and charity institutions in Bethlehem were not unusual. When the Occupation regime was imposed in 1967, the youngest members of this generation had reached their early thirties and the oldest were in their late forties. In the course of the first decade of Occupation the younger among them gave birth to two additional children on average. My discussion centers on a distinct category of newcomers to wage labor that comprised relatively older women, mothers of eight to nine children on average.

CHARACTERISTICS AND CONDITIONS OF EMPLOYMENT

Twenty-six of the fifty-three participants older than fifty-five in my survey on women and employment (49 percent) and thirteen of the thirty-nine interviewees in the core sample (33.3 percent) reported to have worked in Israel and/or the West Bank for periods ranging from one to twenty-seven years. The combined data support the conclusion that approximately 42 percent of the female population of the older generation participated in the waged labor force for varying time periods, and that more than 70 percent of the women who were ever employed worked in Israel.[5] It should be kept in mind, however, that the category of participants in the waged labor force included women who were employed in the relatively distant past and had stopped working since, as well as women whose employment histories were short-lived. Thus, in what follows, the rate of participation in the labor force pertains to employment of varying duration in the distant past, recent past, or present, and not to active participation at the time of the survey.[6]

The phenomenon of employment in Israel of Dheishehian women acquired significant scope in the early 1970s, became commonplace in the mid-1970s, and remained so until the outbreak of the Intifada, with a sharp decline from 1988 onward. High prevalence of wage labor among women of the older generation in the years 1970–88 reflects the high demand for female labor in specific branches of the Israeli labor market during that time period, as well as the extremely high response among camp women to work opportunities. Importance should also be given to the proximity of Dheisheh to Jerusalem—less than fifteen kilometers from the camp to the center of the city—and to the availability of regular and convenient means of transportation (bus and service taxi), conditions that greatly facilitated the accessibility of workplaces.

In the early 1970s many Dheishehian women were employed in fruit picking in moshavim (semicooperative villages) and kibbutzim (communal settlements) in the Judean Mountains, the Ella Valley, and the "Jerusalem corridor." When asked about the locations, women responded, "we worked on our lands," or "we worked in Beit ʿItab, in Zakariya, in Raʾs Abu ʿAmar," referring to names of villages from which the refugee laborers originated. Since after the 1948 war, the land has been part of the Israeli agricultural settlements built on the villages' ruins. Fruit picking is seasonal, lasting regularly from May to September, the harvest time of summer fruits, mainly peaches, apricots, plums, grapes, apples, and pears. The workers were women of all ages, as well as children who joined the pickers during their vacation from school. They were not employed directly by the moshavim and kibbutzim, but rather through subcontractors, Jewish and Arab—some of whom were residents of Dheisheh, known as *raʾis(es)*. Workers received a few liras (the currency that preceded the shekel) per day, were not registered with the labor exchange, and were subject to the power of the *raʾis* who often pocketed as much as half their wages—all in all, making fruit picking one of the most exploitative employment branches.

At about the same time period, Dheishehian women began to work as wage laborers in West Jerusalem, and by the second half of the 1970s service (cleaning) and kitchen work gradually replaced fruit picking. Most laborers of the older generation who worked in West Jerusalem were employed in public institutions, mainly at university campuses, hospitals, government offices, and schools. Others worked in private homes, and a relatively small group worked in factories, mainly a biscuit factory and an underwear factory, both located in the southern Jerusalem neighborhood of Talpiot.

Findings show the Hebrew University campuses and medical centers at Givat Ram, Mount Scopus, and Hadassah hospital to have been the main workplaces of Dheishehian women throughout the years 1976–87. Umm Khader, who cleaned lecture halls, dormitories, and laboratories on all three campuses for more than twelve years, recalled that at some stage there were more than twenty Dheishehians among her fellow workers. Employment was via manpower agencies and contracting companies, and not directly through the public institutions themselves. Recruitment and entrance to the job was often facilitated through personal acquaintance, whereby one woman would bring along a neighbor, relative, or friend. Some agencies worked with local subcontractors from Dheisheh and the surrounding region who were in charge of recruiting the women and providing transportation to the workplaces. Women who were employed in private households usually worked at one or two homes a day, four days a week on average, at cleaning, washing, and other household tasks.

Approximately one-fourth of the female laborers of the older generation worked in the Bethlehem region, mainly as service and kitchen workers at schools, orphanages, and hospitals belonging to charity organizations. Some had been employed by these institutions at the time of the Jordanian regime; others joined in the 1970s and 1980s.

During the time period under consideration (1970–94), women of the older generation were in the labor force for nine years on average. However, the time range was quite varied, with women whose employment spanned over more than twenty years on one side of the scale, while the participation of others in the labor force was seasonal, intermittent, and/or of very short duration. The origin of the extreme differences can be traced to the particular factors that condition women's work outside the home.

The case of Umm Ibrahim, sixty years old in 1994, is typical of women whose labor histories were relatively continuous and lengthy. She was born in Zakariya and married in Dheisheh, where her six daughters and three sons were born and raised. In the 1960s, while she was raising seven children, three still babies, she took part in the grain harvesting in the Jordan Valley each summer: "I used to take at least one baby along with me. We worked from dawn to dusk in the fields and slept in the open every night." During the first years of the Occupation her husband, Abu Ibrahim, worked as a construction laborer in Jerusalem, but in 1975 he was severely injured in a work accident, after which he could no longer undertake physically demanding jobs. In the early 1970s, after giving birth to two additional children, Umm Ibrahim entered the labor force, working at first in seasonal fruit picking, and beginning in 1974, as a cleaning lady. She was a charwoman at the government headquarters for three years, and at the Hebrew University for a total of nine years, during which time she also managed to take on some cleaning jobs in private homes. Her last paycheck, NIS 309, dates from May 1987.

Umm Ibrahim, who was employed by a contracting company by the name of PAB Services, reported to work twenty-three days during May 1987, sixteen of which were full working days, and the others part time. Her gross wage amounted to NIS 379, of which NIS 70 were deducted: 28 in the form of "health insurance" tax and 21.50 as National Insurance tax, while 17 went to "social insurance" and 3.5 to a "union fee." Women's daily wages in cleaning services amounted to between one-half and two-thirds of the already underrated daily wages of nonskilled, or "ordinary" male laborers. The total deduction from a cleaner's wages amounted to about one-fifth of her income, but the single right to which it entitled her was access to the government health system, administered by the disreputably regarded Civil Administration, whose facilities and services were not up to the standard provided by UNRWA. The deduction earmarked for National Insurance went directly to the Israeli treasury, where it remained. Social insurance absolved the employer from setting aside a pension fund for the worker, and served as a fund for scant, one-time compensation upon her/his retirement. The union fee consisted of 1 percent of the gross income, which was automatically deducted from the wages of all registered Palestinian workers on behalf of the Histadrut (General Federation of Israeli Trade Unions). The irony is that the Histadrut never admitted laborers from the Occupied Territories into its ranks.

The paycheck for May 1987, as it turns out, was the highest Umm Ibrahim had ever received. A look at the preceding checks reveals that her average monthly wage stood at NIS 250. In her words: "I still remember the day I cashed the check for May 1987 at the Bethlehem post office branch. All the women from work at the university were there, and they all wondered how it happened that Umm Ibrahim got NIS 309 while they received only 250 or 270." In June of the same year she quit work.

I wanted to continue, and if not for the pains in my legs I would have kept going. I worked for so many years, and it was always hard and tiring work. All day long on my feet, bending my back, my neck, scrubbing, washing, dusting, lifting furniture. My body ached all the time. I slipped on the floor and hurt my knee very badly. At the end the pain was just impossible to bear.

In order to receive the one-time retirement compensation, Umm Ibrahim was compelled to hire a lawyer and sue the contracting agency that employed her.

Compared to the labor histories of men who were employed in Israel, women changed workplaces fewer times and suffered relatively less from layoffs and intermittent employment. The differences can be attributed to the types of employment. Most male laborers worked in construction, which saw periodical fluctuations in terms of the changing demand for manpower, and where demand itself was often highly specific with respect to skill. The supply of workmen was always high, and the older candidates had to compete with the younger and more physically fit. The majority of female laborers, however, were employed through manpower agencies and worked in public institutions. In cleaning services there were no specific demands for skill and competence and at a certain point in time, specifically from the mid-1970s to the late 1980s, supply did not outweigh the market demand for working hands. In addition, all female workers who worked at public institutions were registered laborers, in contrast with many of the men who were not registered with the labor exchange.

Though the status of a registered worker entailed almost no rights whatsoever, it did grant the laborer minimal protection against withholding of payment and a guarantee, at least formally, of one-time compensation upon layoff or retirement. All this is to say that, in comparative terms, women who worked via manpower agencies enjoyed greater job continuity and stability than did their male counterparts who worked in the construction branch. Though the differences in income clearly favored men, and in a sense balanced off the "female advantage," the regularity of the wage was more significant than the wage rate.

Nonetheless, female wage laborers in the cleaning service branch were by no means immune to the plight of arbitrary layoffs and discontinuous employment. Thus, for example, incidents in which workers were dismissed in light of the imprisonment of their sons were not uncommon among my interviewees. According to Umm Khader, who was fired by the manpower agency that employed her for many years: "They received information about our children from the Mukhabarat [Israeli General Security Services, or GSS]. My son's name came up on their computer lists, so they decided not to take a chance with me." Similar incidents, all pertaining to working mothers of prisoners who were sentenced to long terms in jail, appear to corroborate Umm Khader's version. Another common grounds for "discharging" laborers were the "downsizing" policies that were occasionally practiced by the contracting companies.

Ultimately, though, the final blow to the relative advantage of female charwomen at public institutions over male construction workers came in the wake of the Intifada, when the contracting companies laid off all their Dheishehian (and other West Bank) employees, replacing them with laborers from Arab Jerusalem (who, following the annexation of East Jerusalem in 1967, had been classified as permanent residents of Israel). In the course of 1988–89, entrance to jobs in public institutions were sealed off to Dheishehian women. The relatively few who continued to work in West Jerusalem were employed in private homes.

THE HIGH RESPONSE TO WAGE WORK OPPORTUNITIES

Dheishehian women of the older generation shared very similar life experiences. All lived in poverty and extreme overcrowding, almost all were married to day laborers with meager earnings, and all had to feed and take care of many children. Their strong response to work opportunities should indeed be viewed against this backdrop. However, given their situation as mothers of nine children on average (and even if we ignore the grown children the figure remains high), and as those who performed most of the housework at home, women's persistence in the labor force demands closer inspection.

The thirteen interviewees in the core sample who had been wage laborers noted main reasons for joining the labor force: economic hardship, mentioned by all; death of a spouse; disability of a spouse from work-related injury; or chronic illness. Of the twenty-eight (former) wage laborers who were included in the survey, only four reported joining the labor force upon widowhood. Death of a husband or his permanent absence from the labor force was, then, a secondary though not an insignificant factor, whereas the more prevalent cause for women's work outside the home was the insufficient incomes of others in the family, further exacerbated by discontinued employment of the male head of household, and/or by the obstructed entrance of adult sons into the labor force.

Sixty-three years old, Umm ᶜAdel was a wage laborer for more than twenty-two years, from 1971 to 1993. She is a mother of eleven daughters and sons, aged twenty-five to forty-five (in 1995), seven of whom were children and babies during the first decade of the Occupation. When she entered the labor force in 1971, Umm ᶜAdel first worked in seasonal fruit picking, then moved on to cleaning, first at a local hospital in Bethlehem and from 1977 onward at Hebrew University and Hadassah hospital. Her husband, Abu ᶜAdel, was a construction laborer in Israel for several years until illness forced him to quit and take on an easier job at a small factory in the town of Beit Sahour (adjacent to Bethlehem). Two of their daughters, then in their early teens, helped with the smaller children while Umm ᶜAdel was at work. Three of the older children married and left home in the late 1970s.

After Abu ᶜAdel's early death in 1981, the family, then consisting of nine members, subsisted on Umm ᶜAdel's wages, as well as on the income of an unmarried daughter who worked as a teacher, and on remittances from the eldest son, who had become a teacher in Saudi Arabia. In the course of the early 1980s, three adolescent sons were sentenced to imprisonment of varying duration and the working daughter got married. The family relied thereafter almost solely on the income of Umm ᶜAdel, who continued to clean laboratories and lecture halls at the university campus in Haddasah hospital.

In late 1986 the manpower agency that employed her fired Umm ᶜAdel, most probably on the grounds of "confidential" information regarding the imprisoned sons, which was forwarded by the security forces. Shortly afterward she began to work in private homes in West Jerusalem, at which she persisted for seven years. In the wake of the Intifada the three sons, who in the meantime had been released, were imprisoned again for periods that ranged between one and two years. Their entrance into the labor force was further delayed into the 1990s, and for one of them it did not occur until the second half of the decade. Umm ᶜAdel stopped working in 1993, following ongoing deterioration of her health; she suffered from severe nerve inflammation in her leg and was unable to walk without a cane.

The high rate of participation in the labor force among women of Umm ᶜAdel's generation indicates that the circumstance of raising small children, which pertained to the majority of these women at least in the first decade

(1970–80), did not prevent many of them from taking on wage work. Going out to work, however, compelled mothers to find arrangements for their young children, not an easy task in the face of the total absence of day care centers in Dheisheh of the 1970s. The majority relied on their daughters, often themselves not much older than their siblings, and/or on mothers-in-law and other kin. When such arrangements were not available, for example, when all elder children were males, or when the help of in-laws could not be relied upon, women were left with no choice but to stay at home.

On the one hand, then, the expanse of families was among the factors that pushed women to join the labor force at a relatively late stage in their lives. On the other hand, the same factor imposed many limitations that curtailed their movement and availability. Hence, women frequently joined the labor force in the early 1970s as fruit pickers only to "retreat" after one or two seasons. Additional factors such as the limited range of available jobs and the inherent temporariness of employment contracts further explains the relatively short labor histories of many women. However, not less prevalent among this generation were instances of women who, like Umm ʿAdel, held on to full-time wage work long after all their children were adult and well into the late 1980s, in spite of old age and in spite of great physical effort. This perseverance and reluctance to retire among aging women was observed especially in cases when sons who had reached working age did not join the family workforce, or did so on a very irregular basis—that is, when the unfolding of the family's life cycle failed to produce a replacement for the working mother. The phenomenon was closely related to the increasingly marginalized status of male wage laborers, particularly the young and even more so, the politically active, in the Israeli and local labor markets.

Absent from this discussion thus far has been an "attitudinal" dimension that pertains to women's wage labor. Indeed, the very wide scope of female participation in the Dheishehian labor force appears to suggest, a priori, that whatever tradition-grounded objection women may have encountered on their path to work, they ultimately overcame it by sheer necessity. Nadia Hijab generalizes that "wherever there are pressing needs and opportunities for Arab women's work, socio-cultural obstacles do not intrude" (Hijab 1996, 46), a sentiment that is certainly applicable to the camp women. Nonetheless, it is interesting to note differences in attitude with respect to female wage labor that correspond to the divide between families in which women had never worked outside the home and others in which women assumed the role of central providers.

Among the former families one is likely to hear the view, from both men and women, that a woman's working outside the home is disgraceful or a source of shame for her husband and male relatives. It is my impression, nevertheless, that such conventions rarely stood in the way once wage labor became feasible, but rather they reflect an attempt to provide a posteriori idealization for the fact that women did not work. This impression is mainly supported by the testimonies of women who had joined and remained in the labor force. Seldom did I encounter women who complained that their husbands disapproved of their work or pressured them to quit, and rarely did I hear a husband air a negative comment about his wife working outside the home.

When asked whether her employment as a cleaning woman in Jerusalem was met with objection by her relatives and social peers, Umm Ibrahim responded: "I've never heard of such a thing. . . . Almost all the women in our neighborhood worked, it was the most normal thing for everybody." Further support can be found in the fact that wage labor was more or less equally common among elderly women of different kinship groups and from different villages of origin, rather than being concentrated within specific families that are identified with more flexible or less conservative conduct. This is not to suggest that working women necessarily enjoyed the respect or gratitude of male family members, and neither is it to deny the pervasiveness of patriarchal norms that sought to maintain full control of men over women's conduct. Rather, I propose merely that the participation of women in waged employment was not contingent upon any cultural factor.

The Intermediate Generation: Male Wage Laborers

Men aged forty-four to fifty-five (in 1993) belong to the second refugee generation. Some were children (under twelve) at the time of the uprooting from their villages in 1948; others were born during the war or shortly after it. The great majority spent most of their adult lives in Dheisheh. Two of the central social characteristics that differentiate this generational group from the older one are the educational achievements of its members and the high rate of labor migration within its ranks. Whereas very few among the older generation acquired any formal schooling, more than two-fifths (42 percent) of the males of the intermediate generation acquired an education of at least ten grades, and about one-fourth acquired some form of postsecondary education. Seasonal migration from the West to the East Bank of Jordan in search of wage work was rather commonplace among men of the first refugee generation during the Jordanian rule, but almost ceased during the decades of the Israeli Occupation. Among members of the intermediate generation, however, labor migration to the Gulf states, particularly Saudi Arabia and Kuwait, became a salient trend as early as the late 1950s, with migration of the professionally skilled and educated gradually replacing that of manual laborers from the early 1960s and into the post-1967 era. Another factor that carried a profound impact for members of this generation was the affiliation with, and activism in the context of, political parties and organizations that operated in the West Bank and the region as a whole.

The interrelated processes of education, migration, and politicization provide additional contextualization to the analysis of day wage labor among second-generation male refugees who continued to live in Dheisheh. Though the life histories of members of this generation had been affected, to varied extents, by the above mentioned factors, the majority started families that were not significantly smaller than those of their elder counterparts, numbering 7.8 children on average, against an average of 9 among the old generation.

CHARACTERISTICS AND CONDITIONS OF EMPLOYMENT

Only eight of the forty-one interviewees in the core sample (19.5 percent), all holders of a certificate or diploma, were salaried employees in the local public services sector, whereas thirty-one (75 percent) were wage laborers. Almost all the wage laborers (twenty-nine) reported working in Israel and the settlements for time periods that ranged from one to twenty-six years. The average total length of "attachment" to various Israeli employers was thirteen years, but the findings indicate large internal variations in terms of both the total duration and the continuity of employment. Thus, within the category of those who worked in Israel and the settlements for more than ten years (slightly less than 60 percent), one finds laborers who were employed by as many as twenty contractors, and experienced highly intermittent working lives, while others, much fewer in number, enjoyed relatively high job continuity. Following the outbreak of the Intifada, and particularly in the wake of the closure policy, many of those who were previously employed in Israel lost their jobs and sought, often unsuccessfully, opportunities on the local market.

A second category, representing slightly more than 40 percent of the core sample, consists of laborers whose total employment in Israel and the settlements lasted only one to five years, and whose working lives took place mainly within the local labor market.

Twenty-eight of the thirty-one laborers had spent at least part of their working lives in the construction branch. Perhaps the only major difference between them and their elders can be found in the prevalence of skilled workers among their ranks, particularly in trades that were less common among older workers, such as carpentry, painting, plumbing, metalwork, and electricity. The tendency to specialize in specific building trades can be traced to the fact that many within this generation underwent training in their teens and early twenties, either as apprentices in workshops or as trainees in UNRWA's vocational centers. Nonetheless, many of the highly skilled were forced to accept whatever opportunities they encountered on the market at a given moment, alternating between skilled and unskilled jobs and intermissions of unemployment. All in all, it is not easy to find meaningful differences between the labor histories of members of the older generation and those of the intermediate. The difficulty in pointing to a significant trend of change is illustrated by means of a brief examination of four representative cases.

REPRESENTATIVE LABOR HISTORIES

Abu Waʾil, whose family originated from Zakariya, was born in 1950 in ʿEin al-Sultan refugee camp, near Jericho, and lived there for seventeen years. In the aftermath of the 1967 war, most members of his family became refugees for the second time. Abu Waʾil, however, had moved to Dheisheh, where he was married to a first cousin and has lived ever since. Abu Waʾil began to work in Israel in 1970, and for twenty-four successive years stayed with the same contracting company: Eli Brothers. He is a skilled mason, who, he insists, is highly valued by his employers: "They keep telling me that they cannot do without Abu Waʾil." His record experience, supposed indispensability, and close personal ties with the bosses notwithstanding, Abu Waʾil continued to earn his wages on a day basis, and his daily wage in 1995 was only one hundred shekels (the average for an unskilled worker being around seventy shekels). Abu Waʾil is a registered worker who holds a work permit and an entrance permit to Israel. Nevertheless, whenever a closure is imposed on the West Bank the permits automatically expire, and Abu Waʾil sits at home and waits for the Eli Brothers to use their "connections" and obtain the new documents for him. This procedure may take weeks, and at times months. Meantime, Abu Waʾil tries his luck the "illegal" way, and arranges with his employers to meet him at some point on the back roads that connect Bethlehem to Jerusalem.

*

Abu Nidal was born in 1944 in the village of Raʾs Abu ʿAmar. His extended family settled in Dheisheh in the early 1950s and subsisted on the income of his three older brothers, who had become skilled stonecutters and worked together as a team. Having failed to complete more than eight grades in school, Abu Nidal moved to Amman, where he became an apprentice at a carpenter's workshop and trained to become a painter of wooden furniture. Returning to the West Bank shortly before the 1967 war, he started a family in Dheisheh and sought to open his own workshop. However, as the first decade of the Occupation advanced, Abu Nidal joined his mates and neighbors and became a day laborer with building contractors in Jerusalem; only occasionally did he find employment as a painter. In 1981 he found a job at a gasoline station in Bethlehem, which he held on to for twelve years with the aid of his three adolescent sons. Being young veterans of the Israeli prison system, the three, who were barred from entrance into Israel and remained jobless otherwise, were only too eager to join their father. At the same time, Abu Nidal became a small subcontractor, recruiting a team of workers to take on casual painting projects, mainly in West Jerusalem. When the closure policy was enforced in the early 1990s, Abu Nidal and his workers, all of whom were unregistered, were without entry and work permits. Following an extended slack season, they finally took on a project in the (Jewish) settlement of Pisgat Zeev that was within reach via bypass roads. The installing and painting of kitchen cupboards in a newly built residential complex in the settlement was the most promising opportunity they had seen in years, and Abu Nidal, who had passed the previous months playing cards and chain-smoking, was filled with new hope. The Israeli contractor was withholding payment until the date of completion, but he said that this practice was common and there was no reason to be worried: "At the end of the month everything will be settled." The "big day," however, coincided with the imposition of a new and stricter closure, one that nearly halted Palestinian commuting altogether. Abu Nidal and his workers waited patiently, only to discover that they had been defrauded; the checks were without cover, and the contractor was no longer reachable: "At first he told me that I should come and see him in Jerusalem. He knew perfectly well that I had no permit but refused to meet me at the checkpoint [the northern entrance to Bethlehem]. Then he stopped answering my calls and his cellular phone was suddenly disconnected," said Abu Nidal. He was now facing an additional problem. The furious workers paid daily visits to his home in demand of their share: "They are driving me crazy. I told them that I'll take Shimon [the contractor] to court, but everything is against us, because we were not registered in the first place." For some time, Abu Nidal entertained the idea of suing Shimon, but never carried it out.

*

Forty-seven-year-old Abu Hisham was born in ʿEin al-Sultan refugee camp shortly after his family arrived there following their uprooting from Zakariya. He completed nine grades in UNRWA's schools and began to work at age fifteen, at first in road paving on the Jerusalem-Jericho route, with a public works project of the Jordanian government. The 1967 war separated him from his parents and siblings, who found refuge in the East Bank and were not allowed to return. An uncle who had become an Israeli citizen and had lived in Ramleh (Israel) since 1950 adopted Abu Hisham. In the course of the six years at his uncle's, Abu Hisham worked as an agricultural laborer in the fields of several Israeli moshavim and started a family with his first cousin, a refugee from Dheisheh. In 1973, upon rejection of their application for Israeli citizenship, the couple and three children moved to Dheisheh. Between that year and 1995, by which time the couple had five additional children, Abu Hisham changed workplaces and jobs dozens of times. He was employed in two textile factories and in a metal workshop in West Jerusalem for periods that ranged from two to four years, before working intermittently as a construction worker, a driver, and a watchman in the Bethlehem region. He also tried his luck as a vendor of used clothes and furniture. From 1992 onward he was employed as a night watchman at an olive oil press in Beit Jala, where he earned five hundred shekels a month.

*

Abu ʿIsam arrived in Dheisheh in 1955, when he was twelve years old. His family, which originated from the village of Qabu, first found refuge in Nahaline, his mother's home village, but was displaced again following an Israeli retaliation operation. Abu ʿIsam managed to complete secondary school with the aid of his older brother, who had migrated to Kuwait and supported his family in the camp, but he could not afford to go on with his studies. Becoming a construction laborer, he worked alternately in the West and East Banks. Shortly after the imposition of the Israeli Occupation, Abu ʿIsam was arrested and sentenced to four years in prison on the charge of membership in an illegal organization. Two years after his release he was again imprisoned, for an additional three-year term. In between imprisonments and following the second release he worked in construction, and then from 1978 to 1987 as a laborer in a textile factory in West Jerusalem and as a driver who transported laborers to building sites. In compliance with an early call of the UNLU, Abu ʿIsam quit his job in Israel in February 1988 and remained jobless for some time. Unable to find employment in the Bethlehem region, he became a night watchman with UNRWA at age forty-five, a "dead-end" job usually reserved for the old or disabled. Though UNRWA guaranteed secure employment, watchmen were at the bottom of the wage scale. His monthly salary of twelve hundred shekels in 1994 was far from meeting even the minimal needs of his family of eleven.

The Intermediate Generation: Female Wage Laborers

The intermediate generation of women (aged forty-one to fifty-four in 1993) can also be termed a transitional generation, as salient differences among its members demonstrate.

The group includes both women who completed only a few grades of primary school alongside others who attained university education; women who worked at unskilled manual jobs; others who became teachers and nurses in the West Bank, Saudi Arabia, and Kuwait; and yet many others who never joined the labor force. The great majority had been married traditionally, but a small minority did get to know their future husbands through personal acquaintance and choice. The variation corresponds generally, but not consistently, with age differences within the generational group, so that women aged forty-one to forty-five often resembled those of the younger generation, while women over fifty shared many of the characteristics of the older refugee generation.

Women who belong to the intermediate generation came of age in the Dheisheh of the late 1950s and 1960s. Though they enjoyed far better opportunities to acquire education than their older counterparts, the era was still marked by a significant advantage of males over females in respect to schooling. The gender-differentiated gap is clearly reflected in the sample's findings: twenty of forty-one women completed no more than six grades, in comparison with only ten of forty-one men, and only three women acquired postsecondary education, versus eleven of the men.

Most women of this generation were married in the course of the 1960s and the first half of the 1970s, and gave birth to eight (7.8) children on average, the spacing between successive births being approximately two years. Thus, at the time of the research some were still tending small children.

CHARACTERISTICS AND CONDITIONS OF EMPLOYMENT

Results of my survey on women and employment show that of the seventy-five participants aged forty-one to fifty-four, twenty-eight women (37 percent) had been employed for time periods that ranged from two to twenty years. All except one of the twenty-eight, a professional nurse, were wage laborers; twenty worked in fruit picking, cleaning, or kitchen work, and seven were factory workers. Twenty were employed mainly by Israeli contractors and seven by institutions in the Bethlehem region. Of the forty-one interviewees of the core sample, eleven women (26.8 percent) had worked at some point outside the home, one as a nurse and ten as wage laborers in West Jerusalem and Bethlehem. About one-third of all who had ever been employed reported terminating work upon marriage without ever returning to the labor force.

A comparison of these findings with those for members of the older generation reveals that wage labor was relatively more prevalent among the latter women (42 percent against 33.6 percent), while type of employment was almost identical among members of the two generations. The higher rate of participation in the labor force among women of the older generation can be attributed to the availability of employment opportunities in the second decade of the Occupation, coinciding with the end of their baby-rearing years. Indeed, continuous or regular work outside the home was not unusual among women in their late forties, fifties, and sixties. Women of the intermediate generation, however, were at the peak of childbearing during the 1970s, a factor that often hindered long-term ties to waged employment. In their case, the easing of child-rearing responsibilities coincided with the contraction of employment opportunities in the Israeli labor market in the late 1980s rather than their expansion. All in all, however, the figures indicate a considerable participation by women of the intermediate generation in the Dheishehian labor force, implying that home-related tasks, including the rearing of young children, did not bar women from wage labor.

The almost total correspondence between the types of employment in which women of the two generational groups engaged appears somewhat incongruous, given the fact that no less than 50 percent of the intermediate generation went beyond elementary school (six grades), and that 25 percent completed at least ten grades. That these relative achievements in education are not reflected in the types of employment the latter generation found can be traced to the great scarcity of adequate employment opportunities for women (and men) without postsecondary degrees or certificates; the labor market did not favor women with ten years of schooling over those with only five years. Moreover, the late 1960s and 1970s saw a high rate of labor migration to the Gulf by the educated and professionally skilled, giving rise to underrepresentation of the professionally employed among the relevant age group of the camp population.

REPRESENTATIVE LABOR HISTORIES

As in the case of the older generation, entry into the labor force by female members of the intermediate generation and persistence in it was directly affected by the low and irregular income of other family members: husbands, first of all, and later, adult children. Whereas insufficient income was common to many, perhaps for the majority of married women in the camp, the situation assumed extreme dimensions in the case of widows, and even more so for divorcées, who, unless they relied on their own labor, were left without a source of wage-generated income. Hence, there was a very high correlation between divorcée or widow status and labor histories of long duration. The following cases of three laborers—a married woman, a long-time widow, and a long-time divorcée—do not exhaust the possible "archetypes," nor do they provide sufficient detail and social contextualization for a more comprehensive analysis. Rather, they provide some perspective on the more manifest or straightforward aspects and implications of women's working lives.

*

Forty-seven years old, Umm Hisham is married and a mother of eight (one daughter was killed during the Intifada). She grew up in Dheisheh of the 1950s and completed five grades of UNRWA's primary school. From the age of eleven to the age of nineteen, she "sat at home," the common shorthand expression for a girl's social situation in the time period that precedes her marriage. The phrase better indicates where she was confined than her level of activity. Being the eldest daughter at home, she spent her adolescent years doing housework and tending five brothers and sisters. At nineteen she was married to her first cousin, an unskilled laborer who moved from one casual job to another (Abu Hisham of the earlier case history).

At twenty-four, already a mother of three, including a six-month-old baby, she began to work outside the home, first as a cleaning woman at a private hospital and then on the campuses of the Hebrew University. Most of her coworkers were Dheishehian women of the older generation, the "hard core" of cleaners whom we encountered in previous sections. Her younger sister, whom Umm Hisham helped to raise during the time she "sat at home," was now the one who tended Umm Hisham's own children. In 1980 her sister/babysitter married, and Umm Hisham, by then a mother of three additional young children, had no choice but to quit her job. After a four-year interlude she was back at work, this time as a kitchen worker at Caritas Baby Hospital in Bethlehem, where she has been employed ever since. She is a salaried laborer who works eight-hour shifts, earning a monthly wage of one thousand shekels (1995). In the course of this latter period she gave birth to two additional children. This time, however, she was not dependent on the help of relatives, since Caritas, being the workplace of dozens of nurses, many of whom are from Dheisheh, runs a day care center for the babies and children of the employees. The salaried, rather than day basis of employment, the in situ arrangement for young children, and the respectability that this Christian institution has earned for itself in the predominantly Muslim community all make Caritas a sought-after workplace, even for manual laborers such as Umm Hisham. Indeed, the thought of quitting the tedious shifts at the hospital's kitchen does not cross her mind; at least not for the time being, as long as her husband, currently a night watchman, earns only five hundred shekels a month.

*

Umm Nizar, a widow, and a mother of a son, twenty-four, and a daughter, twenty-three, is reserved, especially when it comes to her own affairs: "I am forty-eight. I began to work when I was ten years old and have not stopped working." She was born in the village of Walaje and arrived in Dheisheh as a baby, the fourth daughter of her parents, who in subsequent years had three more daughters and a son.

Her father, thirty years her mother's senior, never entered the labor force after becoming a refugee, and the family subsisted solely on the labor of its female members. Her mother was a laundress and a cleaning lady in the homes of wealthy people in Beit Jala and Bethlehem until 1964, when she became a kitchen worker at Talitha Kumi, an orphanage and boarding school in Beit Jala that belong to a Christian society; she was employed there until her retirement in 1985. Her elder sisters completed no more than four years of schooling each and were sent to work as housemaids in private homes until they were married at the ages of fourteen and fifteen. Umm Nizar completed two grades and left her parent's home at the age of ten to become a maid in the household of a senior UNRWA officer in Bethlehem.

Her marriage at the age of fourteen to a man in his forties was short-lived, however, and she was soon back in her father's household and again at work, this time as a housemaid at a wealthy doctor's home in Arab Jerusalem. There she remained for five years. A second marriage, when she was twenty, ended after four years with the death of her husband. Once again she returned to her father's house, now with her two babies, and once again she returned to work, this time in Talitha Kumi, together with her mother. Only upon her father's death in 1979, some twenty years after her working life began, did Umm Nizar assume control over her own earnings. She bought and renovated an old UNRWA shelter (one room with no indoor toilet), to which she and her children moved, and where she still lived in 1996.

In 1996 Umm Nizar had been working for more than thirty-five years, twenty-two of them in Talitha Kumi. The extreme hardship that accompanied her throughout her life has made her reticent, and little inclined to recall events from her past: "You want to hear about things that no one has ever paid attention to," she told me, "things that I'm not used to speaking about. There's nothing more to tell."

*

Umm Rami is forty-eight years old (in 1996), a mother of four sons and one daughter. She was born in the village of ʿArtuf, the eldest of nine siblings, grew up in Dheisheh, completed nine grades in UNRWA's school, and was married at twenty to a distant relative with whom she went to live in Bethlehem. Her five children were born in the course of an eight-year-long marriage that ended in divorce shortly after her husband married a second wife. It was Umm Rami who demanded the divorce, refusing to live together with the newlywed couple. Consequently, and in accordance with the Muslim shariʿa, she lost rights to her children; with no alternative she returned alone to her family's home in Dheisheh, where she has been living for the last eighteen years. Over time, Umm Rami's brothers, all of whom married and started families, gradually separated from their parents' home, three building a new house on the ruins of the UNRWA shelter that had served the family beforehand, the fourth repairing an adjacent shelter in the same courtyard. Umm Rami, who was not included in the new arrangements, moved, together with her old father and her mentally ill sister, into a deserted UNRWA unit in the middle of that same yard. Each occupied a four-square-meter "cell" without indoor toilet.

In the absence of either alimony provisions from her former husband or any form of regular income, Umm Rami, who had never previously worked outside the home, was compelled to seek employment. For twelve successive years she worked as a scrubwoman at a hospital in Bethlehem. With her income (twelve hundred shekels in 1993), she supported her father and her sister, who both eventually became fully dependent on her wages and on her daily care. Only one of Umm Rami's brothers had a permanent job, and he also had a family of eight to provide for. The brothers took for granted that their divorced sister, who, according to one of them, "makes enough money," would go on supporting their father.

In 1994 Umm Rami was laid off from her job in the hospital, following the "downsizing" that affected many of the employees, including the professional staff. She could not afford to remain jobless for too long and became a worker in a chicken slaughterhouse in the Israeli town of Beit Shemesh, about a forty-five-minute bus trip from the camp: "I received thirty shekels a day, Jewish female workers got forty shekels, and Jewish men sixty shekels," she summarized. As the closure policy became stricter and commuting to Israel was made all but impossible, she was forced to look for another workplace. To my questions about her current work she replied: "Frankly speaking, I'm ashamed to talk about it. I don't care if you write down that I do not work at all, because a job you can not make a living from does not deserve to be called work." Only after much persuasion was she willing to reveal the details: She was working in a textile workshop in Beit Jala for fifteen shekels a day. "Write down that I'm looking for a job as a cleaner of floors, or a secretary—don't forget that I completed preparatory school."

The Younger Generation: Male Wage Laborers

This generational category refers to men whose ages at the time of fieldwork (1993) ranged from twenty-five to forty. All are descendants of refugees who were born at least five years after the 1948 war and who reached working age during the era of the Israeli rule. The mean age in my sample group was 31.6, implying that the average participant had spent his adolescent years and most of his life under military occupation. Two characteristics that distinguish this generational group are the spread of postsecondary education and a high rate of political imprisonment. The leap in educational achievement that was highly manifest among members of the intermediate generation assumed an increased magnitude among the younger generation; only six of the forty participants in the core sample had an education of six years or less, whereas twenty-five acquired either full or partial secondary education, and thirteen of these went on to the postsecondary stage. Labor migration by the professionally skilled was a predominant trend among older members of this age group who completed their education in the 1970s, but it significantly diminished after the mid-1980s. An overwhelming majority of members of the young generation were active, in one way or another, in various political organizations that resisted the Israeli Occupation. An approximate 50 percent experienced some form of detention or imprisonment, of varying duration.

It is still premature to provide an estimate of the changes in family size among members of this generation, since most can be expected to have additional children in the course of the next decade. Whereas among the relatively older participants of the sample, six to eight children are still commonplace, the clear tendency nevertheless is toward a significant reduction in family size, with three to five children becoming prevalent and preferred. The majority live in some form of a linked arrangement with their parents, either in a separate room, an attached apartment, or on the upper floor of the parents' home.

CHARACTERISTICS AND CONDITIONS OF EMPLOYMENT

As of 1993, thirty-three out of the forty (82.5 percent) participants in the core sample were wage laborers. Of the twenty-five among them with secondary and postsecondary education, only seven (17.5 percent) were professionally employed: three teachers, two journalists, an engineer, and an insurance agent. Findings that draw on a much larger sample, which I surveyed to encompass migrant workers alongside the permanent residents of the camp, yielded the following breakdown: 67 percent of the 169 participants were wage laborers in Israel, the West Bank, and abroad; 28 percent were professionally employed, half of them abroad, mainly in the Gulf states, and 5 percent were self-employed contractors or owners of businesses, mainly abroad. Both sets of data show that educational attainments bore little weight for the employment opportunities of young Dheishehians who did not migrate.

The types of employment were very similar to those found among the intermediate generation, with a marked predominance of the building trades, particularly masonry, plastering, metalwork, ironwork, whitewashing, and painting. Almost all construction laborers, however, listed at least two sub-branches or trades as their specialties. Others worked as service workers, kitchen help, waiters in restaurants and coffee shops, drivers, and factory laborers. Those who were employed by UNRWA worked in the sanitation and distribution departments.

The main features that characterized the working lives of members of the older and intermediate generations—perpetual job instability, hard physical labor, low income, and absence of social benefits—found even more extreme expression with respect to laborers of the younger generation. Twenty-seven of the thirty-three laborers in the sample had worked in Israel or the settlements or both, but for more than half of these, the total duration of work for Israeli employers did not exceed four years. Eighteen laborers noted the West Bank or Dheisheh itself as the location where the greater part of their working lives took place, as against fifteen who noted Israel and the settlements. Only five of the twenty-seven who had ever worked for Israeli employers reported having stayed with the same contractor for more than five years. On average, laborers who worked in Israel and the settlements had changed workplaces six times over the years, yet as many as eleven of the twenty-seven (40 percent) had worked for no fewer than ten contractors. Indeed, the builder with the longest history of employment in Israel among my respondents— twenty-four years—recalled eighteen different contractors.

All thirty-three laborers experienced layoffs and described their employment as intermittent. Seventeen reported to have experienced long-term unemployment. Discontinuous employment and frequent changes of workplaces resulted in constant circulation of workers, from skilled to nonskilled jobs and vice versa, followed by the "retreat" of workers who had previously been employed in West Jerusalem and settlements to the dwindling local labor market.

This gradual relocation of the arena of employment—clearly reflected in the finding that relatively more laborers spent the larger and later portion of their working lives in the West Bank—was the forced outcome of the policy of the Israeli military government, which was particularly repressive with respect to these young people. As early as the 1970s, Palestinian political activists and former political prisoners faced various restrictions on their freedom of movement, including house arrests, town arrests, and denial of travel permits. In the wake of the Intifada and the massive level of imprisonment that followed, many additional measures and restrictions were introduced, with the intention of rooting out constituent elements of the uprising. The military government devised a new category of those "barred from entry to Israel," and special, easily distinguishable identity cards were issued to them. Entry into Israel and work there by those who were not on the list of barred persons was now contingent upon the approval of the security forces.

The closure policy, which was enforced in early 1993, had detrimental consequences for laborers of all age groups, but it was harshest for the young. Whenever the political and military authorities decided on a partial alleviation of the closure and issued work permits for a quota of laborers, young people under a specified age were excluded. At times it was all people under thirty; at others all people under twenty-seven or twenty-five were a priori excluded. In addition, under the circumstances that prevailed, long-standing connections with an employer became almost a sine qua non for obtaining a permit, since it was the employer who filed the applications at the military headquarters on behalf of "his" workers. Young workers, who because of their relatively short and highly intermittent work experience lacked precisely such connections, were thus in the most disadvantaged position.

REPRESENTATIVE LABOR HISTORIES

In 1995, thirty-nine-year-old Abu Salah, a father of four, belonged to the category of the unemployed or rarely employed. That had been his status, more or less, for more than eight years, ever since he lost his last regular job. The fifth of eight children, Abu Salah was born in Dheisheh to a family that originated from the village of Zakariya. His adolescence in UNRWA's preparatory school coincided with the early years of the military occupation and with the early wave of resistance among Dheishehian youth, which did not bypass his family. His older brother and his first cousin were among the first in the camp to be sentenced to long prison terms on charges of membership in outlawed hostile organizations. Shortly thereafter Abu Salah, who followed in their footsteps to national activism, was arrested and sentenced to five years in jail. In 1980, as a twenty-five-year-old released prisoner without an occupation and with only partial secondary education, he was married and made his first encounter with the labor market. His steadiest job turned out to be as a worker in an ice-cream shop in the heart of West Jerusalem. Abu Salah still has warm words for his employer at the time, an Israeli of Argentinean origin who treated his Arab and Jewish workers equally well. The ice-cream days lasted from 1981 to 1986, when the business was closed and Abu Salah became jobless. Subsequently, he tried his luck at petty trade, transporting and marketing vegetables to shops in Bethlehem, but without much success. The first years of the Intifada were the worst of times for a fresh start in the Israeli labor market, and Abu Salah, who like others seized every opportunity, waited for better days to come.

But as the days and months went on, one failed attempt—at business or as a worker—followed another. Abu Salah's total employment in the course of 1992 to 1995 did not exceed six months. Although his imprisonment had taken place in the relatively distant past and was not "Intifada-related," he could not obtain an entry permit to Israel on grounds of his and his relatives' security records. Sneaking into West Jerusalem for the sake of a working day's wage remained almost the only option, though on many occasions the effort and risk were in vain. In the early months following the imposition of the first closure in March 1993, Abu Salah remained at home. It was springtime, and he decided to grow seasonal vegetables on a patch of land in his trash-strewn backyard, while expounding on the need to "return to the land" and to rediscover the heritage of his peasant ancestors. The tomatoes and radishes eventually gave way to a small coffee grinder, as Abu Salah considered becoming a local supplier of coffee; this endeavor was later deserted for an old van that he hoped would hold up well enough to transport vegetables from Hebron to Dheisheh. His cogent analyses of the political situation did not deter him from engaging in futile ventures.

It was only in January 1994 that Abu Salah finally obtained a temporary entry permit enabling him to cross the checkpoints. He began work in floor tiling at a construction site in West Jerusalem, toil for which he had little preparation and which left him in constant pain. "Salvation" from the need to adjust to the standards of the building trades came quickly, as in late February of the same year a new and stricter closure was enforced. The remainder of 1994 and most of 1995 were more of the same. Abu Salah now turned his energies to the establishment of a charitable society in Dheisheh, entertaining the hope that it would eventually promote small-scale employment-generating projects. His enthusiasm for entrepreneurial experiments then waned somewhat, and the routine chase after casual opportunities occasionally gave rise to two or three successive weeks of work. How he and his family managed to survive these lean years was not always clear to me, though the secrets of survival lay mainly with his wife, Umm Salah, who cultivated economizing and overeconomizing to the level of an art.

*

Since 1989 Ziyad has been employed as a laborer in UNRWA's distribution and maintenance department. He works alternately in the agency's warehouse in Jerusalem and at the distribution of monthly rations of flour and basic foodstuffs to needy families in the camp that are classified as "hardship cases." While it may not be an inspiring job, it is a secure and salaried one, earning him some thirteen hundred shekels a month and a guaranteed pension allowance.

At age thirty-four, Ziyad has a twenty-one-year work history behind him. It began in 1975, when his father, Abu ʿAbed, was seriously injured in a work accident and thirteen-year-old Ziyad and his two older brothers, aged fourteen and fifteen, dropped out of school and came to the aid of their family. Abu ʿAbed had begun his career at eighteen as a laborer in the local munitions warehouses of the British army during World War II. After he became a refugee in Dheisheh, he worked as a stonecutter in a quarry near Bethlehem, for a short period as a construction worker with the Jordanian army ("The only time in my life that I received a monthly salary"), and from the early days of the Occupation until the accident in 1975, at road paving and construction. The sole provider throughout these years, his injury left his family of eleven members with no income or allowances save for a meager one-time compensation payment that was swallowed up on the spot.

Thus, thirteen-year-old Ziyad became a worker in a soft-drinks factory in Tel Aviv, the first in a long series of odd jobs in the course of the next six years. He was nineteen when the first promising opportunity came along: a position as a waiter in the bar and restaurant of the Holyland Hotel in West Jerusalem, where wages were higher and work less exhausting. Then, one evening when serving drinks at the bar, Ziyad was approached by an army officer. "He pointed at me and shouted so that everyone could hear: 'Hey, I know this guy, he's a terrorist who was in the Russian Compound'" (a detention and interrogation center in Jerusalem). Later, he recalled the man as the soldier who dragged him along the corridor to be interrogated by the General Security Services about a year earlier. After the incident the hotel staff became hostile, and Ziyad was compelled to leave. He worked intermittently at construction sites in West Jerusalem until his arrest in 1986 and subsequent one-year prison sentence on the charge of incitement and illegal activity. His older brothers, who had shouldered the burden of the family's support with him for many years, were now married, and two of the younger brothers were in and out of prisons and detention centers. The situation was so difficult that the disabled Abu ʿAbed returned to work, now in the lowly and poorly paid position of a night watchman.

No matter how arduously he searched for work, Ziyad, now back from prison, was more often in the position of dependent than breadwinner. It took another two years of short-term employment at a cement factory near Dheisheh and at a construction site in Beit Shemesh, and another prison term, before he finally managed to get the job with UNRWA. "Not very long ago people looked down on you if you were a laborer with UNRWA, especially if you were young," he told me. "But nowadays everybody is on their waiting list."

The Younger Generation: Female Wage Laborers

This category refers to women whose ages in 1993 ranged from twenty-one to forty, the mean age being twenty-eight years. Hence, all these women grew up and came of age in Dheisheh under Israeli military occupation. Two main social attributes distinguish this generational group: the educational achievements of its members and a relatively high level of salaried professional or semiprofessional employment. The spread of education to Dheishehian women, which was clearly noticeable in the gap between members of the intermediate generation and those of the older one, received full-blown expression in the younger generation: My survey on women and employment in Dheisheh shows that around half of the 318 younger women completed at least ten years of schooling, and approximately one-fourth had some form of postsecondary education.

In contrast with the experience of men of the intermediate and younger generations, the level of education had a profound bearing on employment. The spread of secondary and higher education among camp women and their integration into professional work will be addressed in Part II, but the magnitude and consequences of these processes pertain directly to the current discussion. Indeed, this is the only one of the six gender/generational groups in which day wage labor, the focus of our interest, diminished in comparison with salaried employment.

CHARACTERISTICS AND CONDITIONS OF EMPLOYMENT

The survey indicated that 106 out of 318 women had at one time participated in the labor force, thirty-eight (36 percent) as manual laborers. Eighteen of these laborers worked as seamstresses, either in their homes, on a piecework basis, or in local workshops in the Bethlehem region. Twenty worked at cleaning, fruit picking, or in factories. Only thirteen, about one-third of the day wage laborers, had worked in Israel. Fully 60 percent of the women who had participated in the labor force were professionally or semi-professionally employed on a salaried basis, among them teachers, nurses, secretaries, and others. All of the latter group worked in the West Bank.[7]

Two findings are striking, therefore, in comparison with the intermediate and older generation. For one, while almost all participants in the labor force from among the earlier generations were wage laborers, mainly day laborers, only slightly more than one-third of the younger women were so employed. The second finding pertains to the predominant type of employment among the younger wage laborers and to venue. Fruit picking, cleaning services, and kitchen work, the leading "industries" for most female laborers of the older and intermediate generations, gave way, by and large, to piecework sewing. And ties to Israeli contractors or manpower agencies and work in West Jerusalem were partially replaced by those to Palestinian subcontractors in the locally based textile industry. These interrelated trends reflect the circumstances in which opportunities for wage labor in Israel for women had been reduced to a minimum. While a few relatively older laborers of the younger generation had worked alongside their mothers in the orchards of moshavim and the campuses of the Hebrew University, for those workers who entered the labor force in the late 1980s and early 1990s such work was a bygone chapter from the history of their elders.

The concentration of an estimated 45 percent of the younger female laborers in sewing had a negative repercussion on their status in the labor market. The majority were hired by local Palestinian subcontractors who produced garments for Israeli firms and who employed laborers either on an hourly or on a piecework basis. Outsourcing in a highly labor-intensive branch such as the textile industry implies that the bigger profits of the firm and the smaller profits of the subcontractor lay in lowering the costs of labor to a minimum. The main consequence for the worker is devalued conditions of employment, first and foremost low income and absence of rights. Wages in the branch in the early 1990s were pushed down to as low as fifteen shekels a day, almost one-third the average daily wage of a cleaner or a kitchen worker in a local institution, and one-fourth the daily wage of a nonskilled construction worker. It is worth noting, however, that the employment of approximately half the women who worked at sewing did not exceed two years, and that about one-third worked at home on an irregular, piecework basis. It would thus be incorrect to suggest that sewing substituted for types of wage labor that prevailed in the past. Rather, its relative weight became more manifest in the wake of the disappearance of other alternatives.

Another significant finding pertains to the marital statuses of workers of the younger generation. Sixty-eight percent of the women who had worked as manual wage laborers and 54 percent of those who were or had been professionally employed were unmarried at the time. However, while some 31 percent of the wage laborers stopped working after marriage, only 5 percent of the professionally employed did so. These results point to the centrality of unmarried women in the Dheishehian female workforce, but also to the negligible effect of marriage on labor force participation once salaried employment is secure.

A Multigenerational Overview

DHEISHEHIAN MALE WAGE LABORERS: INCREASING MARGINALIZATION

For more than eighteen years, beginning in 1969 and ending in 1988, day wage work in Israel, particularly in West Jerusalem and the surrounding settlements, was the primary source of livelihood for more than half of Dheishehian men of the older refugee generation. This part of their working life began when they were in their forties and fifties and was over by the time they had reached their sixties and seventies. Their relatively advanced age notwithstanding, the majority of these men persisted in the labor force throughout the period. Yet despite their particularly high representation, and despite the relatively long duration of their work, the research findings showed that work in Israel did not bring about a gradual improvement in their basic situation.

Employment opportunities in Israel were limited to very few and less remunerative branches in the labor market, first and foremost construction—where inherent job instability, high physical risk, and low income prevailed. Workers were employed on an hourly basis, their wages were much lower than the average wages of their Israeli counterparts, and the wage gap between skilled and unskilled work was small. Throughout their "careers" the majority had changed workplaces many times, sought casual employment, and experienced recurring layoffs and prolonged joblessness. They were denied social benefits, most importantly the right to unemployment benefits and the right to pension insurance, they were not represented by Israeli trade unions, and they were forbidden to organize their own unions.

The personal experiences of the workers testify to the rigid, impenetrable boundaries of the "system" that confronted the individual. When taken together, the case studies and the data demonstrate that even those workers who had accumulated maximum seniority, acquired specific skills, and managed to persist with one contractor were rarely promoted in terms of wages and were not spared dismissal without prior notification. In other words, a combination of perseverance, skill, physical fitness, and luck was insufficient to extend the boundaries of the system and to advance one's individual position via wage labor. Alongside those who showed more resilience, there were many others whose working lives exemplified chronic instability and discontinuity, among them men whose work histories were cut short due to severe injuries at the workplace.

The finding that during twenty years of Occupation preceding the Intifada (1967–87) slightly more than 50 percent of the older men worked primarily as wage laborers in Israel is more indicative of the upper limit of the absorptive capacity of the Israeli labor market than it is of the presence of other alternatives. The nondevelopment of industry, the decline of local agriculture, and the absence of governmental investment in infrastructure— three major outcomes of the Israeli military control over the Territories— had channeled most of those who sought employment inside the West Bank, particularly nonprofessionals, either into construction in the private sector or into devalued jobs, such as night watch and maintenance in institutions and at construction sites. The scarcity of large, long-range construction projects and the concomitant low demand for labor manifested themselves in the short-lived nature of West Bank employment and in the extremely low wages, lower than payment for work in Israel. Findings indicate that for the majority of men of the older generation work in the West Bank served as a last resort, to which they turned in the aftermath of discharge from work in Israel following layoff, physical decline, or work-related injury. It could thus be inferred that the status of a wage laborer in the local West Bank labor market was a derivative of his status with respect to the Israeli labor market and stood at the bottom of the "integrated" economy. At one and the same time, the presence of a reservoir of an underpaid, underutilized labor force in the West Bank enabled Israeli employers to keep wages and working conditions at a minimum level.

A comparative analysis of the findings on workers of the intermediate generation leads to two additional conclusions, one related to the negligible impact of education on the status of these laborers, the other to the absence of upward mobility. Whereas among men of this generation 42 percent acquired secondary education, some 80 percent had worked as day wage workers in Israel and/or the West Bank. This finding, coupled with the data on the high rate of out-migration among the highly educated among this generation, is evidence of the scarcity of opportunities for remunerative employment in the West Bank and the impenetrability of the professions (in both the public and the private sectors) in the Israeli labor market.

Ninety percent of the male wage workers of the intermediate generation had been employed in Israel for at least some time during the Occupation, and more than 50 percent had spent the major part of the period as workers in Israel. Unlike their counterparts of the older generation, these men had entered the Israeli labor market when they were at the height of their physical strength and fitness (aged eighteen to thirty), and a not insignificant group among their ranks had already acquired some training and skills in professions such as carpentry, plumbing, ironwork, and painting. Nonetheless, these skills and capacities, which in other circumstances could have worked in their favor, did not yield them any substantial advantage. Perhaps the best indicator for the instability that permeated their working lives is to be found in the relatively high numbers (close to 50 percent) among this generation of wage workers who had spent more years on average working inside the West Bank than in Israel and the settlements. Unlike members of the older generations, for whom work in the West Bank was a last stage or terminus prior to retirement, the discharging of the intermediate generation from workplaces in Israel implied many more years of confrontation with the conditions on the local market.

The marginalization of members of this generation was exacerbated by the beginning of the Intifada and reached its peak with the imposition of the closure policy. Whereas Intifada- and closure-related layoffs of the elderly had generally coincided with approaching old age, they caught men of the intermediate generation in the prime of their lives, when the majority were parents to both young and adult children and providers for large families. This goes a long way in explaining their willingness to accept any casual opportunity regardless of their skills.

The male wage laborers of the younger generation fared worse with respect to the system than members of the other two groups. The deterioration is reflected in the extremely wide gap between the economic potential of this group and the limited range of job opportunities available to its members, and in the extent to which detrimental treatment by the military authorities had hampered the course of their working lives.

Though educational achievement is one of the outstanding characteristics of this generation, it has not shown itself in the occupational distribution of its members, except for those who had migrated. More than half of this generation acquired at least ten years of schooling, yet around 80 percent of young Dheishehian men who resided in Dheisheh were day wage workers. The finding highlights the contradiction between educational achievement and the impossibility of realizing its occupational and economic potential within the boundaries of the system.

Almost all wage laborers of this generation have gathered some experience working in Israel or the settlements, yet unlike their elders, most of their employment took place in the West Bank. Among those who worked in Israel, rare were the instances of prolonged employment with a single contractor or contracting company, and the prevalence of extended employment was lower in the 1980s than in the 1970s. More common were short-term, frequently interrupted jobs, followed by long periods of unemployment. The "relocation" of the geographical arena of work to the West Bank had begun prior to the closure policy of the 1990s; already clearly noticeable in the second half of the 1980s, it can be traced to the punitive and restrictive measures that the authorities used against political activists and released political prisoners. Thus, it is possible to point at a direct, if not purposeful, correlation between a military policy and the steep contraction of the participation of the younger generation in the labor force in Israel.

The general closure that was imposed in March 1993 and has not yet been officially terminated carried detrimental consequences for workers of all age groups, bringing the unemployment rate in the camp to a record high. Still, young workers found themselves in the most vulnerable position. Having rarely established reliable long-term connections with employers during their interrupted working lives, they had little chance in obtaining entry and work permits.

Comparative scrutiny of the work histories of three successive generations of Dheishehian male wage laborers underscores these histories as processes unable to facilitate accumulation of resources. An hourly basis of employment, denial of basic social rights, dependence on the fluctuating employment opportunities in a single branch of labor, and subjection to the rules and regulations of the military government all militated against the conversion of work histories into cumulative or "ascending" trajectories that could enable advancement. Within the boundaries of the "systemic conditions," factors such as experience, seniority, skill, and persistence did not serve as mechanisms of promotion or as insurance against layoff. Hence the absence of progress along time: the inability of fathers to pave the way for their sons and ensure them a better starting point at work. Quite to the contrary, the case of Dheisheh testifies to a general tendency of regression in the relative status of sons in the labor market when compared with their fathers.

DHEISHEHIAN FEMALE WAGE LABORERS: MARGINALITY IN THE
LABOR MARKET, CENTRALITY IN THE CAMP LABOR FORCE

One of the salient findings on wage labor in Dheisheh is the high rate of women's participation in the labor force: up to 37 percent of the adult female population. Although this figure pertains to all women who had ever worked outside the household, and therefore does not coincide with the rate of active participation at a given moment, the general picture remains unchanged: The representation of women in the Dheishehian labor force during the Israeli Occupation was high in absolute terms.

This finding diverges greatly from the data provided by the Israeli Central Bureau of Statistics (CBS), according to which the rate of employed women in the West Bank stood at 9.5 percent in 1987, at 12.3 percent in 1980, and 14 percent, supposedly its peak, in 1970 (CBS 1988, 722). Smaller, albeit significant discrepancies were also found in comparing my findings with those of Fafo and the Palestinian Central Bureau of Statistics (PCBS). The "survey of living conditions" conducted by Fafo found a female labor force participation rate of around 19 percent in the West Bank as of 1992, but pointed to a generally lower rate of participation among camp women (Heiberg and Ovensen 1993, 210). PCBS labor surveys for 1995–97 found that up to 17 percent of West Bank women were in the labor force, but pointed to significant internal disparities between regions (for example, 17.6 percent for the Tulkarem/Qalqilia district as against only 7.2 percent in the Hebron district) (PCBS 1998, 103–4). The marked differences may be attributed, to some extent, to the local conditions, circumstances, and characteristics particular to the Dheisheh setting, and to a greater extent, to my flexible definition of "participation in the labor force." The main point at stake, however, is that the method of tracing labor histories over time and along generations proved highly fruitful, capturing both the position of women with respect to the two main labor markets under consideration and the significant, although changing, magnitude of their contribution as wage workers. It is highly probable that the application of this method to larger female populations in other refugee and nonrefugee communities on the West Bank would have resulted in similar findings.[8]

Whereas the history of wage labor among Dheishehian men dates to the period prior to the refugee era, the phenomenon of wage labor among Dheishehian women began after the uprooting and was significantly amplified during the Israeli Occupation. Given the refugee condition and the loss of agricultural land as a starting point, the high representation of women in the Dheishehian labor force can be explained against the backdrop of the intersecting impact of three factors: the opening of employment opportunities—albeit curtailed and restricted—in the Israeli labor market, a revolution in the sphere of female education that began to bear fruit from the second decade of refugee existence onward, and the marginalization of male bread-winners within the political economy of the Occupation. While the first factor determined the nature of manual wage work available to women and the second affected the course of change over time in the occupational breakdown of working women, the third factor helps to explain the perpet-uation of the strong response of camp women to wage work opportunities throughout the period.

The highest rate of participation was recorded among women of the older generation, whose employment spanned the fifth and sixth decades of their lives. The fact that almost every second women of this generation per-formed some form of wage labor—even if on a very short-term basis—may be unexpected, given that most were aging mothers of seven to nine chil-dren. Indeed, research pertaining to women, employment, and development in the Arab world has consistently pointed to a negative correlation between high fertility and women's participation in the labor force (see Azzam, Abu Nasr, and Lorfing 1985). Thus, findings from Dheisheh serve as evidence that under certain conditions the correlation may be reversed. True, many women stopped working outside the home following birth and the in-creased burden of child care and housework, as is evidenced by the high percentage of those who left the labor force after very short periods. Yet many women also returned to work after shorter or longer intervals and managed to maneuver between the double load of work outside and inside the household by allocating much of the housework to their older daugh-ters. Thus, the pervasiveness of wage work among relatively older mothers to many children is explained in light of the gender-differentiated structure of labor opportunities in the Israeli labor market and the related pressing need for income.

Much as in the case of male laborers, the working lives of female laborers proceeded in the narrow margins of the prospering Israeli economy. They moved within bounded contours from fruit and vegetable picking in the fields and orchards of moshavim and kibbutzim to cleaning and cooking in public institutions and private homes in West Jerusalem. Like their con-struction-worker husbands, brothers, and sons, they too toiled for an hourly wage and went without social benefits. Moreover, their meager wages were far lower than were those of their male counterparts. Yet, the convergence of circumstances, first and foremost the demand for female cleaners in large establishments and institutions in Jerusalem, combined with the proximity of Dheisheh to the city and the relative ease of commuting, enabled a hard core of workers to persist at the same workplaces for considerable periods. Against the predicament of job instability, which affected almost all male wage laborers, and the double marginalization of young workers in particular, this persistence became a crucial factor in the household economy of many a Dheishehian family. The frequent incidence of women who had passed the age of sixty and continued at exhausting toil, despite deteriorating health and even various degrees of disability, is indicative of the high personal price that was often demanded of them. Family reliance on female wage laborers had far-reaching repercussions for family life (see Chapter 3).

The intergenerational comparison of the work histories of women wage laborers shows that, as with the men, the scope of employment opportunities available contracted rather than expanded over time. The period that could a posteriori (and ironically) be referred to as the golden age lasted slightly more than a decade (from the mid-1970s to the outbreak of the Intifada) and sprang directly from the demand of Israeli manpower agencies for cheap labor. The relatively small number of public institutions and the scarcity of large industrial plants in the local labor market circumscribed the opportunities for those women who did not work in Israel proper, yet, similar to the case of men, the predominant trend among the intermediate and younger generation of female wage laborers was the relocation of work to the West Bank. Proliferation of charity organizations inside and around Bethlehem mitigated somewhat the effect of the otherwise constricted local labor market by absorbing women as manual laborers in hospitals, orphanages, and schools. The fact that conditions of employment in the latter institutions were better (in terms of wages and benefits) than those for workers in Israel is telling.

Among employed women of the younger generation there was a sharp decline in the numbers of day wage laborers, and a sharp increase in the rate of the professionally and semiprofessionally employed, which rose to almost two-thirds of all employed women in the age group. These trends are indicative of the intersecting of two main processes: the gradual closing of the Israeli labor market, and the impact of women's acquisition of secondary and higher education on the patterns of their employment in the local and regional labor markets.

By 1995, in the aftermath of the Intifada-related layoffs and at the height of the closure season, few Dheishehian women continued to work in Israel. These few were mainly elderly, experienced, and resourceful laborers who sneaked into Jerusalem two or three times a week, bypassing military checkpoints in order to get to the private homes where they worked. The impact of the disappearance of job opportunities in Israel for younger women was not as devastating as it was for young men since the numbers of manual wage laborers within their ranks were low to start with. However, the penetration of many educated young women into specific branches of the local professional labor market became a lifeline for numerous Dheishehian families.

CHAPTER 3

Socioeconomic Relationships in the Households of Day Wage Laborers

THE DETAILED FINDINGS on labor histories of three generations of men and women in Dheisheh reveal that nearly every Dheishehian family, at one or more stages of its life cycle, relied primarily on the income of day wage laborers. In 1995 the prevalence in the camp of family households that subsisted solely or mainly on day wage labor was estimated around 35 percent. About two years into the "grand" closure, during the month of Ramadan (February 1995), the Palestinian National Authority (PNA) organized a one-time relief mission in Dheisheh, distributing basic foodstuffs (flour, rice, sugar, tea, and margarine) to families whose main providers had lost their jobs. In order to ascertain which families were eligible for rations, a camp-based society conducted a preliminary survey. According to their numeration, of the fourteen hundred families in Dheisheh, approximately five hundred (35.7 percent) subsisted prior to the policy of closure primarily on the income of day wage laborers who worked in Israel. Another 650 families lived mainly on the wages of employees (skilled, professional, or semiprofessional) who did not work in Israel, and 250 families were on the UNRWA list of "special hardship cases"—families without any wage earner.

While the consideration of hypothetical situations tends to be rejected in the social sciences as speculation, it often provides useful insights. What types of family division of labor would have existed, for instance, if the hundreds of male and female Dheishehian laborers had received monthly salaries rather than hourly wages, unemployment benefits, a pension fund at retirement, and had been entitled to trade union representation? It is safe to assume that under these circumstances many of the processes under discussion here would not have unfolded at all. It follows that familial divisions of labor that actually developed around day wage labor should be understood in view of the fact that <u>continuous employment, regular income, and basic entitlements were beyond the reach of the great majority of the workers.</u>

One is tempted to adopt a functionalist interpretation and suggest that the purpose or telos of familial divisions of labor was to cope with the paucity and irregularity of income and to provide a support system or a safety net for those who needed it—the unemployed, the underemployed, those who were denied work permits in Israel, and former political prisoners who were not integrated into the labor market. While essentially correct in terms of the end results, such an interpretation attributes to the family an unrealistic level of unity and homogeneity. The multigenerational Dheishehian family is faced with conflicts, since its working and nonworking male and female members hold unequal material and cultural claims and resources, leading over time to divergent needs and aspirations. Many interests and goals are realized outside the family as such, while other important individual needs, especially those of the relatively more disadvantaged family members, particularly working un-married and married women, are blocked from realization within the struc-ture of the household economy. My main purpose, therefore, is not to classify familial divisions of labor and roles according to one or another function that can be attributed to them a posteriori, but rather to look into the economic and social origins of specific modes of familial organization and to analyze the mechanisms and power relations that sustain them.

The case studies that follow may be regarded as three subtypes of the more general archetype of family households that subsisted primarily on day wage labor. While these cases are not representative of all subtypes found in Dheisheh, the presentations bring into perspective some of the prevalent con-ditions, problems, and crises that underwrite the unfolding of the family life of laborers in the camp.

A Chain of Working Women: Umm Ahmad, Abu Ahmad, and Their Ten Daughters and Six Sons

In 1995 Umm Ahmad and Abu Ahmad's household numbered fourteen per-sons. They lived in two and a half rooms, all in all 35 square meters, in what had once been an UNRWA shelter. In addition to the parents, there were three unmarried daughters and five unmarried sons between the ages of nine and twenty-five as well as a married son, his wife, and their two young chil-dren. At night, the son's family slept in one room, while the other ten crowded into the remaining space. During the day many of the sponge mattresses were piled up in the corners, with others laid on floors and against the walls to serve as cushions and backrests in the otherwise almost unfurnished rooms. Umm Ahmad, then aged fifty-five, and Abu Ahmad, seventy-two, had been married for thirty-six years, during which time they had sixteen children: ten daughters and six sons. In 1995 the oldest was thirty-five and the youngest nine years old. Seven daughters had married and left home and now lived with their husbands.

Asked who supported this extensive family over these years, Abu Ahmad claimed without hesitation to have been the primary breadwinner, reluctantly acknowledging a role to his oldest son. There was no mention from him of the contribution of others. But this minimalist version, which Abu Ahmad maintains for reasons that have to do with pride, and perhaps shame, does not sustain scrutiny. Throughout the Israeli Occupation, Abu Ahmad, an unskilled worker, took on casual jobs in gardening and cleaning in West Jerusalem. Yet for more than twenty years—from the early 1970s until the mid-1990s—the family subsisted mainly, and at times solely, on the wage labor of its female members.

Between 1960 and 1980 Umm Ahmad gave birth to her first fourteen children, with the intervals between births averaging eighteen months. At first childbearing kept her from working outside the home, but as soon as her eldest daughters—the first six children were all daughters—were old enough to take care of the youngest, she began to work as a seasonal fruit picker. The harvest season regularly lasts from May to October, depending on the fruit, and at its height (June, July, and August) dozens of Dheishehian women, often joined by both younger and older children, would leave the camp at dawn and head for the orchards in the subcontractors' pickup trucks. By the time they entered their early teens, Umm Ahmad's daughters had also joined the picking force, though mainly during summer vacations from school.

In 1979 Umm Ahmad began to work as a charwoman at the Hebrew University in Jerusalem and persevered in that job for more than seven years, during which time she became the steadiest provider for the family. However, her average monthly income at the time was around one hundred dollars, far below the minimum needs of the family. In 1980, the daughters, each in her turn, joined the labor force. Rima, the second in line, became a nurse's assistant at Caritas Baby Hospital and set the pattern that her younger sisters would maintain. With an incomplete high school education, she had no access to more professional employment. Though her job at the hospital enabled her to acquire some skill and experience, it consisted mostly of manual chores. Rima remained at Caritas for a year and a half, until her marriage in 1982. By that time a younger sister, Mona, who had completed only six grades at school and had spent her adolescence at home, took Rima's place at the hospital, working there for two years, until her marriage in 1984. Neither sister set aside any share of her earnings for herself; everything went to their parents. Nor were they "compensated" by dowries at the time of marriage.

In 1986, when she was forty-six years old, Umm Ahmad gave birth to twin boys, her fifteenth and sixteenth children. Kifaya, the fifth sister, replaced her mother at her workplace at the Hebrew University. On campus she met veteran female wage laborers from Dheisheh: "All the women you know were there, Maya: Umm A'del, Umm Ibrahim, Umm Khader, and many others." Umm Ahmad did not go back to work, and after nearly two years of cleaning classrooms and dormitories, Kifaya found employment at Rahabat al-Mahabah, a monastery-orphanage in Arab Jerusalem. Although she had neither completed secondary school nor received any formal training, Kifaya's work as an attendant at the orphanage was semiprofessional in the sense that she was given some responsibility for the children's physical and personal needs. The partially skilled nature of the job, acquaintance with new people, the distance from home, and the fair wage—some four times what she and her mother received as day wage laborers at the university—made the monastery an attractive workplace for Kifaya. Like her older sisters, she too turned her entire wage over to her father: "I did not keep anything for myself, except for the bus or service [public taxi] fare."

When Kifaya left home after marriage, Amani, the seventh daughter, replaced her at Rahabat al-Mahabah. Amani had completed nine grades of schooling (finishing UNRWA's preparatory school in Dheisheh) and, like her sisters, was without professional training. Her job at the orphanage was similar to Kifaya's and lasted for four years, from 1990 to 1994. Apart from her attachment to the children, and the social contacts with other employees, which she cultivated eagerly, what Amani liked best about work was "her" room, where she stayed and slept overnight whenever the work schedule required it. Accommodations at the monastery were very modest, bordering on the ascetic. Workers were asked to economize on electricity, hot water, and heating, and the food was basic and dull. Amani, however, decorated her room with posters, listened to her favorite music on a radio-cassette player that she borrowed, and enjoyed privacy for the first time in her life.

In 1994 Amani quit her job at the Rahabat; the ongoing closure policy rendered commuting to Jerusalem increasingly difficult, and her family preferred that she work closer to home. Within two months she found employment as an attendant in the orphanage section of the Holy Family Hospital (al–Francawi) in Bethlehem, where she was working when I first met her. Now that she rarely stayed at her workplace overnight, she again shared the same living room-bedroom with her seven siblings and her parents.

Amani continued to hand over her wages to her father, and with the Israeli labor market practically sealed off, she became the breadwinner for the entire family. During her years at work, one of Amani's younger sisters was married and another became engaged. All seven married sisters wedded in the traditional fashion, that is, family-arranged marriages with only superficial encounters between the prospective spouses prior to the ceremony. They were married either to distant kin from Fawwar and ʿAida refugee camps or to nonrelatives from Dheisheh and the villages of Beit Omar and Irtas. All the husbands were laborers, and most had worked in Israel prior to the closure. None of the sisters who worked before marriage reentered the labor force.

In 1995 only two of Umm and Abu Ahmad's sons were past eighteen, with the other four boys at secondary, preparatory, and elementary school. Unlike his older sisters, Ahmad, the eldest son, completed high school and holds a matriculation certificate. He entered Bethlehem University in 1986, but his studies were cut short when, a year later, the university was closed down by order of the military authorities. It remained closed for almost four years. Meanwhile, he had given up on the idea of university and tried his luck as a laborer in Israel, but he failed to find long-term employment. With the enforcement of the closure and the difficulties in obtaining a work permit, he remained unemployed for many months. Early marriage (at twenty) exacerbated the problem, since with hardly any income he could not proceed with providing independent housing for his new family. Fuad, the second son in line, lost years of schooling during the Intifada. Failing to procure a steady job, he too could barely contribute to the family's subsistence.

Many years had passed since Abu Ahmad ceased being a major or even minor provider for the family. Nevertheless, he continued to seek casual work in gardening. Chances of finding opportunities were slim, with demand low (particularly for the elderly), and the work was seasonal. The closure years almost brought an end to his irregular working life, further reducing the number of workdays a month to perhaps two or three. On several occasions he spoke of his long walks through the streets of West Jerusalem in search of a job, even a two- or three-hour-long project (our paths once crossed during one of these fruitless attempts in the neighborhood where I lived). When the tight closure of February 1994 was extended into April and May, Abu Ahmad decided to fulfill a religious obligation and what he referred to as a lifelong dream: going on the hajj (pilgrimage) to Mecca.[1] I expected that the costly excursion during days of extreme hardship would enrage his daughters and sons, but, quite to the contrary, none of them seemed to object.

At first glance, Abu and Umm Ahmad's household seems to have changed little since 1975. At that time, the family numbered two parents and eight unmarried children aged one to fifteen; in 1995 the parents and eight unmarried children shared the same home with an extension. In 1975 the family's living space was confined to two and a half rooms (up until 1973 they lived in a single room), and such was the case in 1995. Livelihood in 1975 was precarious; in 1995 the hardship was overwhelming. Yet, a process with a discernible structure took place over the preceding two decades.

The six daughters coming first, combined with the circumstances of extreme poverty and the adult male breadwinner's very low and irregular income, had a direct bearing on the structural features of the familial division of labor. The first six daughters grew up and came of age in the 1970s and early 1980s, at the height of labor opportunities in the Israeli labor market. Yet neither the girls' seasonal work as fruit pickers, nor their mother's more-or-less steady cleaning job could provide for the growing needs of the ever-expanding family. Rather, the entrance of the daughters into semiskilled salaried jobs (as opposed to employment on a day basis) in child care and nursing-related work lent substantial weight to the family's "woman-power" and laid the basis for the chain of work that sustained the family for many years.

The daughters' contribution to the household economy assumed a structure that was defined and delineated by their lack of control over income, and by prospects of marriage, which regulated the extent of their work terms. Indeed, in three out of the four instances, a daughter worked for a period that lasted between one and a half and four years and was terminated upon marriage and departure to the husband's household. The continuity of the work chain was not left to chance; rather, it was enabled anew each time through the replacement of a "retiring" daughter by her younger sister, thus giving rise to a process whereby each daughter in turn raised a kind of capita tax to her family in the form of wage labor. True enough, some daughters were married while very young, barely contributing their "share," yet early marriage and departure somewhat alleviated the family's subsistence burden and could well be viewed as complementing the work chain.

It is not possible to separate discussion of the "work chain phenomenon" from the wider process of the ongoing displacement of men, old and young, from the ranks of the labor force. For many years Umm and Abu Ahmad yearned for a son; they even named their fifth daughter Kifaya, literally "enough," that is, enough daughters: "May God answer our pleas and give us a son!" When Allah finally acceded and Ahmad was born, they groomed him and were more than solicitous in seeing that he completed secondary school and could enter university. They cherished the hope that upon graduation he would find a job that could support the family. Reality failed to comply with expectations: circumstances did not help Ahmad to proceed with higher education or gain professional employment. The ever-contracting opportunities for manual wage labor meant that as a young man in his twenties Ahmad was not even able to become a steady provider. Not only did the female-based work chain remain the viable resource, his own new nuclear family was added to the list of those dependent on the income of his younger sister. Fewer hopes were cultivated for Fuad, with less education and the same unpromising job market. The emergence of the work chain of unmarried daughters should be interpreted, therefore, as an alternative family division of labor that gained ground in the face of the marginalized positions of male family members in the shrinking labor market and under the adverse overall political circumstances.

Central to this analysis is the relationship between the female work chain and the status of the daughters in their parents' household. On the structural-functional level, the chain's modus operandi lies in the unmarried daughters' lack of control over income generated by wage labor. Their earnings did not enhance the economic status of the daughters since all income went in entirety to the family head; unlike unmarried men, the young women did not set aside savings for their prospective marriages and future households. Despite her fundamental contribution, the position of the unmarried working woman within her parents' household remains basically unchanged throughout her term of "service," regardless of its length. She is not entitled to improved material conditions or to greater privacy and continues to share the same living space and belongings with her siblings and parents. While in part this denial is a consequence of the prevailing physical conditions at home, that is, overcrowding and poverty, it should also be attributed to a deep-seated "cultural" block on the part of the family. They persist in looking upon her as a *bint*, a virgin maiden, whose status is frozen in time and resistant to change until her marriage. Thus, the reliance of the family on the wages of its unmarried daughters carries with it the contradiction between their earning power and their inability to realize it in ways that might coincide with their own needs and aspirations.[2]

Nonetheless, the nature of waged employment may carry positive ramifications for such young women. Lacking sufficient education and professional skills, the four sisters entered jobs at the lower level of the occupational scale, which consisted mainly, though not exclusively, of physical labor. Still, especially in the case of the two who worked in the orphanage, the work involved and developed skills and responsibility, created the setting for new acquaintances, enabled a degree of freedom of movement, and induced a sense of satisfaction. Lodging at the workplace provided some opportunity for privacy and for distancing from the burdens of everyday life at home.

How do the young women conceive of the contradictions that inhere in the familial division of labor? According to Mufida, the third sister in line, who in 1996 was married with five children and who participated only partially in the work chain, "There is nothing strange or unique about this . . . each one of us has worked and contributed. I worked in fruit picking every summer and replaced mother whenever she was unable to attend her cleaning job in the university. Now Amani is helping my father and my brother . . . we were all educated to help each other. All of us are united and there is no secret hiding out there." This disregard for contradictions on Mufida's part may well be solidly entrenched socialization at work, or the years that separate her present life from her adolescence in her parents' household. Indeed, the structure of the work chain presupposes that none of the participants, except for the mother, is "trapped" inside for too long and prevents each participant from viewing the "edifice" in its entirety. In other words, marriage, which sets the upper limit of work at the service of the family, does serve to disguise or mask the structure from the women who help create it with their labor.

Moreover, the "framing conditions" wherein prospective marriage demarcates the end of service probably mitigates the burden and allows the unmarried young women to come to terms with their (temporary) role. However, it often happens that the "service period" is extended, as in the case of Amani, almost the single provider for her family over five successive years. The fact that one younger sister married and another became engaged during that period may indicate that the benefits of reliance on Amani's steady income induced her parents to reshuffle the sequence of their daughters' marriages accordingly. Once the chainlike process is brought to a halt due to extended reliance on a single unmarried female member, her own prospects in the (arranged) marriage "market" may be significantly lowered.

Though Amani refrains from directly criticizing her parents and rejects the possibility that her spinsterhood has been intentionally or purposefully prolonged, her perception of her situation is revealing. Amani is on good terms with all her family members and finds much comfort and support in the companionship of her sisters, married and unmarried alike, spending most of her free time with them. Yet, although she appears to be well adapted to her social environment, Amani has also developed a style of her own, which is noticeable in her enthusiastic and relatively unrestrained speech and in her openness, as well as in her modest but matching apparel and in the way she prepares her beautiful long hair, which she keeps uncovered. At twenty-five, Amani is very keen on getting married, though, as she intimated to me on several occasions, she is unwilling to compromise on her right to a marriage of choice, refusing to buy her "freedom" through an arranged match, despite the uncertainties this entails.

As is often the case, the exception may teach us more about the rule. Amani, who got "trapped" in the chain, is the only one among her sisters for whom the inherent but latent structural contradiction has developed into a personal conflict. The more the work is socially or professionally rewarding, and the longer the period of service is extended, the higher the probability that conflict or confrontation will come to the forefront. Such conflicts do not necessarily evolve around the "core problem"—the division of labor and the structure of socioeconomic relationships—but rather, emerge as response to "derivative" issues, such as that of arranged marriage as against freedom of choice.

Since neither the core contradiction nor the conflicts to which it gives rise can be resolved within the family of origin, a solution for the situation of the young working woman depends greatly on the nature of matrimonial life. Will Amani, once she is married (leaving aside the issue of the match), be able to convert the capacities—professional, economic, and social—that she has acquired through work into an improved social status within her new family? A necessary, but perhaps not sufficient condition is that she retains (or upgrades) her position in the labor force. The precedent of her older sisters is not encouraging in this respect, since none of those who had worked previously continued to do so after marriage, and the chances of their reentrance into semiprofessional employment would diminish with time. The local labor market is small and nondiversified, and many women compete for jobs in nursing- and child care–related work. Amani may be exceptional in terms of her motivation and outlook, but she is likely to face difficulties.

The Sons of Umm and Abu Hisham Come of Age

Abu Hisham is a hospitable man. On each of my visits to his home he would come up with the same offer: "Why live in Jerusalem? Come and stay with us, we'll fix a room for you." Within less than three years (1993–95), he has married off three sons, and all three, together with wives and offspring, were living in his house. "But Abu Hisham," I would respond with laughter, "only this summer you celebrated another son's wedding, his wife is already pregnant, and you are looking for more tenants?" It seems that Abu Hisham has grown accustomed to the idea that the number of household members is always on the increase; no matter how many of his sons start families of their own, they seem fated to end up sharing the same house with him.

Umm Hisham and Abu Hisham, both forty-five in 1995, are cousins whose family originated in the village of Zakariya. Both were born as refugees shortly after the uprooting, and thus belong to the second or intermediate generation. They had been married for twenty-six years, during which time Umm Hisham gave birth to eight children: six sons and two daughters (aged eight to twenty-five). Rufaida, their eldest daughter, was killed by an Israeli soldier in April 1989 when she was thirteen years old.

Abu Hisham completed nine grades and has been an unskilled laborer since leaving school at the age of fifteen. In the course of thirty years he has changed workplaces in both Israel and the West Bank dozens of times and

experienced a series of layoffs followed by periods of unemployment of varying lengths. His income has always been low and irregular; in his current job
as a night watchman at an oil press in Beit Jala he earns approximately five
hundred shekels (NIS) a month. Umm Hisham, who completed only five
years of schooling, became a wage worker in 1975, that is, after six years of
marriage and the birth of her four oldest children. Except for a four-year
interlude (1980–84), she has worked uninterruptedly in two workplaces:
five years as a cleaner at the Hebrew University (1975–80), and eleven years
(1984–95) as a kitchen worker in the Caritas Baby Hospital. Though certainly
low in absolute terms, at approximately one thousand shekels, her monthly income is twice that of her husband's, making her the main breadwinner.

When the Intifada erupted in 1987, Umm and Abu Hisham's four older
sons (aged twenty-one to twenty-five in 1995) were junior high and high
school pupils. In the course of the uprising they experienced recurring detention and imprisonment of varying duration, totaling between two and
four years each. In addition to convictions in military courts, two of them,
Hisham and Ahmad, were held under administrative detention (imprisonment of unspecified duration without trial on the basis of the emergency
regulations instituted by the British Mandatory government and maintained
by Israel). "During those years," says Umm Hisham, "there was not a single
day when all four of them sat with us for dinner; at least one, and at times
three, were in prison." As late as the end of 1995, a time when the number
of detainees and prisoners from Dheisheh had significantly diminished, the
family still retained a "representative" in an Israeli jail. The fifth son, seventeen-year-old Bilal, had been arrested in an army and Shabak (General Security Service) raid on the camp shortly before the transfer of parts of the
Bethlehem area to the PNA.

By 1992–93, the end of the relatively long period during which the lives
of the four brothers revolved around political activism, detention, and imprisonment, they were too old to return to school. Since none of them had
acquired a skill or a trade, the alternative was to search for a laborer's job.
But regulations prohibited former prisoners, particularly former administrative detainees, from entering Israel. In the years that followed their release,
none of the brothers succeeded in securing steady employment.

Although he remained unemployed—except for occasional odd jobs—
Hisham, the oldest, got married in 1993. His wife, a secondary school dropout, does not work, and they live, together with their two young children,
with Hisham's parents and siblings, calling "their own" a single bedroom with
no separate bathroom. Ahmad, twenty-three, who remained unemployed for
almost two years after his release from prison and who subsequently found a
job as a cook at a rehabilitation center for the disabled in Beit Jala, followed
suit and married in 1994. With an income of approximately seven hundred

shekels per month, Ahmad, his nonemployed wife and their baby have the same arrangement. The third son, Castro, joined the family workforce only several months before his marriage in 1995: He became a part-time employee in a tourist shop in Bethlehem. Jalal, twenty-one, does not work, apart from the rare occasions when he succeeds in sneaking into Jerusalem.

Until 1987, when Umm Hisham's savings enabled them to renovate, the family of ten members at the time lived in two old UNRWA units. Two new bedrooms, a living room, and an indoor kitchen and bathroom, built over the course of four years, were completed in 1991. The bedrooms currently serve as the multifunctional living spaces for the recently started families of the three brothers. Each contains minimal furniture: a double bed, a chest of drawers, and a free-standing closet, the basic items the groom is obliged to provide for his bride at marriage.

In a visit that took place shortly before Castro's marriage, I wanted to learn how the groom's family was going to cope with the burdensome expenditures, mainly costly gold jewelry and several dresses and other items of clothing for the bride, as well as the bedroom furniture. Umm Hisham told me about the "women's fund" that she and her companions among the workers at Caritas had set up: "On the day that we receive our paychecks, each of us deposits a fixed sum. The idea is to help each other, so that when costly celebrations come along, each in turn can draw a meaningful sum." While the expenditures on her sons' marriages and wedding feasts were high, especially when compared with the family's living costs, the total held to the minimum standard that has become the norm in Dheisheh.

Several months after Castro's wedding, I was surprised to learn of rearrangements in the allocation of space: Umm Hisham and Abu Hisham evacuated their bedroom in favor of Castro and his newlywed wife. Umm Hisham and her youngest daughter, Ruaida, spent the nights together with Abu Hisham at his workplace, the watchman's room at the oil press. From there Umm Hisham left each morning for Caritas Baby Hospital. After work, she returned to her home in Dheisheh, baked, cooked, did the cleaning, and tended to her younger sons, until nightfall when it was time for her to leave. I found it hard to conceal my astonishment: "If Umm Hisham has to give up her room, then why didn't you wait with Castro's wedding?" I confronted the daughters-in-law, who were sitting together in the living room playing with their babies. Castro's wife, barely eighteen at the time, replied without a sign of confusion: "We waited a long time . . . we were engaged for two years." Ahmad's wife, two years her senior, came to her support: "What can they do? We too had to wait for almost two years, and one can not wait forever. All the space is taken up. Jalal, Bilal, and Adham [the three unmarried brothers] sleep in the old room with the damp walls and leaking ceiling, you can't expect that from the newlywed couple." It was obvious that Umm Hisham's situation did not preoccupy them. After all, brides have their rights, which the groom's family is expected to fulfill.

But custom is never that simple. Thus, for Umm Hisham, it was probably a combination of embarrassment and offended pride that prevented her from speaking her mind. Instead, she offered me an alternative account of her nightly excursions to the oil press: the lonely and bored Abu Hisham had asked her to keep him company, a request she could not properly refuse. Considering the fact that for wives to lodge at their husbands' workplaces was novel for Dheisheh (as elsewhere) her version showed quick thinking.

Umm and Abu Hisham's extended family has arrived at the stage of population explosion. Each time a son marries, their living space shrinks, there are additional mouths to feed, additional queuing for the bathroom, and additional sources of friction and quarrels. Finally, the house could accommodate newly married couples only by pushing out the senior spouses. Despite having built up the house with her own wages, Umm Hisham was losing hold of her own bedroom.

In the state of affairs that prevailed in 1995–96, the family's hopes no longer rested with labor market-related opportunities. Rather, they focused on the lingering outcome of the court appeal filed by the family's lawyer in the matter of the death of their daughter Rufaida. In April 1989, at thirteen, Rufaida was shot in the head with a high-velocity bullet while she was walking toward a mass procession on the outskirts of Dheisheh commemorating two youths killed the same week. The army refused to acknowledge responsibility, and the soldier who had shot and killed Rufaida was never brought to trial. However, following persistent intervention by human rights organizations and an appeal by a member of Knesset, the military authorities were forced to reopen the case. History shows that only in extremely rare cases have soldiers been convicted and found guilty of violating the regulations that pertain to opening fire on a civilian population. There is a possibility, however, that the military will offer some financial compensation if the family forgoes further demands.

The case demonstrates the connection between the process that has pushed two generations of male workers to the margins of the workforce and the perpetuation of extended households in Dheisheh of the 1980s and 1990s. The four elder children happened to be males, forefronting the issue of separation of adult sons from their parents' household.

Umm Hisham first joined the labor force in order to provide an additional source of income for a family that already numbered six. Very quickly, however, her earnings became a regular component of the family's livelihood. Moreover, since Umm Hisham's return to work in 1984, the gap between her contribution and that of Abu Hisham widened consistently. This was not the result of her increased earning power, but rather that of the continuous decline in Abu Hisham's situation. In the course of thirty years of work he was unable to rise above the state of a day laborer with intermittent employment and irregular income. Thus, the main positive aspect of Umm Hisham's job was not the amount of her wages but rather the regular monthly basis of payment.

Umm Hisham's role as the permanent and primary provider for her family was directly related to the inability of her sons to become earners. If she had held any hope of their relieving her of the burden developments taught her otherwise. The lack of positive correlation between the potential size and earning power of the family workforce and its actual economic capacity surfaced quickly. The correlation that emerged was in fact negative; while needs were constantly increasing, the means to satisfy them decreased proportionally.

The sons' frequent and lengthy imprisonments during a critical and vulnerable stage in their lives foreshadowed their marginalization even prior to their actual attempts to enter the labor force. Having lost the chance to advance through education, they were later confronted by a policy that further circumscribed their opportunities as day laborers. Such were their personal histories. The longer the instability in the adult sons' work lives, the longer their dependence on their parents' household, that is, on their mother's work and income.

Nevertheless, marginalization did not prevent marriages at what were, by many standards, young ages. In recent decades, families of brides have been stipulating a separate apartment as a precondition for marriage, bringing about a rise in age at marriage for men. However, the ongoing deterioration of the economic situation that accompanied the Intifada led to flexibility and the lowering of demands in regard to bride price and premarital arrangements. As in the case under discussion, the fact that the brides' families were ready to settle for a room rather than an apartment indicates a mutual acceptance of lowering demands and standards.

On the structural level, then, the sons' marriages did not mark the commencement of a new stage in their lives as adult men, but rather the expansion of the household by six members in less than three years. The four nuclear families that reside in Umm and Abu Hisham's household today constitute an extended family. However, this is not an organized productive unit held together by virtue of a well-defined division of labor and roles, nor does it owe its continuity to the patriarchal control of the father over resources and property. Rather, it is a joint residence and consumption unit that subsists on the regular income of one female provider and the extremely irregular incomes of others. Moreover, it would be incorrect to discuss this formation in terms of a transitional stage when separation is not a viable prospect for any of the adults. Longevity, being what it is, may force them into structural solutions.

Unlike the chain of working daughters in Umm and Abu Ahmad's household, the pattern of organization that took root in Umm and Abu Hisham's family revolved, for nearly two decades, around a single female as major provider. The dependence of all other members of the extended family on her income did not, however, give rise to a matriarchal power structure or anything similar. Quite the contrary, her indispensable input to the renovation of the house did not ensure her entitlement to even a single bedroom, nor, apparently, did the financing of Castro's wedding earn her much gratitude from either her son or her daughter-in-law.

Even here, where the husband does not exercise direct control over his wife's income, she is unable to convert this resource into an improved social status. To a large extent the explanation lies in the fact that a "survivalist" household economy, grounded in precariousness, often rules out long-term planning and decision making since wages are regularly consumed on the spot. A level of surplus or welfare is required in order that a woman may determine the allocation of money, rather than be confined to securing its inflow. Moreover, in order that a working woman may enjoy her earning power, adequate channels through which she can realize her personal, private needs are required. Such channels are almost nonexistent in the case of a woman with very little formal education who, on top of the tedious job she held on to for almost the entire period of her marriage, was also burdened with the maintenance of the household and the care of eight children. Beyond the emotional suffering, the loss of her only older daughter left Umm Hisham with no female assistance at home until the marriages of her sons. The nature of the wage labor is also of importance here. A daily eight-hour shift of cleaning or kitchen work is exhausting and does not tend to promote the development of skills or of mental activity. In general terms, the absence of opportunity to convert a woman's income into means that satisfy her personal needs facilitates the propagation of a male-prioritizing patriarchal tradition, even when the economic foundations for this have ceased to exist.

The Closure Closes in on the Hajajra Family

I became acquainted with the Hajajra family shortly after the imposition of the general closure on the West Bank and Gaza Strip in March 1993. By the end of April, with no signs of change in the policy forthcoming, I set out to examine its impact on family life.

"If you want to meet a family that was really hit, you shouldn't come to us," a young friend told me. "We belong to the fortunate 10 percent whose situation hasn't been affected. Go and meet the Hajajras." After a brief consultation with his mother, however, the two agreed that it might not be the best of times for the visit. "Who knows what they think of Jews and Israelis right now?"

But only fifteen minutes later I was sitting with Yusra and Radwan Ha-jajra, who went out of their way to welcome me without any signs of dis-comfort regarding my background. Within another ten minutes or so we were joined by Yusra's parents, two of her brothers, and two neighbors, as well as by a dozen children, daughters and sons of the gathering adults. All of the men present in the room were laborers who up until the closure had worked in Jerusalem and the settlements. This was their fourth week with-out work. A similar scene, with variations, repeated itself in the visits that took place over the years that followed.

Yusra's parents, Umm Jamil, fifty-five (in 1995), and Abu Jamil, sixty-eight, the eldest of my acquaintances among the Hajajras, originated from ʿAjur, a large village in terms of both population (three thousand in 1944) and land, located about thirty-five kilometers southwest of Jerusalem. In the aftermath of the 1948 war they arrived, together with many of the ʿAjurians, at Fawar refugee camp in the Hebron district where they resided for some fifteen years. In 1965 they moved to the Dheisheh camp in order to be in the vicin-ity of others from the Hajajra kin group who had found refuge there earlier.

Yusra's mother was only eleven years old when she was married in 1950 to a man thirteen years her senior. "Three delegations came to ask for my hand, and each time I ran away," she recalled on one occasion. "My family married me off by way of deception, because I was too young according to the law. They forged my age and dressed me in clothes that made me appear older, and that's how they took me to the qadi [religious judge] place, and got what they wanted." Yusra and two of her brothers were born in Fawar camp; two younger brothers and two younger sisters were born in Dheisheh.

Yusra's father, Abu Jamil, was a construction worker from the early 1950s until 1994. During the Jordanian era he worked mainly at road paving and stonecutting. In the course of the Israeli Occupation he worked in con-struction in the Jerusalem area, including seventeen years (1977–94) as a compressor operator with the same contracting company and under the same boss. In the aftermath of the closure he remained unemployed for some six months, after which his employer managed to secure a work per-mit enabling Abu Jamil to return to "his" compressor. A severe work injury in 1994 brought an end to his forty-four-year-long career as a day laborer. At that time, at the age of sixty-seven, Abu Jamil's daily wage was forty-five shekels (approximately fifteen dollars at the time).

Of Umm and Abu Jamil's four sons, only Jamil, the eldest, completed eleven grades at school, the other three dropping out when they were be-tween twelve and fourteen years old. For some fifteen years Jamil worked at gasoline stations in West Jerusalem, twelve of them under one employer and at the same gas station, Oranim. He "opened the door" for his younger brothers who, after several years of intermittent employment in construction and at a chicken factory in the town of Beit Shemesh, joined Jamil at the gas station. Fueling and car washing at Oranim was to become their source of livelihood for many years; Munir worked there from the age of twenty until the time he was thirty-two; Akram, from age fifteen to twenty-five; and Marwan, from age eighteen to twenty-four. Their daily wage in 1993 was thirty-three shekels (approximately twelve dollars), less than half the average daily wage of construction workers, which then stood at seventy shekels. Only one of the four was imprisoned, for a relatively short term during the Intifada, after which his entrance into Israel was prohibited for one year. In the wake of the 1993 closure, the four brothers remained jobless.

Three of the four brothers and their families share residence with the parents in a two-story house built on the remains of an old UNRWA shelter. The private space allocated to each family (four or five persons) is confined to a fifteen-square-meter bedroom, with all fifteen members of the household using the same kitchen and bathroom. The four nuclear families keep their accounts separate, except for special joint household expenditures, which are evenly divided, and except for crisis periods, such as the one initiated by the closure, when the father supported his sons (up until his injury). The fourth brother and his family live in an adjacent house, a relatively new and poorly built structure that suffers from all possible deficiencies: particularly, damp walls, leaky ceilings, and unfinished windows, doorways, and stairs. Yusra's two younger sisters were married to two brothers from the village of Jabʿa (located on the western slopes of the Hebron Mountains), where they reside today with their husbands' family. One completed secondary school and works as a part-time nurse in the village clinic; the other was taken out of school at sixteen for her marriage and is a housewife.

Yusra, my closest acquaintance among the Hajajras, who befriended me from the first encounter, was then a thirty-eight-year-old housewife married to Radwan, a mother of six, five boys and a girl, aged five to fifteen, and pregnant with her seventh child.

Yusra had remained in school up to the ninth grade:

My father took me out of school when I was fourteen years old, even though I was known to be a good student. He bought a sewing machine and taught me how to operate it. For more than six years, I sat at home sewing. In those days people used to have most of their clothes made by seamstresses and purchased very little on the market. There was much work; I remember myself working day and night, but all the money went directly to my father.

When she was twenty Yusra was married to a paternal second cousin. She explained: "I never wanted to marry this person. By God, everyone knew I didn't want to marry him. . . . It was the same with my sisters; they too didn't want the men that our father chose for them. But it was father who decided.

He had no mercy . . . and our mother had no mercy either." Yusra moved into her in-laws' household, just around the corner from her own family's home, a patchwork of old UNRWA units and a storeroom, where she, Radwan, and the firstborn children had no space they could call their own. Some unexpected relief came in 1983, when Radwan's parents left for a family visit in Amman. When they failed to return by the expiration date of their travel permit, the Israeli authorities were only too quick to prevent their reentrance into the West Bank and subsequently to deny them right of residence. It was thus that Radwan and Yusra became the "custodians" of the house.

Radwan Hajajra, Yusra's husband, completed only six grades at school and became a laborer at the age of thirteen. From the time of his marriage in 1978, at the age of seventeen, and until 1989, he worked at a biscuit factory in West Jerusalem. Though his daily wage never exceeded thirty shekels, Radwan's factory days are recalled with great nostalgia by Yusra, as "the time when we were 'high'" (using the English term). The factory shut down in 1989, and Radwan remained unemployed for a long period. In fact, for four straight years he hardly worked at all, until in January 1993 his brother-in-law arranged a job for him at the gas station. Two months later, in the wake of the closure, Radwan was again without work. It took him more than one year to get hold of a work permit, which proved to be of little use when harsher restrictions on movement were imposed in the course of 1994. Sneaking to construction sites in the suburban Jewish settlement of Maᶜale Adumim in search of a day's work remained Radwan's only option in the years that followed.

In the course of her married life, Yusra rarely worked for wages. Occasionally, she took on some sewing work, mainly dresses for camp women, but it was very limited and the income marginal. Over nine years she gave birth to six children, a circumstance that tied her down to child care and housework and left little opportunity for wage work.

Six years with hardly any income brought Yusra and Radwan's family to the verge of hunger. For months their diet consisted of bread, rice, lentils, and tomatoes, some of which they received through UNRWA's hardship rations, some by pleading for credit from local storeowners. Their electricity was cut off, leaving the Hajajras without light and with a single kerosene heater for the winter. The children wore second-hand clothing and shoes that Yusra purchased for a pittance at the Bethlehem market, and she and Radwan bought nothing for themselves for years. Amid all this hardship, they nevertheless continued with the construction of a second floor begun eight years earlier. Costs remained low since relatives and friends did most of the work, and they managed to get building materials either as gifts or on long-term loans. The outcome was in accord with the investment, however, and the new walls afforded little protection against even the mildest of rains.

It was during a visit from me in late November 1993, about eight months after the closure, that Yusra spoke her mind. Though it was well past midday, Radwan was asleep, or pretended sleep. Cigarettes, sleep, and tea in the company of men in a similar situation were the signposts of bitter days of unemployment. Yusra said:

I can not remember the last time we saw a hundred shekels enter this house. People look at Radwan as if he is to blame, but I know he is not at fault. If he had the opportunity he would work at this moment. He has become very nervous, with fits of anger and the like. Imagine, even when he wants to get from Dheisheh to Bethlehem he has to borrow two shekels from someone. . . . But the hardest thing is the way people start avoiding you because of your miserable situation.

You act by pretense. As long as you pretend, you can adjust to the expectations of others. It's the dress you wear, the presents you exchange, and the celebrations you attend that matter, not the real things that make up your everyday life. People don't care. They know that Radwan has not worked for one single day in nine months, they know that we have nothing coming in, but they expect me to act as if the world spins for me as it does for them, to attend wedding feasts and birth celebrations and to show up with the proper present, a sack of sugar or a sack of rice. But there is no way I can show up with a present these days, so I simply stop attending feasts, and people respond by avoiding me; they stop paying visits, stop asking questions, keep distance. As we become poorer, I lose my standing among women of the camp.

Umm Nidal invited me to her son's wedding feast and I attended it in spite of myself. I watched the rice and sugar sacks piling up in the corner and felt so ashamed; I didn't know where to put down the two kilos of sugar I brought for the occasion. . . . The other day Umm Akram stopped by and told me she was angry because I failed to congratulate her on her big day. After all, her daughter graduated from university with distinction and has just been accepted for work at the hospital. I decided not to remain silent this time and told her that she should know better, that it's about time she shows some understanding for my situation. And besides, she has been celebrating many special events lately: the graduation of her son from university, the completion of a new house, the birth of grandchildren. As for me, I have had no occasion to celebrate since the birth of my youngest son six years ago.

But worst of all is what I get from my parents. My mother is a ruthless and heartless person without feelings. . . . It is they who took me out of school so that I would work and help them raise my younger brothers. But nowadays they do not show any regard for my family and me. They keep providing my brothers with fresh fruits and vegetables, sometimes with cooked meals as well, while they never offer me any help whatsoever.

In each of our subsequent meetings, Yusra would lament her family's deteriorating situation and, in the same breath, would inform me of the (supposed) growing prosperity of others: one who got a work permit, a wife whose kitchen is always filled with fresh vegetables, a neighbor who has opened a store, another who built a henhouse with chickens laying eggs around the clock. There were also days of renewed hope, whenever Radwan managed to get an entry permit to Jerusalem or found a short-term job with a contractor in Bethlehem. Yusra would welcome me with a beaming smile. "Come on, ask about Radwan," she would say, and then complete her sentence, impatient to break in with the good news: "Radwan is not at home today. This is his third day at work." And two weeks later, Radwan was at home sleeping, and Yusra was trying to figure out how to make do with yesterday's leftovers. Never losing her sense of humor, she once spoke of her great fear: What if the Israeli authorities changed their mind and permitted family reunion for her exiled in-laws, adding them to her family scene?

Nor does she spare Radwan, blaming him for her latest pregnancy and his failure to use contraceptives. Yusra had hoped that she could put infant care behind her and had entertained the idea of going out to work. Now she would have to face up to the facts and all they implied. "Radwan is selfish," she said with her husband present in the room, "he thinks only of himself . . . not of me and of our children." Radwan shrank silently in his chair.

However, it was the encounter with Maysun, one of Yusra's two younger sisters who live in the village, that helped me gain a better perspective on Yusra's fate. As it turned out, Maysun's visits to her parents in the camp are among the happier days in her life. In Jabʿa she experiences almost total isolation, especially since her in-laws, with whom she lives, have recently terminated ties with most of their kin group. As a childless housewife she is idle for most of the day and solely in the company of relatives. Her husband, an unemployed laborer who studied in a religious *sharʿi* college in Hebron, prevents her from completing her secondary education, cut short at her marriage, forbids her to wear trousers even at home, and makes sure that she never leaves the house without a *mandil* (headscarf). "If he could see me now, in pants and without the *mandil*, he would go crazy," Maysun said.

"Life in the village is hell in comparison with Dheisheh," Yusra filled in. "You see, our camp is an easygoing place, everybody comes and goes as they wish, women may leave their house at any hour of the day. . . . See what our parents have done to us?" She continued, "I told you that my sisters never wanted this match." Yusra and Maysun's mother, who was present throughout the conversation, ignored her daughter's accusations, as though she had had no part in hammering out the marriage deals. According to her, the marriage of two sisters with two brothers is the optimal match, allowing the sisters to remain together and within the same family. "It is me who suffered more than anyone," she said suddenly. "I am the one they took away when she was still a little girl who didn't understand a thing."

Yusra's parents' household represents a subprototype different from that of Abu and Umm Ahmad's or Abu and Umm Hisham's. This is a family whose male head was economically active, almost without intermission, throughout the years of the Occupation, and whose four sons entered the labor force at a very young age and persisted in their jobs as day laborers for a very substantial time period. This is a family whose routine life was (almost) uninterrupted by detention and imprisonment of its members, a family whose subsistence did not depend on female wage work.

Two of the above factors could have led, at least in theory, to developments other than those that materialized on the ground. It could be expected that the steady employment history of the male head of the household, despite the low wages, would enhance the chances that his children complete their schooling, including some form of higher education. The fact that none of the sons completed secondary school and that three dropped out before that level indicates that early dropout is affected by other causes, among which is the lack of a family tradition of schooling, that is, the absence within the narrower family, as well as wider circles, of a sensibility that values, prioritizes, and facilitates education. Under such circumstances and against the backdrop of inherent instability and insecurity in the labor market, working at what appeared to be a stable workplace (the Oranim gas station) was regarded as an appealing opportunity, one justifying leaving school. The attrition of the sons led to the father's withdrawal of the younger daughters from school in favor of marriage.

A second potentiality that did not materialize was that associated with the sons' continuous employment. Unlike many youths in Dheisheh whose work lives were severely interrupted by long imprisonment and its aftermath, and yet others whose employment histories were checkered with layoffs and lengthy unemployment, each of the four brothers had persisted in the same workplace for years. It might have been expected that this would facilitate the physical and economic separation of the adult sons from their parents' household upon their marriages. In reality, however, the marriages were followed by the expansion of the family-household unit, at least in terms of joint living. It can be inferred that job continuity is not a sufficient condition for dissociation and independence. Other limiting factors must be taken into account, among which are the extremely low income earned by the working sons—in this case, less than half the average wages of construction laborers—and the scarcity, indeed the near absence, of building space in the vicinity of the parents' home. The only territory on which one can build a house in Dheisheh without having to purchase land is that to be found within the courtyard or surrounding space of the housing unit that was allotted to one's parents and grandparents in the past. The Hajajras, specifically, live in a highly overcrowded section or neighborhood of the camp, where very little empty space is presently available for construction. Under these circumstances, sons often prefer to delay dissociation from their parents' household until they have saved an amount of money sufficient for land purchase, either inside the camp or in the adjacent residential area of Doha.

In the aftermath of the 1993 closure, Abu Jamil's extended family was turned, virtually overnight, from a family of four providers to one without a single jobholder. The crisis that hit so many Dheishehian families during the years of the Intifada, and to a lesser, though not insignificant, extent, during earlier periods as well, invaded the lives of the Hajajras at a relatively late stage. Since the four brothers were at the same workplace, they fell together; the blow was sudden. The return of the aging father to work, while his sons remained jobless, meant a state of dependence on his unbelievably low day wages, thus postponing independence to an unknown date.

The previous case studies explored aspects of patriarchal control in families of laborers whose major providers were women. Patterns of familial control over the wage-generated income of female members were significant factors that diminished the emancipatory element that inheres in women's employment, thereby facilitating the reproduction of the gender-differentiated familial hierarchy of social statuses. Yusra's parents' household subsisted, throughout the years, on the wage income of male providers. Major manifestations of patriarchy within this household were not centered, therefore, on the control over the family's female labor power as much as on the father's capacity to dominate major (and interrelated) junctures in the lives of his daughters, namely, educational attainment and marriage. Interrupted schooling denies women access to social, economic, and personal resources, thereby rendering them more available for the fulfillment of "traditional" roles, such as cementing interfamilial ties and alliances by means of arranged marriage, as in the case of the double match of Abu Jamil's daughters with the two brothers from Jabᶜa. The embodiment of familial control in the denial to unmarried daughters (and to women in general) of access to resources is a more ancient or "classic" expression of patriarchy than is the appropriation of the daughters' resources and income. The former relies on exercising power over the weak who subsequently become more powerless; the latter feeds on the contradictions that permit exploitation of the relatively more "empowered" and resourceful.

Yusra's instance speaks to her high level of awareness of her situation, even if this consciousness is imbued with powerlessness. Though by no means a rebellious woman who defies conventional conduct, Yusra is cognizant of the fact that things could have been otherwise, and is capable of pointing, with great sophistication, to the specific turning points that circumscribed the realm of opportunities available to her. Although the unfolding of her life appears to jibe with a predetermined pattern, Yusra does not attribute the pattern to destiny but rather insists on relating it to the deliberate deeds of humans. Her critical viewpoint does not, however, stop the completion of a cycle. Although Yusra has never forgiven her father for withdrawing her from school and preventing her from acquiring an adequate education, twenty-five years later, now as a mother of adolescent sons, she herself lacks the means to guarantee them opportunities or to spare them early dropout. Although she despises her father for the six years during which he exploited her work as a seamstress, under the current circumstances she is tied to housework and does not possess even the limited advantages associated with casual labor. Yusra outspokenly condemns arranged marriage, but, as a mother of six, she can only bemoan the expected birth of the seventh.

Yusra's tendency to blame her misery on injustices and deprivation that befell her in the past can be attributed, at least partially, to her "borderline" generational status: she may be counted either with the older women of the young generation or with the younger of the intermediate generation. Among members of the latter group fewer women acquired secondary and higher education and were integrated into professional and semiprofessional employment; the majority, like Yusra, were either taken out of school early or dropped out. Among those five to ten years younger, the incidence of educated and professionally employed women is significantly higher. The criteria that serve Yusra in her critical assessment of her situation were defined by the direction of development in Dheisheh, a trend from which she was excluded. Yusra places the blame on her father, since the Dheishehian standard enables her to make a comparison with the educational accomplishments, employment opportunities, and married lives of her contemporaries and especially of younger women.

Yusra senses that she was a victim of traditional patterns and norms of patriarchal control that are gradually losing their grip on family life in Dheisheh. Indeed, the manifestations of patriarchy that she and her sisters experienced, though not extinct, represent a patriarchy in withdrawal, a "specie" of paternal control over the lives of daughters that can persist only within enclaves. This kind of patriarchy has gradually given way to "novel" modes of familial control that center on the appropriation of wage labor-generated income, as I illustrated in the discussion of the "chain of working daughters."

Two additional, interconnected issues received emphasis in Yusra's monologue. One pertains to economic differences between families and the other to the custom of exchanging gifts at social events. Previous case studies addressed the consequences for the situation of individuals and families of layoffs, work-related injuries, imprisonment, closure, and denial of work permits. I focused mainly on the economic dimension and the impact on division of labor in the family. Yusra gave special weight not solely to deteriorating economic conditions, but also, and perhaps mainly, to her growing sense of alienation and isolation within a community in which people not only distance themselves from the unfortunate but also carefully measure their social behavior.

Have significant differences arisen in standard of living among families in Dheisheh, or is it that in times of ongoing crisis relatively small differences acquire exaggerated importance? Looking at the individuals who were the objects of Yusra's chagrin, I found her sense of affairs distant from reality. One who got hold of a work permit soon lost it, the flourishing business went bankrupt after a few months, and the owners of the chicken coop soon targeted the hens for slaughter because of their low egg yield. Nonetheless, there is no doubt that the closure policy furthered differences in the standard of living among families in the camp. Families that subsisted mainly on the work of professional and/or salaried employees—teachers, nurses, and clerks in public and private institutions—were almost unaffected by the closure. The families that were hardest hit were those that subsisted solely on the wages of day laborers who had been working in Israel. The situation was exacerbated when family members and more distant relatives all shared a similar fate and could not extend a hand. Moreover, the closure policy led to the relative leveling in the situation of most families who relied on daily work in Israel; small but not insignificant differences, such as those between a laborer who earned fifty or seventy shekels a day and a skilled carpenter or stonecutter who earned 120, were erased once all had become jobless.

The estrangement and the absence of solidarity that Yusra reported testify to the existence within the camp society of a social standard, which, if not maintained, imputes defective character. Even though it is drawn very close to the bottom of the economic scale, the pervasiveness of this standard is socially real. An income as low as eight hundred shekels a month in 1989 (the days when they were "high") was enough to maintain Yusra's "worthiness." Once there was virtually no income Yusra was expected to hide the signs of her extreme poverty, or at least to avoid discussing it openly, regardless of the fact that many in the camp share her plight. The custom of gift giving at festive events reflects the standard of what is and what is not regarded as a suitable gift, who is a welcome guest and who faces declassing, and who has been declassed in the past—and many women have long memories and spiteful tongues, as Yusra was learning.

Gift exchange, or reciprocity, in a small and relatively closed community such as Dheisheh is considered to be an expression of mutual commitment among equals or relative equals. Most of the occasions mark stages in sociobiological life cycles: engagements, marriages, births, marriages of children, and so on (though achievement-based celebrations such as graduation parties are also common). The element of reciprocity is evident: one hosts a celebration and likewise takes part in the feasts and celebrations of others.

Hence, there is an obligatory nature of participation: I dance at your son's wedding party today, and you shall dance at my son's party tomorrow. Indeed, people keep lists of obligations to be repaid. Not to repay a debt or to give a gift is taken as a hint of ill will and perhaps of malicious intention. The principle of equal distribution and the obligatory nature of the events seemingly render the exchange value of the gift secondary. I was witness to instances where the same gift "circulated" at several parties—families that received sacks of sugar and rice on the occasion of a son's marriage feast kept them in stock, only to draw on them for the next occasion. Yusra's case teaches, however, that the gift issue is marginal only on the surface. Yusra feels obliged to take part in Umm Nidal's festivity, but she cannot maintain the standard demanded. Her loss of face is a bitter matter.

PART TWO

Occupation, Education, Employment, and Family Life in Dheisheh

WHEN DHEISHEH came into being in 1949, the vast majority of its population, adult and school age, was illiterate or partially so. The exceptions, few in terms of number but quite resourceful in terms of the role they came to play, were those men, all in their teens and twenties, who back in their villages of origin had managed to enter and to complete the British Mandatory basic school program of four to six grades.

Less than a decade and a half later, in the early and mid-1960s, Dheisheh was already represented, mostly by men but not exclusively so, at the universities of Cairo and Beirut, as well as in the local and regional professional labor force, especially among the ranks of teachers. By the late 1970s and early 1980s, the trends that emerged in the 1960s had become greatly amplified. The gap between the rate of enrollment of girls and boys in secondary schools had all but closed, and students from Dheisheh were obtaining degrees from universities and colleges not only in the West Bank, but also in locations as varied and distant as Arab capitals, the Socialist bloc, Western Europe, and even India and Pakistan.

Given the particularly low starting point—the extreme hardships that accompanied refugee existence in the camp, especially during the first period, and then what we have learned about the highly vulnerable status of Dheishehian female and male laborers in the labor market—the profound transformation in the sphere of education calls for investigation. Chapter 4 is devoted to an examination of the institutional and circumstantial factors that affected the spread of education in Dheisheh and sheds some light on this intricate process. It places my research findings on the Dheishehians' educational acquisition and trajectories of schooling within wider contexts and processes. Salient among these are: (1) the historical role of UNRWA as provider of educational services and the impact of these services on the acquisition of elementary and preparatory education among Palestinian refugee communities; (2) the Israeli military government's political and administrative control over the Palestinian educational system and the attendant consequences for the acquisition of secondary education in the Occupied Territories; and (3) the contribution made, first by institutions of higher learning in the Arab countries and later by the locally based Palestinian universities, to the spread of tertiary education among Palestinian refugees.

The restriction of UNRWA's schooling program to nine years, the poverty of state services during the Jordanian regime, and above all, the nondevelopment policies of the Israeli authorities—particularly the denial of governmental investment in education and welfare—all bring to the forefront the question of active participation by refugee families in the acquisition of education by their sons and daughters. How, in the face of such negative input on the part of the regime, could refugee families put four, five, and at times eight or nine children through high school and in some cases even through university? The gravity of the circumstances intensifies when we call to mind that familial divisions of labor that rested solely on income from daily wage labor were incapable of generating an accumulation of resources beyond the immediate requirements of subsistence. Chapter 5 is for the most part given over to the emergence and consolidation in Dheisheh of family divisions of labor and patterns of organization centered on facilitating high school and higher education for members of the intermediate and younger generations. These emerge as chain-style processes whereby the family harnesses the employment of one son or daughter for the education of the next in line, which in turn may yield the possibility of educating another sibling. Preceding this exposition is a brief exploration of the Dheishehians' attitudes regarding the values and virtues of education. The process by which women's access to schooling acquired legitimacy among the camp residents is explored as well.

If the spread of education in Dheisheh can by no means be taken for granted, this is all the more true with respect to the realization of the potential returns that inhere in it, that is, the conversion of education into an economic and social resource. Chapter 6 studies the structure of employment opportunities that awaited Dheishehian high school, college, and university graduates, starting with the period of the Jordanian regime, but focusing mainly on the era of the Israeli Occupation. In a manner similar to that employed in Chapter 4, I examine the problems faced by educated Dheishehians who sought professional employment against a background of factors and processes of a much broader scope. Chief among them are the determinants of the market for qualified labor power under the Israeli Occupation and within the economies of the oil-producing Gulf states.

Focusing mainly on structural factors, Chapter 6 attempts to show how the political economy of the Occupation and that of labor migration to the Gulf directly affected the modes of family organization around education in

Dheisheh. Thus, for example, the near absence of a governmental service sector under the military occupation rendered high school education, as well as many spheres of academic specialization, almost irrelevant for white-collar employment, hence reducing the prospective "returns" on education. The restricted and nondiversified options in the local labor market had a direct bearing on the preferences of individuals and families regarding where, what, and how long to study, whether or not to migrate, destinations for migration and modes of arranging it, and other such issues. The already extremely limited employment opportunities were differentiated along gender lines and prone to constant fluctuations, thereby affecting the gender and age composition of the family labor force in Dheisheh.

The families of origin of those second- and third-generation refugees who acquired higher education were, almost without exception, very large, and they lived under harsh conditions, subsisting on meager and irregular resources. The relative scarcity of permanent employment with a regular salaried income led to the emergence of new familial divisions of labor with some novel attributes. Already outlined in Chapter 5, these are further examined in Chapter 7, which discusses the long-term, cumulative consequences of steady employment for educated Dheishehian women and men and their families.

Unlike families that subsisted solely on income from daily wage labor, those that could rely on the salaried income of a professionally employed family member found it possible to accumulate some savings, at least in certain instances. A major manifestation of this garnering of resources is found in the success of such families in enabling most or several of their sons and daughters to acquire high school and tertiary education. They thereby guaranteed the necessary conditions for the continuity of the process and secured an opening, albeit a modest one, for the upper mobility of the young. Accordingly, these familial divisions of labor may be viewed as ongoing, active confrontation waged against the dictates of the politico-economic system. Following this interpretation, I seek to assess the capacity of such family ventures to improve standard of living and to change the social situation of those involved.

While the divisions of labor under consideration provide support for family members and enhance their opportunities in life, the endurance of the patterns is shown to be contingent upon the family's ability to exercise patriarchal control over the resources and behavior of its working, unmarried daughters, and to a lesser extent over its working sons. An additional purpose of Chapter 7, therefore, is to unravel the contradictions and explain the tensions that imbue familial divisions of labor involving educated wage earners. The near impossibility of resolving these within an unmarried worker's family of origin suggests that examination of the course of social change should continue within the new nuclear families that such workers eventually started. Consequently, the chapter concludes by looking into the social status of professionally employed married women within the setting of the newly founded nuclear family, using comparative indicators, such as a wife's control over income, the allocation of resources, and childbearing.

All the topics addressed in Chapter 7 arise from a single case study. Tracing the schooling and employment histories as well as the matrimonial lives of both males and females, it presents the story of one multigenerational family in Dheisheh from the early 1960s to the 1990s.

CHAPTER 4

Acquisition of Education by
Dheishehian Refugees

UNDERSTANDING THE STRUCTURAL CONTEXT

Reviewing UNRWA's Services: A Comparative
and Historical Perspective

FROM REHABILITATION TO EDUCATION:
A SHIFT IN UNRWA'S GOALS

Two schools currently operate in Dheisheh camp: one for boys and one for girls, each with an elementary level (first to sixth grade) and a preparatory level (seventh to ninth grade). Both were set up by UNRWA, which has run them since the 1950s. In the first part of the 1990s, the dropout rate of girls and boys from the elementary level was negligible, and the dropout rate from the preparatory level was very low, with more than 80 percent of all girls and boys who started the seventh grade also completing the ninth. This means that—setting other limitations aside and without assessing the quality of schooling—the path to high school is open to almost every fifteen-year-old in the camp. One cannot appreciate this achievement without recognizing the developments that made an "obligatory" standard of nine years of schooling an established fact for the majority of refugee children in Palestine and its Diaspora.

A factor that goes a long way in explaining the success of this process was the shift in the goals and the resource allocations of UNRWA. From an initiative originally set up by the United Nations to facilitate the resettlement/reintegration of Palestinian refugees in the Arab "host" countries, it became an agency that directs most of its funds, efforts, and human resources to the provision of social services, primarily education and health.

The shift was already well manifest in the mid-1960s, when the relative expenditure on education constituted about 40 percent of the agency's total budget, in comparison to 17 percent in 1957–58 and only 3.3 percent in 1952–53. This tendency continued throughout the 1970s and early 1980s, reaching its peak in 1985, when 67 percent of the agency's total expenditures were allocated for education. Subsequently, the relative share declined somewhat, stabilizing around 55 percent in the early 1990s (UNRWA 1951–95; Schiff 1995, 51–52).

The operative capacities of UNRWA were circumscribed from the very beginning by its status as a subsidiary organization with a temporary mandate. Funding was entirely dependent on annual voluntary contributions by donor countries rather than on a permanent and regular allocation from UN headquarters. Set up in the early years of the cold war, UNRWA was by and large a venture of the United States, which subsequently became the prime donor state—contributing more than 70 percent of total pledges to the agency during the first decade. Its establishment should be viewed in light of the U.S. effort to gain control in the Middle East and combat Soviet influence (Buehrig 1971; Schiff 1995, 111–37). These intentions notwithstanding, donations were maintained on a very small scale from the very beginning. With an average annual income of thirty-five million dollars throughout the first decade of its operation, UNRWA could do very little to materialize the objectives it initially set out to advance. The built-in vulnerability of the agency exposed it to repeated budget crises that were only exacerbated as the years went by and the size of the needy refugee population swelled. No steps were taken toward the implementation of UN Resolution 194, which stipulated the "right of return": the repatriation of the refugees and/or compensation to them. The number of refugees registered with UNRWA quadrupled over fifty years (from 960,000 in 1950 to 3,625,600 in 1999) while the real value of the agency's annual income has remained almost unchanged throughout most of the period.[1]

The decline of the "reintegration/resettlement option" and its eventual abandonment by UNRWA as early as the mid-1950s can also be explained against the background of the economic conditions that prevailed in the so-called host countries and by the policies that their regimes adopted. Absence of modern industries, underdeveloped infrastructures, and soaring unemployment in Jordan and the Egyptian-ruled Gaza Strip, where the largest concentrations of refugee populations settled, implied very low "absorptive capacities" unless investments on a grand scale in developmental schemes were made available via external aid, and were followed by compatible governmental policies. Lebanon, a third and comparatively more developed host country, opted, nonetheless for the exclusion of its refugees: it denied them citizenship and social rights, prevented their access to most sectors of the economy and restricted their residence mainly to the "camp zones."

One should also bear in mind the strong objection, widespread among the refugees and representatives of their communities, to what they justly perceived as attempts to liquidate the political essence of the refugee problem and to undermine their right to repatriation. This stand was shared, at least officially, by the Arab regimes. At the same time, the needs of the growing refugee population for basic provisions, especially food, water supplies, shelter, and medicines, called for immediate intervention.

Forced to shelve ambitious proposals for grand development schemes that aimed at absorbing hundreds of thousands of refugees in agricultural projects (Buehrig 1971, ch. 5; Schiff 1995, 21–47), UNRWA did not generate employment on the large scale originally envisioned, at least not until the first cohorts of its educational system came of age. Even then, the agency's role as an employer was restricted to its own institutions: its school, health, distribution, sanitation, and administration systems, all of which could absorb only a very small fraction of the employable refugee population.[2]

Throughout the 1950s UNRWA ended up directing most of its financial resources to relief, primarily by constructing elementary infrastructure in the camps, distributing monthly food rations, and providing basic housing units, or shelters, which were simply cement blocks measuring three by four meters with roofs of asbestos or metal. However, as the years went by the organization significantly cut back its expenditures on housing and living conditions. It stopped short of building additional shelters for newly started families or renovating the existing substandard units, which contained neither kitchens nor indoor toilets. It also minimized its investment in roads, sewage systems, and other public facilities. For thirty years the agency continued to provide various relief services, such as rations of basic foodstuffs, milk distribution for babies and nursing mothers, and the operation of public kitchens, particularly for the benefit of schoolchildren (UNRWA 1986, 74–79, 179–80). However, most of these services were gradually ended in the 1980s, in the wake of the prolonged emergency situation created by the Israeli invasion of Lebanon, which necessitated a reallocation of funds in order to provide greater resources to the devastated refugee population there.

Since the mid-1980s direct relief in the form of regular rations, special allowances, and house repairs have been provided solely to an extremely needy population, defined as "hardship cases." In 1991–92 these amounted to no more than 6.4 percent of the registered refugees (UNRWA 1992, 56). The agency does renew distribution of rations temporarily, however, whenever specific refugee communities are exposed to emergencies, such as the extended curfews imposed on most refugee camps in the Occupied Territories at the height of the Intifada (Schiff 1989, 70–73), and the ongoing closure of the Gaza Strip in the post-Oslo years. All in all, the relative share of relief in the annual expenditures of UNRWA (not including allocations from emergency funds) declined from 97 percent in the first years, to around 55 percent in the mid-1960s, 35 percent in the mid-1970s, 25 percent in 1980, and between 10 and 15 percent in the years 1985–95. At the same time, the relative share of education and health increased incrementally to constitute 75 percent of all expenditures by the early 1990s (Schiff 1995, 51–52).

Dependence on the fluctuating political goodwill of donors, unfavorable economic and political conditions in the host countries, and operation under ongoing turbulent circumstances, then, all militated against the consolidation of UNRWA as an agent of reintegration and resettlement, or even as a provider of significant amounts of material aid. Although the causes that eventually brought the organization to prioritize education may warrant separate research, it seems safe to assume that the relative cost of investment in this sphere, as well as in community health services, proved to be much lower than in all others. The reorientation toward education should therefore be understood in terms of the blocking of other avenues or their lack of feasibility, rather than seen as preference. Within a relatively short time, however, the shift yielded outcomes of fundamental long-term significance for the refugees, as well as for the agency. The focus of UNRWA on educational services became a major determinant of the "profile" of second- and third-generation refugees in Dheisheh and elsewhere. Young men and women who grew up in living conditions not much better than those experienced by their elders a generation earlier nevertheless came to be distinguished by a level of education that compared favorably with that of their peers in the host countries as well as that of nonrefugee Palestinian populations.

UNRWA AND ELEMENTARY EDUCATION:
A HISTORICAL ASSESSMENT

The first goal of UNRWA was to enable basic six-year schooling for all refugee children of relevant age. With the professional and administrative assistance of UNESCO (United Nations Educational, Scientific, and Cultural Organization), the agency set up its own school systems in Jordan, the Gaza Strip, Lebanon, and Syria. Schools were built inside the refugee camps, though UNRWA covered, at least partially, the tuition costs for refugee children who resided outside camps and studied in other institutions. Although the agency's schools were financed and administered independently, the curriculum they followed was similar to that observed by the governmental educational systems of the host countries, primarily in order to ensure standardization that would enable refugee children to proceed with higher studies (UNRWA 1986, 114–27).

The initial conditions were especially difficult. In 1951 only sixty-one schools were operating in the four districts; the majority functioned in tents and huts. There was a severe shortage of qualified staff and a near absence of equipment and facilities (UNRWA 1951). The great majority of the refugees, and nearly all those among them who now dwelt in refugee camps, originated from villages, where only a very small fraction of the population, almost exclusively male, had access to elementary schooling (Al-Haj 1995, 41–45). According to one assessment (Ibrahim Abu-Lughod 1973), this inferior position of the villagers with respect to education—especially when contrasted to the Jewish sector, but also in comparison with the Palestinian urbanites—was on the verge of changing in the last years of the British Mandate, mainly due to local pressure on the government to extend its services. But such developments, if they were to have materialized, were cut short in the wake of the 1948 war and its consequences (Abu-Lughod 1973, 103–4). Most students of the initial cohorts at UNRWA's schools were therefore the first in their families to acquire education. Although UNRWA started from scratch, it is important to note that in the years under consideration the elementary education in the governmental school systems of the host countries was of a very poor standard. This found primary expression in the low rates of enrollment of school-age children in general, and in the low proportion (25–30 percent) of girls among all students (UNESCO 1970, table 2.5).

A leap forward in the elementary education of refugee children took place as early as the first decade. Thus, for example, the total enrollment in UNRWA's schools multiplied by a factor of 2.5, while the number of schools increased from sixty-one in 1950–51 to 386 in 1958, with most of the temporary structures replaced by permanent buildings. The number of teachers rose from seven hundred in 1951 to four thousand in 1960 (UNRWA 1958; 1961). Nonetheless, up until the mid-1960s high dropout rates of girls from the fifth and sixth grades were commonplace in the agency's schools.

My data for a sample of male and female interviewees from Dheisheh who studied in UNRWA's elementary schools during the 1950s and 1960s corroborate the aforementioned trends of significant increases in enrollment rates and a persistent gap between boys and girls. Of forty-one men from the intermediate generation in my core sample, only ten (less than 25 percent) completed six or fewer years of schooling, while thirty-one completed at least seven grades. However, as many as twenty of the forty-one women in the core sample (48.7 percent) had completed no more than six years of schooling.[3]

From the 1970s onward the rate of increase in the number of pupils in the agency's schools slackened, pointing both to the stabilization of the system after the years of accelerated growth and to a gradual closing of the gap between the enrollment of girls and boys. The percentage of girls increased from 24 percent of all pupils in 1951, to 38.9 percent in 1958, 47.8 percent in 1975, and 49.4 percent in 1991. It was around the mid-1970s, then, that the agency succeeded in meeting the goal of providing elementary schooling to the great majority of its target population. A comparison with the overall situation in the Arab countries shows that this achievement is not to be belittled. For example, in 1976 only 56 percent of Egyptian girls of elementary school age were enrolled, as opposed to 88 percent of the boys (Sanabary 1985, 96–97).

Notwithstanding the accomplishments in terms of enrollment rates and gender equality, UNRWA's school system continued to suffer from a multitude of severe defects emanating from a budget shortage that was constantly growing because of dwindling incomes and an ever-expanding student population. In the late 1990s, with the organization running 649 schools, double shifting was introduced in 75 percent of classrooms as a result of shortage of space, and triple shifting was considered. Overcrowding implied an average of 43.6 pupils per classroom, with the figure for the Gaza Strip standing at 49.6. The structures are old, most have not undergone renovation since their construction in the 1950s or 1960s, and some are dilapidated beyond repair. There are neither heating facilities nor air-conditioning, furniture is less than adequate, and libraries and laboratories are antiquated, lacking in basic equipment and auxiliary supplies (UNRWA 1999).

The situation in Dheisheh can serve as an illustration. The boys' school and girls' school, originally built during the 1950s, were not renovated before the mid-1990s. By that time each housed around twelve hundred pupils (elementary and preparatory levels together) and operated in double shifts. A special extrabudgetary donation enabled UNRWA to replace the old girls' school with a new modern building, one of the most attractive in the camp. Throughout the more than one-year-long period of construction (1996–97), the old boys' school hosted the girls, a situation that resulted, in addition to double shifting, in the shortening of each shift to four hours. After the girls finally moved to the new building in early 1998, no funding was yet forthcoming for the replacement of the dilapidated boys' school, where some of the walls had fallen into ruin and many classrooms were by all standards unfit for use. Ongoing protest by the teaching staff, as well as street demonstrations by the pupils and their families (and there is not a single family in the camp that was not affected), finally compelled UNRWA, in 2000, to raise the funds to initiate the construction of a new building. This in its turn implied the hosting of the boys in the girls' school for more than a year.

UNRWA AND POSTELEMENTARY EDUCATION

The problem of postelementary education emerged in the second half of the 1950s, as the first cohorts of girls and boys were graduating from the agency's elementary schools. Faced with growing demand among the refugees and the absence of adequate solutions within the host countries' governmental systems, UNRWA took on the responsibility for providing continued schooling toward the end of the decade. The decision taken was to expand the schooling services by an additional three-year cycle, from seventh to ninth grade (UNRWA 1958; 1965). High school (upper secondary) education was therefore left outside UNRWA's commission, compelling those who sought it to enroll in governmental and private schools. However, around the turn of the decade the agency committed itself to setting up its own teaching training centers (as well as several vocational training centers) in the host countries. This step would eventually render it "self-sufficient" in terms of educational staff and held far-reaching implications for the academic and professional tracks of its client population.

The record of UNRWA should be evaluated in light of the pronounced transformation in the spread of postelementary education that took place in most Arab states from the 1960s onward, and especially during the 1970s and 1980s. Propelled by substantial increases in governmental expenditures on schooling at all levels, the scope of change was indicated by spectacular growth in the absolute numbers of secondary school pupils, the ever-rising proportions of pupils enrolled, the steady growth in the ratio of girls, and the incremental increase in the number of teachers (UNESCO 1981, table 3.8; UNESCO 1994, table 3.7).

Nonetheless, factors such as the size of the population, its class composition and geodemographic distribution, and the economic resources at the disposal of the regimes determined, to a large extent, the upper limit of development. This led to significant differences between states. In the late 1960s girls constituted less than a third of all secondary school students in Syria, Jordan, and Egypt, and the total rate of enrollment was less than 40 percent (Sanabary 1985, 96). The breakthrough in Jordan took place in the years 1975–85, during which the gap between boys and girls was closed and the total rate of enrollment rose from 45 to 78 percent. In the manifestly more populous Egypt, with its largely rural and peasant-heavy demographic composition, progress was made at a much slower pace despite massive governmental investment; in the mid-1980s girls' enrollment (54 percent) lagged far behind that of boys (77 percent). Speedy expansion of the student population was recorded in some of the oil-producing Gulf countries, where up until the 1970s the rate of illiteracy was the highest in the region (and perhaps in the world as well). The turning point took place in the wake of the tremendous profits that were generated during the oil-boom years, some of which were reinvested in the public sector, including in education. Thus, in Kuwait, for example, the number of girls enrolled in postelementary education multiplied fivefold, from 11,500 in 1965 to 50,000 in 1976, and their relative share among all students rose to 46 percent.

Lacking the means of governments and states and constantly battered by insufficient funding, UNRWA's endeavor to foster secondary education among Palestinian refugees looms large. This is all the more true given the crises that befell camp dwellers throughout the years under consideration, including the 1967 war, Black September (1970–71), the Lebanese civil war (1975–76), the Israeli invasion of Lebanon (1982), and "the war of the camps" in Lebanon (1985–89). The catastrophic consequences suffered by the refugees—heavy casualties, mass uprooting, wide-scale destruction of homes and infrastructure, and at times the total demolishing of camps—all disrupted the course of UNRWA's regular operations and demanded emergency intervention on its part (UNRWA 1968, 1971, 1983, 1985, 1989). The numerous obstacles notwithstanding, in 1980, within two decades of the inception of its preparatory schooling program, 73 percent of all refugee children who attended UNRWA's elementary cycle continued studies at the next level, with the relative share of girls being as high as 47 percent. By 1985 the respective figures were 86.5 percent and 48.5 percent, implying that the agency had more or less achieved the goal of rendering nine years of schooling obligatory, or standard.[4]

The achievements of UNRWA, which surpassed those of government schools in all host countries (perhaps with the exception of Jordan), may be attributed in part to free-of-charge provision of all school-related needs and the great accessibility of the agency's schools. However, the rapidity of the process by which (lower) secondary education became widespread was greatly facilitated by the relative homogenization of the life situation of the camp refugees throughout the regions of dispersal. The sharp transition, from village-based agricultural subsistence to the cramped camps where they were dependent on wage labor opportunities and relief assistance, created fertile ground for UNRWA's educational system in all five of its fields of operation. Unlike UNRWA, the government educational systems operated within heterogeneous societies split by class, regional, and at times ethno-religious divides that often aggravated existing disparities between sectors through discriminatory allocation of services, hence the slower and uneven spread of secondary education in these countries.

My findings from Dheisheh are in line with the general tendencies that marked the development of UNRWA's lower secondary program, though their institutionalization in the camp appears to have taken less time than on average. The data pertaining to the intermediate generation provide information on women and men who were in their early teens during the initial period in the late 1950s and through the 1960s. A very high rate of enrollment is seen for boys of this generation—thirty-one of my core sample of forty-one male interviewees (75 percent) attended the preparatory (lower secondary) level. (By way of comparison, the average rate in UNRWA's institutions in Jordan was 36 percent in 1966.) But only twenty-one of forty-one female respondents had done so, indicating a marked gap between the sexes. The big leap forward is demonstrated by the men and women of the younger generation who were in their early teens in the 1970s and 1980s. Thirty-three of my core sample of forty men (82 percent) studied at the preparatory stage, as did thirty-six women out of forty (90 percent), indicating that by the late 1970s preparatory schooling had become almost obligatory in the camp.[5]

Acquiring Education Under Israeli Military Occupation: The Government School Bottleneck

Among the central factors that determined the state of education in the Occupied Territories were absence of a sovereign Palestinian educational system, subjugation to the control of the Israeli military government, and the internal split of educational institutions between three subsystems—government, UNRWA, and private. Imposed in June 1967, the military government immediately assumed administrative control over the government schools—previously run by Jordan in the case of the West Bank and Egypt in the Gaza Strip. The bulk of students, some 80 percent and 50 percent, respectively, attended these schools. In 1981 this control passed to the Civil Administration. In addition to budgeting, allocation of resources for development, the appointment of staff and regulation of employees' wages, and so forth, the political-military dimension of administration entailed the direct intervention of the security forces in the hiring and firing of teachers, censorship of books and programs, prohibition of teachers' unionizing, subjection of schools to military closure orders, and sanction of military action within school confines. The only sphere that was not determined by the Israeli military was the curriculum, which continued to follow the Jordanian and Egyptian programs. Hence, even here there was not the slightest measure of autonomous management in the government schools.

The scope of intrusion into the affairs of UNRWA's schools, attended by some 12 percent of the student population in the West Bank and 50 percent in the Gaza Strip, was significantly less, since they were administrated, financed, and to an extent protected by an international organization. The private schools attended by a small minority, under the auspices of churches and charity societies, also suffered less interference. Nonetheless, these institutions, and particularly UNRWA's, were by no means immune to direct military intervention in the form of closure orders, the permanent presence of armed troops in school vicinities, and at times incursions into school compounds.

Rather than focusing on the consequences of military interference to education in the Occupied Territories, I scrutinize certain structural aspects of the Israeli administrative control. Of special concern here is the high school (upper secondary) level, spanning the grades ten to twelve, since this is a definitive stage with respect to the prospects of young people. Unlike the elementary and preparatory levels, which are split between the three subsystems (though unevenly, as noted), education in the upper level was almost exclusively under the control of the military government. This is because UNRWA does not maintain high schools, and the relative proportion of those who attend private institutions is small.

The most noteworthy feature with respect to the spread of high school education in the Occupied Territories is that it did not undergo a profound transformation that resembles or even approaches elementary and preparatory education under UNRWA's auspices. West Bank data for 1985–86 show that fewer than half of those who attended the preparatory level continued in the upper one. And dropout rates soared in the transition from tenth to eleventh grade. Of every hundred who entered elementary school, only thirty completed twelve grades, and fewer still passed the matriculation examination (PLO, Economic Department, 1988, 23–29).

A comprehensive survey conducted by the Norwegian research institute Fafo in 1992 revealed that Palestinian men aged twenty to twenty-nine (from all sectors of society) had slightly fewer years of schooling on average than did men aged thirty to thirty-nine, indicating that those who reached the upper level during the 1980s had no better or even a worse chance of completing high school than their predecessors of the previous decade (Heiberg and Ovensen 1993, 136). More recent statistics point to the persistence of this "legacy" from former years: Data compiled by the Palestinian Central Bureau of Statistics (PCBS) for 1996–97, the third year after the establishment of the PNA, show only 41 percent of the relevant age group attending the upper level, which since 1995 consists of the eleventh and twelfth grades (PCBS 1998, 49).

The above figures provide ample evidence of a "bottleneck" at the high school stage under the Israeli military government, which reversed the marked trend of growth achieved on the elementary and intermediate levels. This effectively served to block the opportunities for higher education for the majority of youth in the relevant age groups. This grave outcome should be attributed, first and foremost, to a long-term policy on the part of the responsible authorities of nondevelopment and deprivation of all spheres of the government education system. So, for example, while the student population in all government institutions (elementary through secondary) more than doubled between 1967 and 1992 (growing from 165,307 to 362,688), throughout these twenty-five years of Occupation the number of government schools increased only from 746 to 979 (CBS 1970, 643; 1993, 804). This indicates the minuscule investment in construction of new facilities—nor were resources allocated for the repair of existing structures, the replacement of dilapidated furniture, or the upgrading of equipment. Most schools lacked science laboratories, proper libraries, ball courts, and sports equipment, not to speak of extracurricular activities or advanced devices such as computers. The Civil Administration did not set up a single vocational school throughout the entire period; except for UNRWA's vocational training center in Ramallah, with its modest capacity of a few hundred trainees, virtually all secondary schools were academic. Nor was a single teachers' training center established, despite the fact that the teaching staff in government schools greatly outnumbered that in UNRWA's system. In Jordan (as well as in most Arab states), the decades under review, particularly the late 1970s and the 1980s, were years of vast government investment in the expansion of the educational system, reflected in the increase and diversification of institutions and the unprecedented growth in the number of secondary students.

The scope of neglect and discrimination can also be inferred from the degrading employment conditions in the government system. During the last year of Israeli administration (1993–94), teachers' monthly wages ranged from seven hundred to eleven hundred shekels, less than one-third of what their Israeli counterparts earned and about 35 percent less than the wages of their colleagues in the UNRWA system. Unlike UNRWA's staff, teachers in the government system were not entitled to a pension fund and were denied the right to organize in unions. Moreover, eligibility for employment required that one's "security record" and that of immediate relatives be untainted; imprisonment of a teacher (or that of immediate relatives) entailed the loss of the teaching post. Like measures were extended in the 1980s to incorporate the expulsion of secondary students who were imprisoned on charges of nationalist activity. Repression and intimidation were therefore built into the school environment, both as a workplace and as an educational institution.

My findings from Dheisheh with respect to the spread of high school education in the camp cover two main time periods—the late 1950s into the early 1970s and the mid-1970s to the early 1990s—corresponding to the eras of the intermediate and young generations, respectively. Surveys conducted among several sample populations show that between 40 and 50 percent of the male population of the intermediate generation and some 25 percent of the females have an education of at least ten years. These men and women were all graduates of the first cycles of the UNRWA elementary and preparatory schools in the camp; they continued their secondary education at the Jordanian government high schools in the Bethlehem region or, to a far lesser extent, at church-run institutions. The achievements of both sexes far exceed those overall for West Bank residents of the relevant age groups; according to one source, the average figures stand at 30 percent for males and 10 percent for females (CBS 1993, 802). Indications that acquiring secondary education became commonplace for Dheishehian boys and not uncommon for Dheishehian girls, far before the phenomenon became widespread in the population as a whole, is an achievement that can be attributed to a large extent to UNRWA's gradual institutionalization of the preparatory stage in the camp. Nonetheless, the marked difference between the enrollment rates of the two sexes shows that during the years under review (the 1960s), the universalization process was still a long way from completion. Far fewer girls were finishing ninth grade and entering the upper level than were boys.

My findings with respect to the younger generation—Dheishehian women and men who entered the upper level during the 1970s and 1980s and studied under the authority of the military government—are not unequivocal. The most significant change that occurred in these decades was the closing, if not the slight reversal, of the gender gap. Fifty-two percent of a survey population of 318 women aged between sixteen and thirty-nine (participants in my survey on women and employment in Dheisheh) reported acquiring at least eleven years of schooling, and twenty-eight of my core sample of forty female interviewees (70 percent) reported acquiring at least ten years of schooling. That is, the rate of girls attending at least part of the upper level rose from some 25 percent in the 1960s to around 60 percent in the 1980s.

As for the educational attainments of men of the younger generation, findings show that the extent of change was much more modest beginning in the mid-1970s than in earlier decades. Twenty-five of my core sample of forty interviewees (60 percent) attained at least ten years of schooling, a result corroborated by the findings for larger population samples and indicating that the rate of men enrolled in the upper level rose by approximately 15 percent, far less than the dramatic increase shown for women.

The educational attainments of Dheishehians, then, compared favorably with the average for the West Bank, a result consistent with findings for the refugee camp population in general (Heiberg and Ovensen 1993, 137). However, the fact that around 40 percent of the young generation completed no more than ten grades is further evidence for the aforementioned blocked progress of secondary schooling under Israeli rule.

Acquiring Higher Education in the Diaspora and in Palestine

In the aftermath of the 1948 war—the uprooting and the dispersal in the host countries—higher education gradually came to play an increasingly central role in the social history of the Palestinians. As early as the mid-1950s Palestinian professionals, most of them recent university graduates, were conspicuously represented in the developing economic and administrative sectors of the Gulf states, first and foremost in Kuwait (Kossaifi 1980; Aruri and Farsoun 1980; Brand 1988). Indeed, a salient common denominator among the founding leaders and activists of the Palestinian national movement was the intersecting of their political paths with their schooling and labor-migration trajectories. The historical leadership of the Fatah movement, for example, comprised mainly educated professionals—engineers, teachers, economists, and others, many of them refugees—who acquired their education in Egyptian universities in the early 1950s and sought work later that same decade in Kuwait, where they first set out to build their organization (Abu-Iyad 1979).

The schema by which Palestinians came to acquire higher education on a wide scale, and the broader consequences of this development, first gained the attention of scholars in the early 1970s when the process was already in full force. It appears that the researchers, almost all Palestinians themselves, were inspired and motivated by another process taking root during the same period: the political and institutional consolidation of the PLO and its constituent organizations as the recognized representatives of Palestinian national aspirations. Accordingly, in these pioneering studies (for example, Shaath 1972; Abu-Lughod 1973; Zahlan and Zahlan 1977), Palestinian higher education was intimately connected to pressing social and political issues, such as the economic and class transformation of the Palestinians in the Diaspora, the long-term development of Palestinian human resources, and the impact of the latter on the composition and potential of the emergent national movement.

The first quantitative findings on Palestinians and higher education pertain to the second half of the 1960s. The total number of Palestinian university students in 1965–66 was estimated at thirty thousand, with thirty-three thousand by 1968–69 (Shaath 1972, 92; Abu-Lughod 1973, 108). The number of students per thousand Palestinians in 1969 was estimated at 11.4, a high ratio not only in comparison to that found in 1970 in Egypt (7.11), Iraq (4.54), Syria (6.82), and Jordan (1.97), but also in comparison to the ratio in most developing countries and in some of the more developed ones (UNESCO 1981, table 3.10). At the time, approximately two-thirds of the Palestinian postsecondary students attended Arab universities, first and foremost Cairo, ʿEin Shams, Al-Azhar, and Alexandria universities in Egypt; Damascus University in Syria; and Beirut Arab University in Lebanon. Most of the remaining third studied in Europe and the United States. In the fifteen years that followed, between 1966 and 1981, the number of students multiplied by a factor of more than 2.5; in the latter year the ratio of students to population was estimated as no lower than 17.8 per thousand (Tahir 1985, 34).[6]

The coinciding of a number of internal factors during a highly critical period contributed to the accelerated growth in both the absolute number of Palestinian university students and in their relative weight in the population. Emanating from the transformation of Palestinian society in the postwar decades, these factors were amplified by external ones, the most significant being the unprecedented availability of opportunities for higher learning. Having by and large become urban-centered political-national minorities without land, property, or influence, the Palestinians were forced to struggle in the tight and competitive labor markets of the host countries. Under these debilitating conditions higher education was rendered a valuable asset, perhaps the only one that could guarantee survival in the long run.

Given the boost already provided by UNRWA's universalization of basic education, one can easily understand the growing propensity among members of refugee communities to engage in university studies. Such an undertaking would not have been possible, however, had opportunities to enroll in universities not been opened to Palestinians on a wide scale and at low cost. Indeed, the spread of tertiary education in Palestinian communities as early as the late 1950s and throughout the 1960s and most of the 1970s should, to a large extent, be attributed to the official state policies of several Arab regimes. First and foremost among them was Nasser's Egypt, which opened the gates of public universities and colleges to Palestinians free of tuition charges and on terms equal to those enjoyed by the state's citizens.[7]

The relative educational advantage of the Palestinians over their Arab brethren diminished significantly during the 1970s, with figures for 1980 showing the ratio of students in the population to have risen to 17.5 per thousand in Egypt, 16.1 in Syria, and 16.5 in Jordan (UNESCO 1994, table 3.11). In Egypt and Syria this ascent continued into the mid-1980s, with the respective ratios standing at 18.4 and 17.3 per thousand in 1985 and dropping somewhat toward the end of the decade. In contrast, in Jordan the ratio continued to rise into the next decade, with the figures for 1990 reaching a peak of twenty-five students for every thousand residents (however, the greater number of Jordanian students were of Palestinian origin). The sharp growth was enabled by vast investment on the part of most Arab governments in the expansion and diversification of tertiary education during the period under consideration—in itself a combined outcome of regime policies and the oil boom-related prosperity that lasted approximately a decade. The gradual closing of the educational gap between Palestinians and Arab citizens of various nationalities probably reflects the upper limit of the spread of higher education in the absence of a supportive state system, although the downward trend in the rate of student enrollment in most Arab states in the post–oil boom years indicates that state sponsorship is not without its own contradictions and limitations.

HIGHER EDUCATION IN THE WEST BANK AND GAZA STRIP

The institutional history of postsecondary education in the West Bank and Gaza since 1948 can be roughly divided into two periods:

From the 1950s to the early 1970s.   During these years there were no local institutions of higher education other than teachers' training colleges. While the number of those who studied abroad is not known, it probably amounted to many thousands. The lion's share studied in the Arab capitals, primarily at Cairo University, Beirut Arab University (BAU), Damascus University, and Jordan University (opened in 1962), though a substantial proportion were enrolled in the external program of BAU, suggesting that they did not physically attend the university except for the final examinations. The majority (some 70 percent) of those who studied in Arab universities specialized in the humanities (especially Arab literature, history, geography, and education), with the minority concentrating on the natural sciences, engineering, and medicine (Shaath 1972).

In a second category were those who studied in the Soviet Union and the rest of the Socialist bloc, usually through the assistance and mediation of the Jordanian Communist Party. These students benefited from full scholarships and living stipends provided by the host governments in the framework of the support extended to young party cadres in the third world. Most went on to specialize in spheres that demanded long academic and practical training, mainly medicine and the natural sciences, but also jurisprudence, engineering, journalism, and other fields. In yet a third category, quite substantial in size, were those who studied in the United States and Western Europe, as well as in Italy, Greece, and Spain.

From the mid-1970s into the 1990s.   In the wake of the steady increase in the number of high school graduates and the growing demand for higher education, six Palestinian universities were established during the 1970s, five in the West Bank (Birzeit, 1972; Bethlehem, 1973; Al-Najah, 1977; Hebron, 1979; Al-Quds, 1980) and one in the Gaza Strip (Gaza Islamic University, 1978). The students enrolled in these institutions totaled some twelve thousand in the early 1980s and around twenty thousand in the early 1990s. The last decade saw the establishment of the Open University, where the largest number of students is currently enrolled, as well as a second university in Gaza and several other institutions for technological education. The replacement of the military government with a Palestinian Ministry of Higher Education greatly enhanced this process of expansion and diversification, leading to a sharp increase in the enrollment of university students, which in 1996–97 numbered forty-six thousand (19,643 of whom were women—42.5 percent) (PCBS 1998, 58).

At the same time that local institutions were taking root, opportunities for acquiring higher education abroad dwindled significantly, primarily as a result of changing political circumstances. Israel and Egypt's signing of the Camp David Accords in 1979 led to an immediate deterioration in the relations between the latter country and the PLO, and to the subsequent closing down of the gates of Egyptian universities to Palestinian students. Upon the dismantling of the Soviet Union, slightly more than a decade later, another important sponsor of Palestinian higher education had been lost. The Israeli military authorities often mounted obstacles for Palestinians who wished to travel abroad by imposing various restrictions on the length of stay, linking "the right of residence" in the Occupied Territories with inordinate demands for renewal of personal documents, and at times denying travel permits altogether.

Thus, although thousands continued to enroll in universities and colleges outside, especially in Jordan, where the number and size of institutions kept expanding throughout the 1980s, and in the West, the core site for the acquisition of higher education was eventually transferred to the Occupied Territories. This relocation also greatly facilitated the accessibility of higher education to women of the Occupied Territories, as reflected in their relatively high share of the total student body in the Palestinian universities since the early 1980s.[8]

The Palestinian universities were quick to become centers, perhaps *the* centers of political, national, and cultural activity in the Territories. This served to turn their student populations, as well as the teaching staff and the institutions themselves, into targets of systematic repression and harassment by the military government and the Civil Administration. If, during the 1980s, universities were subject to occasional military closure orders ranging from several days to several months, during the Intifada all institutions were ordered closed for more than three successive years (1988–91). Moreover, army troops were routinely employed to put down student demonstrations and gatherings on campuses and in their vicinity; live ammunition was repeatedly used by the military to disperse crowds of students, often leading to severe casualties within their ranks; student leaders and activists were regularly subject to surprise raids, and hundreds were sent to prison. Faculty members were occasionally summoned for interrogation, threatened, put under various restrictions, and in several cases imprisoned or deported; and an attempt was made (by the Civil Administration) to intervene in the hiring procedure of teachers (Order 854). Heavy censorship was imposed on library books and periodicals (Sullivan 1988, 1991, 1994; Rigby 1989; Gerner 1989; Baramki 1992; Johnson 1987a, 1987b, 1988a, 1988b; Graham-Brown 1984a; Fasheh 1984; Al Haq 1988a).

All Palestinian universities were founded as private institutions and relied for financing on a combination of sources: primarily the rich Arab states (first and foremost Saudi Arabia), the PLO (through various indirect channels including the joint PLO-Jordan fund and the Saudi government), private donors and nongovernmental organizations (including the Vatican in the case of Bethlehem University), and income from tuition fees (Sullivan 1988). The absence of governmental budgeting and support seriously harmed the ability of universities to develop the faculties of natural, physical, and applied sciences; to promote research; and to offer advanced or graduate programs, all of which require fairly large investment in laboratories, equipment, and staff. The result was the channeling of the majority of students into specialization in the humanities and social sciences, especially Arab and general literature, and in education. (In the 1990s, however, commerce and business administration became increasingly popular.) Up until the mid-1990s none of the universities had a medical school, only two (Bethlehem and Hebron) offered an academic degree in nursing (with complementary practical training), and another two offered a degree in engineering (Birzeit and Al-Najah). The students' opting for the humanities should be attributed not only to limited choices but also to the relative weakness of the scientific subjects taught in the government secondary schools. Another major problem that resulted from the denial of sovereign administration was the low level of interuniversity cooperation and the consequent near absence of comprehensive planning (and implementing) policy on a national scale (Sullivan 1988, 1994; Anabtawi 1986).

The most problematic aspect of higher education in the Occupied Territories, then, emanated from the political and economic conditions within which academic institutions operated. Indeed, there was a negative correlation between the expanding number of university graduates, on the one hand, and the depleted opportunities for the realization of their qualifications in a contracted underdeveloped local market, on the other.

Postsecondary Education: The Case of Dheisheh

One outstanding socioeducational attribute in Dheisheh is the large number of graduates from postsecondary institutions (universities, colleges, training centers) among members of the intermediate refugee generation, and even more so within the young generation. The first to acquire postsecondary education were those men, and to a far lesser extent women, who completed the UNRWA preparatory cycle in the late 1950s and early 1960s and who graduated from local high schools during the 1960s. The majority of those who continued their studies attended the teachers' training centers for men and women that UNRWA had set up in the West Bank earlier in that decade, institutions that granted their graduates a teaching certificate at the end of a two-year program. Others enrolled at universities in Egypt, Syria, and Lebanon, most in pursuit of a bachelor's degree in the humanities. Many first graduated from UNRWA's teachers' training college and later enrolled, while working, in an external university degree program.

Approximately 25 percent of the men from the intermediate generation acquired some form of postsecondary education, indicating that slightly more than half of those who completed the upper (high school) level went on with their studies. In contrast, among men in the entire West Bank of the relevant age group (forty-five to fifty-four), only 9.9 percent were estimated to have an education of thirteen years (CBS 1993, 802). As to women of the same generation in Dheisheh, roughly 11 percent acquired some form of postsecondary education, suggesting that approximately 40 percent of those who completed high school continued with their studies. Although the percentage of highly educated Dheishehian women of this generation is by far smaller than the corresponding percentage for men—reflecting retention of the gender gap from earlier stages—it is still significantly higher than the West Bank average for the age group, which was estimated at 2.1 percent (CBS 1993, 802).

Data for the young generation (aged twenty-five to forty in 1993) pertain to women and men who acquired their postsecondary education between the second half of the 1970s and the early 1990s. The majority studied in the West Bank at UNRWA's teachers' training centers, Bethlehem University, Birzeit University, and Hebron University, as well as in local hospitals and training centers that offer a diploma in nursing, such as the Caritas Baby Hospital in Bethlehem and Augusta Victoria Hospital in Jerusalem. It would be safe to estimate that more than 60 percent of those Dheishehians who completed their postsecondary studies in the West Bank hold a two-year diploma, with 30 to 40 percent holding bachelor's degrees. Of those who studied abroad, many attended colleges and training centers in Jordan, a relatively large number acquired advanced degrees (master's, doctorate, and medical) in the Soviet Union and other countries of the Socialist bloc, and yet others completed their higher education in Western Europe. Egypt, Lebanon, and Syria figured less and less in the educational trajectories of young Dheishehians.

The findings are impressive on both an absolute (Dheishehian) and comparative scale. They show 36.5 percent of Dheishehian men of the younger generation to have obtained some form of higher education. An astounding 80 percent of those who completed the upper (high school) level successfully went on to acquire postsecondary education.[9] In comparison, the rate of men (aged twenty-five to thirty-four) with thirteen years or more of education in the West Bank was estimated at 23.2 percent (CBS 1993, 802). My findings for camp women of the young generation show around 23 percent to have postsecondary education. Between 50 and 55 percent of the women who successfully completed the upper level went on to higher studies.[10] Again, in comparative terms the Dheishehian figures for women with postsecondary education stand far above the West Bank average, which was estimated at 12.1 percent (CBS 1993, 802).

The data on camp women indicates a very significant leap forward in the spread of higher education during the 1970s and 1980s and a gradual closing of the gender gap. The fact that meaningful differences remained can be attributed, to some extent, to the still-prevalent phenomenon of early marriage for females. Although extremely early marriages, of girls between the ages of thirteen and sixteen, are very rare, engagement and marriage at seventeen to nineteen, that is, precisely at high school age, are commonplace in Dheisheh. Although this does not necessarily preclude the option of studies at a later stage in a woman's life, it certainly lowers the probability of such an undertaking.

The very high proportion of those among graduates of the upper level who pursued higher education provides further evidence for the bottleneck effect of Israeli policy. Government high schools became a threshold that many (as noted, around 60 percent throughout the West Bank) failed to cross; those who succeeded in doing so usually did not halt there, and continued with their studies.

Finally, Dheishehian women and men competed very favorably with their West Bank peers in terms of higher education.[11] This finding is supported by the results of Fafo's comprehensive survey (1993), which indicate that the camp refugee population in the Occupied Territories has the highest rate of persons with an education of thirteen years and more, even slightly higher than the rate for Arab Jerusalem (Heiberg and Ovensen 1993, 137). On the systemic or structural-institutional level, the explanation for the relative advantage of Dheishehians (and possibly of other refugee camp communities) should be traced back to a combination of UNRWA's contribution and facilitating local factors, including those elaborated upon below.

One may justly argue that, to start with, socioeconomic conditions in the camp(s) were more conducive to the spread of education than, for example, those characterizing rural and partially rural communities (where more than 50 percent of the West Bankers still resided during the 1990s). This chapter, however, highlighted the role of UNRWA in actualizing this potential. I have particularly stressed UNRWA's success in making standard a minimum of nine years of education in the camps, at an earlier stage than in government systems, along with the concomitant accomplishment of a rapid closing of the gender gap. In the local arena of the West Bank, this implied that in the 1970s and 1980s the percentage of refugee camp girls who graduated from the preparatory level and went on to the upper one was by far higher than that of village girls. Eventually, this advantage found expression in the relatively higher rate of high school graduation, and subsequently, candidacy for postsecondary education among the refugee camp girls—as the Dheisheh findings and the data for camp refugee population in the Occupied Territories well reflect.

No less vital in terms of UNRWA's contribution were the teachers' training colleges for women and men, providing an opening for higher education exclusively to refugees. Four to five hundred women and men were regularly enrolled in the agency's biannual program, bringing the total number of graduates over the last thirty-five years or so to many thousands. In the face of the near absence of equivalent training colleges for the wider (non-refugee) public throughout the period of the Israeli Occupation, UNRWA's institutions became an invaluable asset for the refugees. Indeed, the graduates of UNRWA's teachers' training center in Dheisheh outnumber those from any other single institution for higher education in the West Bank or abroad, amounting to a substantial percentage of all Dheisheh graduates (I would estimate around 30 percent). Recently, UNRWA has upgraded the academic standard of its training centers, which now offer a four-year program leading to a full bachelor's degree and a teaching certificate.

A third factor conducive to the spread of postsecondary education among young Dheishehians was the camp's geographic location not far from (Arab) Jerusalem, in the vicinity of Bethlehem, Beit Jala, and Beit Sahour. The latter communities are known for having a relatively large number of public institutions, particularly hospitals, clinics, and rehabilitation centers, the majority of which were set up by churches and charitable societies. Some of the hospitals introduced training tracks for nurses, usually lasting from one to two years, during which time the interns were integrated into the employed staff. This opportunity, combining the acquisition of certification and a profession with work, was seized upon by dozens of young women from Dheisheh (and not a few men) from the early 1970s onward, accounting for the very high proportion of nurses among women with a postsecondary education in the camp. During the 1980s opportunities for academic degrees in nursing opened at Bethlehem and Hebron Universities. Here too, the geographical accessibility played in favor of the young Dheishehians.

All this notwithstanding, it would be wrong to take for granted a continuing upsurge in postsecondary education among young Dheishehians. My research covered the developments from the 1950s to the early 1990s, providing an assessment of the relative educational achievements of two generations in the camp, but leaving out the still younger generation, those who came of age during the 1990s. Several factors worked to the detriment of these young men and women, starting with the school closures imposed from 1988 to 1991 and with the aftermath of long-term destabilization lingering on well into the mid-1990s; continuing with a significant worsening of economic conditions during the Intifada and post-Intifada years; and culminating with the deterioration of UNRWA's financial situation and organizational status in the wake of the Oslo Accords, which posed (and continues to pose) a serious threat to the agency's operations.

The transfer to the PNA of responsibility for the national education system may in the long run bring about positive results in terms of the acquisition of education by all sectors of society, including camp refugees. This could counterbalance the deleterious effects of the factors enumerated above. The evaluation of the PNA's role, however, was beyond the confines of the present study. Changes in the educational accomplishments of Dheishehian youth in the last decade await complementary research.

CHAPTER 5

The Human Factor

DHEISHEHIANS, young and old, frequently speak in praise of educated people and of education. Already in my first meetings with families in the camp, and before I had managed to raise the subject, my hosts presented me with "lists" of those among their sons and daughters who had acquired higher education. They provided names of the universities and the degrees obtained, often fleshing out matters with a full "genealogy" of the educated people on their family tree. Apart from the subject of political prisoners—which was then the signal item on the agenda for the Dheishehians—higher education of family members was a topic of choice.

Showing how well versed they were on the details, men and women who did not know how to read or write easily elaborated the exact course of study of their younger siblings, their sons and daughters, as well as of distant relatives.

My brother studied in the humanities track in high school and came second in his class. After matriculation, he was accepted by the teachers' seminar in Ramallah [where applicants were four or five times the number of those admitted], but a diploma didn't satisfy him and he went on to take a correspondence course for his bachelor's degree in history, sitting for exams every year in Damascus University.

Such was not an unusual reply, here from a fifty-five-year-old illiterate woman, to the question: "Did your younger brother study?"

So it was that I heard of doctors, both men and women, who studied in the Soviet Union, in Bulgaria, and in Greece; of nuclear physicists who studied in Czechoslovakia; of engineers who studied in Damascus, in Cairo, or in New Delhi; and of teachers, male and female, who studied in the capital cities of all the Arab countries. I learned during my first visits to Dheisheh that it was hard to find a family in the camp (in the extended sense of family) lacking at least one member, man or woman, with higher education.

The great appreciation for education is of course related to its instrumentality in promoting employment prospects and the concomitant potential for personal advancement. But this is far from the full explanation. In the reality of Dheisheh, the link between education and employment has been far from clear-cut, and many are the parents with university graduate sons who are unemployed or construction workers. Indeed, the virtues ascribed to education often exceed the advantages it confers.

At least three prevalent attitudes toward education could be identified in Dheisheh. Some spoke of it as an attribute or trademark that, if not exactly hereditary, was nonetheless comparable to other qualities of character, such as diligence, perseverance, and wisdom. This view was common among members of the older generation in the camp, some of whom linked past kin and village background with the achievements and failures of the present generation. Thus, there were those who originated from the village of Zakariya who felt secure in the knowledge that Zakarwas are known for their great love of the written word and respect for education, while the ʿAjajra, their former neighbors from ʿAjur, were portrayed as ignorant to the core. Such stereotyped conceptions overlook, among other things, the fact that in the 1930s and 1940s a child from Zakariya could acquire, at best, four to six years of study at the Mandatory boys' school, that a similar school existed in ʿAjur, and that in effect few pupils attended school, and only a small number of these completed six grades.

Another interpretive mode, one common to all three generations in the camp, with much to sustain it, links education to the efforts of others, stressing the connection between the attainments of a family member and the work of his/her parents, brothers, and sisters. I heard the words "I put my sons and daughters through university" dozens of times, voiced especially by older women who had labored for years at cleaning or kitchen work. Fathers and mothers spoke of their eldest daughters who "taught all the younger brothers and sisters," and younger siblings spoke with admiration of an older brother or sister who "enabled us all to study." These are shorthand expressions referring to the income of an older sister or brother that was invested in the schooling of younger siblings. The deep appreciation of such support reflects a widely held recognition that the most effective and useful gift a parent or sibling could bestow on younger family members was to facilitate acquisition of higher education. Although grounded in reality, this perception inclines to idealization. Success in the realm of educational achievements can indeed be described as a "family project" rather than as a "family attribute"; however, by omitting the details of how the family division of labor operates, which is the nexus of the matter, only the "end product" is left, in the form of a degree or certificate, along with the "sacrifices" made by those who bore the burden.

Yet a third mode of relating to education differs substantially from the first two in its focus on content, meaning, and capacity for general enlightenment, rather than on certificates, titles, and degrees, or on the conversion of schooling into an economic asset. Special reference was made to the education acquired by political prisoners serving terms in Israeli jails, in spheres such as politics, history, political economy, and philosophy. In terms of this viewpoint, what mattered most was the role of education in generating political and social consciousness. Those autodidacts among former prisoners who had attained competence and authority on various subjects were highly esteemed, and their opinion was frequently consulted on current affairs. This approach was most common among the young; among the older parents of political prisoners, some shared the enthusiasm for informal political education, but many others lamented the "lost years" sons spent in prison.

The attitudes of Dheishehians with respect to education and the educated reflect the generation gap, change over the years, and the impact of political socialization, alongside the material as well as symbolic returns of education. The variety of views offers insight into the centrality of this factor for family and community life in the camp.

First Years, First Conditions, First Teachers

A large open tarpaulin tent supplied by the Red Cross served for the first school in Dheisheh, shortly after the arrival of the first hundreds of refugee families in the spring and summer of 1949. The initial staff of teachers was partially recruited from among the camp population. They were men in their twenties and thirties with four to eight years of education acquired in Mandatory schools in their home villages or in adjacent towns. The atmosphere in those times is conveyed in the story of Mahmud al-Khatib (aged sixty-eight in 1992), one of the first teachers.

Al-Khatib studied for six years in the Mandatory village school in Zakariya, subsequently working with his father on the family lands. When his family was uprooted from the village, he was twenty-four years old and married. Together with his wife, the baby daughter who was born to them shortly after the flight, his parents, and six of his brothers and sisters, al-Khatib fled to the Hebron district and from there to the Nu'eima refugee camp in the Jordan Valley, where they stayed for six months. Arriving in Dheisheh in the summer of 1949, he became one of the refugee representatives to the Red Cross, responsible for the allocation of food rations. Later that summer, Mahmud and three other men in the camp with similar levels of education were appointed by the Red Cross as teachers. They taught in the open tent without chairs and tables. The refugees themselves purchased such basic equipment as books, notebooks, blackboards, and chalk.

Several months after opening the school, the Red Cross decided to close it, claiming that there were no funds.

For four months they did not pay us a salary. A kitchen worker suggested that we demonstrate. The truth is that I knew nothing about demonstrations . . . he taught us how to prepare placards and write slogans such as "We Want Books," "We Want Our Salaries," and "We Want to Return to Our Homeland." We had no food and were really hungry. Anyone who has not experienced hunger is unable to understand the meaning of the word. In fact, on the day of our demonstration we planned to set fire to the car of the Red Cross supervisor, but disturbances broke out between residents and Jordanian soldiers, and the car couldn't get through. We were arrested on the spot and taken by foot to the office of the Jordanian military governor in Jerusalem. Eventually, the school was reopened.

Al-Khatib continued as a teacher in the UNRWA school after the agency took over from the Red Cross. He studied on his own, completed his matriculation examinations, and taught Arabic in the first sequences of primary school in the years 1950–57. His relatively radical social views are illustrated by the following comment: "Britain didn't establish schools for women in our villages. In my opinion the British knew full well that having educated women is a vital condition for assuring progress. Such progress was of course opposed to their interests." His eldest daughter, Sara, was the first woman in Dheisheh to study nursing, at the Augusta Victoria Hospital in Jerusalem. In 1957, following the imposition of martial law in Jordan, al-Khatib was arrested together with seven other teachers and the headmaster of the Dheisheh school on a charge of subversive activity. He was never to return to teach in Dheisheh after his release from prison.

Al-Khatib is the only one of the "first teachers" who was living in Dheisheh when I conducted my research. Some have died, some emigrated even before 1967, and others, who left the camp during the 1967 war, were not permitted to return. But the residents of the camp, particularly those who attended school in the 1950s, well remember them as self-made educators and public figures with an understanding for and an involvement in politics. Few fail to mention, for example, the name of Subhi Nashef, the headmaster, who was not a camp resident and who eventually, following his dismissal and arrest, was forced to leave the area. Portrayed as an educator who had spared no effort in attending the individual needs of each pupil, including food and clothing, he is also recalled with admiration as a leading activist in one of the opposition parties to the Jordanian regime.

The stereotyped image, then, of those from a traditional village upbringing, an agricultural or semiagricultural way of life, and with only limited education of the Mandatory village school, does not fit the first teachers. Nor did they all come from a peasant background; there were some nonrefugee urbanites among the early teaching staff. The personal achievements of al-Khatib, like that of other colleagues among the teachers, surpassed those of many of his generation. Most were and remained illiterate and became casual manual workers during their first decade in Dheisheh. In many respects, the biographies of the teachers are more similar to those of educated people from the intermediate generation who grew up in the 1960s.

Boys and Girls in the UNRWA Schools

Schools, one for boys and one for girls, were among the first permanent buildings to be established by UNRWA in Dheisheh. In photos of the camp from the mid-1950s, one can clearly distinguish the rectangular concrete structures near the Jerusalem-Bethlehem-Hebron main road surrounded by hundreds of tents, row upon row. During the first years the schools took in boys and girls aged six to eleven, allowing entrance into the first grade for all of that age group. Thus, children with no prior schooling started on the regular track; however, children over eleven years of age in 1950 did not enjoy this opportunity. Those young people age eleven and above who arrived in Dheisheh constituted a "lost generation" in terms of education.

But nearly all the children younger than eleven years of age in 1950 entered primary school and completed at least a few grades. As witnessed by Mahmud al-Khatib and by those who were pupils in that period, and as demonstrated by my statistical data, there was a very high response by the parents to the opportunity for sending their sons to school, and a somewhat lesser one for sending their daughters. Two major factors account for this: first and foremost the physical proximity of the schools to the homes of all pupils, and secondly, the fact that the entire cost was covered by UNRWA. The importance of the location of the school within the camp cannot be underestimated. It saved travel and transportation outlays and, moreover, helped dissipate objections by parents to sending daughters to school in an "unprotected" environment. In addition, being the only public institutions (apart from the mosque) within the confines of the refugee camp, the schools' good reputation was closely associated with the prestige of the public figures comprising the nucleus of the first teaching staff. In addition, UNRWA's provision of all necessities, including notebooks, textbooks, writing implements, and school uniforms, as well as a hot meal at lunchtime, was of key significance. One can say that the agency took upon itself the full burden of the education of refugee children and relieved the parents of the responsibility.

An additional element contributing to the high level of response was rooted in the lack of any significant "competition" to the school in the form of wage work opportunities. There were many children who nonetheless dropped out and sought jobs, but given the situation of unemployment and underemployment that prevailed in the region, the impact was negligible. The housing distress, with people living in tents and in the UNRWA shelters that replaced them, also had its effect. Unlike the peasant household, in which boys and girls also participated in outdoor and indoor chores, family life in the refugee camp was crowded into the narrow confines of a single room, leaving children with little to occupy them, although the situation of girls, pressed into housework at a very young age, differed substantively from that of boys in this respect.

Lars Wahlin's research (1987) on the spread of government education in the rural regions of Jordan during the years 1946–80 provides perspective on the speed of the institutionalization of primary education in Dheisheh. In 1946 some two-thirds of the population of Jordan lived in villages, yet there were only forty-five government schools in rural regions, and the number of pupils was as low as 3,115. Dozens of new village schools were added in the 1950s, but nearly all were solely for boys. In 1954 girls made up 5 percent of all students in village government schools, and by 1960 their relative share had risen only to 20 percent. An accelerated change took place in the late 1960s and in the course of the 1970s. By the end of this period, the number of girls learning in village government schools reached 45 percent of all pupils.[1]

Comparison with Dheisheh is instructive, since the refugee camp is also home to a population of village origin that until the early 1950s was barely exposed to public educational services. As demonstrated by Wahlin's data, the spread of elementary education in rural Jordan was characterized by a slow and uneven rise in the rate of pupils' enrollment, insufficient increase in the number of schools, and a marked discrimination against the schooling of girls in terms of allocation of government resources. In Dheisheh, however, schools have functioned within the community from the very first year of its existence, with girls and boys enjoying the same opportunities, at least on a formal level. While most of the boys and girls in the relevant age group in Dheisheh acquired some elementary education in the course of the 1950s, in rural districts in Jordan this result was achieved only in the 1970s.

Somewhat incongruently in light of the empirical data above, those of the intermediate generation in Dheisheh (aged forty-three to fifty-five in 1993), when asked to describe their childhood, often objected strongly to the mere notion of childhood. In the words of Abu ʿImad, currently director of Dheisheh camp on behalf of UNRWA:

We didn't have a childhood in the accepted sense of the word. The significance of childhood, as I understand it, perhaps abstractly, but as many children live it, is that a child is guaranteed protection, studies in relative quiet, wears clean clothes, plays, and has some living space of his own. As for us, we were without all this. We went barefoot in summer and winter, and when a father bought his son new shoes, the boy put them under his head when he went to sleep.

Deprived childhoods notwithstanding, studies and school became an integral and normalizing aspect, indeed routine, for the sons and daughters of the refugees. Nonetheless, and even though the families were not required to finance their children's studies in the UNRWA school system, the first fifteen years (1950–65), were marked by a sharp difference in the attitude of families to the education of boys versus girls. The data presented in detail in Chapter 4 show that half the girls from the intermediate generation dropped out of school somewhere between the first and the sixth grades, with dropout at its peak among fifth and sixth graders. In contrast, some 75 percent of the boys completed at least six years of schooling.

In those days it was still commonplace for families to withdraw their daughters, particularly the oldest, from school as soon as they reached the fifth, sixth, or seventh grades, either for the sake of early marriage, to help in the household, or in response to traditional demands. The phenomenon was related not only to low, or rather negative, awareness of the importance of female education, but also to the fact that the maintenance of the refugee household in the camp fell mainly on the shoulders of women. Only in rare cases were girls taken out of school for wage work outside the household. But cleaning, cooking, baking, child care, and carrying water buckets from the spring in the adjacent village of Irtas, or from the central container that UNRWA placed in the camp (piped water was provided only after 1967)— all were "women's work," often carried out by several women: the mother, the older daughters, and the daughters-in-law.

Fieldwork acquainted me with a number of families in which all the children completed at least a basic nine-year school program—except for the eldest daughter, who was generally taken from school when she was ten or eleven and spent the remainder of her childhood and youth at housework and tending her younger or older brothers as well as her younger sisters. Indeed, the oft-employed phrase "it was my sister who brought us up" refers in many cases to a sister who was younger than the male speaker. I can also point to numerous examples of families that compelled all daughters to leave school at an early age, though seemingly their labor could have been spared.

The common expression "she/they 'sat' at home" was coined to connote the "static" role of the girls during this stage of their lives, that is, as they awaited marriage.

The extent to which families removed their girls from elementary and from preparatory school gradually declined from the mid-1960s onward, though without ceasing entirely for many years. Toward the end of the 1970s, the discrepancy in the ratio of boys and girls enrolled in the preparatory level disappeared completely. I interpret this relatively rapid change in the attitude of families to their daughters' schooling as a product of two main factors. The first is the institutionalization of preparatory education for girls in the social landscape of the camp. When UNRWA opened the intermediate level of schooling (grades seven to nine) in the latter part of the 1950s, it invested efforts in advancing a standard nine-year study track. The number of girls who continued on to the preparatory level remained small initially, but after several years girls who both started and completed preparatory school ceased to be exceptional.[2] The second interrelated factor was the gradual recognition of the economic potential latent in the education of women. A not insignificant number of girls who started school in the 1950s completed the secondary level in the first half of the 1960s. Some continued studies and found employment, mainly as teachers with UNRWA; several among them became the main breadwinners in their families, at least until marriage. This potential had a direct influence on the attitude of many families in regard to the education of daughters. And, of course, families became aware that the increasing number of educated males sought educated spouses.

Students of Arab-Muslim societies have often pointed out the connection between the inferior position of women with respect to education and the patriarchal traditions and norms rooted in the culture and religion. Denial of education to girls is considered to be a prime manifestation of family control over the life chances of women, and is seen as integral to their relegation to domestic spheres and socialization into secondary roles within family and community. Further, the juxtaposition of patrilocality with patrilineal descent and patriarchy encourages devaluation of education for the daughter since she is destined to marry into another family. (See, for example, Azzam, Abu-Nasr, and Lorfing 1985; Rugh 1985; Warnock 1990; and Joseph 1993.)

The wide recognition and legitimization accorded the education of women in Dheisheh since the 1970s indicates that norms and values regarding the acquisition of education are the result of ongoing, multiple developments, subject to constant and cumulative changes and influences. However, substantive shifts in norms pertaining to female education do not necessarily, in themselves, provide a sufficient basis for a parallel ascent in the overall social status of women. Changes in the social and political status of women develop more slowly; the contradictions are more complex.

Secondary and Postsecondary Education and Their Relation to Family Structures

Secondary and postsecondary education became established among Dheishehian men starting in the early 1960s, and among women starting in the late 1960s and the early 1970s (see Chapter 4). From the latter part of the 1970s and into the 1990s, enrollment of both men and women from the camp in institutions of higher education was at a comparatively high level. The correlation between the increased incidence of graduation from the preparatory cycle and the subsequent growth in secondary and postsecondary enrollment is significant, but does not, in itself, provide a full explanation for either the scope or the rapidity of the process.

The role of UNRWA and of foreign governments and institutions in facilitating the studies of those seeking advanced education is not to be underestimated. Both tuition and living costs of those enrolled in the UNRWA teachers' training centers were covered by the agency; academic studies in communist countries were almost always financed through full grants by the host governments; Egypt and Syria opened their government universities to Palestinian students on terms equal to those offered to native citizens; tuition fees at the universities in the Occupied Territories, all of which are private, were fairly low. Nevertheless, the absence of government agencies committed to investing in, promoting, and directing education—combined with the extreme hardships of living in the refugee camp, the size of the refugee families, and the denial of government welfare provisions—counterbalanced the favorable factors, shifting the center of gravity to a large measure onto the students' families.

Almost all the university students, college graduates, and professional workers I interviewed came from very large families, of eight to twelve persons on average. Almost all fathers and many mothers had been day wage workers at the time of the Jordanian regime and throughout the first and second decades of the Israeli occupation. Familial divisions of labor that developed within households that subsisted solely on incomes from day wage labor failed to generate an accumulation of resources sufficient to procure a meaningful rise in the standard of living. The pooling together of unstable and meager resources could guarantee survival but lacked the capacity to engender more than that.

In order to sustain the prolonged schooling of four, six, or eight children, families required a minimum of economic security in the form of steady income, but the earnings of day wage laborers were devoid precisely of that potential. Secure income in the form of a monthly salary could therefore only come from the professional employment of those who acquired higher education, outside the nexus of day wage work in general and employment in the Israeli labor market in particular. Such regular salaries were to be found in either the local impoverished public sector or in the much larger public sectors of the Gulf states.

Two case studies illustrate how the acquisition of education beyond the intermediate level in Dheisheh rested, to a large extent, on the capacity of families to adopt and articulate structured chains of labor, relying on different sons and daughters in turn. By harnessing the yields of the skilled, professional, or semiprofessional employment of these unmarried family members, the families ensured the "production" of secondary and postsecondary education for the next children in line.

THE SOCIAL COMPLEXITY OF REMITTANCES

I never had a chance to meet Amira. Ever since the 1967 war she had been living outside the West Bank, fifteen of those years in Saudi Arabia where she taught in a girls' school for daughters of the upper class ("a school for princesses," as her family termed it), and the remainder of the time in Jordan. Her story was reconstructed with the assistance of her older sister, Jamila; her eldest brother, Mahmud; and other relatives and acquaintances, all of whom live in Dheisheh.

Born in Zakariya in 1943, Amira arrived in Dheisheh at the age of six with her parents and four unmarried siblings—two older and two younger than herself—as well as with Mahmud al-Khatib, her oldest brother, whose story appears early in this chapter, and his family. Her father, Abu Mahmud, then in his late forties, did not work after being uprooted from his land and becoming a refugee, although he lived for another twenty-four years. In fact, Abu Mahmud had given over physical work to his older sons when still a peasant in Zakariya.

Until his imprisonment in 1957, it was Mahmud who continued to support his father's family, along with his own family of five, from his work as a teacher in the local school. During those years the two families lived side by side in tents and maintained a joint household. Following Mahmud's arrest and dismissal from work, the burden of providing for the family fell upon his brother Muhammad, who had meanwhile married and established a family. Muhammad was a construction worker who went from job to job in both the West and East Banks.

Amira was the first girl in the family to attend school. Her eldest sister, Khadija, who was already married in 1948, never received formal education in the village. At age ten when she arrived in Dheisheh, Jamila, the second sister in line, was on the border of the unfortunate age group that was considered too old to be admitted to UNRWA's schooling system, and she was kept at home. Amira entered UNRWA's school in 1950 and completed high school in 1962, a rarity in those days when normally a girl's schooling did not exceed the preparatory stage. Mahmud, Amira's senior by more than fifteen years, who had completed the Mandatory school in Zakariya, credited himself for at least some of his sister's perseverance, pointing to his role in providing constant encouragement.

Amira continued at the UNRWA teachers' training college in Ramallah, completed her studies in 1964, and immediately after started work. She found a job in Saudi Arabia through the assistance of UNRWA. Her mother accompanied her there as per the Saudi government's requirement for work contracts for unmarried migrant female workers. Returning to Dheisheh a year later, Amira was given a post in the local UNRWA school, where she taught for the next two years. While working, she enrolled in the external studies program at Beirut Arab University (BAU), majoring in history. The 1967 war found Amira in Beirut sitting for her summer exams, whereupon the Israeli authorities deprived her of resident rights on grounds of "absence from the region." Amira eventually settled in Jordan, where she had family, and was accepted as a teacher at the school for refugees in Karameh, a position she held until her marriage in 1972. Her parents and youngest sister (who was born in Dheisheh) followed her to Jordan, remaining there until the father's death and the subsequent return of the mother to the West Bank under the rubric of "family reunion."

During the eight years preceding her marriage, Amira was the sole regular breadwinner for her parents and siblings. Throughout this period, she transferred her entire monthly wages to her parents. In addition to covering living expenses, Amira's remittances enabled the family to keep her younger siblings in school and subsequently to support at least one of them through long-term studies for a doctorate. Like Amira, her brother Ibrahim also studied at the UNRWA teachers' training college and at BAU. However, he married soon after his appointment as a teacher in Amman, and he did not share in the burden of supporting his parents' household, at least not on a regular or significant basis. Years later, Mahmud al-Khatib, the eldest son, would remark: "Ibrahim could avoid helping the family because Amira was there and mother could rely on her." The younger brother, Youssef, graduated from high school in 1966 and went on to study in Yugoslavia, supported by a grant and by small, albeit regular and ongoing, remittances from his sister. He completed a doctorate in electrical engineering and did not return to the West Bank. Noha, the youngest, specialized in laboratory studies in the Soviet Union, where she met and married a Syrian student of Palestinian descent; they established their home in Syria.

When I attempted to understand why Amira remained unmarried until she was twenty-nine, I learned that the delay was by no means a chance matter. While still a teacher in UNRWA's school in the mid-1960s, a colleague of Amira's had asked for her hand in marriage. Her family, reluctant at first, later gave their consent to the proposal on condition that the engagement contract explicitly stipulate a five-year delay. The reasons were not specified in the contract, and Amira's close relatives were reluctant to disclose them, despite the many years that had passed. In any case, shortly before the five-year term expired, and against her wishes, Amira's brothers called off the engagement. In 1972, after eight years of teaching, Amira was wed to a relative, a migrant teacher, and went to live in Saudi Arabia, where she taught for another fifteen years. On different occasions, she sent gifts and money to her family.

In tracing family divisions of labor that enabled and sustained the acquisition of education, it is easier to interpret patterns and mechanisms in motion than to point to the catalyst. If, as suggested above, the steady, salaried employment of at least one family member was a necessary condition for facilitating the prolonged schooling of others, how did the first son or daughter overcome the entrapment of adverse circumstances and go on to complete college or university? Whatever the answer in a particular family, once the first—not necessarily the eldest—crossed the hurdle, the second, third, and others usually followed. Thus, it is not uncommon to find in Dheisheh families in which seven or eight children completed some form of higher education. At the same time, families in which not even one out of eight children completed high school are not unusual.

Amira represents a watershed in the family's history. She was preceded by two sisters and a brother whose life courses were not affected, at least not in a direct manner, by the factor of formal education, and succeeded by three others who were to become among the best educated of their generation in the camp. The exception in terms of the chronological sequence was Mahmud, Amira's eldest brother, whose presence and accessibility, as both closest kin and an educator, undoubtedly played a significant role in fueling the process. Nonetheless, Mahmud stands more as a precursor, while it was Amira who brought about the great change.

During its first fifteen years in Dheisheh, the household was maintained as a supported segment of an extended family. It was first dependent on the teacher-son and later on the worker-son, even though both had families that expanded year by year. The situation altered when Amira began to work in 1964. Small as was the salary of a starting teacher, it was the first time that her parents enjoyed a steady and secure income. Soon enough, household affairs revolved around the daughter's employment opportunities, as evidenced by

Amira's mother's journey to Saudi Arabia in the role of guardian, and the family's later resettlement in Amman in the wake of Amira's forced migration.

Amira's income not only provided the material foundation that allowed long-term schooling for Ibrahim, Youssef, and Noha, but also "exempted" Amira's siblings from direct participation in the household economy during the period of their studies. Yet, it is precisely in this respect that the instance before us is atypical rather than representative. The expected and "logical" course of development is that each sibling benefits from the labor of his/her predecessor, only to replace her/him later in enabling the schooling of a younger brother or sister. As we have seen, for different reasons the "benefits" from Ibrahim and Youssef failed to materialize, rendering Amira's initially temporary role as breadwinner an ongoing one. With no foreseeable "replacement" for Amira's service in sight, the family could not afford to lose Amira's earning power through marriage. Indeed, our claim is that the family deliberately "extended" Amira's spinsterhood. The household division of labor rested on the family's capacity to exercise control over the resources of the working daughter as long as she remained single. Amira's higher education and professional work were not sufficient to grant her freedom and control over her personal affairs.

By some standards, the case of Amira and her younger siblings is a success story; four members of one refugee family, three of them born in Zakariya and one in Dheisheh, received full academic education in the 1960s and 1970s and acquired professions. It can be rightly claimed that the education and work experience of the first daughter paved the way for the others. Such an assessment, while in line with the final outcomes of the process, nonetheless disguises the familial power structure. Analysis of the foundation on which this family division of labor rested exposes the contradiction between the economic potential that higher education confers upon women and their social-personal status within their family of origin, wherein "traditional" forms of control continue to be imposed.

"NINE OUT OF NINE" CONTINUE THEIR STUDIES

Umm Walid, in her early sixties, and Abu Walid, fifteen years her senior, were both born and raised in Zakariya and married in Dheisheh in 1952. Between 1953 and 1969, Umm Walid gave birth to six girls and three boys, all of whom completed high school and acquired postsecondary education. Three daughters are graduates of teachers' training colleges, two hold diplomas in practical nursing, one has a certificate in secretarial work, and the three sons are university graduates. This achievement of nine out of nine family members who continued their studies is not that common, but neither is the case exceptional in Dheisheh, where a range of similar examples of eight out of eight, nine out of ten, or even ten out of ten can be found.

During the 1950s and 1960s the family lived in dire poverty. For more than a decade both the father and the mother worked at harvesting and olive picking—seasonal work during the summer and autumn months—in the fields of large landowners in the Jordan Valley and elsewhere. At the beginning of the season the entire family, children and infants included, would travel and camp out in the fields, not returning to Dheisheh until the harvest was over. Receiving payment in kind, they would have to cope through the dead winter season until the next year's round of work. In the early 1970s Abu Walid found employment as a construction laborer in Israel, but a severe injury on the job forced him to quit physical labor in 1975. Subsequently, Umm Walid became the steady, at times sole, breadwinner, working as a cleaning lady, first at a Bethlehem hospital and later, for more than twelve years, at the Hebrew University and at Hadassah hospital in West Jerusalem.

Their oldest daughter, Zeinab, born in 1953, studied at the UNRWA school in Dheisheh and at the Bethlehem secondary school. She then acquired training as a practical nurse and began work at the government hospital for the mentally ill in Bethlehem. While still at the internship stage, Zeinab was married to her cousin, a construction worker who had barely completed six grades of elementary school. Giving birth to six children did not stop her work at the hospital, where she had accumulated twenty-two years of seniority, when I became acquainted with the family in 1993. At that time, Zeinab's husband, who had been fortunate enough to work for the same contractor for almost twenty years, had just lost his job in the wake of the closure imposed by the Israeli government, which prevented Palestinians from entering Israel.

Walid, the eldest son and Zeinab's junior by two years, first studied for a diploma in engineering at the UNRWA vocational training center in Kalandia (Ramallah). He had wanted to become an engineer but the family could not afford the cost. Huda, a younger sister, graduated from UNRWA teachers' training college in 1978. With the aid of the agency, she applied for and received a teaching position in Saudi Arabia, where she went escorted by her father. Huda taught at a government school for girls in an isolated zone, several hours of travel from an urban center. She and her guardian father, who found odd jobs in maintenance work, lived in a rented house without electricity or running water.

Not long after Huda started working and sending money home, Walid registered for academic engineering studies at a university in New Delhi, and Fatma, two years younger than Huda, enrolled at a private teachers' training college in Amman. Huda remained in Saudi Arabia with her father for four years. Her remittances covered the education expenses of her brother and sister and enabled the family to add two relatively large rooms to the original

UNRWA shelter. "What would you have done without Huda?" I asked Umm Walid. "What would we have done without Huda?" she repeated, sighing. "Without Huda nothing would have come of the children. All of them studied thanks to Huda." She paused and added, "But it was because of me that Huda studied. I would come home from work in the afternoon and do most of the heavy housework by myself, cooking, baking, washing. Neither I nor Abu Walid can read or write, but we have always wanted our children to be better than us."

After four years, Huda was married to a Palestinian from the Tulkarem region who was a migrant construction worker in Saudi Arabia. As of 1996, the couple and six children born in the intervening years were still living there. Huda continued to teach in government schools, in various parts of the kingdom, in keeping with the changing demand over the course of the years and as stipulated in her annually renewed employment contract.

Her place in "family support" was taken by Fatma, who received her teaching certificate in 1982. She too went to Saudi Arabia, again accompanied by the now-established family guardian. Her earnings over the next two years helped keep Naᶜma, one year younger than Fatma, at the same teachers' college in Amman and to finance the building of a living room and a kitchen. In 1984 Fatma married a resident of Ramallah (a marriage of choice) and returned to the West Bank. For a while she taught in a government school, but she was eventually dismissed on grounds of her husband's and her younger brother's security records as political prisoners. She returned to teaching only in 1994 following the transfer of authority over the education system from the Israeli Civil Administration to the PNA.

With the marriage of Fatma came the turn of the teacher Naᶜma; in 1984 she set out for Saudi Arabia, accompanied by the veteran Abu Walid. This third venture turned out to be the shortest in terms of the family income, lasting only a year. Naᶜma was then married to a maternal cousin who followed her to the Gulf, where he became a petty merchant. Naᶜma was to remain in Saudi Arabia for another ten years, teaching in government schools. Living conditions and the general quality of life were of an inferior standard, she explained to me on her summer visit to her parents' home in 1994. She worked in a remote and backward rural area, and the house she rented from the government was unsuitable for the extreme desert heat: the supply of electricity came only from generators and at limited hours of the day. The absence of day care centers in the vicinity left her no choice but to leave her four small children with a village nursemaid. A year later, in 1995, Naᶜma was notified that her work contract was terminated, most probably in the wake of a general decline in the demand for foreign teachers. She received compensation (six months' salary) and left for Jordan with her family.

Naʿma's marriage marked an end of an era in the household's economy. In fact, for a brief time the family returned to reliance on the meager wages of Umm Walid, who continued to clean floors and laboratories at the Hebrew University until she retired in 1987. Hanan, who studied to be a secretary, married before graduation and skipped altogether the stage of working at the service of the family. Amina, who became a practical nurse, was married in 1986. ʿAdel was arrested in 1985 when still at high school and sentenced to five years in prison. Jamal, the youngest, went to study veterinary medicine in the Soviet Union in 1988 on a scholarship granted by the Soviet government; tragically, he was killed in a road accident in Ukraine in 1993, half a year shy of graduation.

Walid's return from India in the mid-1980s as a certified engineer accorded his family of origin no measure of prosperity. Rather, in the absence of means to build a house of his own, he, his wife, and four children crowded into his parents' home for another ten years. "Rescue" came unexpectedly through Amina's divorce, only one year after she married, and her subsequent return to her parents' home. In the following decade, Amina worked continuously at a local hospital as a practical nurse, serving as the only regular provider for her family. At the end of each month she handed over her salary to her parents, apart from a small sum kept for herself. Supported by a scholarship granted to former prisoners, and relieved from contributing the family income while studying, ʿAdel, who was released from prison in 1990, completed a degree in sociology at Bethlehem University.

Tracing the family's history over the last thirty years helps to unravel the conundrum (or at least the spring of its mechanism) of how nine out of nine children went beyond secondary education. The acquisition of this education—in terms of type of study, timing, and duration—appears here to be intricately connected to the social and gender-based division of labor within the family, as well as to the more general conditions of living in the refugee camp. Here, then, is a multiple-staged family organization, structured around the professional or semiprofessional employment of four daughters, supplemented by the contribution, peripheral, yet by no means marginal, of the mother's decades of waged labor.

Unlike the parents from the previous case study, for whom the uprooting from the village marked a complete disintegration in the sense that they never after "retrieved" their working lives, Abu and Umm Walid supported their family in Dheisheh for many years, though their wages were meager and insecure. A younger couple of the same first refugee generation whose married life commenced in Dheisheh, they provided their offspring with a "smoother" starting point than could a family in which the sole lifeline was the generosity of the children. Another difference of import is the generation "statuses" of the children in each case study. Whereas Amira's academic achievements were indeed pathbreaking in the early 1960s, Abu and Umm Walid's children—all from the young generation with the possible exception of Zeinab, who borders on the intermediate generation—acquired their education at a time when secondary as well as postsecondary schooling for both boys and girls was established and fairly widespread in Dheisheh. Thus, the issue here is no longer the introduction of education into a refugee family's "agenda," but rather the division of labor that perpetuated the acquisition of education over and over again.

One may justly point out that the case of Zeinab, the oldest daughter, is outside the "chain mechanism," since she married prior to entering the labor force and therefore did not contribute to the upkeep of her family of origin. Yet Zeinab's marriage, and more so, her life history as a married woman, is of interest, in view of what we know about the traditional marriage system from the "days of the village," which continued to prevail in the refugee camp after the uprooting. With an arranged marriage to a first cousin, Zeinab was traditionally wedded in the full sense of the term *tradition*. However, when compared with the great majority of the Dheishehian brides of the 1950s and 1960s, and indeed the overwhelming majority of brides in the village, Zeinab entered matrimony with a novel asset in the form of her earning power as a semiprofessionally employed woman. One may indeed speak of her—and of the many camp women like her who followed a similar course of schooling and training, particularly from the early 1970s and onward—as brides who came to marriage with a "dowry" in hand. In a social and cultural system wherein the transactional aspect of the marriage contract, and of the negotiations that precede it, traditionally revolves around the bride price (a payment given to the woman's family, part of which goes to her), the novelty is even more pronounced in the case of Zeinab, for as a barely educated laborer, the groom's economic potential was lower and less secure than that of the bride.

For many decades the family, which in 1969 numbered eleven persons, depended for subsistence on the daily wage labor of the parents, and increasingly on that of the mother. The fact that UNRWA provided postsecondary education free of charge in its colleges enabled Huda to earn her diploma in education and Walid to earn his in engineering, in spite of these harsh conditions. Yet the two certificates also marked the upper limit of feasible opportunities at first, since UNRWA restricted such aid to only two members of one family, and there were six more children at home.

The barrier was lifted in 1978 with Huda's journey to Saudi Arabia. Why was it Huda who traveled, thus beginning the chain of salaried professional work, and not Walid, her senior, who was as well qualified? This was not the norm in Dheisheh. In the majority of instances, the first to migrate for the purpose of work and family assistance was a male. Walid, however, did not have a job or a contract for work in hand, and perhaps he envisioned the academic possibilities that eventually were his lot when he enrolled at the university in New Delhi. Since Walid was "exempt" from participation in the work chain, its start and then its perpetuation depended, to a significant extent, on the "female-heavy" composition of the family, with five "intervening" daughters before the other two sons at the end of the line. Clearly, the division of labor would have differed had the age and gender order been reversed and six sons had preceded two daughters.

Still more essential to an explanation is the manner in which the education of the daughters was geared to the benefit of the family's immediate needs. Except for Hanan, who studied secretarial work, all the daughters studied either teaching or practical nursing, functional professions that required relatively short periods of training and usually led to rapid integration into the labor force. The choices should be attributed more to the narrow structure of job opportunities on the local as well as the regional labor markets (see Chapter 6), than to family preferences. Nonetheless, one cannot avoid comparison with the sons. All three attended academic, rather than semiacademic or vocational, institutions, and they chose to specialize in spheres that demanded relatively long studies. And in at least one instance—ʿAdel's choice of sociology—the applicability to the job market was tenuous.

The temporary migration to the Gulf of the educated and skilled unmarried daughters deserves closer inspection. The escorted journey to Saudi Arabia appears here as an "ideal type," a pure expression of the subordinated position of the young women with respect to both their family and the dictates of the ultraconservative "hosting" state, with the protective guardian role of the father epitomizing both. Not only did the young women working in Saudi Arabia transfer their income to the family, they also had to cope with social isolation, loneliness, difficult physical conditions, gender segregation, and close supervision.

Unlike Amira's family in the former case study, this family did not "need" to delay the daughters' marriages, since it had ample qualified female offspring at its disposal. However, the case represents the same "system," one that rests on the family's control over the working and earning power of its unmarried daughters. In a marked qualitative contrast with the work chains among families that subsisted solely on daily wage labor (see Chapter 3), those relying upon professionally (or semiprofessionally) employed unmarried family members did not function only to guarantee survival. Rather, their added value rested on the family's capacity to give their young women and men higher education and professions. It was the pace of this reproductive process, in fact, that regulated the length of a daughter's service on behalf of her family. In this case, Huda, who enabled Fatma to acquire postsecondary education, assumed the role of main provider for four years, by which time her sister had graduated and was ready to take her place and "release" her for marriage. Two years later, Naʿma, whose studies were made possible by Fatma, held the necessary qualifications to take over. The reference is therefore to an active mediation by the family of a process wherein education begets salaried employment, which is then harnessed to produce the education of younger family members, who, in their turn, produce work—all within an external, larger context that determined the structure of job opportunities for the refugees.

In many instances, however, the "tribute" of the working daughter (or son, for that matter) to her family of origin is not limited to the period of time in which she hands over her income. The end of the term of economic service to her parents' household is also the end of the daughter's unmarried days. In all the instances thus far introduced, the entrance of a new daughter into the chain coincided with the marriage of the one who preceded her, although one need not suggest that the "enactment" or timing of marriage is necessarily conditioned by the availability of an employable substitute. She is relieved from her duty, one without reward (except in the form of that deep-seated, obligatory, Durkheimian-Maussian sense). Yet marriage is not always an outcome of a daughter's independent decisions and will. This could be directly inferred from the instances of Zeinab, Naʿma, and Amina, all of whom were wedded to close family relatives of not exactly comparable statuses, at least with respect to education. In such instances, the replacement of a working daughter by her younger sister is liberating and binding at one and the same time.

Nonetheless, marriage, even when arranged, is a safety net for a young woman, as we gather by way of negation from Amina's story. Her place in the chain of work could have been minor, but for the failure of her matrimonial life. For lack of an alternative that is considered respectable, the only "solution" for a divorced woman from Dheisheh, or elsewhere in the Occupied Territories (or in the Arab Middle East, for that matter) is to return to her parental home. Amina came back at a point in time when all her sisters were married, her older brother had established his own family, her younger brother was in prison, her father was not working, and her elderly mother was on the verge of retiring. Her role as main breadwinner resembled that undertaken by her sisters in the past, but the passing of time was to her detriment, and her status as a provider lacking social independence was stabilized.

All that has been said notwithstanding, the work chain is not a profit-generating mechanism, wherein the products of female labor are reaped and retained by men. In none of the stages of the chain did the family become one of means and neither did its male members turn into property owners. Income from the salaried work of the women served to cover the ongoing expenses of the family, including everyday subsistence, the postsecondary education of its children, and the improvement of its housing conditions. The three successive journeys to Saudi Arabia were vital for ameliorating the family's standard of living; yet they were not sufficient to procure a surplus guaranteeing affluence or long-term economic security. Clear-cut evidence for this is seen in the long-delayed retirement of Umm Walid from her job as a cleaning woman, indicating that throughout the entire period when the family was sustained by a flow of remittances, her miniscule income was not a superfluous contribution to the household. It seems that there could be no better proof than the renewed dependence of the aging parents for their survival on the monthly salary of their divorced daughter.

CHAPTER 6

Circumscribed Avenues for Mobility

DHEISHEHIANS WITH TERTIARY EDUCATION IN
THE LOCAL AND REGIONAL LABOR MARKETS

SINCE THEY BECAME refugees in the 1948 war and took up residence in Dheisheh, the inhabitants of the camp have had to depend on wage labor for their living. From the early 1960s, the time when the first cohorts of Dheishehian youth completed their secondary education, and into the mid-1990s, the camp's workforce could be divided into two major categories. The first and larger group comprised day wage laborers of three generations (see Part I). In the second group were men and women with postsecondary education and/or professional training who were employed in public and community services. For the sake of brevity, this latter group will be referred to as "the professionally employed" or "salaried employees," so as to differentiate between them and laborers who receive their wages on a nonsalaried basis. While the relative weight and gender composition of these two groups underwent several changes throughout the period, they remained the only significant categories. Self-employed workers were a rarity in Dheisheh; their numbers included few subcontractors in the building trades or transport services, as well as shopkeepers and petty merchants. There were virtually no Dheishehians who practiced the so-called liberal professions in the local private sector.

In the years that followed the establishment of the Palestinian National Authority (1994), and especially since the end of 1995, when Dheisheh was incorporated into zone A, where the PNA assumed control, another category of salaried wage workers was added to the Dheishehian occupational structure. It includes the employees of the PNA, particularly employees of the various security forces—intelligence, preventive security, police, and so on—and of the administration and various government ministries. The great majority of the security force employees are former political prisoners and activists who had served long terms in Israeli jails. The considerable changes to the composition of the camp workforce resulting from their recruitment into the apparatus of the PNA are outside the scope of this research.

In order to understand the changes in the distribution of occupations in Dheisheh during the decades under consideration (from the early 1960s to the mid-1990s), one must examine the structural factors that determined the opportunities for professional employment available to the camp's young men and women. In the period that preceded the 1967 war, two salient factors intertwined: the absence of a developed economic infrastructure in the West Bank, which significantly reduced the absorptive capacity of the local market, and the opening of job opportunities in the growing government sector of the oil-rich Gulf states. In the era of the Israeli Occupation, the effects of the underdevelopment of the West Bank economy intensified, while the economic development of the oil-rich Gulf states accelerated, reaching its peak between 1973 and 1983. This latter process relied almost in its entirety on the labor power of millions of migrant workers, among them hundreds of thousands of Palestinians from the Diaspora and Palestine, including tens of thousands from the West Bank. The mid-1980s recession in the Gulf oil producers' economies following reduction in revenues from oil sales, the expulsion of the largest Palestinian expatriate community from Kuwait in the buildup and aftermath of the Gulf War (1990–91), and the gradual "nationalization" of the government sector in Saudi Arabia in the early 1990s dealt severe blows to labor migration of professionals from the Occupied Territories, all but blocking this route to the younger generations among the educated.

Apart from the major structural factors, secondary factors took on unanticipated import and centrality in the absence of statehood and in the face of restricted development. I refer specifically to UNRWA's contribution to the "production" of a camp refugee teaching force, and to the welfare institutions of Christian charitable societies in the Bethlehem area, which served as a catalyst for the employment of camp women in nursing.

The Jordanian Era: The Onset of Labor Migration to the Gulf

In Jordan of the late 1950s and 1960s most state investment in economic development went to the East Bank, where a modern road infrastructure was developed, a number of industrial plants were established, and agricultural projects started. Relatively more resources were directed to the region of the capital, Amman, center of the state administration and apparatus. Nonetheless, the scope of development in a poor country, which lacked natural resources and which witnessed a trebling of its original population in the wake of the 1948 war, was limited. High rates of unemployment and of underemployment led, from the 1950s onward, to a wave of internal migration from the West to the East Bank of the Hashemite kingdom, and to a widening phenomenon of out-migration. Indeed, some scholars viewed out-migration as the most significant among the determining demographic attributes of the West Bank (Sabatello 1984, 3).

The internal migrants, whose numbers were estimated in the hundreds of thousands, included both refugees and nonrefugees (mainly villagers) from the West Bank, the majority of whom sought employment, which was more often casual than permanent, in the expanding Amman and Zarka regions. An increase in out-migration was recorded as early as the 1950s; the population census of 1961 found that sixty-one thousand Jordanians were employed abroad (about 9 percent of the labor force) (Kanovsky 1989, 43–44). In 1965 there were 63,568 holders of Jordanian citizenship, mostly West Bankers, in Kuwait alone, about half of whom were in the labor force (Share 1987, 33, 34). In the three years that preceded the 1967 war, an annual average of twenty-six thousand migrants, the majority Palestinians from the West Bank, left the kingdom, mainly for Kuwait and Saudi Arabia (Seccombe 1987a, 119). The massive outflow from the West Bank was reflected in the fact that throughout the seventeen years of Jordanian rule its population increased by only a hundred thousand, despite a very high annual rate (3.5 percent) of natural growth (Sabatello 1984, 2).

The 1960s predate the oil-boom era in the Gulf states, yet as early as the middle of that decade hundreds of thousands of migrant workers were working there, the majority of them coming from the "labor-rich" and otherwise poor or relatively poor Arab countries. When the production of oil on a commercial scale commenced (shortly after the end of World War II), the sparsely populated, tribal-based emirates and monarchies in the Gulf—Saudi Arabia, and the then-British protectorates Kuwait, Oman, Bahrain, Qatar, and the sheikhdoms and emirates that were later to form the United Arab Emirates—were all severely lacking in qualified manpower and devoid of modern infrastructure. Oil revenues were eventually followed by large-scale investments in development and state building; first the construction of roads, ports, and airports, and gradually the establishment of state administrations and institutions, modern-equipped armed forces, and state-sponsored social services. With the exception of the armed forces, the operation of these depended on imported labor power.[1]

Jordan became a significant exporter of migrant workers, the majority of whom were Palestinians. Among them were skilled, semiskilled, and nonskilled laborers, technicians, professionals and semiprofessionals—all this before the regional division of labor between oil-rich and labor-exporting states reached its full-fledged pattern of development.[2] Already in 1971 the value of remittances from workers working in the Gulf (predominantly in Kuwait) amounted to more than 43 percent of Jordan's exports (Share 1987, 35).

The employment prospects for the first generation of Dheishehians to complete secondary and postsecondary education were bleak. In fact, job opportunities within the local Bethlehem region and the adjacent districts of Hebron, Jerusalem, and Ramallah became available mainly through the auspices of UNRWA, which assumed responsibility for the placement of graduates of its training centers, in either its own school system and other departments or abroad (UNRWA 1986, 130–31, 143). In this respect, once again, the refugee population enjoyed a relative advantage over the non-refugee one, since at the time the governmental educational system lagged behind that of UNRWA; it produced far fewer graduates (in relative terms) and was not accountable for their integration into the labor force. Indeed, under the conditions that prevailed during the 1960s, study at UNRWA's teachers' colleges and training centers was among the very few tracks with relatively good prospects for employment.

Notwithstanding its seminal contribution, UNRWA could not cater to all its graduates. Neither could it provide solutions for the thousands of refugee high school graduates nor for the hundreds of university graduates who completed their studies abroad. Some of the latter were absorbed in the Jordanian government school system in both the West and East Banks. Lars Wahlin, who studied the development of government school services in one of the rural districts of the East Bank, noted that as early as 1963 about one-third of the teaching force in that district were Palestinian refugees. This reflects a trend that was continued into the 1970s, pointing to the contribution of Palestinian migrant teachers to the spread of education in the rural regions of the kingdom (Wahlin 1987, 162–64). Yet, this is the period that preceded the "educational revolution" in Jordan, which was to begin in the mid-1970s, so annual vacancies in the government system could by no means accommodate the growing supply of qualified teachers among the refugees.

The migration of young educated Dheishehians to the Gulf during the 1960s should therefore be located within the wider context of labor migration in the Middle East. The scope of this migration in Jordan alone encompassed hundreds of thousands. It should also be viewed against the backdrop of the local arena, marked by an ongoing stream of migration from the West to the East Bank, also driven by the search for employment. Belonging to the category of highly skilled manpower, educated professionals showed different patterns of migration to the Gulf than did nonskilled laborers. Whereas the latter relied predominantly on family relations and on social networks among veteran migrants, the placement of professionals was usually precoordinated through state and other agencies (Owen 1985, 5). Here too UNRWA had a role in assisting its graduate teachers to secure positions in the Saudi and Kuwaiti school systems (UNRWA 1986, 143).

PROFESSIONAL EMPLOYMENT AMONG THE INTERMEDIATE REFUGEE GENERATION FROM DHEISHEH DURING THE 1960S

Any assessment of the prevalence of professional employment among secondary school and college and university graduates from Dheisheh during the 1960s is bound to be imprecise, given the extreme demographic changes that followed the 1967 war. It is estimated that between one-quarter and one-third of the inhabitants left the camp as a consequence of the war. Among the latter were people who fled the West Bank during the fighting and were later prohibited from returning by Israel and people who were temporarily absent from the region when the war started and whose resident status was subsequently denied by the Occupation authorities. Many, probably the majority, of the Dheishehian migrants who were professionally employed in the Gulf at the time of the war belong to the second category of those who lost residency rights, hence the difficulty in providing a reliable depiction of the occupational breakdown for this generational group. The quantitative data at my disposal pertains to the population that remained in the camp and therefore does not reflect the prevalence of labor migration in the 1960s. However, insight into the scope of this phenomenon and its centrality to socioeconomic development in the camp can be gained indirectly through interviews with relatives of the former migrants. I believe it is safe to assume that one out of every four families had at least one migrant son or daughter with postsecondary education who worked in the Gulf.

Three salient features emerge from my sample data pertaining to women and men of the intermediate generation who did not migrate: the irrelevance of secondary (high school) education for employment; teaching as the major opportunity for those with postsecondary education; and the underrepresentation of women in the professional labor force. Not one of the nine men (in my core sample of forty-one) with ten to twelve grades of schooling obtained a job that required any formal education. They either entered the construction and building branch or worked in transport. As for the eleven men with postsecondary education (ten of whom held a diploma and one a bachelor's degree), five worked as teachers, two as nurses, another two in land surveying, and the remaining two as day laborers. Not one of the seven women (of forty-one in the core sample) who completed ten to twelve grades joined the labor force, and only one of the three who attained higher education worked at her profession (nursing), the other two were not employed. As noted, however, the qualitative research shows far greater participation of women of that generation in the professional labor force than the above figures suggest.

In my attempt to explain the process by which young Dheishehians climbed up the educational ladder, I have stressed the fact that advancement beyond the basic level of nine grades most often depended on family support in the form of a specialized division of labor and allocation of resources. The findings on the relationship between educational attainments and the occupational breakdown indicate that despite the effort and hardship that acquiring secondary education entailed, especially in the first decades of refugee existence, it was an insufficient prerequisite for professional employment. Male graduates of elementary, preparatory, and secondary schools alike became manual laborers, whereas female graduates remained largely outside the labor force. Tertiary education alone carried the potential for integration in professional employment, and this too mainly in teaching.

The Era of the Israeli Occupation: The Detrimental Consequences for White-Collar Employment

In the aftermath of the 1967 war the administration of public-government service systems in the Occupied Territories was taken under the auspices of the military government, which would later (in 1981) extend the authority to its supposedly civilian appendage, the Civil Administration. This is not the place to settle a historic account with these apparatuses, yet it is nevertheless important to emphasize a central consequence of the policy: public services were allowed to deteriorate, to the extent that their level in 1994 was relatively lower than that in 1967—despite the fact that the military government and Civil Administration imposed on the population of the Palestinian Territories, via military orders and decrees, an extensive collection system of fees and taxes.[3] Evidence for the detrimental effect of this policy on the government school system was provided in Chapter 4. Suffice it to note that the situation in the sphere of the public health system was by no means better; throughout the entire period not a single government hospital was added to those that operated prior to 1967, with the number of hospital beds remaining the same despite a 2.5-fold increase in population.

A central indicator for the underdeveloped state of the public services emerges from an examination of the employment in this sector. In 1970 employees in the public and community service sector amounted to 12.7 and 15.2 percent of all employed persons in the West Bank and Gaza Strip, respectively (CBS 1988, 697). In 1992 the respective rates were 10.9 and 9.5 percent (CBS 1994, 809, 811). In absolute numbers, 23,600 employees were serving a population of around one million in 1970, and 33,200 were serving an estimated 2.2 million in 1992.

In both developing and developed countries, the public and community service sector, which encompasses the government administration and the education, health, and welfare systems, is a major employer, with the level of employment often serving as an indirect indicator of the job opportunities for high school and university graduates. The contraction of this sector at the hands of the Israeli authorities meant an ongoing depletion of the opportunities available for the educated on the local market. This retrogression was particularly pronounced against the backdrop of the continuous growth in the numbers of high school and university graduates, the absence of job opportunities for skilled manpower in the local industrial sector, and the scarcity of such opportunities in the local business sector. In research he conducted in the early 1980s, Sabatello found that only one out of every five high school or university graduates could find employment in a given year. He estimated actual white-collar vacancies at a mere thousand per year, due to an extremely low recruitment rate of some three hundred per year in the military government and Civil Administration apparatuses (Sabatello 1984, 4).

Israel and Jordan are natural candidates for comparison. Each has a unique historical position vis-à-vis the West Bank, and while Israel is a prosperous welfare state, Jordan's economy became dependent on the exportation of highly qualified manpower to the Gulf. In Israel, throughout the 1980s and into the mid-1990s, approximately 30 percent of all employed persons and 35 percent of all salaried workers were employed in the public service sector, which constitutes the largest branch in the labor market.[4] The rate of female employment in this sector is higher than that of males and stood at 45 percent of all employed women and around 50 percent of all female waged workers. These figures underwent very slight changes throughout the period (CBS 1994, 376–79).

Data for Jordan shows that the relative weight of employment in the public sector (including employees in the security forces) rose from 34 percent in 1972 to 46 percent in 1986 (Kanovsky 1989, 58). This growth was a byproduct of the "readjustment" of Jordan's economy in the wake of its becoming a main exporter of professional workforce to the Gulf. Government investment in higher education was by and large directed to export, and the local market absorbed only a fraction of the highly qualified manpower that this investment produced. Nevertheless, "returns" in the form of generous aid extended by Saudi Arabia and Kuwait enabled incremental expansion of the government sector (Farsoun 1988, 158, 166; Seccombe 1987a, 122–25).

To gain further insight into the scope of deprivation of the Palestinian public sector under Israeli rule, it is sufficient to glance at the changes that have taken place since the establishment of the PNA in 1994. In late 1997 the number of employees in the government sector of the PNA, including employees in the security forces, was around one hundred thousand (Hilal et al. 1998, 52), an addition of approximately seventy thousand jobs in comparison with the figures for 1992.

Yet another aspect of the political economy of the Israeli Occupation, the selective, restricted opening of the Israeli labor market to Palestinian workers, worked to the detriment of the highly educated. Only limited branches of Israel's economy were accessible to Palestinians, with the government-state sector and the licensed liberal professions remaining utterly sealed off. Facing few choices, many thousands of high school and college graduates were forced to try their chances as day laborers.

THE PROMINENCE OF UNRWA AND NONGOVERNMENTAL INSTITUTIONS

Given the scarcity of white-collar positions in the government sector (Civil Administration), and the blocking of Palestinian employment in the Israeli public sector, the role of UNRWA and several other nongovernmental organizations looms large in the creation of job opportunities for educated refugees in the Bethlehem area.

Under adverse circumstances, UNRWA became the prime local employer of Dheishehians with postsecondary education, especially graduates of its own colleges. Of those who were accepted for work, the majority were assigned teaching posts in the agency's schools in the camps of Dheisheh, ᶜAida, ᶜArroub, and Fawwar, and the villages of Surif and Batir— all in the Bethlehem and Hebron districts—while others took on jobs in the agency's headquarters in Jerusalem. In addition, UNRWA absorbed university graduates in its preparatory schools and colleges and employed graduates of nursing schools in its local network of clinics.

The moderate number of women and men from Dheisheh who found employment with UNRWA's educational institutions greatly exceeded the number who worked in government schools. This point deserves special emphasis, given the relative sizes of the two systems: UNWRA, which catered to only 12 percent of West Bank pupils, offered more job opportunities than the Civil Administration that was in charge of 78 percent of the student population. Not only in the "education market," therefore, but also in the job market UNRWA managed to provide some kind of safety net, albeit limited in range and scope, for its refugee clientele. Perhaps no lesser importance should be attributed to the private hospitals and rehabilitation centers in Bethlehem and neighboring Beit Jala and Beit Sahour, the majority of which are run by Christian charity organizations.[5]

SEASON OF MIGRATION TO THE GULF: THE "BRAIN DRAIN"
FROM THE WEST BANK IN THE 1970S AND EARLY 1980S

Figures on migration from the West Bank reveal that following the mass flight during and immediately after the 1967 war (when the number of refugees was estimated at around 250,000), out-migration stabilized around an annual average of twenty-five hundred for the years 1969–74. It rose significantly to an annual average of twelve thousand for the years 1975–79, reaching a peak average annual rate of sixteen thousand for the years 1980–81. Altogether, 136,000 persons left the West Bank between 1968 and 1982, a process that counterbalanced natural growth and placed the rate of population growth at half its otherwise expected value (Sabatello 1984, 4). The extremely uneven age distribution of the emigrants, and in particular the overrepresentation among them of young males with secondary and postsecondary education, led Sabatello to dub the phenomenon of migration as a "brain drain" from the West Bank.

The Political Economy of Labor Migration to the Gulf

The intensified rate of out-migration of Palestinian inhabitants of the Occupied Territories between 1975 and 1983 should be viewed in the wider context of the unprecedented growth in the scope of labor migration, at first from various Arab countries and later from South and Southeast Asia to the oil-producing Gulf states. Whereas some six hundred thousand migrant laborers were estimated to have worked in the Gulf in 1970, the figure for 1975 stood at 1,250,000 (Owen 1985, 4).[6] Drawing on various sources, researchers calculated that in 1985 some 5.1 million migrant workers were employed in the six member states of the Gulf Cooperation Council (GCC; Kuwait, Saudi Arabia, Qatar, Bahrain, Oman, and the United Arab Emirates), 3.5 million in Saudi Arabia alone. These workers constituted 70, 80, and 90 percent of the labor force in Saudi Arabia, Kuwait, and the Emirates, respectively (Birks, Seccombe, and Sinclair 1988, 267).

Indeed, it was the command over the labor of millions of migrants—professional, skilled, and nonskilled—that enabled the backward oil-producing monarchies and emirates in the Gulf to become modern (albeit autocratic) state systems and to amass regional and global economic-political power. In the wake of the post-1973 war and coordinated action taken by the Organization of Petroleum Exporting Countries (OPEC) to raise oil prices and to improve their shares vis-à-vis foreign producing companies and conglomerates, revenues from oil sales increased steeply, rising from 9.3 billion dollars in 1972 to 170.7 billion in 1980 (Farsoun 1988, 156). Much larger investments were directed during those boom years to the development of infra-

structures—physical, industrial, military, administrative, and public—a transformation that entailed an unprecedented expansion of the imported labor
force and a concomitant change of its composition.

Up until the mid-1970s the majority of workers in the Gulf states originated in the relatively poor Arab countries (some of which were "rich" with
highly qualified manpower and developed in other significant respects):
Egypt, Jordan, Lebanon, Syria, North Yemen, and the Occupied Territories.
In 1985, however, the number of Arab labor migrants in the GCC states was
estimated at approximately 1.5 million, against around 3.5 million workers
from non-Arab Asian countries. Birks, Seccombe, and Sinclair estimated
that in 1985 the relative share of workers from South Asia, particularly India,
Bangladesh, and Pakistan, was 43 percent of the entire expatriate labor force,
compared with 20 percent whose countries of origin were in Southeast Asia,
particularly the Philippines, South Korea, and Thailand, and 30 percent who
came from Arab countries. According to their calculations, at the time around
29 percent of all migrant workers in the GCC states worked in the construction sector, against some 30 percent who were employed in the service sectors
(including community services, financial services, and personal services). Fourteen percent were absorbed in wholesale and retail trade, 9.4 percent worked
in manufacturing, and 8.9 percent in agriculture (Birks, Seccombe, and Sinclair
1988, 268, 274).[7] The government service sector employed Arabs almost exclusively, and it was within this category of professional employees that migrants
of Palestinian origin—primarily teachers, clerks, accountants, doctors, and engineers—were overrepresented, alongside significant numbers of Egyptian, Jordanian, Syrian, and Lebanese migrants. At the other extreme, and equally noticeable, was the concentration of workers from the Philippines, Bangladesh,
and Indonesia in the "domestic services," regardless of their level of education.

The political economy of the oil-producing states in the Gulf was underscored and sustained by a sharp dichotomy. At one pole were the large populations of labor migrants, who, although they greatly outnumbered the local
labor force, were denied all political and civilian rights. At the other pole
were the small native populations, a relatively wide strata of whom enjoyed
extensive privileges and ample opportunities for amassing wealth. Despite
the internal differences in status between labor migrants in the various sectors of the economy and of the relatively advantaged position of Arab workers, whose countries of origin maintained bilateral agreements with the labor-importing states, the situation of all foreign employees was marked by
inherent insecurity and lack of protection. Discrimination against them was
legally institutionalized in the immigration, residence, citizenship, property,
and labor laws of the oil countries. Naturalization in the Gulf states was all
but sealed off to expatriate laborers, who were denied access to any form of
political participation or to the social rights and benefits to which citizens

were entitled. Residency in the labor-importing countries was contingent upon annual renewal of the migrant's work contract and was immediately rescinded in the case of job loss. Expatriates were prevented from owning real estate property, including businesses. Hence, it was temporariness, above all, that characterized the situation of the migrant worker, one that stemmed from the terms of his/her work contract, and was reflected in the especially high rates of turnover in the construction sector, where short-term hiring was the rule, as well as in the insecure positions of employees in the public government sector. Even veterans among the latter group were hired on an annual basis, with no tenure or cumulative benefits. Migrant workers were not allowed to form trade unions or to join local ones and were prohibited from holding strikes and demonstrations. The majority were prevented from bringing their families with them (professional employees being the exception) (Owen 1985, 8–13).[8]

The vulnerability of migrant workers was most acute at times of crisis or market instability. Thus, for example, the decline of oil prices in the mid-1980s was followed by a recession that cost hundreds of thousands of laborers their jobs and led to a sharp decrease in wages (Birks, Seccombe, and Sinclair 1986; 1988, 272). Another quintessential case is seen in the expulsion of an estimated 350,000 Palestinians (workers and families) from Kuwait in the aftermath of the Gulf War (1991). Theirs was the largest, oldest, most well-rooted community of migrants in the country, with the highest proportion of professionals and strongest representation in the government sector. It was to their skill and expertise that the Kuwaiti state owed much of its prosperity. Yet in the absence of acknowledged legal rights, none of these credentials could guarantee them a measure of security (Lesch 1991; Feiler 1993; Le Troquer and Al-Oudat 1999).

The appeal of work opportunities in the Gulf, however, was in the comparatively high wages that, in the heyday of the oil-boom years, exceeded those in the countries of origin many times over (Ibrahim 1982; Seccombe 1987a), mitigating, to some extent, the subjugation of migrants to discriminating and exploitative terms of employment. In the case of the labor-exporting Arab states remittances transferred by migrants constituted significant parts of the gross national products (GNPs), and in some states, particularly Jordan and North Yemen, the value of remittances was much higher than the income from all other exports (Share 1987, 36–39; Farsoun 1988, 157). Moreover, in some states the migration of professionals became a quasi-institutionalized solution for the intensifying unemployment among the ranks of university and college graduates.[9] Of perhaps no less importance to the institutionalization of the inter-Arab regional division of labor was the especially generous aid in the form of grants and long-term loans, totaling many billions of dollars, which the "labor importers" extended to the exporters, and which were anchored in bilateral agreements and Arab summit decisions (Seccombe 1987a, 123; Farsoun 1988, 157–58).[10] Indeed, contributions of foreign aid from the Gulf states, first and foremost Saudi Arabia and to a somewhat lesser extent Kuwait, enabled the labor-exporting states to expand and sustain significantly large state sectors. Some scholars argue further that the relative economic stability achieved by the latter regimes was accompanied by substantial amplification of their repressive capacities, on the one hand, and the amassing of economic and political power by new strata of entrepreneurs and intermediaries that emerged from within the national bourgeoisie, on the other (see Farsoun 1988, 155–68).

HEIGHTENED VULNERABILITY IN THE
ABSENCE OF STATE HINTERLAND

Whereas oil boom–generated prosperity in the Gulf effected relative prosperity and stability in the labor-exporting Arab countries, particularly Jordan and Egypt, the migration of the teacher, technician, engineer, and laborer from the Occupied Territories was not accompanied by similar outcomes. The benefit from their migration was confined to personal savings and to the remittances transferred to the family back home. In other words, migration from the West Bank and Gaza to the Gulf did not generate development and new workplaces in these territories; the migrant only vacated his or her place. Thus, although many of those who left the Territories for the sake of work in Saudi Arabia and Kuwait did not lose their "rights of residency," some preferred not to return upon the termination of their contracts and eventually settled in Jordan.

Moreover, notwithstanding the fact that in most cases labor migration of Palestinian professionals to the Gulf enhanced their economic position, at least temporarily, the denial of rights and freedom in the countries of migration prevented the translation of this gain into social independence and mobility. The contradiction between the economic potentials of migration and the absence of a concomitant social transformation will be discussed in Chapter 7. This contradiction fostered a twofold dependency: on the one hand, that of families on the economic support of their migrant sons and daughters; on the other, that of migrants on the familial social ties and connections in the homeland. One of the results is the prolonged preservation of traditional patriarchal relations within the family despite the physical separation of young family members and despite the latter's economic advantages.

Dheishehian Graduates of the Younger Generation in the Local and Regional Labor Markets

MEN

An examination of the occupational breakdown in my core sample of forty interviewees shows that only nine of the twenty-five with either secondary or postsecondary education had salaried employment.[11] An additional sample that encompassed 169 men, including migrant workers, provided the following data: Forty-seven of the 169 (27.9 percent) were salaried employees, twenty-four in the West Bank and twenty-three outside the region (predominantly in the Gulf). Nine of the 169 (5.3 percent) were self-employed (contractors, merchants, owners of businesses) either in the West Bank or abroad. The remaining 113 men (66.8 percent) were laborers.

The findings give rise to several conclusions: Notwithstanding the prevalence of secondary and postsecondary education, the rate of salaried and professional employment among men of the young generation during the period of Israeli Occupation was definitely low. It would be safe to assume that this rate did not exceed 20 percent of the locally employed and 30 percent when migrants are taken into consideration. Secondary schooling turned out to be almost irrelevant to employment, given the finding that the lion's share of men with secondary education became day laborers. The implication: Family investment in the education of its young members was futile in terms of the job market unless a minimum threshold of fourteen years of schooling was surpassed.

The "employment profile" of the educated among the young generation is similar to that among the intermediate one, a finding that underscores the scarcity of salaried and professional employment opportunities on the local market throughout the era of the Occupation. Finally, there is sufficient evidence to assume that for every Dheishehian man of the young generation who was salaried or professionally employed in the West Bank there was another who migrated in search of such employment. In addition to those who became migrant professionals in the Gulf, this category included a significant subgroup of people who studied in the Socialist bloc and extended their stay for the purpose of further specialization in the sciences and medicine.

Since the mid-1980s the rate of labor migration from the camp to the Gulf has decreased profoundly, following, first, the periodic recession and declining demand for an expatriate workforce there, and subsequently, the mass expulsion of the migrant Palestinian community from Kuwait in the wake of the Gulf crisis and the increasingly discriminatory immigration laws adopted by the GCC states since the Gulf War. The dismantling of the Soviet Union at the beginning of the 1990s all but sealed off the unique track of higher education and long-term specialization previously made available to Dheishehians through the Socialist bloc. Consequently, the second half of the 1980s and first half of the 1990s offered ever-diminishing job opportunities to educated Dheishehian men.

WOMEN

An examination of the occupational breakdown in my core sample of forty interviewees shows that fifteen were in the labor force (37.5 percent). Of these fifteen, ten had postsecondary education (one university and nine college graduates) and five had secondary schooling. Only one of the fifteen was a laborer, against fourteen who were employed in the public services sector: eight nurses, three teachers, one secretary, and two journalists.[12]

The results of the survey on women and employment, which included 318 married and unmarried women between the ages of sixteen and thirty-nine, provide a wider (and more reliable) data base.[13] Fifty-two percent of the sample acquired secondary or postsecondary education (some were students when the survey was conducted), and 106 (33.3 percent) were in the labor force. Of the latter group, sixty-three (59.4 percent) were professionally or semiprofessionally employed (salaried employees): twenty-six nurses (41.2 percent), eleven teachers (17.5 percent), and nine secretaries (14.3 percent), while seventeen (27 percent) had miscellaneous jobs. All worked in the West Bank (including Arab Jerusalem). Thirty-eight of the employed (35.8 percent) were laborers in the West Bank and Israel (twenty-five and thirteen, respectively), and five worked at small family businesses in the camp. Fifty-four percent of the salaried employees were unmarried at the time the survey was conducted.

When interpreted in context and compared with the findings about their male counterparts, the above data support the following conclusions: The representation of salaried employees among all employed women of this age group is particularly high (60 percent), and especially so when compared with the rates for men. This can be attributed first to the relatively more abundant opportunities for Dheishehian women on the local professional and semiprofessional labor market. More than 40 percent of the salaried female workers were nurses, the majority of whom found employment with the hospitals and health care centers of nongovernmental charity organizations. There was no equivalent "dominant branch" in the case of salaried male workers. Indeed, this relative advantage in terms of access to opportunities in health care "channeled" the course of education and training track for many, probably the majority of those who took on postsecondary education, to nursing (at times against their aspirations and natural inclinations). The second reason for the marked difference in the occupational breakdown of women and men can be traced to the very low incidence of day laborers among women with education beyond the preparatory level. Most women in this category who could not find suitable jobs did not join the labor force, while there were high numbers of laborers among men with similar academic attainments.

Notwithstanding the high representation of the semiprofessionally and professionally employed among all young female wage workers, and their relative advantage on the local market, the survey results show that only about 40 percent of the women with secondary and postsecondary education were in the labor force.

The relative irrelevance of secondary education for employment was valid in the case of women as well, yet not to the same extent as for men. Here again the difference stemmed from the structure of opportunities in the nursing and paramedical branch, since some hospitals hired practical nurses without diplomas or even with partial secondary education (ten to eleven years). It should be stressed, though, that the standard prerequisites for acceptance have risen significantly in the past decade, and nowadays preference is clearly given to holders of bachelor's degrees in nursing.

The "employment profile" of women of the young generation differed conspicuously from that of their elders. Whereas the majority of workers in the latter age group were day laborers in Israel and the West Bank, the majority of young workers were professionally employed in the West Bank and in the Gulf.[14] The marked change reflects the leap forward in spread of secondary and postsecondary education among women in the camp during the 1970s and 1980s.

Finally, although women accounted for only about 30 percent of the young labor force in Dheisheh (female and male workers of the young generation), their relative share as breadwinners was much higher, and in periods of crises, such as during the Intifada and in the aftermath of the closure-related mass layoffs of laborers, it exceeded that of men. This conclusion draws on the findings presented in this section as well as on the analysis of the employment situation of young Dheishehian laborers as presented in previous chapters. The majority of young male workers were underpaid day laborers who worked intermittently and experienced long and recurring terms of unemployment. In contrast, semiprofessionally and professionally employed young women, although most often underpaid, enjoyed steady employment and a regular monthly salary.

FIGURE 1. Dheisheh in the mid-1950s, a view from northeast. Most refugees are still living in tents. The rectangular buildings near the main road are UNRWA boys' and girls' schools. Source: Ibdaᶜ Cultural Center, Dheisheh. Reprinted with permission.

FIGURE 2. Dheisheh in the early 1960s, a view from northeast with recently built UNRWA shelters in the background. Source: Ibdaᶜ Cultural Center, Dheisheh. Reprinted with permission.

FIGURE 3. Main entrance to Dheisheh camp in the late 1980s, blocked by Israel Defense Forces (IDF). Source: Ibdaᶜ Cultural Center, Dheisheh. Reprinted with permission.

FIGURE 4. IDF troops during a daily patrol in Dheisheh's main street in the late 1980s. Source: Ibdaᶜ Cultural Center, Dheisheh. Reprinted with permission.

FIGURE 5. Another entrance to Dheisheh camp blocked by the IDF, 1987. Photograph by Maya Rosenfeld.

FIGURE 6. Dheisheh in 1993, a view from the southwest. Photograph by Maya Rosenfeld.

FIGURE 7. Metal shield attached to the fence erected by the IDF along the entire western side of the camp, 1992. Graffiti (in Hebrew) reads, "It is cheaper to kill them." Photograph by Maya Rosenfeld.

FIGURE 8. Cactus in a flowerpot—Dheisheh in 2000, a view from inside the camp. Photograph by Miri Yehuda.

FIGURE 9 (left). Dheisheh in winter, 2000. Photograph by Miri Yehuda.

FIGURE 10. Children of the camp, 1987. Photograph by Maya Rosenfeld.

FIGURE 11 (above). The street as playground for Dheisheh children, 1987. Photograph by Maya Rosenfeld.

FIGURE 12. Grandmother and grandchildren at the entrance of a renovated UNRWA shelter, 1993. Photograph by Maya Rosenfeld.

FIGURE 13 (above). Carrying homemade bread (*raghif*) from the bakery, 1990. Photograph by Maya Rosenfeld.

FIGURE 14. Sister and brother, 1987. Photograph by Maya Rosenfeld.

FIGURE 15 (above). Mother and children against the wall of their UNRWA shelter, 1993. Facing months and years with little income, a family had to wait a long time before constructing a new house. Photograph by Maya Rosenfeld.

FIGURE 16. Mother and children in an improvised kitchen attached to an old UNRWA one-room shelter, 1993. Photograph by Maya Rosenfeld.

FIGURE 17 (above). A Dheisheh family at *iftar* (the meal
that breaks the Ramadan
fast), 1994. Photograph by
Maya Rosenfeld.

FIGURE 18. Mother saying
her prayers on the day before
visiting her imprisoned son,
1987. Photograph by Maya
Rosenfeld.

FIGURE 19 (above). Woman
preparing traditional pita
bread, or *raghif*, 1987. Photograph by Maya Rosenfeld.

FIGURE 20. Woman dressed
in traditional *fallaha* dress,
cutting off thyme leaves
before crushing them into a
powder, 1994. Photograph
by Maya Rosenfeld.

FIGURE 21. Grandmother and grandchildren on the roof of their home on a sunny winter day, 1994. Photograph by Maya Rosenfeld.

FIGURE 22. Memorial wall for the *shaheed* (martyr) Muhammad Abu-ᶜAker, in his parents' living room, 1992. Muhammad was lethally wounded by IDF soldiers in August 1988; he died in October 1990, at the age of eighteen. Photograph by Maya Rosenfeld.

FIGURE 23. Each generation and its ideologies and beliefs; top, a page from the Quran; bottom, a sketch of Lenin's head drawn by a young Dheishehan while in prison. Photograph by Maya Rosenfeld (1987).

FIGURE 24. Eleven-year-old Muhammad doing his homework outside his crowded two-room home, 1993. Photograph by Maya Rosenfeld.

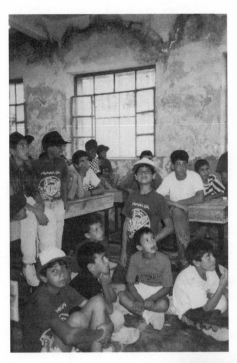

FIGURE 25. Children attending a summer camp in Dheisheh's old boys' school, 1991. Photograph by Maya Rosenfeld.

FIGURE 26. Summer camp for Dheisheh children in the courtyard of UNRWA's old boys' school, 1991. Photograph by Maya Rosenfeld.

FIGURE 27. At the courtyard of UNRWA's old boys' school, 2000. The newly built girls' school is visible to the right. Photograph by Miri Yehuda.

FIGURE 28. Dheisheh's new UNRWA girls' school, 2000. Construction was completed in 1997. Photograph by Miri Yehuda.

Professional Employment, Labor Migration, and the Multigenerational Family in Dheisheh

The Nine Children of Sheikh Abu Ibrahim Make History

THE SHEIKH'S SONS SET AN EARLY START

Since the death of his wife, Muhammad Abu-Laban, better known as Sheikh Abu Ibrahim, the retired imam of Dheisheh, divides his time between the homes of his sons, Saleh and Amjad. The first, in his midforties, had spent sixteen years in Israeli prisons and is currently a high-ranking officer with the PNA; the second, ten years younger, is an UNRWA official. Four other sons and one daughter have either migrated, were expelled, or left for studies abroad: "Nowadays, you can find us Abu-Labans wherever you go," the sheikh told me. "We have representatives in Eastern and Western Europe, in Africa, Saudi Arabia, and Jordan." Two other daughters, nurses by profession, live in Dheisheh and daily attend to their father's health problems.[1]

Muhammad Abu-Laban was in his late thirties, married and the father of three sons, when he arrived in Dheisheh in the summer of 1949 with his mother, two younger brothers, Ahmad and Mahmud, and their families. Back in Zakariya, their village of origin, Muhammad's father, the village sheikh, owned an average-sized plot of land as well as livestock, which the three brothers continued to own and tend together after his death in 1945. During the 1940s, however, each found employment outside the village, and agricultural cultivation became a secondary source of income up until 1947. Muhammad, the oldest, worked in Jaffa port and in construction in Jerusalem until his father's death, whereupon he inherited the sheikh's mantle. Ahmad, the only one in the family to complete school, became a policeman in the British forces, and Mahmud worked intermittently as a laborer and supervisor at an armament warehouse of the British army and as a shepherd in the village. The Abu-Labans fled Zakariya in October 1948 shortly before the arrival of the Jewish forces, seeking sanctuary in the village of Surif, which remained under control of the Jordanian army. From there they moved on to a central camp set up by the Red Cross near Jericho, and later to Dheisheh. The three families were provided with adjacent tents, which were eventually (in 1957) replaced by standard one-room UNRWA "shelter units" bordering on one another. "We carried out all our activities in that one room," the sheikh recalled. "There we slept, washed, cooked, and ate, and that was where the children read and did their homework."

Work was hard to find, and like the great majority of men in Dheisheh the three brothers sought whatever casual jobs they could get. Each worked intermittently in construction, forestation, and road paving in and outside the area. Toward the end of the first decade, Muhammad was appointed as imam of the Dheisheh mosque, a low-paying post financed by the Waqf, which he held on to for more than thirty-five years. The literate Ahmad became a low-ranking official—a registrar of marriage certificates and contracts in the Shari'a Court in Bethlehem, while Mahmud bought an oven and set up a small bakery in the camp, where he worked until 1967.

In the course of the 1950s and 1960s, Abu Ibrahim and his wife, Dalal al-Khatib (sister of teacher Mahmud al-Khatib), had three more sons and three daughters. The three oldest sons, the ones born in Zakariya, started elementary school during the 1950s and continued their studies through preparatory and high school. The eldest, Ibrahim, was among the first cohort of Dheishehians to graduate from high school (in 1961), and Mustafa, the second son, followed in his footsteps a year later. Ibrahim left for Saudi Arabia immediately after completing his studies and began teaching in a state-run school there in 1962. Every month he sent his parents a fixed sum, which enabled the younger siblings to continue their studies and allowed the family to add two new rooms to their home and to renovate the old UNRWA unit. Zohra, Ibrahim's sister, who was present during my conversation with her father, and who was only five years old when her brother left, broke in to make the point that "it was Ibrahim who lifted us from the depths. He was the first to leave, and a very big responsibility rested upon his shoulders." Indeed, the sheikh's family was among the first to build a new house in Dheisheh. What was to become a common phenomenon during the 1970s and 1980s was still a rarity in the mid-1960s when the first educated youngsters paved the way for those who would follow them to the Gulf states.

In Saudi Arabia, Ibrahim met and married a young teacher from Dheisheh who was working in the same district. They planned to return to the West Bank, Ibrahim sending money to his family so that they could build a house for him alongside theirs. However, being "absent from the area" at the time of the census conducted by Israel in September 1967, Ibrahim and his wife were denied their right of residence. When I interviewed family members, he had been teaching in Saudi Arabia for thirty-three years running. His wife and the four children live in Amman, where the family established its home. The degree and frequency of Ibrahim's financial assistance to his family in the camp significantly lessened after he married and started a family of his own, but he has not ceased assisting them, whether through sending personal gifts or through one-time sums that he gives on the occasion of his visits to the camp and at family reunions in Amman.

Mustafa, who completed high school in 1962, studied for two years at Birzeit, which at the time was still a teachers' training college. In 1964 he left for Bahrain, where he taught in a private school and held a second job as a clerk in a private firm. At the same time, he registered for external studies in English at Beirut Arab University, which he completed over the course of five years. During the period that he lived in Bahrain, Mustafa, like Ibrahim, the firstborn, also sent his family a fixed sum of money each month. When his work contract expired, Mustafa went to Jordan, and in 1969 he moved from there to Algeria, where he had been offered a teaching position in a state school. The salary in Algeria was substantially lower than what he had earned in the Persian Gulf, and the government also limited the amount of money residents could take out of the country, so that the value of the remittances that the family received declined.

Mustafa married a maternal cousin from Dheisheh. His sister, Yusra, intimated that he had wanted to marry an educated Algerian woman but that his father, the sheikh, had objected, and his mother then arranged the traditional match for him. During the 1970s the family hoped that Mustafa's resident wife would make it possible for him to rejoin his family, but the security forces, with the Abu-Laban family in their sights, conditioned "family reunification" on receiving "services" that Mustafa was loathe to provide. During the 1970s he remained in Algeria, where he was appointed school principal, and in the 1980s he worked in Jordan, Libya, and again in Jordan, where he lived in the mid-1990s with his family.

Sadeq, the third son, was in the last grade of high school when the 1967 war broke out, and his family, afraid of what might be in store, entreated him to leave Dheisheh and flee to the eastern side of the Jordan River. After the war, Sadeq was "stuck" in Jordan. He planned to study in Damascus but was late in registering for university and was conscripted into the Jordanian army. He visited the West Bank in 1971 after completing his army service and was arrested by the Israelis, interrogated, and expelled to Jordan. There too the authorities arrested him, even though he had the requisite papers attesting to his military service. Eventually, Sadeq did get to study, at first in Yugoslavia and later in Czechoslovakia. He had a partial scholarship and continued to receive assistance from his older brothers for many years. He married a Czech woman, to the great chagrin of his father, the sheikh, and a son was born to them: "You see," the sheikh smiled, "there is an Abu-Laban in Czechoslovakia too." After completing a master's degree in agricultural engineering, Sadeq worked for a while in Libya, returned to Czechoslovakia, completed a doctorate in veterinary sciences, and went on to work in a number of countries in Africa. Sadeq did not send money to his family in the camp. His studies extended over a period of many years, and it was only during the 1980s that he achieved economic independence.

BACK TO SQUARE ONE

In April 1970 Saleh, the fifth child of Abu and Umm Ibrahim, then seventeen and an eleventh-grade student, was arrested. Accused of membership in an armed organization, he was sentenced to twenty-five years in prison. One of those sentenced along with Saleh was his cousin Muhammad (son of Ahmad, the official in the Shari'a Court), who was the same age and lived next door. A short while after the beginning of the trial, the Israeli authorities dynamited the family homes of Saleh, Muhammad, and a third boy from Dheisheh who also belonged to the group.

Nothing remained of the new house built with money from the labor of Ibrahim and Mustafa. Even furniture and personal possessions of members of the household were buried beneath the rubble, and the family, then numbering nine persons, moved into an abandoned UNRWA shelter. Only five years later did the authorities permit them to rebuild their home.

THE SHEIKH'S DAUGHTERS GET THE FAMILY BACK ON ITS FEET

The same year that Saleh was arrested, his sister Yusra (born in 1951) completed high school. Yusra was the eldest of the daughters in the family, and her memories of childhood abound with descriptions of the burden of the household chores that were her lot. It was she who helped her mother with the difficult work, baking bread, lugging water home, cleaning and cooking, and especially caring for the five younger brothers and sisters. "I remember that wherever I went, at least two infants trailed behind me. To this day my younger brothers call me 'mother.'" She was not a good student in high school, nor did she recall receiving any special help or encouragement, but despite it all she completed her studies and passed her matriculation exams. Her brother Mustafa, then working in Algeria, suggested that she join him and teach Arabic in the school where he worked, but the sheikh objected to the idea.

Yusra decided to study nursing in the Caritas Baby Hospital in Bethlehem. She and another young woman from Dheisheh were the first ones from the camp to study and work in that institution, thereby paving the way for dozens of other Dheishehian girls. Nursing was not yet accepted as a female profession, and those of Yusra's classmates who continued studies did so mostly in the teachers' college for women. Her father was not happy with the idea of a young woman working among men: "They preferred teaching, work in a girls' school, without contact between males and females. I told my father that I wanted to try it. After he learned that the entire staff consisted of women, some of them nuns, and that the doctors were present only during the daily visits, he gave his consent."

Studies at Caritas lasted for two years, and Yusra saw them as a personal challenge no less than a professional one. She received high grades and, as she took pains to note, she avoided socializing with men in order to ensure that gossip would not reflect on her behavior. While still studying, Yusra received her first student training salary, and in 1972 her certificate (as Dheishehians say, "diplom"). She began full-time work in the hospital and thereby became the main provider for her family; except for the meager salary of the imam, there was no other regular source of income. Yusra did not marry until 1977, and for the six intervening years her entire salary went to her parents, who, among other things, managed to rebuild their home. In retrospect, she has no complaints, explaining that it was both her choice and her duty; moreover, she rejected several marriage proposals in order to continue supporting her family. A similar process took place in the household of Ahmad, the sheikh's brother and neighbor, who died shortly after his home was demolished in 1970. Ahmad's daughter Jamila completed high school in 1971, a year after the arrest of her brother Muhammad, comrade of Saleh, and the demolition of the house. She studied nursing in Caritas and became the main provider for her family until her own relatively late marriage.

In 1977 Yusra married Ahmad, a teacher in Dheisheh who is not a relative. It was a traditional marriage arranged by her eldest brother and her father, although the behind-the-scenes matchmaker was actually a female colleague of Yusra's at work. Once married, Zohra, the next daughter in line, took Yusra's place. Born in 1956, Zohra was fourteen years old when their home was demolished, and the details remained vivid for her: "In the afternoon jeeps, armored cars, engineering units, and security forces arrived and closed off the neighborhood. They gave us half an hour to remove what we could, moved the people away from the detonation site, and blew up our home. Afterward the people assembled as if at a funeral . . . it was the first house demolished by the army."

She too went to high school but did not complete twelve grades due to the family's economic situation: "Saleh's arrest and the demolition of the house set us back ten years," she explained. In 1975 Zohra registered to study nursing at Caritas, and this time the move had the support and encouragement of her father and mother. She started working full-time in 1977, the year of Yusra's marriage, and like her sister, she turned over all her earnings to her parents. In 1978 Zohra became engaged to Ahmad, her paternal cousin (son of Mahmud who had owned the bakery), a preferred match for both families; but she was obliged to wait three more years to marry until he could build a room.

Ahmad had been imprisoned for two years (1974–76) for membership in an illegal organization, headed by Youssef, another paternal cousin and neighbor (son of his uncle Ahmad). Having taken his matriculation exams in prison, Ahmad studied nursing after his release and then sought work in the Gulf. Failing to secure employment, he returned to the West Bank, where he faced additional difficulty; because of his prison record, the security forces prevented him from being hired at any of the government hospitals. He finally found work in Makassed hospital in Jerusalem, saved his wages, and built a separate room next to his father's house. Ahmad describes his marriage to his first cousin as "free choice": "I married my wife, who happens to be my paternal cousin (*bint-ʿammi*), because she appealed to me. Over the years I met many women who weren't relatives, but she was the only one I wanted. With us Dheishehians, there's no obligation to marry a relative."

The third to study at Caritas was Khawla, five years younger than Zohra (born in 1961). This time it was the sheikh himself who urged his daughter to study nursing. Khawla commented that she would have preferred going to university, but economic hardship eliminated the possibility. "On the other hand, in Caritas you learn, work, and earn money at the same time, and that's considered a real advantage." But after one year of training, she was married to a Dheishehian and followed him to Saudi Arabia. Her early marriage and the interruption of her studies were not of her choosing. Khalil, the bridegroom, was the cousin of Yusra's husband, and the match was agreed upon between the families. Ibrahim, Khawla's eldest brother, sanctioned the arrangement from Saudi Arabia where both he and Khalil were working, Ibrahim as a teacher and Khalil as a translator for a foreign investment concern.

MARRIAGES AND NEW HOUSEHOLDS

Following the marriages of the three daughters, only Amjad and Ziad, the two younger sons, then students in secondary school, remained in the Abu-Laban household. The family managed somehow on the salary of the sheikh, who was already in his seventies. They lived in the new house built with the salaries of Yusra and Zohra: two very small bedrooms, a kitchen, and bathroom; the top floor remained unfinished for another fifteen years.

Yusra and Ahmad.   Upon her marriage in 1977, Yusra went to live with Ahmad in his parents' home. For the first six years, the couple and their two small children lived with Ahmad's parents, his six brothers and sisters, and his grandmother. At the time, Ahmad's father was a day laborer working in Israel, and the family lived on his earnings and those of Ahmad, who was then employed as a teacher in an elementary school in Beit Jala. After completing his studies, Ahmad's brother left for work in Saudi Arabia and began to support the family on a regular basis. Yusra, who continued her job at Caritas, did not contribute money to the household of her in-laws. She saved most of her salary, and when the sum reached a thousand Jordanian dinars she and her husband began to build a new house next to that of his parents. The construction extended over a period of three years and was almost solely the work of Ahmad himself, with Yusra's salary covering most of the costs. In 1983 they moved into their new and relatively spacious home of three bedrooms, a guest room, a kitchen, and a bathroom. Ahmad and Yusra had six children, three boys and three girls. The boys were all born with serious physical deformities, and the eldest (who died at age fifteen) also suffered from severe mental retardation.

As of 1996, Yusra has been working at Caritas for more than twenty-five years, accumulated maximum seniority, and has attained the status of deputy chief nurse in the hospital. She has worked continuously, except for short maternity leaves lasting a number of weeks. This was made possible because Caritas maintains a day care center for infants three months and older, and a nursery school that goes up to age five for the children of the nurses and the other female maintenance and service employees. Ahmad continued working as a teacher in government schools, and today he teaches English in an elementary school in Doha, located next to Dheisheh. Until the period of closures, he would work in Israel as a construction worker during summer vacations. In 1992, with twenty-two years of seniority in teaching, Ahmad was earning about one thousand shekels a month (approximately $350), without any pension fund contributions. Yusra's salary, the maximum that a practical nurse could earn in Caritas, was then about twelve hundred shekels a month; the hospital also set aside a monthly sum in pension funds for its entire staff.

Yusra loves her work in Caritas. She is greatly appreciated by the administration and the staff, and her attitude toward the profession is imbued with a sense of responsibility and devotion. According to her, she has not missed one workday since she began to work and was late only once, a day when there was a heavy snowfall. Over the years she has acquired considerable knowledge of pediatrics and quite a broad English medical vocabulary. Her way of life is spartan, the work exhausting, with day and night shifts lasting six and a half hours, and she devotes to her household hours that equal or surpass the time she spends on the job. Before and after her work shifts, she cooks, bakes, launders (she has a washing machine), and bathes and cares for the children. The home of Yusra and Ahmad is well looked after and pleasant.

The guest room is modestly and simply furnished and, like the rest of the home, meticulous.

Bassel, their eldest, was born retarded and deformed, a severe blow to the couple. In the absence of treatment and rehabilitation institutions in the West Bank, the burden of raising the child fell completely upon the parents and the younger siblings. Yusra speaks with envy and anger of the medical and social services available to retarded children in Israel compared with the complete neglect in the Territories. The degree of Bassel's retardation necessitated constant supervision; though he was able to walk and run he was unable to speak, control his bodily functions, or feed himself. On more than one occasion he was the cause of anguish when he disappeared from the house during a curfew, wandered around the camp, and was held by soldiers. Yusra notes that, to Ahmad's credit, he did not leave her after she brought what she refers to as "abnormal children" into the world: "The Arab man usually remarries and leaves the wife who has given birth to abnormal children. But my husband is different . . . he loves me and helps me a lot. He would feed Bassel, bathe him, and change his clothes. He has always gone out of his way to treat me well."

Bassel died in the summer of 1994 after a fall that caused a cerebral hemorrhage. During the ten days preceding his death, Yusra set up an "emergency treatment center" in her home after finding that her son was poorly supervised in the hospital. She consulted the doctors, attached her son to intravenous drips herself, and shared the "duty roster" with Ahmad. During the first days after Bassel's death, hundreds of mourners from Dheisheh visited their home; indeed, the entire camp made its appearance.

Zohra and Ahmad.   Although Zohra and her husband, also named Ahmad, started their marital life in their own separate, albeit very small space, they continued to shoulder the burden of his parents' household for several years. Ahmad's father had stopped working in the mid-1970s, most of his brothers were youngsters still in school, the older brothers and sisters had not yet found regular work, and the entire family (nine persons) was crowded into two old UNRWA rooms, compelling Ahmad to give a substantial part of his salary to their support. The situation improved in the middle of the 1980s, after two sons sought work abroad, one in Saudi Arabia and the other in Jordan, and one daughter, a teacher, joined the family workforce. With their savings Ahmad and Zohra built two additional rooms, and for the past ten years they have been living in relatively comfortable conditions.

Ahmad and Zohra have similar seniority and similar salaries (in 1992 Zohra earned twelve hundred shekels per month, and Ahmad earned about thirteen hundred). They keep track of the household expenses and savings together, and together decide on all matters concerning family planning. At the time that I interviewed them in the summer of 1992, they had one daughter and two sons, and Zohra indicated that that would suffice. In the meantime, another daughter has been born. Zohra commented that the "old ladies" (her mother-in-law and her aunts) kept pressing all the time for her to have more and more children. She has friends who married after her and today have six or seven children, but there are also others, teachers and nurses, with fewer children—two or three. If she hadn't been working, she would have five children, Zohra declared.

The work in shifts makes it necessary for Ahmad to share the responsibility for the household, but Zohra says that his participation is minimal, being limited to supervising the children. "He does not clean and does not cook. I need to prepare everything in advance." Unlike her sister Yusra, Zohra does not particularly enjoy her work at Caritas. While suitable due to the relatively short shifts, she finds the work boring.

Every month Ahmad turns over a fixed sum of money to his father, as does the brother living in Saudi Arabia and the brother who has returned from Jordan. But this is a small sum; today Ahmad's parents' household is sustained mainly by the salary of his sister, Inshirah, who has remained single and for the past ten years has lived with the family and worked as a teacher.

Khawla and Khalil. I met Khawla in the summer of 1992 during a family visit she made with her husband and children to Dheisheh. Between their marriage in 1980 and this visit, Khawla and Khalil had changed their residence four times, living in three Saudi Arabian cities following changes in Khalil's place of work. Khalil had completed his high school studies with distinction, studied English in a Jordanian university, and had gone to Saudi Arabia in the mid-1970s to work as a translator. After his marriage to Khawla, the couple lived in Riyadh where Khalil worked in the office of an American investment firm. Two years later he signed an employment contract with a Norwegian company, and the family moved to the city of Buraydah. With their high income the family rented a spacious home. When the contract terminated, Khalil was engaged as personnel manager in a large Saudi Arabian investment and development company owned by the royal family, and his family moved to the city of Jiddah. Indirect influences of the Iran-Iraq War led to cutbacks in the company and reduced salary, and Khalil left to work in Riyadh with an American investment firm; there he was employed at the time I met his wife.

Khawla had very little to say of the twelve years spent in Saudi Arabia. A housewife, she raised four children in relative comfort, with excellent housing conditions, private school for the children, and a family car. At the same time, Khawla says that the outlays for rent, the children's education, and so on, were extensive, and that Khalil also turned over part of his earnings to his family in Dheisheh. She did not work because she did not have a diploma and the pay scale for nonprofessional nurses was particularly low; according to Khawla, Egyptians and Filipinos commonly do such work. She has suffered especially from the Saudi laws limiting women's freedom of movement. She leaves her home only when accompanied by her husband and must wear traditional Islamic attire. In Dheisheh the fact that her father was an imam at a mosque had never prevented her from wearing jeans or from coming and going as she chose. In Saudi Arabia all her acquaintances and those of her husband are Palestinians, some of them relatives living and working in Riyadh. She has almost no contact with either male or female Saudi Arabians. Every month Khawla and Khalil set aside about two hundred dinars toward building a home for themselves. They have bought land in Bethlehem and plan to return to the West Bank when they have enough money to build and furnish a home.

I doubt that Khawla's life in Saudi Arabia could be called luxurious, but that is how it seems to her sister Yusra. "Khawla lives a life of luxury in Saudi Arabia. Her husband gives her everything. I work and everything goes to the family, and my whole life revolves around that. That's the difference."

Saleh and Fadwa.   Saleh was released from prison in the Jibril exchange of May 1985, fifteen years and one month after he had been arrested. A short time after his release he married Fadwa, his maternal cousin (daughter of Khadija, she too a sister of Mahmud al-Khatib, the "first teacher"), who was then nineteen, thirteen years his junior. Although the kinship ties, significant age difference, and short premarital acquaintance are usually indicative of traditional marriages, Fadwa says that hers was one of choice and not an arranged match. According to her, the two families had not been on good terms, and if not for Saleh's persistence in wanting her for his wife the wedding would not have taken place.

Fadwa is the daughter of the late Ibrahim Youssef, a self-educated intellectual, a local leader of the Jordanian Communist Party, and a male nurse by profession; he died shortly before her marriage. Youssef was in prison for seven years during the period of Jordanian rule and for two more years under the Israeli Occupation, when he was already in his fifties. At home he kept a fairly extensive library that attracted many of the educated and young in Dheisheh, who sought the wisdom of the librarian no less than the use of his books. Fadwa recalls her father as nurturing social and political awareness in her and her sisters and brothers, encouraging them to acquire a wide-ranging education while treating daughters and sons equally.

At the beginning of the 1970s Fadwa went to a private kindergarten in Bethlehem, something very unusual at the time. She and a number of her siblings completed their secondary studies at a private school and not in the government school, as was the general rule. Her oldest brother and her three sisters studied at a university in Moscow; the brother studied medicine, her oldest sister studied pharmacy and laboratory management, her second sister studied communications and journalism, and the third sister studied dentistry. At the time of the interview, her younger brother was studying nuclear physics in Germany. Except for the youngest, all four received scholarships through the Palestine Communist Party. The exceptional emphasis placed on education and achievements is outstanding, in view of the family's situation. For many years (during the time that Ibrahim Youssef was in prison and after he became ill), the family managed on the mother's earnings as a cleaning woman in institutions and private homes in both the West Bank and Israel.

The transition from her parents' home to the home of Saleh's family was not easy for Fadwa, who was used to having a great deal of freedom and independence. Her father and mother had permitted her to invite male friends and colleagues from school and from work to visit in their home, which was unthinkable in the home of the sheikh. The atmosphere in her parental home, the way in which resources were allocated, and the attitude toward women were much more liberal than in Saleh's family.

When I pointed out to Fadwa that the sheikh's daughters had also acquired an education, she responded that they had studied nursing, a manifestly feminine profession. It was indeed very hard for Fadwa to get used to the change: "People would say to me that another woman wouldn't agree to live this kind of life, but I made an effort to overcome the problem. There were times when I was hurt, but that's nothing unusual." Her relations with Saleh were partial compensation for the difficult transition. Fadwa found many qualities in him that reminded her of her father: an ideological and emotional maturity, openness, willingness for partnership, and an egalitarian, nonexploitative attitude toward her.

Saleh, who had completed his matriculation exams in prison, began to study education at Bethlehem University in 1985, only a few months after his release. The couple, living in cramped conditions—a room created by the use of a moveable divider in the overcrowded home of Saleh's parents and younger brothers—made their living from a small stationery shop. After the birth of their first daughter, Fadwa began taking courses in computers and typing at the UNRWA vocational center in Ramallah and worked as a typist. At the beginning of the Intifada, Saleh was placed under administrative detention and remained in prison for a year. Fadwa found work at the UNRWA headquarters in Sheikh Jarah (in Arab Jerusalem) and later in another institution in Jerusalem, where she continued working after Saleh returned home and until he completed his studies in 1991. She also learned to drive and bought an old Fiat in order to get to work.

Meanwhile, Saleh's mother had died, his father retired from work in the mosque, Amjad married and left home, and the youngest brother, Ziad, went to Switzerland to complete his studies, marrying a local young woman there. Saleh traveled to Germany, where he earned a master's degree in education. In the wake of the Oslo Accords, he took on the management of the office of Fida (an offshoot of the Democratic Front for the Liberation of Palestine that supported the accords) in Bethlehem, a position he held until his later appointment as a high-ranking official in the PNA.

Fadwa, now a mother of three, enrolled in the department of social work at Bethlehem University and completed her degree in 1997. According to her, Saleh proved to be a supportive partner:

Our society is a male society. . . . Almost all the men believe that housework was intended solely for women, but there are also exceptions, and Saleh is certainly one. At times I would come home from the university very tired, and Saleh would tell me to go to sleep, and he would do all the housework. Because he has been in prison, he is used to taking care of himself and knows how to do all kinds of work. Prison turns out two kinds of people—either they are of outstanding qualities or else they are men with many emotional problems. I always told Saleh that prison turned him into a sensitive and friendly person, even as it made him tough and perhaps rigid . . .

Are the sons and daughters of the sheikh making history or is it that history has made, and continues to make, the sons and daughters of the sheikh? Marx's well-known observation, that people make history but under conditions and circumstances not of their own choosing, would seem applicable to the spirit of the following discussion.

The Sixties: Decade of the Migrant Sons

A number of factors combined to kindle the hope that the 1960s heralded a better era for the Abu-Laban family. Already at the beginning of the decade, when most Dheishehian families existed on the insecure income of day laborers, two mature sons were part of the professional salaried workforce. Another son completed his high school studies during that time, which should have ensured further continuity and stability of income.

What conditions were necessary in order that a family reap the benefits of the education and salaried work of its migrating offspring over an extended time period? The history of the Abu-Laban family shows that only to a small degree were these conditions under the control of the family or of the skilled workers themselves. In order to gain suitable employment, the sons were obliged to migrate, but there was no guarantee of success. On the face of it, the difference in the employment histories of Ibrahim and Mustafa was a matter of chance, but this chance reflects in microcosm the nature of the

Palestinian migration in search of work in the Gulf states. Some, like Ibrahim in Saudi Arabia, found quasi-permanent positions, and some, like Mustafa in Bahrain, stayed in the Gulf only for relatively short periods. From the standpoint of personal advancement, it is unclear which of the two "came out ahead," but as far as the family in the camp was concerned, work in Algeria, Mustafa's second migratory station, was a somewhat disappointing source of income. It is hard to predict what would have been the course of Sadeq's studies and employment had he not lost his right of residence in 1967 or been arrested and banished in 1971, but what *is* clear is that his extensive studies in Czechoslovakia removed him from the roster of family supporters and added him, at least for part of the time, to the list of those requiring support.

The land of migration thus determined, to a considerable extent, the scope of the assistance that the migrant workers could transfer to their families, but the decisions and wishes of these workers were of secondary importance—and sometimes of no importance at all—in determining the route of migration and the length of time spent in the countries in which they found work. Migration to Saudi Arabia and the other Gulf states was more profitable for the family, not only because salaries there were higher and because there were no limitations on the transfer of money from these countries, but also, and perhaps mainly, because of the temporary status of the migrant worker, who, without rights of citizenship, could not make full use of his income where he worked. Unable to become permanent residents, the migrants sent their savings to their families in Dheisheh where they also planned to build their future homes.

The degree to which the family in the camp would have the benefit of income transferred to it by a son depended not only upon the country of migration and the nature of the job, but also upon his commitment to his family. One might ask why a young man who had completed a course of study and found a well-paying position in a distant land would each month transfer a considerable portion of his salary to his family; why would he not make efforts toward rapid economic independence; why not free himself from family shackles? These questions may sound somewhat out of place when speaking of a pattern of behavior that was so pervasive that it might even be called normative. When asking a man why he turned over a large part of his salary to his family, the usual answer was "It was my duty," or "I owed it to those who raised me. They fed and taught me all those years and I paid them back," or "That's how it is with us Arabs, not as with others, where each is concerned only about himself." Some emphasized being the eldest as the reason for their greater obligation to paving the way for their younger brothers and sisters.

Indeed, there are well-defined social and cultural expectations of sons who have completed their studies and emigrated in search of work. I have listened to more than one mother label a son who could not find work in Saudi Arabia or Kuwait as "a failure" and lament that "all that we invested in him has been for naught" or "no good ever came to us from him." A son's departure for one of the Gulf states is, in the eyes of most Dheishehians, synonymous with remittances. These expectations, of course, also feed the consciousness of the migrant workers, who do not want to disappoint or to give themselves and their families a bad name.

Yet, the very fact that in many instances the obligation is only met partially, or for a brief period of time, and in some cases not at all (for example, in the case of Sadeq), indicates that the matter has additional facets, some of them more practical in nature than the cultural explanations that rest chiefly on deeply rooted norms and traditions. Ongoing financial support from the migrant son for his family in the camp is perhaps less an expression of past traditions than it is the product of the conditions and constraints of migrant labor. Those who acquired academic skills and worked in socialist countries, or who worked in less prosperous Arab countries, did not become regular participants in their families' support. The regular transfer of remittances by sons who worked in the Gulf states and "fulfilled their obligation" was linked to the dependence of these sons upon their families.

While the family in the camp was indeed lacking in means, the migrant son in Saudi Arabia, a foreign, temporary resident excluded from local society, often needed his family to arrange his marriage and build his house. The incongruence of the relatively high income of the migrant worker in the Gulf and the denial of civil and political rights there contributed to the ongoing dependency upon the family in the camp, which in turn further strengthened the obligation of remittances. This perspective does not exclude the moral and cultural components of the obligation, but rather attempts to enmesh them within their practical and other complexities.

Thus, consideration of the sons migrating in search of work reveals a process replete with contradictions; related, at least in the above instances, to the incongruity between amelioration of the migrant's economic position and his circumscribed social status. One of the salient manifestations of this anomaly, which yielded reinforcement rather than disintegration of ties with the family of origin, was the custom of endogamous marriages and arranged marriages, well in place even for the migrant workers living thousands of miles away from the camp. There are, of course, examples where migration and the ensuing distance from the family helped create new and independent ties between men and women (as in the case of Ibrahim himself). But even in these instances, the new ties are primarily relations between migrants and other migrants, and mainly of those with a common background—such as between men and women from the same refugee camp. The formalization of these ties was dependent upon the approval and involvement of the families in the camp. Mustafa, for example, was forced to accept the dictates of the family and forgo a marriage to the Algerian woman he loved. His temporary status and his uncertain future as a migrant worker brought him to subordinate his personal affairs to the wishes of his family.

The intertwining of the economic dependence of the families upon their migrant children with the social dependence of the migrants upon their families of origin contributed greatly to the preservation of patriarchal relations within the family. An indication of the perpetuation of social relations of authority and hierarchy, despite the stay abroad, can be found in the instance of Khawla's marriage. Ibrahim, who had left Dheisheh for Saudi Arabia in 1961, the year his sister was born, arranged her marriage in 1980, approximately twenty years later.

Israeli policy, which prevented the return to the West Bank of Palestinians who were living outside the country in 1967, made its contribution to these emigrants' separation from their families. But at the same time another process was taking place. Almost every family in Dheisheh included a branch that had sought refuge in the East Bank of Jordan following the 1967 war. These family branches settled in Jordan, especially in Amman and Zarka, and often became a second tier of social support for the migrant workers in the Persian Gulf. Those, like Ibrahim, who lost their right of residence as a result of the 1967 war or following it, built their permanent homes in Jordan, usually with help from, and in close proximity to, their relatives.

Distance had a greater impact upon those who acquired an education and training in the socialist countries and who remained there for extensive periods of time. This group had not arrived in new countries as migrant workers but rather with the status of foreign students. The education of such individuals was in spheres demanding lengthy training (medicine, science, engineering, law)—in certain cases (especially medical specialization) lasting for more than ten years. The studies usually took place in settings that included foreign students from many countries, especially those of the third world, alongside local students, creating opportunities for acquaintanceships and the possibility of forming romantic ties.[2]

Also significant was the duration of the migrant sons' regular support for their families in the camp. Usually, the marriage of the son constituted the limiting factor in the ongoing transfer of remittances, as in the instance of Ibrahim. As long as the son was single, he sent home a fixed sum at regular intervals, with part of that money usually being set aside for building a house or rooms for him. After marriage, and especially after the birth of children, the assistance would lessen and gradually become occasional support in the form of one-time allocations and/or generous gifts bestowed at family gatherings and during holiday seasons.

The importance of the assistance sent by the married sons should not be underestimated, whether as expenditures for building rooms for younger brothers or for financing their studies (as in the case of Sadeq). But regular support of the family comes to an end. Thus, the significant contribution of the migrant son to his family's income is made during the time between his migration and his marriage. The "golden age" of the Abu-Laban family was therefore short, lasting for the few years when both Ibrahim and Mustafa were single and Mustafa was employed in Bahrain.

Regular income arriving from the migrant workers was channeled into meeting the immediate needs of the family—first and foremost improved living conditions and current expenses—thus enabling the younger siblings to continue their studies. Despite the structural limitations described here, the changes in the standard of living of the family of origin were definitely significant during the period under discussion, that preceding the 1967 war, especially in light of the poor living conditions in the camp. The outcome of the war and the Occupation policies severed the chain that Sadek was in line to continue, while the collective punishment that accompanied Saleh's arrest destroyed, together with the house, the relative advantage that had accrued to the Abu-Laban family during the 1960s.

The Seventies: Decade of the Working Daughters

Zohra's comment that Saleh's arrest and the demolition of the house "put us back ten years" encapsulates the extremity of the setback that marked the turn of the new decade. Yet "the decade of the working daughters," which succeeded that of "the migrant sons," was to put the Abu-Laban family back on its feet.

Yusra was one of the pioneers among the Dheishehian women who would study nursing and do their internships at the Caritas Baby Hospital. Her confrontation with her family before and during her studies, and the supreme efforts she made to please her father, puts the earlier discussion of the nursing profession in a slightly different light. In discussing the structure of employment opportunities during the Israeli Occupation, I described nursing as a markedly "feminine" profession that became the most accessible employment alternative for Dheishehian women with an education. But the case of Yusra shows that what was to become a common enough phenomenon by the end of the 1970s, a fact of life, was achieved by means of a resolute struggle. Interestingly enough, the development transforming nursing into a profession that was recognized, legitimate, and even preferred took place within a brief number of years. The rapidity of the change can be seen in the experiences of the Abu-Laban family. Abu Ibrahim, who had feared for his eldest daughter's reputation, gladly accepted the idea that Zohra, five years Yusra's junior, would go off to study and work in Caritas, and it was he who pressed Khawla, five years younger than Zohra, to follow in her footsteps.

The Abu-Laban family did not invest a great deal in the education of its daughters. The fact that Yusra completed high school while caring for her younger siblings and also doing burdensome housework deserves special mention. Zohra did not complete high school, and Khawla did not have the opportunity for university study as she had wished. The girls' postsecondary studies were channeled in advance to bringing home an income. In fact, nursing is the shortest course of higher education that also provides an opportunity for immediate wage earning. The combination of a minimum investment, a quick return, and the fact that the nursing studies and the work in the hospitals took place in what was predominantly a feminine and "protected" setting can explain why Sheikh Abu Ibrahim changed his mind within such a short time.

For six consecutive years Yusra turned over her entire salary to her parents and was the main wage earner for her family. A working unmarried daughter transfers her entire income to her parents, except for small amounts that she keeps for minor expenses. Unlike her unmarried brother, she does not set aside any funds toward her future marriage and the building of her house. The explanation commonly proffered for this difference by Dheishehians, including the working women themselves, is that the costs of the marriage always fall upon the groom/husband, and the woman, being free of them, can release her income for the sake of her family. While congruent with the Quranic imperative that places the burden of providing for the family exclusively on the shoulders of men, this widely accepted rationalization does not stand the test of the Dheishehian reality, wherein the share of family support provided by working women often outweighs that of their spouses, fathers, or brothers. Rather, I attribute the difference in the patterns of income appropriation mainly to the family of origin's capacity to exercise maximum control over the lives and resources of its unmarried daughters, despite the conspicuous changes that have occurred in the realms of education and employment of women.

Anchored in religion and tradition, this ability to control is sustained by the conditions defining the situation of the unmarried working woman; primarily, the institutions wherein the women acquired their professional training, their work settings, and their continued residence in their parents' homes during the entire period of "spinsterhood." In the large majority of cases, acquiring postsecondary training and engaging in (semi)professional work has taken place in settings that do not afford the women an opportunity to enjoy social freedom and independence: colleges and seminaries set up for women only, schools for girls, and hospitals employing women nurses almost exclusively. To a certain extent, these institutions contributed to the persistence of the social control over women and neutralized the liberating potential of acquiring an education. From another perspective, lacking any alternatives, single working daughters continued to reside in their parents' homes, that is, in the bosom of families raising numerous children, under difficult housing conditions and without privacy. In such circumstances, it is difficult, perhaps impossible, for a young single woman to utilize her income for her own needs—for example, to purchase her own table or cupboard, or such items as a radio, television, or videocassette recorder, not to mention the building or furnishing of a room of her own. The only personal expenses appearing in her budget are likely to include her clothing and shoes.

Family control over the unmarried working daughter's resources notwithstanding, the entire household economy was dependent on the salary of one entry-level nurse, which was extended to cover the immediate expenses of eight persons. During the mid-1970s, more than a few Dheishehian families whose members were day laborers in Israel repaired their homes or built new ones, thereby "overtaking" the Abu-Labans, who had held an advantage during the previous decade. Yusra's employment enabled her family to get by, but little more than that. While it is true that the familial framework acted to constrain and dominate the single working daughter, this was not a system that conveyed profits and property to the strong at the expense of the weak.

Still, taken together, the years of the unmarried daughters' employment granted the family a full decade (from 1971 to 1981) of steady income, something that not even the migrant sons had been able to provide. This lengthy continuity was also made possible by means that might be called artificial, first and foremost the prolongation of the unmarried status of the working daughters. It is doubtful whether Yusra and Zohra would share this assessment—Yusra believes with all her heart that she remained single until age twenty-six by her own choice in order to help her family. Yet in a community where arranged marriages are the norm and where the average age of women at first marriage has remained low, it is difficult to accept that the extended unmarried period was a matter completely outside the family's calculation and interest.

The common practice of arranged early marriage, rather than that of delayed marriage, has received the most attention from students of kinship and patriarchy in Arab societies and cultures. Family-arranged early marriage in the context of patrilocal residence and a patrilineal descent system has been identified as a salient manifestation of the control of family over the lives of its daughters (and sons). The prolonging of the spinsterhood of women with higher education and a profession emerges here as an expression of similar control in circumstances and conditions that underwent profound transformation.

The fact that the three daughters in the family, all with postsecondary education, were wed in traditional marriages—one marrying her first paternal cousin—is consistent with the explanation suggested here for the social status of single working women. In short, while far-reaching changes have occurred in the realm of education and employment of women belonging to the middle and younger generations, no similar transformation has followed in the domain of social relations within the family of origin. This is, in effect, a case of uneven development.

Upon Zohra's marriage, her family of origin went back to bare subsistence on the low salary of the elderly imam, and the relative stability of the "decade of the working daughters" gave way to the decline of the 1980s. On the face of it, the retreat can be attributed to the sociobiological life cycle—the parents reach old age and the adult sons and daughters leave home—in other words, an inevitable natural process. But of interest here are the structural limits of the socioeconomic process that determined the standard of living of the family of origin.

Absent, or nearly so, were factors that would help enable the single migrant teachers and locally based nurses to reap the social potential of their earning power. As long as they remained unmarried, relations of control and dependency—differentiated along gender lines and other variables, and nourished by a paramount notion of obligation—bounded these sons and daughters to the family of origin. Intrafamily mechanisms and extrafamily circumstances thus stretched to the limits the "life span" of the multigeneration family of origin as a joint economic unit of parents and their adult working children. Translation of the economic potential of professional work into changed social status was postponed until the next stage: disengagement from the family.

The duration of the Abu-Labans' period of relative prosperity notwithstanding, the improvement in their standard of living depended upon elements that were essentially temporary. Once the migrant sons established families of their own, and the working daughters finally left home, no reserves remained that sufficed for the aging father to give up his low-paying job. The family of origin was forced to retreat.

Transforming Socioeconomic Relations Within the Family

New families were established by professionally and/or semiprofessionally employed men and women in Dheisheh. In examining the socioeconomic relations within these families, the perspective again centers on the status of women.

The starting point is far from promising. The daughter who leaves her father's home does so only when she marries; in most cases marriages are arranged by the family. It is not only that the family of origin controls the present of the employed single daughter; it also places its stamp upon her future. Apart from denial of independence and freedom of choice for the young woman, marriage commonly entails a high degree of compliance with those in another extended family. Most often the first stage of matrimonial life ensues in the husband's family of origin, either within a joint home or in a room or apartment appended to it. In cases involving a couple in which the husband or both spouses are day laborers, this first stage is likely to persist for decades.

Upon her marriage, Yusra, who until age twenty-six had worked for her father's household, became a part of an extended family, also with numerous children and very limited resources. The lack of privacy that had been her lot in the home of her parents became more severe when she became a wife and a mother of two crowded into an apartment occupied by the family of her father-in-law. Zohra also shared a household with her in-laws, despite living in a separate room with her husband. As long as her husband's brothers and sister did not enter the labor force, Zohra and Ahmad's separate living space remained more symbolic than actual.

The premarried years of Saleh's wife, Fadwa, were very different from those of the Abu-Laban daughters, since her family had granted its daughters exceptional opportunities in the realms of education and personal freedom. Nonetheless, it lived and functioned inside the much more conservative environment of the camp. The family did not force Fadwa to marry, but neither could they protect their daughter from the daily ramifications of the match she chose. Even the fact that Fadwa married a released prisoner—one with relatively radical social beliefs concerning the status of women—was not sufficient to spare her the difficulties of adjustment imposed by life in the common household with his family.

Though the stage of common domicile in the household of the husband's family is characterized more by continuation than by change in the social status of the newlywed working women (or by retrogression, as in the case of Fadwa), with hindsight it can be seen as a transitional period. The goal of almost every married woman in Dheisheh, young or old, educated or not, with or without waged work, is to live in her own home. For a non-wage-earning woman, construction of a separate house or apartment depends upon the economic ability of the husband and is influenced by the situation of his parents' family and the extent of his obligation to them. In the case of Yusra, it was her income that enabled the building of the new separate house and hastened the end of the transitional stage; had she not been working and saving her money for this purpose, moving out of her in-laws' household would have been delayed for many years.

The case of Zohra illustrates the same point. Had she not earned money after her marriage, it is reasonable to assume that the need to manage on her husband's salary alone, and his commitment to his parents' household, would have delayed their house building. In fact, had Zohra not continued working, her marriage to her first cousin would have become a double bind for her. Marriage to such a close relative is thought to inhibit conflicts between wife and in-laws and is taken as a guarantee of her obedience and compliance. She is expected to refrain from complaining when her husband contributes to his parents' household rather than to the couple's personal needs. Being a working woman with a monthly income allowed Zohra to concern herself with her own future without entering into conflict with her in-laws. Thus, women who remain in the labor force after marriage facilitate the process of separating their nuclear families from their extended family.

In the final analysis the status of an employed married woman in her new family is determined by her work and her income. While her education and her role as provider do not lead to a significant change in her social situation within her father's household, these elements are decisive in improving her position in her new family. The corollary is that even though arranged marriage is a clear expression of the inferior status of an employed single daughter in her father's household, and despite the initial impact upon the daughter's future, such a marriage does not block the path of an employed married woman to various advantages in managing her life within her own nuclear family.

Since the marriages of Yusra and Ahmad in 1977 and of Zohra and Ahmad in 1981, their family lives have differed substantively from what they knew growing up. Each family now depends upon the regular salaries of two semiprofessionals. The family's daily schedule revolves around the work shift of the mother outside the home, and there is family planning. The homes are more spacious and well equipped, enabling a certain degree of privacy and comfort even for the children. Decisions are taken together, with joint planning of current expenses and of more long-range allocation of resources. Finally, the husband helps, even if only to a limited degree, in the care and supervision of the children.

It might be argued that such changes and improvements, or some of them, would occur in time even if the woman was not working and if the family was dependent upon the income of the man alone. But such an argument is not supported by my findings in Dheisheh, which, as indicated in Chapter 6, point to the increased proportion of women among the members of the younger generation in the camp who hold steady positions of employment. The emergence in the 1970s of a "new" type of household that was guaranteed regular employment is thus largely understood in this context. Moreover, the income of a single wage earner is not sufficient to maintain a reasonable standard of living for a family. Work in public institutions such as hospitals and schools brought in salaries that ranged between approximately one thousand shekels in "government" institutions and about thirteen hundred shekels in private institutions in 1995, a time when a family of four required more than two thousand shekels simply to cover basic current expenses. In other words, two regular salaries were an essential precondition for ameliorating the low standard of living characteristic of the camp, and a minimal basis for long-term planning.

One of the salient expressions of the transformation in such households with two breadwinners is reflected in the link between employment, on the one hand, and family planning and the conditions for women as mothers, on the other. A woman's salary earned her a say in the matter of birth control. The decrease in the number of children in the family, which reduced the burden of home and child care substantially, was directly related to the women's daily schedule as wage earners employed outside the home. In families that were started by members of the middle and younger generations in which the man was the sole breadwinner, women gave birth to seven or eight children.

The case of Khawla and Khalil is an example of a different course of development, one that could not have materialized under the conditions then existing in Dheisheh. Here a sharp rise in the standard of living and a change in lifestyle were not attained through the work of the woman. The integration of Khalil, the migrant worker, into the private labor market in Saudi Arabia—a path much less accessible than employment in the public-government sector, albeit replete with its own hazards—rendered rapid economic mobility possible. But while Khawla was not obliged to work, her relative material comfort was secured at the cost of social isolation, marginality, and adherence to the Saudi regulations—both official and unofficial—that discriminate against the woman and constrain her, especially if she is not employed.

It was not the mere participation of women in the labor force, however, but rather their relatively stable and protected position within it and the (semi)professional nature of their employment that served as impetus to, and vehicle for, the changes in the standard and style of living of the new families in Dheisheh. This conclusion is strengthened by comparison with the findings pertaining to the work life of female day laborers and their central role in supporting their families. Though crucial for the livelihood of many Dheishehian families, the returns from female day wage labor were shown to be insufficient to ensure family economic security and to promote significant changes in the social status of its carriers.

The venue for professional and semiprofessional work for women was public institutions, especially hospitals and schools, which guaranteed steady, long-term employment and income. Although the salaries themselves were low, they amounted to double or more the average wages of day laborers. Moreover, institutions not administered by the Civil Administration granted their employees various social welfare benefits. It was this improved position of the female employee in the labor market that became a necessary condition, even if not always a sufficient one, for inducing changes in family life.

Furthermore, unlike the work life of a cleaning lady, kitchen worker, or harvest hand, the work of a nurse or a teacher (the two most common professions) in a public institution involved the accrual of seniority, status, and possibilities—albeit limited—for advancement. In their turn, all these influenced society's attitude toward the woman as well as her own consciousness and self-esteem. Thus, for example, a male teacher who earned less than his nurse wife, and who was cognizant as well of her social ties and her professional abilities, would find it difficult to exclude her from family decision making. The woman, for her part, assesses her situation in comparison with that of her female colleagues, cultivates her own preferences for herself and for her children—some of which she can implement by means of the money she earns—and may well regard her husband from a "competitive" perspective, weighing his earning power against her own.

Another compelling advantage that working women gain from employment in certain institutions (for example, hospitals) is child care arrangements for infant and preschool children. Institutionalization of the use of day care centers also has long-range ramifications. It frees married working women from dependence on their mothers-in-law (who would ordinarily serve as nannies), and/or removes the task from her oldest daughter (who has traditionally borne the burden of raising younger siblings), and it reduces to a minimum the hiatus from work following births.

It is not my intention to idealize semiprofessional salaried work by ascribing to it absolute power to change the social status of married women within their families. The instances described here are replete with references to the inequities in the division of household labor. Yusra and Zohra work a daily "double shift" consisting of six and a half hours in the hospital, and just as much time in cleaning, cooking, baking, laundering, and child care. The work shifts in the hospital, which necessitate their absence from the home during various hours of the day and night, have not transformed their husbands into housework partners. This is notable in the case of Zohra's husband, Ahmad, who is employed in work identical to that of his wife but barely lifts a finger at home. Yusra's words of praise for her husband—whom she considers to possess rare virtue because he has not taken a second wife, even though she has given birth to "unnatural" children—show just how far from equality are the relations between men and their working wives. They also indicate the extent of their deep-seated fears lest husbands avail themselves of "rights" that tradition offers.

The Prevalence of the Two-Breadwinner Family in Dheisheh

In the first half of the 1990s, families in which both wife and husband were professionally employed were not exceptional in Dheisheh, but by no means were they a widespread phenomenon. I estimated their incidence among couples of the young generation to range between 10 and 15 percent. The estimate was based on the finding that 17 to 25 percent of the married women and 14 to 20 percent of the married men of this generation in the camp were professionally or semiprofessionally employed, and on the relatively higher prevalence (though not predominance) of marriages by women in this category to men of like or similar occupation. Around 80 percent among the married men of the young generation who had participated in the labor force (migrant workers who worked abroad excluded) worked as day wage laborers, in comparison with a very low percentage (probably as low as 5 percent) of married women of the same age group who were so employed. The prevalence of two-breadwinner families among day wage workers of the young generation was therefore extremely low. Moreover, the fact that the late 1980s and 1990s were marked by the continuing expulsion of young Palestinian workers from the Israeli labor market, and soaring rates of unemployment among their ranks, implied an ongoing decline in the standard of living of families that relied on day wage income for subsistence. Thus, in comparative terms, households that were organized around two salaried wage earners were a small minority that enjoyed a far better economic standard than the greater lot. I would further suggest that their relative weight among households that were started by the young generation (10 to 15 percent) represents the upper limit of what could have been attained by Dheishehian refugees struggling through the obstacles to acquire education and professional employment under the extremely discriminating power structure of the Israeli military occupation. All the means that were at the disposal of the refugees were exhausted, including UNRWA's services and institutions for postsecondary education, on the one hand, and their own "agency," on the other—that is, familial divisions of labor and patterns of organization to facilitate education and training—implying that any further widening of the narrow social layer of the professionally employed would be contingent upon massive state investment in the creation of adequate workplaces.

Employment opportunities (mainly those for men) in Dheisheh were certainly affected by the establishment of the PNA, and the incorporation of the camp into the areas under its control, at the end of 1995. The main change, so far, has been the recruitment of dozens of former political prisoners and activists into the ranks of the Palestinian security forces (intelligence, secret service, police), and the incorporation of others into state ministries and agencies (as clerks, managers, directors). Formerly, the great majority of these men were either unemployed or were employed on a very partial basis, so that their entrance into the labor force as salaried employees has meant a significant improvement in their situation and that of their families.

However, employment with the security forces is almost exclusively confined to men, particularly those with certain political credentials and affiliations. And no less important, salaries are extremely low, since the total revenues and resources of the PNA are meager. Job openings in the government public sector—the PNA's apparatus, ministries, and agencies—absorbed only a small fraction of the potential candidates, and here, too, average salaries are very low. Therefore, and though I do not have statistical data on which to base my estimations, I believe that it is safe to assume that thus far employment via the PNA has been unable to produce a profound increase in the relative prevalence of the two-breadwinner family in Dheisheh, or to raise substantially the standard of living of those two-breadwinner families that presently exist. Faced as the PNA is with the obstructions to the implementation of the intermediate Oslo Accords (not to speak of a more comprehensive settlement), a very restricted sovereignty over territory, meager external support and internal resources, a near absence of infrastructure and industry, and a very high rate of unemployment and underemployment, the PNA is not very likely to meet the challenge, at least not in the near future.

PART THREE

Occupation, Political Imprisonment, Politicization, and Family Life in Dheisheh

Introduction

ONE OF MY EARLY visits to Dheisheh took place in July 1987, some six months before the outbreak of the Intifada and long before I decided to do research in this refugee camp. I had come to do a journalistic piece on a community clinic operated by the outlawed Fatah movement. A young man who gave me directions also invited me to join him and his family for coffee. The gate to his home opened onto a small courtyard with three tiny "shelter units" that were set up by UNRWA in the 1950s. "Here's my home," said my host. "My oldest brother and his family live in one room and the rest of us—my mother, father, and seven brothers—live in the second room and the kitchen. . . . It's been very roomy in our home lately, though," he continued, laughing along with his brother who had joined us. "With five of our brothers in prison, there's much more space."

I learned that the youngest of the brothers who were in jail were fourteen, fifteen, and sixteen years old; one was eighteen; and the eldest was twenty-five. Three were arrested during an army raid on camp activists and sentenced to six to eight months in jail, the fourth was serving a two-year sentence on charges of attempting to attack an officer on duty, and the fifth was held under administrative detention.[1] My hosts told me that their father worked as a janitor in a hospital in West Jerusalem and then turned to me with a question: "Don't you want to know where mother works?" Impatient for my response, they went straight on and solved the riddle: "Mother works on the busses . . . five sons in prison are a job for the entire week."

Their mother—a lady in her fifties who, it turned out, had worked for many years as a cleaning woman in Jerusalem—added the detail: "Last Friday I visited Raziq in Khalil [Hebron] prison. Yesterday I visited Raed and Hisham who are also held in Khalil, but in the youth wing that has separate visiting days. Today I've been to Jneid prison [near Nablus] to see Muhammad, and on Thursday, *in sha° Allah* [God willing], I'll go to Tulkarem prison to see Ziyad."

Later on, I met Isma°il Ramadan, then twenty-five years old, with four and a half years of prison behind him, at his mother's place: two very small, dilapidated rooms, where she, a widow in her late fifties and for many years a wage laborer in Israel, lived with four of Isma'il's younger siblings. The first thing that struck me upon entering the practically unfurnished living room/bedroom was the sad expression on Che Guevara's face on the large wall poster. Next to Che was a portrait of Ghassan Kanafani, the renowned Palestinian novelist and playwright, a refugee (from Acre) who was killed in 1972 when his car was booby-trapped by Israeli agents. The crowning jewel—hanging just to the right of Ghassan—was an amateur sketch of Lenin's head, drawn by Isma'il's youngest brother, who at the time was in prison. On the same wall, on the mother's side, and about thirty centimeters above Lenin, within an improvised frame, was an excerpt from the Quran.

My early encounters with former prisoners and prisoners' families provided clear enough evidence that political imprisonment of Dheisheh residents was not confined to periods of marked upheaval and unrest but rather was a widespread phenomenon throughout the era of Occupation. I realized then that while political activism took place principally within the context of modern organizations and parties—formations that in general promoted non-kin-based ties and affiliations—its consequences, in the form of political imprisonment, had a profound impact on family life and family relationships.

The pervasiveness of political imprisonment in the life history of many men from Dheisheh has already received attention in previous parts of this book, yet not as a subject in its own right. Rather, central importance was accorded to the detrimental consequences of imprisonment for employment opportunities, job security, economic independence, and so on, and hence for the maintenance and functioning of family households. In this third and last part of the book, the perspective is inverted and the thus far "passive" political prisoners take center stage. The main focus is on the intricate interrelationship between the systematic subjection of generations of activists from Dheisheh to the experience of lengthy imprisonment in Israeli jails and the politicization processes experienced by individuals, families, and an entire community.

The structure here is similar to that of the previous sections. The point of departure is a brief exploration of the systemic context, here referring to the historical conditions at the time when the local, West Bank– and Gaza Strip–based branch of the Palestinian national liberation movement came into being. The context refers as well to the power structure in which the movement operated. Chapter 8 seeks to highlight the centrality of the exposure to military repression—first and foremost in the form of imprisonment—to the development of organized resistance to the Israeli occupation.

Chapter 9 addresses the particular experiences of individuals, in this case political activists and former prisoners from Dheisheh. I trace the phenomena of political activism and imprisonment in the camp, starting from the early days under the Jordanian regime, continuing with the first and second decades of the Occupation, and ending with the Intifada. Just as the labor and schooling histories seen in previous sections were given to differentiation along generational lines, so it is possible to discern characteristic profiles or prototypes of activists and prisoners along this divide. As I further attempt to show, the scope of political imprisonment in each age cohort, together with the findings on the personal, social, and generational backgrounds of activists and prisoners, portray a microcosm—albeit one with some unique Dheishe-hian features—of a much broader historical process: that of the emergence and consolidation of the Palestinian national movement in the West Bank.

The major finding—that political activism in Dheisheh, regardless of pro-found changes in its content and expression over the years, was almost invari-ably followed by imprisonment—serves as a point of departure for the re-maining chapters. Political imprisonment is in itself a means of repression, punishment, and intimidation concentrated exclusively in the hands of the occupier. The approach I offer for consideration, however, analyzes it as a platform for the spread of organized patterns of resistance, both among the ranks of the imprisoned and within the families and community to which they belong. The various modes of participation in this resistance—material-practical, ideological-political, and social—and their consequences for partic-ipants of both sexes and the various age groups, lie at the heart of the politi-cization process. The process, in turn, provides a setting for potential social changes. Thus, my main emphasis is on interpreting politicization as "praxis," as modes of involvement and participation in politically meaningful action that are generated in response to imprisonment and produce changes in con-sciousness and behavior.

Accordingly, Chapter 10 is devoted in its entirety to the exploration of the prison experiences of men from Dheisheh who were sentenced to long terms in Israeli jails during the years 1967–87. Based on diverse testimonies of former prisoners, the chapter traces the efforts to confront imprisonment through the establishment of a comprehensive alternative order that per-tained to all aspects of life in prison, drawing its legitimacy from the prison-based branches of the political organizations with which the prisoners were affiliated.

That the internal world of political prisoners was not confined to prison territory is suggested by the prestige that the prisoners and their leaders en-joyed "outside," as emerges in Chapter 11, which returns us to family life in Dheisheh. As many as 85 percent of Dheishehian families have experienced the imprisonment of at least one family member, and as many as 60 percent have experienced the imprisonment of two or more members. Thus, political imprisonment has had a direct bearing on the daily lives of the great majority of families in the camp. Consequently, the chapter follows the steps that constituted the process through which imprisonment precipitated the politicization of family life and family relationships.

As illustrated by the chapter's case studies, the day-to-day confrontation with the realities of having imprisoned sons, brothers, and spouses drew their relatives, especially women, into active participation. This gave rise to the emergence of new gender roles, as well as to novel extrafamilial social ties and relationships. Because it was mainly female relatives who took on the responsibility of maintaining regular contact with the imprisoned and who sustained the networks of prisoners' families, the examination of politicization of family life is bound to raise the question of the long-term consequences of this process for the social status of women.[2] The overarching question of whether political participation leads to social emancipation of women a priori invites, in my opinion, a negative answer, and was therefore discarded. Instead, I ask in what ways participation precipitates political radicalization. What are the concrete expressions of "radicalization" in a woman's social behavior and contacts? And, given the material and social setting, can resources attained through political activism shake and undermine patriarchal family relations, and hence be translated into social gains?

These questions are addressed through a series of representative case studies that examine how the political participation and consciousness of female relatives of prisoners intersects with their conduct and self-perceptions with respect to various aspects of family life. Deep incongruities emerge between, on the one hand, the resourcefulness of the women and their radicalized political outlook and, on the other hand, their relative powerlessness and far less developed consciousness in the sphere of gender and family relationships. The disparity between political radicalism and conservative social conduct and outlook is not less manifest among men, and is even more distressing in their case, given their much wider exposure to systematic political indoctrination. Yet, as is shown in several examples from this and the following chapter, the practical consequences of "hosting" such a duality are far less to the detriment of the individual male than to his female counterpart.

Can one trace the impact of political imprisonment years after prisoners are released and have restarted their lives in the camp? If so, in which spheres is this possible? How did former prisoners confront and/or adjust to the changing social and economic realities they found at home? These questions are addressed in Chapter 12 through a major case study, the unfolding family life of Lila and Ibrahim, both former prisoners from the intermediate generation, and through examining major trends that were found among former prisoners of the younger generation.

The conclusion integrates the findings and attempts to provide the basis for a comparative evaluation of politicization, as generated by varied levels of political participation. Are the various resources bequeathed to individuals, the family, and the community through politicization commensurable with the resources attained via wage labor, the acquisition of education, and professional employment? The section concludes with critical assessment of the relative capacity of politicization to transform the life situations of those who partake of political life.

A major part of my fieldwork on this topic was carried out in 1992–93. At the time, all Palestinian political organizations in the Occupied Territories were outlawed, and mere membership in any of them was a punishable offense that could lead to long-term imprisonment. Consequently, in the course of the dozens of interviews that I conducted with activists and former prisoners, I never asked them to report about their organizational affiliation or that of others. While I encouraged my interviewees to speak about their political views, I never asked them to relate specifically to the official ideology of any given organization. I did want to learn the specific accusations that led to the conviction of my interviewees by military courts and to their imprisonment, but I avoided the specifics of their organizational roles and ranks. Wherever full details pertaining to organizational affiliation and role do appear in the text, this should be attributed to the initiative and preference of the interviewee. Only in this way could I guarantee that my interviewees were not endangered and thereby obtain their basic confidence. Accordingly, this work is not concerned with the "mapping" of Dheisheh in terms of the distribution of activists and supporters along organizational lines, nor does it examine the institutional development of the Palestinian organizations in the camp.

CHAPTER 8

The Palestinian National Movement
in the Occupied Territories

*Aspects of the Rise of the Palestinian National
Movement in the Aftermath of the 1967 War*

As has been widely acknowledged, the outcome of the 1967 war—primarily, the Arab defeat and the Israeli occupation of the West Bank and Gaza—marked a turning point in the history of the Palestinian national movement. In its wake the gate was opened for the emergence and consolidation of the Palestinian guerrilla organizations and mass political movements. Taking on considerable weight and influence in the politics of the Middle East, the new groups and ideologies inspired Palestinians in the Diaspora and in Palestine, commanding identification and support.

During the period between the wars of 1948 and 1967, political activism of Palestinians, refugees and nonrefugees, took place mainly within the political parties and movements that operated in opposition to the regimes in the major "host countries" and elsewhere in the Arab world. In some instances, salient examples being those of the Arab Nationalists Movement (ANM; *harakat al-kawmiyin al-arab*) and the Jordanian Communist Party, Palestinians, predominantly members of the intelligentsia and university students, played a fundamental role in the establishment and sustenance of the entities.[1] Most political movements with which Palestinians were affiliated at the time did not champion a separate, explicit Palestinian nationalism (*wataniya*), the notable exception being Fatah with its emphasis on Palestinian "self-reliance." Rather, many endorsed Arab nationalism (*kawmiya*) and unity as a unifying element and as a precondition for the struggle over the liberation of Palestine. This latter trend was largely affected by the victory, in the early 1950s, of the revolution in Egypt. The combination, embodied in Nasser's leadership, of Arab nationalism, rejection of Western imperialism, and social radicalism appealed to millions throughout the Arab world, among them the Palestinian refugees, and led to a proliferation of pro-Nasserist movements and organizations. However, the failure of the unification of Egypt and Syria in 1961, and more so, the defeat of the Egyptian army six years later, precipitated disenchantment with Arab unity, reevaluation and self-criticism, and the subsequent decline or disintegration of leading pan-Arabist movements. Indeed, in the postwar epoch, "Arab unity" became associated more with the (coincidental) convergence of interests of regimes than with an expression of popular revolutionary sentiment and outlook.

While as early as the mid-1960s Fatah, as well as the Palestinian wing of the ANM, set up commando units that carried out a series of assaults against Israeli targets, the breakthrough in terms of mass recruitment to the ranks of the *fidaʾiyyun* (guerrilla fighters) took place only after June 1967.[2] The timing of the dissociation of the Popular Front for the Liberation of Palestine (PFLP) from the ANM (December 1967) and its emergence as one of the more influential, independent Marxist Palestinian organizations was in itself a war-related outcome. In other words, the postwar political and geographical setting led to reorganization in the ranks of those political forces within which Palestinian nationalism was previously articulated.

The historical shift found institutional expression in the takeover in 1968 of the PLO—formerly under the tutelage of the Arab regimes—by the recently established or empowered independent Palestinian organizations, and in its transformation into an umbrella organization. Yasser Arafat, who headed the largest movement, Fatah, was elected its chairman in 1969. The allocation of seats in the central representative institutions of the PLO, notably the Palestine National Council (PNC, the equivalent of parliament in exile) and the Executive Committee (the equivalent of government in exile), was altered to reflect the relative sizes of the various Palestinian organizations. Alongside the more significant factions (Fatah, the PFLP, the Democratic Front for the Liberation of Palestine [DFLP], which had split from the PFLP in 1969, and the Syrian-supported Saiqa) were included small splinter organizations, some of which were sponsored by various Arab states. The PNC, numbering hundreds of members, also included representatives of the Palestinian mass organizations, such as the General Union of Palestinian Women, the General Union of Palestinian Workers, and the General Union of Palestinian Teachers, as well as independents who were not officially affiliated with any organization. Revolutionary at the time, the composition of the council and committees, and particularly its quota system of representation, was later to become the subject of sharp criticism.[3]

Shortly after the war, the Palestinian organizations set out to build an infrastructure for guerrilla warfare in the Occupied Territories, Jordan, and

Lebanon. In the West Bank they confronted outright failure as early as the first months of the Occupation. Massive deployment of the Israel Defense Forces (IDF) throughout the region, lack of military tradition and training among the Palestinian activists, and a topography and geography that did not facilitate the creation of a "strategic hinterland" led to the rapid exposure of the embryonic underground network by Israeli intelligence and to the subsequent imprisonment and expulsion of thousands. In the Gaza Strip the Israeli forces met with pockets of armed resistance that were sustained, in part, by former recruits of the Palestine Liberation Army (PLA), as well as by significant civil disobedience. Resistance persisted until their final violent suppression in 1971.[4]

Having the longest border with Israel and with a population that was half Palestinian, Jordan took top priority for Palestinian institutional and military organizing during the years 1967–70. The training camps that were set up throughout the country by the various political factions attracted thousands of young Palestinian volunteers from all over the Diaspora, and the guerrilla assaults they conducted across the border line with Israel enjoyed soaring popularity among Palestinian communities. The operation of Palestinian institutions—and especially military training camps for Palestinian guerrillas—on Jordanian land could not have been possible without the consent of King Hussein. However, this military and political presence created the potential for a revolutionary upheaval that would destabilize the regime or bring its downfall, especially since a development of this kind matched with the political prerogative of the PFLP and DFLP.[5] The king, who throughout the 1950s and 1960s oscillated between a pro-Western, anticommunist orientation and support of Arab nationalism, and who at some stage expressed explicit sympathy for the Palestinian *fida'iyyun*, finally opted for the services and guarantees offered by the United States. Enjoying covert cooperation from the Israelis, he waged a total war against the Palestinians, known subsequently by the name of Black September. Lasting from September 1970 through 1971, it left thousands of Palestinian casualties (fighters and civilians), with thousands of others imprisoned or exiled and the organizational infrastructure destroyed.[6]

Lebanon was the only state where the PLO—as an umbrella organization and each of the factions that comprised it—succeeded in building and maintaining military infrastructures and setting up a broad network of civic institutions. This was facilitated mainly through the Cairo Agreement—mediated by Egyptian president Nasser and signed in November 1969 by the Lebanese army commander, Emil al-Bustani, and by the PLO chairman, Yasser Arafat—which institutionalized the PLO's presence in Lebanon. The freedom to organize politically and militarily in the refugee camps and in specified zones on Lebanese land, which the agreement granted to the Palestinian organizations (in return for their noninterference in state affairs), balanced to some extent the extreme discrimination to which the refugee population was officially and unofficially subjected. Palestinian refugees were not granted Lebanese citizenship, were denied access to all state institutions and government services and prevented from practicing all free professions, and were excluded from participation in (official) politics.

In the wake of the Cairo Agreement the Lebanese forces withdrew from the camps, and the Palestinian organizations took charge of ensuring the security and safety of their dwellers, who up until then were subjected to the direct control of the Lebanese police and security services. The organizations provided the refugees with a network of services and institutions; primarily hospitals, clinics, rehabilitation centers, and centers for vocational training, as well as special welfare provisions for families of martyrs (members of organizations killed in combat). Although the outcome of the Lebanese civil war of 1975–76 was detrimental for the Palestinians, who allied with the defeated side (the Lebanese National Movement [LNM]) and suffered very heavy losses, the agreement was eventually restored. It was the Israeli invasion of 1982—designed to annihilate the PLO's infrastructure, military and civilian, and leading to loss and destruction on an unprecedented scale, as well as to the forced exile of the Palestinian fighters from Lebanon—that rendered the Cairo Agreement invalid.[7]

The PLO began to garner recognition and political status in the international arena primarily after the 1973 war and the changes the war engendered for the strategic balance of power in the region. In July 1974, following long internal debates, the PNC adopted the Ten-Point Program, which included the goal of establishing "the peoples' national, independent, and fighting sovereignty on every part of Palestinian land to be liberated." The wording implicitly indicated a readiness to settle for a "ministate" in the West Bank and Gaza Strip, at least as an intermediate solution. The outcomes of the 1973 war brought to the forefront high expectations of an opportunity for a comprehensive territorial and political settlement between the Arab states and Israel. These were linked with the then-viable initiative to convene an international conference in Geneva under the auspices of the United Nations and the two superpowers. An effective campaign launched by the DFLP and diplomatic pressures from without (mainly on the part of the Soviet Union) to acknowledge the potentialities of an apparent new opening, as well as fear of losing the West Bank to Jordan through failing to adopt a pragmatic program, were major factors that led the Fatah leadership, and eventually the PLO institutions, to opt for a change in strategy.[8]

Notwithstanding the divisive consequences that this strategic shift carried in its wake for the PLO—primarily, PFLP withdrawal from the PLO's Executive Committee and its move, together with smaller factions, to set up an internal opposition (subsequently known as the Rejection Front)—the benefits overshadowed the burdens. The Seventh Arab Summit, which convened in Rabat in October 1974, granted the PLO unanimous recognition as "the sole legitimate representative of the Palestinian people," Arafat was invited to deliver a speech to the UN General Assembly (November 1974), and official or semiofficial diplomatic relations were established between the PLO and most of the Western countries, the United States remaining a salient exception for many more years. It was the Intifada, the popular uprising that erupted in the Occupied Territories in December 1987 that drove the PLO to complete the move it had embarked upon in 1974, by accepting UN Resolutions 242 and 338 and endorsing the "two-state solution": a Palestinian state in the West Bank and Gaza Strip, alongside Israel. This historic decision of the PNC (November 1988) eventually compelled the United States to enter into dialogue with the PLO and facilitated the commencement of Israeli-Palestinian negotiations several years later.

An Essentially Nonmilitary Venture

A different course of development can be discerned in the Occupied Territories from the mid-1970s onward: an essentially nonmilitary, civic-political venture. While it was Israel's ultimate military superiority that thwarted the early Palestinian attempt to establish guerrilla strongholds in the Occupied Territories, the unique features that came to characterize the local branch of the movement can be traced to the interplay of three central structural factors: (1) subjection to the highly restrictive conditions for organizing under the Israeli occupation regime, and specifically in the face of military government, military law and judicial system, and the omnipresence of the IDF; (2) the existence in the Diaspora of a ramified and (at least until 1982) stable political, military, and institutional Palestinian "center," with continuous and intensive interaction taking place between the leaderships of the various political factions and those branches in the West Bank and Gaza Strip; and (3) rapid processes of, on the one hand, proletarianization, and on the other hand, the spread of secondary and postsecondary education, which transformed the class structure and societal attributes of the West Bank and Gaza Strip. Evolving against the backdrop of the denial of civil rights and the Israeli policy to undermine development of the productive and public service sectors, these processes contributed to a relative homogenization of the life circumstances (and life chances) of wide social strata and provided the human foundation for the national movement.

As suggested before, it was the interplay of these structural components, rather than the isolated impact of each, which determined, to a considerable extent, the development of organized resistance to the Israeli occupation.

Thus, for example, the cumulative experience of operation under Israeli military rule informed and shaped the positions that local leaders and activists propounded in their ongoing dialogue with the organizations "outside," positions that were eventually taken into consideration in PLO decision making. The amelioration of the PLO's political and economic status in the 1970s assisted in the empowerment of political-organizational infrastructure in the Occupied Territories, yet it also enhanced the repressive countermeasures that the Israeli military government put into practice. The establishment of universities in the West Bank and Gaza and the rapid increase in the number of students created a platform for political activism, which in turn produced its own culture of resistance, leading to more persecution at the hands of the military.

The emergence and history of the Palestine National Front (PNF), which arose in 1973 as a result of local initiative, can serve as a classic case study of the trends underscored above. Bringing together public figures, heads of municipalities, and representatives of trade unions, professional associations, and student committees, the PNF introduced three innovations to the local political arena: (1) it was the first public body that openly supported the PLO and looked up to it as the sole legitimate representative of the Palestinians in the Diaspora and in Palestine; (2) it encouraged and extended support to informal grassroots organizations, such as students' and voluntary committees, as well as to charitable societies, trade unions, and associations of artists, writers, and journalists; (3) it supported the establishment of a Palestinian state in the West Bank and Gaza Strip, much in line with the historical position of the Palestinian and Jordanian Communist Parties, and it played a role in the PLO's move toward relinquishing the old maximalist formula and adopting the new strategy. On the local level the PNF also organized public gatherings and protest demonstrations against land confiscation, political imprisonment, and the Israeli program to set up a Civil Administration. The military government employed a number of means against the PNF, including the deportation of leading members, imprisonment and detention of many others, and the prohibition of PNF-sponsored public gatherings. The PNF was finally dismantled in 1977 as a combined consequence of these measures, internal rivalries, and a negative shift in the position of the PLO toward it.[9]

The absence of a military option distanced activism in the Territories from armed struggle and prioritized the public–civilian channel. Submission to the authoritative center in the Diaspora, notwithstanding the relations of dependence it produced, reaffirmed the ties of belonging to the wider Palestinian national movement. At the same time, societal change, primarily the emergence of new social forces with pressing, unattended needs, propelled the historical dynamic of organized activism in the direction of popular decentralization.

This was well reflected in the growth, spread, and consolidation, from the late 1970s and onward, of local, nonclandestine organizational structures for popular action, all of which were further divided along the line of political affiliation/identification. Thus, each of the major political factions (primarily, Fatah, PFLP, DFLP, and the Palestine Communist Party [PCP]) set up associated university student committees, trade union branches, women's committees, high school pupils' committees, neighborhood and village-based "voluntary committees," medical clinics, and more. The dispersal of the foci of activism, the diversification of the spheres of action, and the fierce competition between organizations over the provision of social and cultural services attracted wide populations to the circles of the national movement and eventually drew many Palestinians into the ranks of the organizations that comprised it. Among these were women, villagers, and residents of refugee camps and poor urban neighborhoods whose participation in organized political activity in the early 1970s was limited.

In many respects, the Intifada—a popular national uprising of an unarmed populace against the Occupation and for Palestinian independence—which continued after its outbreak in 1987 with varying degrees of intensity until the signing of the Oslo Accords in 1993, can be conceived of as the culmination of the modes and vehicles of resistance that preceded it. Outstanding, especially during the first year of the uprising, was the broad participation of different populations and sectors (urban, village, and refugee camp dwellers; students, workers, merchants, professionals), of both sexes and all ages, covering the widest geographical area. Under the authoritative direction of the Unified National Leadership of the Uprising (UNLU; the joint command of the uprising comprised of high-ranking representatives of the leading political factions: Fatah, PFLP, DFLP, and the PCP), the rebelling masses showed extraordinary perseverance in the face of unprecedented military repression. Novel patterns of action were developed and older ones were renovated or "upgraded"—notably the general strike days (encompassing all commercial and business activity), which were scheduled by the UNLU on a weekly basis and strictly adhered to by the public, and the specialized popular committees that formed in almost every community and locale.

APPROACHES TO THE ANALYSIS OF POPULAR
RESISTANCE TO THE ISRAELI OCCUPATION

The development and expansion of popular organizations and institutions in the Occupied Territories have been the subject of varied analysis and commentary, especially in the wake of the Intifada. Only a sample of the literature, and not necessarily a representative one, is addressed below. One line of argument, represented here by Hillel Frisch (1989, 1990), views the history of the national movement in the Occupied Territories primarily in terms of a struggle over hegemony, control, and leadership between the "outside"—the PLO and particularly Fatah, which dominated its central institutions—and the "inside," namely, political organizations based in the West Bank and Gaza Strip. According to this view, the struggle was determined in favor of the "outside" leadership only after the latter was finally wise enough to adopt, in the early 1980s, the practices of recruitment, organization, and mobilization employed by competitors from the "inside," and especially the Communist Party. The latter was known for the high importance it attached to the political education and training of its cadres and for the priority it accorded to organizing members of the working class over social issues, primarily in the framework of trade unions.

Like Frisch, Emile Sahliyeh (1988) also builds on the thesis of the tension and rivalries between contenders over hegemony. The central local competitors were the new national "urban elite" that emerged and took root in the 1970s (replacing the pro-Jordanian "notables"), the Palestine Communist Party, and the student movement in both the universities and secondary schools. According to this interpretation, a debilitating "crisis of local leadership" predominated since none of the rival groups succeeded in attaining sufficient power. The PLO under the leadership of Fatah, as well as the Hashemite kingdom and Israel under the Likud government, each motivated by its own interests, worked to either subordinate or get rid of the new local elite. Employing a "society-centered" rather than a "politics-centered" conceptual apparatus, Baruch Kimmerling and Joel Migdal (1993) attribute the manifestations of tension and dissonance between the PLO "outside" and the institutions and leadership "inside" to an inherent difference in roles and orientation. While the PLO was engaged in state building, the local leadership and constituency were laying the institutional foundation of civil society.

Lisa Taraki (1991) and Joost Hiltermann (1991a) both emphasize the demonstrated capacities of popular organizations to penetrate, sink roots in, and mobilize diverse sectors of society, as well as to provide much needed social services and to disseminate political-national consciousness. These achievements help in explaining the especially high level of mass participation, as well as the endurance and perseverance, of the Palestinian public during the Intifada. Taraki points to the decentralization of the national movement's institutional infrastructure as a qualitative transformation, in the course of which popular structures of open and democratic nature became preponderant. Hiltermann applies Charles Tilly's model of "collective action" to the Palestinian case, claiming that it was the mobilization of organizational and human resources, along with the collective experience of the population under military occupation and the unifying political leadership of the PLO, that enabled drawing the entire Palestinian public into open confrontation with Israeli rule.

Salim Tamari's analysis (1991) accords centrality to the contradictory orientations that permeated the national movement and to the expressions they found in the arena of resistance to the Occupation. The early 1970s were marked by a conflict between the "strategy of liberation," which prioritized the goal of liberating the whole of Palestine by means of armed struggle, and the pragmatic, "statist" strategy of "struggle for sovereignty," which accorded priority to the establishment of a national entity on part of Palestine. This conflict was determined in favor of the latter strategy in 1974, as noted above. The relative prosperity that the PLO enjoyed in the latter part of the 1970s guaranteed a steady inflow of financial support to a selected array of institutions (and persons) in the Occupied Territories, primarily those affiliated with Fatah. Among other things, this facilitated the fostering, particularly by the privileged beneficiaries, of a passive strategy of resistance, which became known by the (somewhat misleading) term *sumud* (steadfastness). The antithesis to *sumud* emerged in the late 1970s in the form of a "populist" orientation and strategy that underscored the role of grassroots organizations and reached its peak during the Intifada.

ACCORDING CENTRALITY TO POLITICAL IMPRISONMENT

In spite of their pronounced divergences in orientation, emphasis, and outlook, writers tended to focus on the institutional development of the national movement in the Occupied Territories, thereby distancing themselves from systematic treatment of the conditions of political activism and organization. This disregard applies in particular to the absence of a military option and the subjection to the Israeli military rule. Never in its history did the resistance movement to the Israeli occupation control a "liberated zone" inside the Occupied Territories, nor could it ever provide its followers with the protection of fighters and guerrillas. In the absence of military backing, therefore, political activists were extremely vulnerable. Moreover, and again unlike the organizational structures that prevailed "outside," the opposition to the Occupation did not lean on official functionaries and salaried employees, since civic-political organization was for the most part illegal and outlawed. Those who sustained the resistance were perforce predominantly unarmed grassroots activists who were regularly exposed to persecution and punishment at the hands of the authorities.

Among the means of punishment and repression that Israeli authorities used throughout their rule over the West Bank and Gaza, imprisonment was the most extensively and systematically employed. In the course of these years hundreds of thousands of Palestinians spent time in Israeli jails and detention compounds—starting with most members of the underground cells that were set up in the late 1960s; proceeding with the public figures, activists, and followers of the leading political networks of the 1970s, the PNF and the National Guidance Committee (NGC); continuing with the leadership, constituency, and sympathizers of the popular committees of the 1980s; and culminating with the participants and supporters of the Intifada. The centrality of imprisonment to Palestinian political activism under Occupation calls for its incorporation into the sociohistorical analysis.

CHAPTER 9

A Multilayered History of Political
Activists and Prisoners in Dheisheh

IN 1988–89, THE height of the Intifada years, hundreds of Dheishehian residents were in Israeli prisons, among them boys between fifteen and eighteen years old and men between the ages of eighteen and thirty, as well as those in their thirties and forties. According to many, Dheisheh played a pioneering role in the national struggle in the Occupied Territories. As they put it: "In Dheisheh the Intifada was already going on in the 1980s." When I returned to the camp in 1992 to undertake field research, young men who were fifteen and twenty years old when the Intifada erupted would tell me of their political activities and multiple arrests at the hands of the Shabak (General Security Services) and the Israeli army during the mid-1980s. Those who were some ten years older claimed that it was their generation that took an effective part in initiating public action in and outside the camp during the late 1970s and early 1980s. Most of them had histories of ten and more years of intermittent arrests and imprisonment.

Although the younger people rarely acknowledged the influence of the generation that preceded their own (that of activists over age forty-five), there were a significant number of men (as well as several women) who were politically active in the late 1960s and who spent long years in prison during the first decade of the Occupation. Among this group—"the generation of the Occupation," in their lexicon—there were those who gave little weight to their own forerunners, regarding them as prehistory," "the generation before 1967." But throughout the period of Jordanian rule there was active opposition to the regime, accompanied by persecution and imprisonment. The history of resistance in Dheisheh knew no lacunae years.[1]

This chapter is not a comprehensive history of activism in the camp. I do not attempt detailed documentation of the formation of political and social institutions in Dheisheh or of organizational structure of the committees that were active over the years, nor do I go into detail concerning the purposes and worldviews of the different political streams. Aspects of political activism in Dheisheh during the Jordanian period, certainly a topic that deserves separate research, are highlighted only briefly. Moreover, my presentation here deliberately excludes a full discussion of the role of female activists and women's organizations and committees in the camp.[2] (This arguably unjust omission is partially redressed in Chapter 11.) Rather, the focus on "profiles" of male political activists and prisoners of three generations in the camp enables one to reconstruct major themes of three eras of activism.

First Activists, First Prisoners

> The objective truth, although I don't know to what extent
> people will admit it, is that the role played by the Communists
> in the 1950s and 1960s served as the nucleus for all the national
> activities that followed afterward in the camp. But this role didn't
> necessarily benefit the party itself; at times there were no more
> than three or four Communists in the camp.
>
> —AHMAD MUHAISAN, ACTIVIST AND FORMER PRISONER,
>   HELD IN PRISON MORE THAN EIGHTEEN TIMES

LEFT-WING OPPOSITION TO THE JORDANIAN REGIME

Educated Palestinians, often school teachers, and self-taught intellectuals (what may be termed the "autodidactic intelligentsia") figured prominently as activists in the left-wing opposition to the Jordanian regime and as key personages in the political life of Dheisheh in the 1950s.[3] Mahmud al-Khatib's first contact with the "post-1948 politics," for example, was in 1949, during which time he was with his own family and that of his parents in Nuʿeima, one of the refugee camps in the Jordan Valley:

I met a number of teachers from the refugee camps in the Jericho area, and they were saying that everything was determined and that the matter of the refugees was not a coincidence but a British plan intended to give the West Bank to [Jordanian king] Abdullah, who was a friend of British imperialism from the start, and that afterward it fit in with American imperialism. It seems that this was so, since after Abdullah annexed the West Bank to Jordan he opposed the partition plan and called those who supported it "traitors." Let me tell you that there were many among us who supported the partition plan of the United Nations, but Abdullah didn't want an independent Palestinian state to arise.

The political reflections that al-Khatib initially heard when meeting teachers in the camps complement the stand of the League of National Independence, a major faction that broke with the Palestine Communist Party in 1943 and set up the Jordanian Communist Party in 1951 (Sahliyeh 1988, 88–90). Following the 1948 war the Communists strongly opposed the annexation of the West Bank by Jordan and continued to support the establishment of a Palestinian state alongside Israel in accordance with the 1947 partition plan.

After arriving in Dheisheh later in 1949, al-Khatib was appointed as a teacher in the first school established by the Red Cross in the camp, and later worked in the UNRWA school. Based on the recollections of al-Khatib—the only one of the "first activists" who was still living in Dheisheh when I was doing fieldwork—it appears that activism in the camp started in the 1950s with a group of teachers in the UNRWA school who were in their twenties and early thirties and whose basic education had been acquired in Mandate schools. Most were refugees of village origin; al-Khatib had completed elementary school in his home village, Zakariya. These teachers' own students remember them as assertive, committed, and as having great influence upon them.

Teachers as political activists were not a phenomenon limited to Dheisheh. Aruri (1972, 96) indicates that the majority of supporters and activists of the Communist Party, which was the most organized and developed of the opposition parties to the Jordanian regime in the 1950s, were intelligentsia—teachers, students, and professionals. Both Cohen and Sela, who utilized the Jordanian secret police files from the 1950s and 1960s, found a high proportion of teachers among the leaders and activists of the Baʿth and the Communist Parties on the West Bank (Cohen 1980, 39–40; Sela 1984, 90–94, 105, 110).[4]

Jordan of the first half of the 1950s experienced ongoing political unrest and ceaseless parliamentary and governmental crises, concurrent with army and police oppression and strained relations with surrounding political regimes. Some of these circumstances were related to extensive demographic changes in the aftermath of the 1948 war and the tensions between Palestinians, who now constituted two-thirds of the population, and "original" Jordanians; between Bedouins and city dwellers; and between refugees and locals. Yet at the core of the rivalry lay the ongoing political confrontation between the Royal Palace, its local conservative supporters, and its colonial military backers, on the one hand, and the secular opposition parties and movements, primarily the Communists, Baʿthists, and the National Socialist Party, on the other. Allied with the radical notion of Arab unity associated with Nasser or with other versions of anti-imperialism and protest of Western domination, these parties garnered widening public support, especially among the Palestinian refugee, and some of the nonrefugee, populace. Marked ideological differences divided the opposition, but in its consistent objection to the military and political alliance of Jordan with Britain, as well as in the call for cooperation with the Nasserist regime and in the struggles over the democratization of political life, it was united.

In early 1956 teachers from the Dheisheh school and dozens of others from the Bethlehem area were imprisoned for demonstrating against King Hussein's intention to join Iraq, Turkey, and Iran in the British- and American-sponsored Baghdad Pact. Faced with mounting opposition from within, including that of parliament members, and pressured by the counterdefense alliance formed by Egypt and Syria, Hussein backed off, deposed the Arab Legion's commander, General Glubb (Glubb Pasha), and eventually permitted relatively democratic parliamentary elections. A radical national cabinet/government headed by Suleiman Nabulsi of the National Socialist Party and including representatives of the Ba'th and the Communist Parties (running under the guise of the National bloc) came into power (Aruri 1972, 128–35). Political prisoners and detainees were released, among them Mahmud al-Khatib and his colleagues, who returned to their teaching positions.

In the five months of its existence (November 1956–April 1957), the new government canceled the emergency defense regulations, thereby legalizing the political activity of all parties and movements; established an alliance with Egypt; and called off the bilateral agreement with Britain. However, in the spring of 1957 the king once again disbanded the parliament, purged the army, and reinforced the military regulations that outlawed opposition movements (Aruri 1972, 134–46; Cohen 1980, 20–24). These measures were accompanied by extensive arrests throughout the kingdom. Mahmud al-Khatib, a number of his fellow teachers, and the principal of the UNRWA school in Dheisheh were among those imprisoned. He explained, "The king removed Nabulsi and imposed the martial law that had served him many times before. All of a sudden large numbers of people were detained and we were among them. They transferred me with another 430 prisoners to the Jafar prison in the desert, and dismissed every government worker who had been arrested." After a year al-Khatib was freed but discharged from his teaching job in the camp. He required security clearance for a teaching position in Saudi Arabia. But with his brother-in-law on a wanted list, it was made clear to him that this would not be forthcoming: "You'll never receive clearance or a passport as long as Ibrahim Youssef is your sister's husband. We'll make sure that you'll lose every job you find." For eight years, up until the time he got a job in a private school, and with the exception of some temporary work, he was unemployed.

Before his imprisonment, al-Khatib had been the sole supporter of his parents' family of eight persons and of his own of six. After he lost his job, his parents' family lived on what his brother (a building worker, and himself a political activist) could provide, and later on they relied on the wages of his sister, who had become a migrant teacher. After the 1967 war, al-Khatib obtained a job in a government school and continued teaching until his retirement in 1985. When I interviewed him in 1992 and 1993, he and his family lived on a meager monthly pension of 180 shekels, and a similarly minuscule support allowance through UNRWA.

Al-Khatib did not remain a Communist, and in the mid-1990s it was possible to meet him on his way to the mosque, although he did not become a religious man and held on to radical social beliefs. He demonstratively supported higher education for women; his sister, Amira, twenty years his junior, and two of his daughters attained university degrees. He openly regretted that he had nine children, and supported family planning and the use of contraceptives. Over the years he acquired broad knowledge and was regarded as one of the outstanding autodidacts in the camp. As one young Dheishehian put it: "Whenever you meet Abu Nabil [al-Khatib], he's always carrying a book." Al-Khatib's preference, as he confessed on one occasion, was classic Russian literature: "Translations into Arabic of Chekhov, Dostoyevsky, and Tolstoy that Nidal [a son with a doctorate in chemistry from the Soviet Union] used to send me when he was in the Soviet Union."

His brother-in-law, the "wanted" Ibrahim Youssef, married Khadija, al-Khatib's sister, in an exchange (*badal*) marriage (that is, Youssef's sister married al-Khatib), and as refugees they reached Dheisheh in the beginning of the 1960s. Youssef, who worked as a medic in the UNRWA clinics in the Hebron, Bethlehem, and Ramallah areas, was jailed several times and sentenced to fifteen years imprisonment for Communist activity, but was released in the context of a general amnesty for political prisoners in Jordan after the 1967 war. He was known in Dheisheh as a "doctor" who provided free treatment and as an intellectual whose library was open to all. Muhammad Laham, who was making his first steps as a political activist in the early 1970s, recalls that "In Ibrahim Youssef's library we found books on liberation movements throughout the world, the Soviet and Chinese revolutions, anything you looked for. . . . He was imprisoned in Jordanian jails for almost eight years, and we respected his courage and his knowledge." Ibrahim Youssef served an additional two-year sentence in 1973–74, imposed by an Israeli military court on the grounds of membership in the PNF, the non-party roof organization that was the first to give open support to the PLO.

Over the years of Youssef's imprisonment, his wife Khadija worked as an agricultural laborer, as a charwoman and laundress in the Crimizan monastery, and in the Talbiah hospital in Jerusalem. Khadija and her children visited Ibrahim every month at the Zarka prison in Jordan (the "cursed" prison, in al-Khatib's words, where the leaders were held) and later at the Hebron prison. Family life and her work to a great extent revolved around his intermittent and extended imprisonments. Together they were concerned with the education of their sons and daughters; one daughter studied sciences, another journalism, and a third dentistry, all in the Soviet Union. When I interviewed her, Khadija extended her arms to me, ringless and without bracelets, miming how she sold everything she possessed to provide for the family.

LIMITATIONS TO AN ACTIVE OPPOSITION: THE IMPACT ON THE SECOND GENERATION

Structural and existential obstacles to taking part in an active opposition abounded for the next age cohort in Dheisheh. The Communists had a strong impact on literate members of this group as well—those who were children during the 1948 war and who received their secondary, vocational, and higher education during the late 1950s and the 1960s. Some became active while still in the local school and in secondary schools, influenced by teachers, friends, and relatives, and through contact with urban intellectuals from Bethlehem and Jerusalem, where the Communists had strongholds. For others, the impetus was when they studied at local colleges and at the universities in Egypt and Beirut. As well, there were those whose exposure to communism came when they received scholarships for higher education in the socialist countries, a possibility that became extensive in the 1970s.

Ahmad Muhaisan, thirty-seven in 1994, describes pervading influences in his home in the 1960s: "In our family the atmosphere was patriotic and nationalist, and we were absorbed by the struggle carried on by the Communists. My older brother was in prison, my cousin was in prison." His older brother had studied in the UNRWA vocational school on the West Bank at the beginning of the 1960s and later went to work in Kuwait and sent remittances back to the family. Ahmad commented on the secularizing impact of a Communist role model: "I didn't fast during Ramadan even once in my life, and that was due to him."

Muhaisan's association of a national atmosphere with Communist influence is not surprising. Nationalism and patriotism were identified with opposition to the Jordanian regime, especially with the struggle to democratize political and public life, and with an anti-imperialist line—elements that were paramount to the political agenda of the Communists. Particularistic Palestinian nationalism, which was to gain prominence in the post-1967 era, was seldom endorsed by the nationalist parties and movements that were active in Jordan in the 1950s and 1960s. The two additional identifying trademarks of the Communist Party mentioned by Muhaisan—the imprisonment of its members and its atheism—accompanied the party for long years. The first forced it to operate in underground conditions; the second exposed it to antagonism not only from the regime, but also from "sister" opposition groups (Aruri 1972, 139–40; Cohen 1980, 14–26).

Most salient figures whose names were linked to Communist activity in Dheisheh during the 1950s and 1960s were from the same large kin group that originated from the village of Zakariya. Since the same *hamule* (patrilineal clan) contained hundreds of people with different degrees of kinship and connection, and the majority were not politically active at the time, one should beware of attributing too great a significance to political camaraderie among kin. Nevertheless, it is possible to find a correlation between the number of educated persons in specific families and party attachments. Moreover, as several of the above examples indicate, family ties of the first and second degree and endogamous marriages within the *hamule* increased the circles of the actively involved.

However, alongside political activism and having a wider effect was the phenomenon of labor migration outside the boundaries of the West Bank (see Chapters 6–7). The two processes drew the educated of the generation in directions that were often, although not necessarily, contradictory. Thus, for example, vying for places in the migration countries' job markets eventually distanced many of the young from political activism.

The Ba'th Party and the Arab Nationalists Movement, which had supporters in Dheisheh, were also illegal during most of Jordanian rule. Ibrahim Abu-Ghalus, who was to become a central figure in the Fatah movement, pointed out that during the 1960s (when he was in his teens and twenties) the repression of political activists was very harsh:

People were apprehensive about joining political groups or parties, but when it came to protest demonstrations, they would show their support. I recall being jailed during the protest wave that broke out in the wake of the Israeli raid on the village of Samu' (in 1966). When I arrived at the prison there were already 150 detainees from Dheisheh inside.

Parties were very small—for instance, membership in the Communist Party did not reach two thousand throughout the West Bank, while for the Ba'th there were a few hundred, and in periods of decline and persecution, fewer still (Cohen 1980, 38; Sela 1984, 102–4). Apart from the oppressiveness of the regime, the noted gap between the small size of opposition parties and mass participation in antigovernment protest can also be traced to attributes of Palestinian social structure, including the virtual nonexistence of a middle class, a weak proletariat, and patriarchal control.

Their peasant-village origins and limited formal education notwithstanding, to say nothing of the appalling circumstances they confronted, a group developed within Dheisheh possessing the identifiable characteristics of an intelligentsia. It appears that the human factor was critical in the instilling of political awareness in the camp: the efforts of some (perhaps no few) to gain a political-social education, and their willingness to act and to endanger themselves in order to spread their views and ideas, left its imprint on the enculturation of the middle and younger generations.

Initial Forms of Resistance to the Israeli Occupation

> When I entered prison there wasn't a "national movement";
> there were only underground cells that performed clandes-
> tinely. When I got out I found a world full of organizations,
> committees, and community institutions.
>
> —Saleh Abu-Laban, a prisoner in Israeli
>   jails during the years 1970–85

AFTER THE 1967 WAR: THE FIRST NUCLEI OF RESISTANCE

Resistance to the Israeli Occupation emerged in Dheisheh shortly after the 1967 war. The backdrop was mass dislocation of residents of the refugee camp, the enforcement of a repressive military rule in the West Bank, and the sharp political changes that were wrought by the Arab defeat. The conquest of the West Bank in June 1967 led to the uprooting, for the second time in twenty years, of thousands of the inhabitants of Dheisheh who sought temporary refuge in the East Bank of the Jordan Valley. An Israeli policy of nonreturn was soon to follow and resulted in the permanent relocation of the majority of these refugees, who ended up in the camps and neighborhoods of the Amman region.[5] Nearly every Dheishehian family suffered fragmentation and separation. There are men and women in the camp whose siblings all fled to the East Bank during the war, thereby losing their "right of residence"; other families sought refuge for weeks in the mountains and desert and then infiltrated back. There are numerous cases of families that for years expended every effort to obtain a "family reunification" permit from the military government for their kin. Uncertainty prevailed not only at the level of personal and family fates, and at that of basic means of livelihood, but also in political terms. At the time, no one thought that the Israeli Occupation would be long lasting. As well, the Arab defeat brought in its wake the discrediting and decline of the movements that were associated with the notion of Arab unity; meanwhile support weakened, at least temporarily, for the once highly influential Jordanian Communist Party.[6] Nonetheless, concomitant with the latter process was the ascendance in the popularity of the independent Palestinian organizations.

Rosemary Sayigh describes 1969, the year the Palestinian organizations gained control over the refugee camps in Lebanon, as "the year of the revolution." The camp inhabitants were carried along on a political-national wave of enthusiasm and hope (Sayigh 1979).[7] Gerard Chaliand, who followed the guerrilla fighters of the Palestine organizations in the late 1960s and remained with them in their Jordanian training camps, speaks of the practical, ideological, and political effects of the "revolution" on the new recruits to its ranks (Chaliand 1972).[8] The West Bank during the first years of

Occupation was a different story. Massive Israeli military deployment throughout the territory, the excessive means at the disposal of the occupying power, and an early failure of the emergent Palestinian organizations to set up guerrilla bases inside the West Bank thwarted the option for a Palestine-based military resistance. Nor was there, at that stage, the institutional infrastructure needed to sustain political and social activism, at least not on the local and regional level. It is against this void that one can explain the emergence of the secretive, clandestine, locally based small cells that became typical of resistance in Dheisheh in the first decade of the Occupation. Change would not take place until the latter half of the 1970s.

SMALL-SCALE LOCAL SECRET ORGANIZING

The majority of Dheishehians who were to engage in resistance during the late 1960s and early 1970s adhered to a certain pattern of underground organization: small groups numbering only several persons, young people in their teens, friends, relatives, neighbors, classmates (in many instances these ties overlapped). It is necessary to qualify the term *underground organization*. Overall, there were no military or even quasi-military structures that carried out training or followed a fixed routine or schedule of activities. Training camps, experienced military personnel, and facilities for instruction did not exist on the West Bank, and even though some Dheishehians sought them individually with the armed Palestinian guerrillas in Jordan or Lebanon, their efforts did not have significant impact on local organizing. Only in rare cases did secretive groupings manage to get hold of weapons or ammunition, which more often than not consisted of improvised devices, and rarer were the occasions when these were actually put into use. Neither was it common for members in the groups to live in hideouts. Furthermore, the local Dheishehian cells were detected, almost without exception, shortly after their formation.

One of the better known and oft-recalled groups in Dheisheh, no doubt due to the heavy sentences imposed on its members, included Saleh Abu-Laban, his paternal cousin and next-door neighbor, Muhammad Abu-Laban, and Noah Salameh, their friend and classmate. Recalling his teenage days in post-1967 Dheisheh, Noah Salameh, now a director in one of the Palestinian National Authority (PNA) ministries, related,

There were many tough experiences; a police post was set up near the camp and each day we would witness beatings and brutalizing of the people by policemen and soldiers. At the time I was still in preparatory school, and Saleh and I used to sit together and talk of what could be done. We began with very simple things, distributing handwritten leaflets, painting graffiti on walls, raising flags and banners. We did not belong to any political organization . . . what united us and a few other friends was a compelling urge to resist and act.

In 1968 Noah entered the UNRWA vocational secondary school in Kalandia, where he socialized with peers from all over the West Bank and Gaza Strip. By 1969, now aged sixteen, Saleh and Muhammad, who attended another high school, had joined Noah and several other schoolmates to form a clandestine cell, which eventually got hold of explosives. According to Noah, even by that time he was not ideologically or politically affiliated with an organization; neither does he recall receiving guidance or instruction. The group was short-lived. An abortive action led to the arrests, interrogations, and confessions of some of its members and to the consequent imprisonment of the entire cell. Accused of membership in a subversive armed organization, Muhammad and Saleh were each sentenced to twenty-five years in prison and Noah to eighteen. The army demolished their family homes in Dheisheh shortly after they were convicted. The families were not allowed to rebuild for five years, and they were denied travel permits and other licenses. The three were not released until the 1985 prisoners' exchange, better known as "the Jibril deal." By then they were thirty-three years old.[9]

DIVERSE MOTIVES, SIMILAR PATHS

In 1974, some four years after Muhammad's and Saleh's imprisonment, Youssef Abu-Laban, Muhammad's younger brother, set up a small local cell comprising himself, a cousin who was a neighbor, and a few other young friends living nearby, all in their teens. The secret cell was formed after Youssef's return from a brief trip to Lebanon, where he met people from the Palestinian organizations. The members of the group, who in the past had scrawled slogans on walls and distributed leaflets they had written, now got an antiquated rifle and practiced with it on the mountain near Dheisheh. They were caught a few months after they formed their cell and were sent to prison for terms of two to five years.

From the perspective of twenty years later, Youssef, today a senior clerk in the Welfare Ministry of the PNA, explains how his personal story is linked to the history of his family as an entity or unit. Youssef's interpretation of the period is unusual; family categories were not often entertained in the analyses of others. He returns to the time after the 1948 war when his father and uncles became refugees and arrived at Dheisheh:

My grandfather was a religious figure in Zakariya and the region, and his son, my uncle, inherited the position. With the Nakba [the tragedy of the 1948 war] came the downfall. Although the family remained large and even grew in the camp, it lost the religious office and social influence it had in the village; they no longer had their land and position. Everyone became dependent on the sacks of flour from UNRWA. Each to his own tent. A man and his brother were no longer joined together. To put the family back together was difficult, almost impossible.

In Youssef's understanding, since the family lost the identity it held in Zakariya, it sought ways to reunite, so as to "put themselves on the map again." Family members tried, for example, to get his uncle the job of imam for the camp or, alternatively, to enter into Jordanian politics of the early 1950s. "Since both attempts failed, the family had to break new ground."

The groundbreakers were his older cousins and brothers who grew up in the 1950s and 1960s and who were influenced by, and became active in, parties of the new national movement—the Communists, the Baʿthists, and the Nasserists; but they migrated from Dheisheh in the beginning of the 1960s in search of work in the Gulf and elsewhere. The great change took place, in Youssef's opinion, when his brother Muhammad and his cousin Saleh joined an underground cell. He himself learned about the course taken by his brother only after Muhammad was jailed. Brother and cousin became well known and highly regarded as leaders in the prisons. Youssef recalled: "The people of Dheisheh acknowledged those in our family who succeeded in achieving reputations as true national leaders both within and outside prison. People saw us as a tightly knit unit." Youssef did not claim that he joined the movement in order to represent a kin group, but he sees himself as continuing the earlier course of family solidarity and leadership.

Ahmad, Youssef's cousin, who belonged to the same cell and was arrested when he was sixteen, mentioned the arrest of another cousin in 1970, when he was still a child:

The visits to prison and the suffering affected me. I was also very impressed by Arafat's [1974] speech before the United Nations. I began to ask myself: "Why are we in a refugee camp? Why don't we have a state? Why do Jews come from all over the world to a Jewish state?" Questions like these occupied my thoughts and those of my friends and fed my national emotions, and finally I joined the organization and then to prison. I went in with emotions and I came out with knowledge and understanding.

When I drew his attention to his cousin's explanation, Ahmad replied promptly: "One always thinks of his family's good name and of its place in society, but the purpose and reason for action doesn't come from that."

Ahmad Muhaisan, who was in prison for two years (1974–76) and belonged to the same group, was highly critical of Youssef's interpretation: "All this talk about family and *hamule* [patrilineal clan] is beside the point. No *hamule* stands on its own, as an independent entity, though rivalries and conflicts that divide people who belong to the same class tend to reinforce such an illusion. It's not only Youssef, my mother too glorifies the *hamule* she comes from, but, as I see it, it is ridiculous."

While all interviewees emphasized "the need to act against the Occupation," Muhaisan maintained conceptions held from early boyhood. His brothers and relatives had been members or followers of the Jordanian Communist

Party. Reading newspapers, journals, and Egyptian literature were part of his growing up in Dheisheh. In late 1971, the time after Black September when Hussein carried out his assault against the Palestinian organizations, Muhaisan visited Jordan. He witnessed the hanging of three Palestinian fighters in the town center, an event that remained engraved in his memory. He was then a boy of fourteen who was drawn to Marxist thinking: "What attracted me at first were the Marxist activists and not Marxism; they were educated, understanding people, and they had important tasks. I wanted to be like them." He also relates the attraction of the written word for a young boy: "The vision starts from a simple and very clear point which is opposition to the existing evil and exploitative rule, and the call for economic equality, social justice . . . these formulations had a powerful effect on me." In the years after his release from prison, he became one of the central activists identified with the Palestine Communist Party, wrote for the newspaper a-Tali'a, and was active in the trade unions in the Bethlehem area. He was arrested eighteen more times and was held several times for weeks on end without trial.

Youssef and Ahmad Abu-Laban and Ahmad Muhaisan bear evidence of the multiple influences (ideological, personal, familial), experiences, and individual considerations that motivated young people from Dheisheh to join initiatives of resistance to the Israeli Occupation during its first decade. There were individual differences, but the paths taken to active participation by those of the generation were much alike. Without local movement organizing for social and political activity as an option, the youths turned to clandestine channels. Although they identified with the ideologies and political purposes of the Palestinian organizations, they were not exposed to the potential contribution of an organization upon individual action. Lack of experience and the absence of means, accountability, and orientation, not to speak of the confrontation with a strong military rule and its legal handmaiden, set these young people with their youthful ideals on a brief and abruptly interrupted path, straight to prison.

Exceptional, in this respect, was the imprisonment of local activists who took part in the PNF. Since it represented an open and public structure, not an underground one, the PNF was a forerunner to the popular organizations of the 1980s. The aforementioned Ibrahim Youssef was sentenced in 1973 for his activity in the PNF, and other senior members (none from Dheisheh) were exiled from the West Bank.

ARREST AND IMPRISONMENT IN THE FIRST DECADE OF THE OCCUPATION

My findings pertaining to the rate and duration of imprisonment among Dheishehian men during the first decade of the Occupation are based on results of a survey, which encompassed the core sample of forty-one interviewees and a larger sample, together totaling 299 men.[10] The combined data shows that seventy-five of the 299 (25.1 percent) experienced some form of imprisonment ranging from several weeks to sixteen years.[11] Of these, fifty-three (70.6 percent of the seventy-five men) were imprisoned for relatively short terms; the majority were held in custody for several weeks and eventually released without charges. Others were sentenced for minor offenses and held in prison for periods that did not exceed one year. Twenty-two of the seventy-five (29.4 percent) were imprisoned for periods longer than one year: nine (12 percent) spent between one and three years in prison; five (6.6 percent) were held in prison for three to five years; and eight (10.6 percent) were imprisoned for between five and sixteen years.

To generalize, then, short-term arrest and imprisonment were definitely a regular occurrence for Dheishehians during the first decade of the Occupation, although to a far lesser extent than in the decade that followed. It was mostly those on the "periphery" who were detained; people suspected of contact with activists. More than being indicative of how the nuclei of resistance spread in the camp, however, the multitude of arrests attests to the massive means employed to suppress those nuclei, including the extremely common procedure of arresting family members and friends of suspects; hence, too, the notable proportion of detainees who were eventually released without charges.[12]

Imprisonment for extended terms was the lot of activists or those involved in underground associations. Because of the conspiratorial nature of these associations and the paucity of members in any organized group during those years, long-term imprisonment involved a relatively small, though certainly not insignificant, segment of the male population of the age category in question (7.3 percent of the surveyed men). The majority of those found guilty of membership in these associations were sentenced to particularly long confinements.[13]

The survey findings show a significant impact upon families. Every other family in the surveyed sample (thirty-nine of seventy-eight families) experienced some form of imprisonment (arrest, short-term, long-term) of at least one family member.[14] Moreover, the figures also show that 27 percent of the surveyed families experienced the imprisonment of two or more sons. In numerous instances, there was an "induced" relation of influence, that is, the activity and arrest of an older brother leading to the activity and imprisonment of a younger brother.

The testimonies of the activists and prisoners of the early 1970s demonstrate that it was not activism in the full sense of the word that characterized the underground clandestine efforts in Dheisheh. The formation of Dheishehian cells did not yield large-scale mobilization among the camp's people, nor were their members effective in challenging the Occupation soldiers on the streets. Rather, what distinguished them, perhaps more than any other attribute, was their having served as easy prey for the Israeli security forces. The majority of the groups were apprehended in their infancy, and their members were handed especially heavy sentences, so that there were many whose connection to a group was counted in weeks, while their sentences numbered years. With hindsight, one can say that the connection between affiliation to a group and imprisonment was more automatic than in any other time period, perhaps with the exception of the Intifada years. Simply, the "activist" became a prisoner before experiencing political activity.

These are reasons why the fairly high number of Dheishehians detained and imprisoned during the 1970s is liable to lead to an exaggerated picture of organized activity in the camp over the same years. At the same time, and here a matter of consequence, the multiple arrests, on the one hand, and the heavy sentences meted out to those in the groups, on the other hand, gave rise to a social phenomenon with a significance of its own. Family after family underwent the experience of having a family member in prison and joined the growing "community" of prisoner families. Entrance into this fraternity was no passive calling. Its impact was far-reaching, inflicting clear emotional effects and engendering a process of politicization of an entire public.

From Clandestine Cells to Popular Committees: The Pre-Intifada Years

> We wanted to abandon the clandestine frameworks, which the Occupation demolishes so easily, and to engage in activities that involve the public as a whole.
>
> —HASSAN ABD AL-JAWWAD, JOURNALIST,
> FORMER PRISONER, FORMER DEPORTEE

New patterns of activity manifested themselves in the second and third decades of Israeli Occupation. Armed struggle remained the "nonoption" it had been during the first decade, yet as the years went by the void in the sphere of organized political activism gradually filled.

The late 1970s marked the founding and spread of political associations, organizations, and committees, at first by the Left and then on the part of all factions of the national movements, echoing and expanding the "voluntary committees" that had formed earlier in 1972–73.[15] It was the time when labor unions, as well as professional associations and societies, amassed strength, women's committees were founded, university students' and secondary school students' committees proliferated, and local Palestinian newspapers gained in circulation. This was also the period of peak activity for the National Guidance Committee (NGC), the public-political umbrella body that led the opposition to the Camp David Accords and popular protest against it and the Israeli policy of control. Its leadership, which adopted a left-wing political orientation not unlike that of its predecessor, the PNF, included the more outstanding of the elected mayors of towns and townships, trade union leaders, representatives of women's organizations, heads of university students' councils, and public figures.[16]

Fed by the expansion of the working class and the rapid spread of education, locally based committees and institutions in the Occupied Territories came into being against the backdrop of the PLO's success in garnering recognition for and maintaining its extended quasi-state infrastructure on Lebanese soil. At the same time, Israel, now headed by the right-wing Likud government, was well along in institutionalizing its military, political, and economic control over the peoples and lands of the West Bank and Gaza Strip. An extensive campaign of suppression was soon to confront the newly established Palestinian modalities for action. Between 1980 and 1982 Israel removed from office or deported all but four of the elected municipal mayors in the West Bank, including three who were targets of an assassination attempt by the "Jewish Underground" in 1980. Members and activists of the NGC, which was finally outlawed in 1982, underwent harassment, arrest, and confinement throughout its existence. The Civil Administration was set up in 1981 as an appendage to the military government, in a move to further strengthen Israel's hold on the Territories; the same year saw the formation of the Village Leagues—a puppet institution designed to counter the growing support for the national movement—armed, trained, and provided with privileges by the Israeli authorities. Settlement expansion received an unprecedented boost, as it now became a prioritized government project. In its turn, resistance to all of the above facets of the Israeli policy was articulated through popular, local, grassroots committees, which were eventually to form the backbone that sustained the Intifada.

Though it could hardly be attributed to any specific person's deliberate decision or action, the transition from clandestine cell to open committee in Dheisheh was nonetheless facilitated by a score of "forerunners," activists whose experiences spanned both the first and second periods and who became increasingly critical of the shortcomings of their predecessors. One of them was Hassan Abd al-Jawwad, a journalist by profession, who was forty when I first interviewed him in May 1993, shortly after he returned to Dheisheh from an eight-year exile in Jordan. He had been deported in 1985, under what became known as the Iron Fist policy of the Israeli "unity" government (a coalition headed by the Likud and Labor Parties). His return to the West Bank in April 1993 was facilitated through so-called confidence-building measures that preceded the Oslo Accords.

Hassan was fourteen at the outbreak of the 1967 war. His elder brother, Faiq, was put under a two-year-long administrative detention on suspicion of membership in the PFLP and deported immediately upon his release in 1971. His father underwent interrogation in 1969 and was beaten, losing his hearing in one ear as a consequence. Hassan's first arrest took place in 1970 when he and dozens of other family relatives of PFLP-affiliated activists from Dheisheh were detained in the course of a crackdown on the organization.

In 1972 Hassan left for Beirut, where he studied journalism for a year. Upon his return to Dheisheh he was arrested, tried, and sentenced to eighteen months in prison on counts of membership in a hostile organization. After his release he worked as a journalist for the daily *a-Sha'b* and studied sociology at the recently established Bethlehem University, where he became one of the founders of the Progressive Student Action Front, a pro-PFLP student bloc. In 1979 he was elected the chairman of the Bethlehem University student council, as well as chairman of the West Bank confederation of the Action Front's student unions. Hassan also continued to pursue journalism and was a founding member of the Palestinian Journalists Association in the Occupied Territories. During those years of activism he was incarcerated for several short periods until an order of deportation was finally issued against him in 1985. While in exile, Hassan worked for a Palestinian research institute that was set up in Amman by another deportee, Abd al-Jawwad Saleh, the former mayor of Al-Bireh, who was exiled in 1973 on account of his activism in the then-influential PNF. In 1988 the Jordanian authorities put Hassan under administrative detention, employing the notorious emergency regulations—an inheritance from the times of British colonial rule that Jordan, like Israel in its own turn, was reluctant to relinquish. He was released in 1989 after two years of imprisonment.

Hassan's entrance into the world of activism was affected by the imprisonment of his brother, his father, and others, as well as by what he refers to as "a deep natural resistance to the Occupation and to oppression." However, as he explains, his political consciousness developed mainly during his student days in Beirut and during his first imprisonment:

In Lebanon there existed a wealth of opposition movements, parties, and organizations, and each had its own papers, magazines, and bulletins. University life was highly politicized. These were also the days when the Palestinian national movement was becoming more influential among the masses . . .

I was jailed in 1973 and released in 1975, a time when the fear of prison and of the Occupation had waned in comparison with the postwar days. In prison I received practical training for political thinking. It was then that I first began to think less about the ideological disputes, which divided the national movement and more about organizing people on a large scale . . .

We reached the conclusion that ideology was not enough. The Occupation maintains plans and a policy, and we also require a practical program. The test was how to make this concept operative. We wanted to abandon the clandestine frameworks that the Occupation demolishes so easily and to engage in activities that involve the public as a whole, so that if I and others went to prison there would be many, many others who would take our places.

We examined all the institutions and social settings that existed in the Bethlehem region at the time and tried to figure out how it would be possible to bring them together; how to link youth clubs, women's unions, student organizations; how to make use of a foundation that already existed, at least in an embryonic form, and to push it forward.

Upon his release and following his revelations, Hassan became involved in student committees at Bethlehem University as well as on a wider scale in the West Bank. He also became a central figure in the local youth or *shabab* club of Dheisheh. The club initiated a variety of voluntary activities in the camp, such as sanitation and street-paving projects, raising funds for needy families, printing a local newsletter, sports, and trips for youths and adults (the most popular excursion took in Tiberias and the Sea of Galilee, Acre, and Jaffa).

FACTORS IN THE GROWTH OF A NEW GENERATION OF ACTIVISTS

Institutions, movements, and literature influenced a new generation of activists. The opening in 1973 of Bethlehem University—the second of the five institutions of higher learning inaugurated in the Territories during the 1970s—in the very proximity of the camp, was among the factors that bore a major effect on the social and political life of young adults in Dheisheh. The university's students came from all over the Occupied Territories (including the Gaza Strip), with a high representation of urbanites, especially Christians from Bethlehem itself, and, unlike in the sex-segregated UN-RWA and government schools, male and female students shared the same classrooms and cafeteria. Perhaps most crucial in the context of this study, from the mid-1970s the universities became major centers of political activity in the Occupied Territories.

The student organizations that were affiliated with the national movement (as opposed to those affiliated with the Islamic movement) are commonly acknowledged as a leading factor in the legitimization and public acceptance of the PLO and in the organized resistance to the Occupation. University campuses served as not only arenas for dissemination of propaganda and the recruitment of young people to the various political factions, but also as battlegrounds for the ongoing competition between the national and the Islamic blocs and, according to some (see Frisch 1989), for the struggle over leadership between the "local" and "outside" forces.[17] The pro-PLO student blocs included the Progressive Student Union (pro-Communist), the Progressive Student Action Front (pro-PFLP), the Student Unity (pro-DFLP), and the Student Youth Movement (pro-Fatah). Emile Sahliyeh (1988) portrayed them as exhibiting revolutionary potential, readiness for sacrifice, conspicuous organizational talent, and novel initiative for mobilization against the Occupation; as abiding by democratic principles and practices; and as being imbued with a sense of a mission.

Of no less importance was the success of the student movement in converting university campuses into major foci of cultural and social activities. These attracted wide circles, beyond the student body itself, from the adjacent localities; mainly, but not solely, high school students. Art and folklore exhibitions, performances, seasonal festivals, and political and cultural gatherings commemorating events of national significance were inseparable from the agenda of student life and bound it to the larger community. Indeed, in the absence of (legal) national-cultural centers of similar vitality in the Bethlehem region, it was not uncommon to meet Dheishehians of all age groups and vocations, including parents of students, on their way to parties, assemblies, and exhibitions on the Bethlehem University campus.

Literature—"high," political, and philosophical—had a place of its own in bringing young men and women closer to active politics. Alongside modern Palestinian writing, especially the works of Ghassan Kanafani and Emile Habibi and the poetry of Mahmud Darwish, Samih al-Quasim, Rashid Hussein, and Tawfiq Zayyad, many were drawn to the stream of social realism in Arab literature, the Egyptians Nagib Mahfuz and Yusuf Idris, the Syrian Hanna Mina, and the Sudani Tayib al-Salah, and to the poetry of the Syrian Nizar Qabbani and the Iraqis ʿAbd al-Wahhab al-Bayati and Buland al-Haidari. As for theoretical studies, priority was given to translated Marxist works and especially to interpretations of Marx, Engels, and Lenin. Books and pamphlets were discussed, but it is fair to say that, prior to prison, most individuals were not acquainted with theoretical literature. However, less demanding political writings, pamphlets, periodicals, and circulars from the "outside" organizations and movements were required reading for every young activist or supporter, male and female, and almost everyone had a hand in either composing, printing, copying, or circulating political materials—all punishable activities carrying prison sentences.

ENTERING POLITICAL AND SOCIAL ACTIVITY

The activist Hassan Abd al-Jawwad spoke of the need to replace clandestine activity with public action that "could not easily be dissolved," and indeed by the early 1980s the transition to popular frameworks was well under way in Dheisheh. Concomitant with this change and with the attendant steep rise in the number of activists, however, was the exacerbation of repressive measures by the Israeli authorities, as is evident from numerous recollections.

ʿAdnan Ramadan, age thirty in 1995, spent a cumulative period of three and a half years in prison. He is a graduate of the sociology department at Bethlehem University and since the early 1990s has been working as an instructor in the YMCA rehabilitation center for the handicapped in Beit Sahour. For ʿAdnan, the early 1980s were years of initiation:

This was a time of upheaval in the West Bank, following the entrance of General Sharon into office as [Israeli] minister of defense. The scope of the demonstrations that took place in the spring of 1982 resembled those we were to see during the Intifada. Many events were organized by the general confederation of high school student committees, which was especially active. Whoever wanted to be effective and make a difference found his way to the committees. In my second year in high school I became the head of the confederation.

ʿAdnan has four brothers and six sisters, but books were his other close companions during those days: "Our two-room home was always crowded and noisy, so I got into the habit of taking books out to the nearby hill—Jabl Anton. My favorite was a series on philosophy that was published in Moscow. We always sought after Marxist literature, and it was through Marxist critique that we came to know other orientations."

According to ʿAdnan, Dheisheh was overrepresented in the local and regional committees: "I do not have a full explanation for this; maybe we were more experienced than others, maybe more courageous, but the fact remains that wherever I went, there were always Dheishehians playing key roles in committees and councils."

Nasser Laham, the same age as ʿAdnan, and his friend, adds:

Our age group is more intellectual, so to speak, than that of our elders and that of the still younger generation, whose education was interrupted during the Intifada. We read a lot, formed our own study groups, acquired wide knowledge in world literature, in philosophy, in the arts. We lived the rise of the revolutionary movement and believed that all obstacles and difficulties can be overcome through a combination of struggle and reading . . . and we proved that it's so. We brought credit to the camp. During the 1960s and even the beginning of the 1970s, the word *camp* carried something of a stigma. In the city we were ashamed to say we came from a refugee camp. Later on, the expression "son of the camp" became a source of pride. The older activists didn't benefit from this transformation.

Today, Nasser, together with others, runs a local television station in Bethlehem, after several years as an editor at the Voice of Palestine (the official Palestinian broadcasting station). A graduate in social work from Bethlehem

University, he has five years of prison behind him. Like ʿAdnan Ramadan, Nasser was active on the secondary school committee, and later on the Progressive Student Action Front at the university. His portrayal of his youth and activities prior to imprisonment focuses on the camp:

Most of our free time was spent on the street. Jews can't understand what our "street" is like. The street is childhood, friends, love, and the whole world . . . even when there is total curfew you can find children from the Salam neighborhood of the camp playing out on the street without anyone bothering them. Seven kids can't play in one room. The child, the boy, and the old man as well; it's impossible to be anywhere other than on the street. The old man goes and sits in front of a shop on a street corner, a woman who wants to speak to her neighbor stands on the street. And the same street is also poverty, crowding, no room to do anything, no place to go. . . . The small child doesn't understand the reasons, but over time he becomes acquainted with other things and sees the difference. He compares the private school in Bethlehem with his school in Dheisheh, a playground in Jerusalem with the fact that there is nothing similar in the camp, the paved roads and sidewalks in Jerusalem with the neglected street and potholes in Dheisheh. A fifteen-year-old looks for answers. He doesn't have much of an alternative other than getting involved in with whatever one calls "political."

Nasser's street and that of his friends was also the arena of their activity in the face of the constant presence of army forces that, already in 1981, under the orders of the military governor, had closed down the *shabab* club in the camp for an indefinite time. He continued:

Take the school courtyard, for example. They would use loudspeakers [bullhorns], to summon all the men from age fifteen to fifty-five to the schoolyard. When I would leave the house and meet up with a bunch of soldiers, they'd ask me where I thought I was going, and then they would beat me. Later I would come upon a second group of them, and then a third, and each time they beat me. When I would finally get to the schoolyard they would beat all of us with sticks, clubs . . . we would remain in the yard until seven in the morning, and then they would leave us.

The political activities of ʿAdnan and Nasser as students were repeatedly interrupted by long periods of imprisonment. ʿAdnan was arrested for the first time when he was seventeen, a high school senior. He was taken for questioning at the Farʿah prison and released after eighteen days, and then two months later the army came for him again. He ran away and hid out for three months, during which time he prepared for his matriculation exams. After failing them, he turned himself in. Under interrogation, one of his friends gave his name, a confession that led to a fifteen-month sentence for organizing a demonstration, incitement, and stone throwing. Over the years 1980–84, when he was between fifteen and nineteen years old and a student activist, Nasser was placed under arrest five times. Again, a companion's confession led to lengthy imprisonment. Nasser and a number of comrades were found guilty of membership in a hostile organization and of attacking a policeman and were sentenced to five years, served in full.

ʿAdnan and Nasser represent a prototype, perhaps a major one, of young activists in Dheisheh during the early and mid-1980s. The background to their activism entailed study, especially personal reading, intensive participation in student political activity, and the day-in and day-out military intrusion into their homes in the camp. Yet the constituency of young participants in both the organized and spontaneous political activity in the camp was much wider, encompassing adolescents aged twelve to fifteen, as well as youngsters who dropped out of school, both those who found and those who could not find work.

The imprisonment of others—especially of brothers, cousins, parents, friends, and neighbors—was of key importance in setting the direction taken by these youths, as is illustrated in the case of Fuad Laham. Thirty-one in 1996, and an officer in the Palestinian security forces, Fuad spent his teen years, from age fifteen to twenty, in prison. About political escapades when in school, he said,

Our family was known for this; my cousins on both sides, who live close by, were all activists who went to prison. Every boy in the camp wanted to belong to one of the organizations and the active groups. When you're thirteen and fourteen you tend to imitate those who are older. I remember how I wanted to be like Muhammad [his cousin who was sentenced to fifteen years], to take part in the struggle . . . for us, it was our dream to be like him . . . we went to see him [in prison] without fail every visiting day.

Since Muhammad was in prison, ʿAdnan, Muhammad's younger brother, took over the job of instruction: "He taught me and some of my friends. He was the first to bring me books. The day I was arrested, I had twenty books on politics at home."

Nidal Abu-ʿAker, twenty-seven in 1996 and a student at Bethlehem University, also spoke about the effect of the atmosphere at home:

I grew up in the reality of a refugee camp where everybody breathes and talks politics day and night, and when my mother and grandmother speak politics, how can it be that I won't? At the beginning my mother tried to stop me from taking part in the meetings of the students' committee, in demonstrations, and so on, but the grownups also gave their hearts to the struggle, to Palestine, the revolution, and suffered from the Occupation. At the same time, they feared for their children.

While most of those interviewed emphasized the role of organized groups and/or of family, friends, and so on, there were others who described their youthful course of action as highly individualistic. Burhan ʿAtallah, thirty in

1994, who was first taken into custody when he was thirteen years old, commented: "I saw life differently from my friends. I used to believe that one's decisions and personal behavior mattered most. I wasn't afraid of soldiers then at all, but today I've changed. I've not become a coward, but I consider things in a different light. I entered prison at an age when you think that you alone can change the world."

THE EXPANSION OF ARREST AND IMPRISONMENT IN DHEISHEH IN THE 1980S

Just as it was clear to me that every living creature eventually dies, it became evident that every Palestinian man would eventually be taken to prison.

—SHAᶜBAN ᶜATALLAH, FATHER TO FOUR SONS IMPRISONED DURING THE 1980S AND IN THE COURSE OF THE INTIFADA

Notwithstanding their dominance on secondary school committees and on university and college councils, young people from Dheisheh were overrepresented above all in the detention centers and prisons, and their numbers grew with the years. The findings here pertaining to the prevalence of imprisonment among men of the younger generation are based on the results of the survey, which included the core sample and two additional sample populations, altogether encompassing 539 men.[18] They show that 258 of the 539 men (47.8 percent) experienced some form of imprisonment, for periods ranging from several weeks to fifteen years. An almost even distribution of the results for the three samples indicates that one out of every two men of this generational group spent time in jail.

A breakdown of the data according to duration of imprisonment (the total sum of time periods spent in prison) reveals the following: Of the above 258 who were imprisoned, 133 (51.5 percent) were held for periods ranging from several weeks to one year. Sixty-eight (26.3 percent) spent between one and three years in prison, forty (15.5 percent) spent between three and five years, and seventeen (6.6 percent) were imprisoned for more than five years.

The pervasiveness of imprisonment as a factor affecting family life was calculated for a sample of thirty-nine families. Results show that nearly 85 percent of the families experienced the detention or imprisonment of at least one son. Moreover, 58 percent of these experienced the imprisonment of more than one son, while close to 40 percent saw the imprisonment of three or more sons (the average number of imprisoned sons per family standing at 2.6). Indeed, the period from the end of the 1970s culminating in the Intifada was characterized by such an extensive rise in detentions and imprisonment that one may speak of a social fact affecting almost every family in the camp.

Two major categories of imprisonment may be discerned: detention for a period of up to eighteen days that could be extended at the request of the Shabak and that did not eventually lead to standing trial, and prolonged imprisonment. The testimony of the interviewees indicates that intermittent arrests for periods of several weeks each were a common procedure, systematically applied by the authorities as a means of punishment, intimidation, recruitment of informers, and disruption of daily life. Though extreme, the case of Burhan ʿAtallah is not an exception:

They would take someone for questioning for eighteen days, let him go, arrest him again, and so on and so forth. Me, for example, I spent a year in prison just like that . . . they picked me up for questioning fourteen times, each time for from eighteen and up to thirty days. If we take an average of twenty days it makes fourteen times twenty, that's 280, and that's almost a year. In that way they succeeded in wrecking a person's life. As a result, it took me five and a half years to get my degree, from 1982 to 1987. I began by studying chemistry and because of the time in jail I didn't meet the requirements and I changed over to education. On my transcript you'll see that I stopped a lot of courses in the middle.

Repeated arrest and interrogation was mainly the lot of those who were in preparatory and secondary school during the years 1982–87.[19] Among them are many who did not complete secondary school, either due to recurring absence during their last year of studies, expulsion from school in the wake of arrest, or failing to pass final exams. There are also those who completed their matriculation exams at a later stage, commonly when in prison.

An additional sign of the inordinate use of arrests during the second decade was extension of the measure to especially young boys, in fact, children by any definition. Ahmad Jaʿfari was only thirteen upon his arrest in 1983:

I was the youngest in the group they arrested. They put me on a truck with other detainees. When they placed us up against a wall, it was clear that I was the smallest. They put iron handcuffs on me, but they slipped off, so they brought plastic ones . . . they set me free after fifteen days. The problem was that I didn't know how to get from Nablus to Dheisheh by myself. This was the first time I was such a distance from home, and alone.

Detention was followed by trial and imprisonment whenever the authorities produced "evidence"—usually in the form of confessions taken from the detainee or his companions during interrogation—that the accused joined a specific organization or took part in a prohibited activity. The lion's share of young people from Dheisheh who were sent to prison in the course of the second decade (1978–87) received sentences ranging from one to five years for one or more charges such as the following: membership in a hostile or illegal organization, participation in outlawed activity, organizing demonstrations, throwing stones, throwing or possessing incendiary bombs (such as Molotov cocktails), attempted attack upon a soldier or policeman, and so on. Instances of indictment for membership in an armed group (one that possessed weapons other than Molotov cocktails or a makeshift gun) or for planning or carrying out terrorist acts against civilians are unknown to me.

IMPRISONMENT AS AN INEVITABLE CONSEQUENCE OF POLITICAL ACTIVISM

A Dheishehian activist of the early 1970s would have most likely joined his cousins and friends to form a secret group. A Dheishehian activist of the 1980s usually joined a student committee at his or her high school, a student union at Bethlehem University or UNRWA's teachers' training college, or a regional voluntary committee. The salient representation of Dheishehians in student committees, so evident in the interviews, is as indicative of the remarkable educational achievements of this refugee generation as it is of the scope of its activism. There they stood—children to parents of the camp's elder generation of a peasantry turned into day wage laborers, and siblings to brothers and sisters of the second refugee generation, who acquired higher education in Cairo and Beirut and sought job opportunities in the expanding economies of Kuwait and Saudi Arabia. Now, and against many odds, these youngsters were present in ever-growing numbers in governmental high schools, UNRWA's teachers' training colleges and the four main West Bank universities.

Membership in the various committees socialized these young Dheishehians into a new milieu and integrated them into the growing network of organized resistance to the Occupation. It also sharpened their political and ideological identities, introduced them to political and world literature, and engendered local and regional leaders from within their ranks. However, neither the popular civilian attributes nor the public nature of this activism provided immunity for the participants. The transformation in the patterns of Palestinian political organizing did not yield a corresponding shift in the policies of the Israeli authorities. And so the young activists were not spared the fate of their clandestine predecessors. Indeed, one may easily argue that it only led to the contrary.

As a regular participant in gatherings, assemblies, demonstrations, and rallies—events that more often than not ended in a direct confrontation with the military—the typical Dheishehian activist of the 1980s experienced his first detention at a very early age and a second and third one a little later, in a course that would finally lead to his conviction and long-term incarceration. My statistics on political imprisonment in Dheisheh indicate that in the second decade of the Occupation the Israeli military government "readjusted" its policies, now directing the bulk of its repressive means against the newly formed committees. The proliferation of activism and of activists was matched by the unprecedented numbers of the imprisoned. The quasi-inevitable link between resistance to the Occupation and political imprisonment was not severed, therefore, irrespective of the dividing line that separates two significant periods in the history of the national movement.

Dheisheh During the Time of the Intifada and Mass Imprisonment

In spite of the Dheishehians' oft-mentioned aphorism, that the camp already knew the Intifada in the mid-1980s, there is no doubt that the first years of the uprising in the camp differed profoundly from those that preceded it, in terms of the intensity of events, the nature of the demonstrations, the number of casualties, the means of punishment used against the camp inhabitants, and the scope and extent of imprisonment. Although my fieldwork in Dheisheh began only in 1992, more than four years after the outbreak of the Intifada (December 1987), I made numerous visits to the camp at the height of the uprising as well, and I was witness to what took place during the time. That period and those events require separate research, and what follows does not, in any respect, displace that need; rather, it is an attempt to present some of the main configurations of daily life in the camp at the time, and to amplify the discussion regarding imprisonment.

Dheisheh of 1988–89 displayed many of the characteristics that distinguished the Intifada: Thousands of the camp inhabitants, among them women of all ages, took part in the almost daily demonstrations and confrontations with the army (sometimes with dozens of participants, sometimes with only a few, and often with hundreds). Additional committees were formed ("popular committees") and assigned to tasks of mutual aid, distribution of food during periods of curfew and shortage, and help and support for families of prisoners, the wounded, and bereaved. The inhabitants obeyed the declarations, and those of the Unified Leadership, in all matters pertaining to observance of strikes, organizing demonstrations, protests, and the like.

The IDF's reaction was extremely fierce and remained so long past the decline in the scope of popular resistance among the camp residents, which was already noticeable in the second year of the uprising. An army camp was set up opposite the entrance to Dheisheh and remained in situ for some five years; squads of soldiers patrolled the streets day and night; all the entrances to the camp were sealed off with concrete blocks, barrels, and barbed wire fences; the western side of the camp, that which borders the Bethlehem-Hebron main road, was encircled with a six-meter-high barbed wire fence, making impossible direct passage by foot between the camp and the road (a person wishing to leave the camp had to walk a long distance to an exit point on the camp's boundary or to a revolving door placed close to the entrance to the UNRWA offices); and giant tin panels were placed on the fences, giving the camp the appearance of a large detainee compound.

Cruelest of all for the inhabitants was the use of firearms by the army and the repeated imposition of extended curfews. Eleven Dheishehians were killed as a result of the soldiers' use of live ammunition (almost all very young people, three between the ages of ten and thirteen), and hundreds were wounded either by live ammunition or rubber-coated bullets. Curfews lasted for periods ranging from a few days to two weeks; for several months during 1988 and 1989 the number of curfew days exceeded "normal" ones. With and without the pretext of curfew, soldiers carried out house-to-house searches for demonstrators and stone throwers, and/or in order to intimidate. Usually, damage resulted from the raids—doors broken in; closets, windows, and furniture smashed; radios and television sets, refrigerators, and washing machines broken. Valued objects disappeared, and often enough the home dwellers were beaten with sticks, struck with rifle butts, kicked, and punched.

Primacy should be given to the extent of the detentions and imprisonment that were the lot of the people of the camp. In 1988 I met families with three, four, and even five sons in prison at the same time. The most salient development was the stretching of the age boundaries of the imprisoned to include hundreds between the ages of thirteen to forty.

The Intifada prisoners can be divided into three major subgroups:

1. Activists of the 1980s—young men who were seventeen to thirty years old when the Intifada broke out and who had been detained or imprisoned a number of times during the decade for organizational activity in the camp. Throughout the Intifada many in this group were active in the local and regional popular committees, which were outlawed shortly after their appearance.

2. Older activists, mainly men imprisoned during the 1970s. These were long-time political activists and prisoners who married, raised families, and were seemingly distant from the daily affairs of the 1980s, which mainly revolved around youngsters and young people. Some returned to fill central positions in the different committees that were formed during the Intifada, while others were not really involved in the hubs of activity but were imprisoned on grounds of security due to their past records.

3. Young boys who were from thirteen to sixteen years old when the Intifada broke out—the Intifada generation, too young to have played roles in the early 1980s. They were students in preparatory school or early secondary school in 1987 and lost two full school years during the uprising. For many of these youths, arrest during the Intifada was their initial experience with detention. Something

of the nature and the size of the group involved can be understood from the reports from forty-one parent couples of the middle generation about thirty-seven of their children who were sent to prison: Thirty-four of them were Intifada prisoners, while only three served sentences in the period that preceded it.

Three types of imprisonment can be identified:

1. Administrative detention: Holding prisoners without trial under the 1945 Mandatory emergency regulations. The overall number of the administrative detainees during the five years of the Intifada (until October 1992) was estimated at more than fourteen thousand (B'tselem 1992), which gives some idea of the very extensive use of this measure by Israel. In Dheisheh, thirty-two of a sample of seventy-six Intifada prisoners (42 percent) were held under administrative detention for one or more terms of six months. There were several cases in the camp of people held under administrative detention for three to five terms totaling eighteen to thirty months.

2. Regular detention: This category includes all those who were arrested during the Intifada, placed in detention camps, held there for periods ranging from days to months, and released without having been brought to trial and without undergoing administrative imprisonment. It would probably be fair to estimate (extrapolating from the sample examined) that several hundred Dheishehians, young and old, were in this category.

3. Regular imprisonment: Those who stood trial during the Intifada and were sent to prison. This group was relatively much smaller than the other two categories.

An additional category cannot go unmentioned: "wanted" individuals, those sought by the army for arrest who had not been apprehended. Dozens of Intifada activists from Dheisheh went underground; in constant flight, they kept away from the camp especially at night. Since the area was not blessed with many natural hiding places and since the Intifada did not proceed along lines of guerrilla warfare with a strategic home front, and many of the "wanted" were family men with children, most were picked up after weeks or months.

The Organized Struggle of Palestinian Political Prisoners and Its Influence on the Politicization of Dheishehian Activists

In prison we created an internal regime that touched upon
all areas of life: cleanliness, food, politics, studies, social life.
In spite of the tough conditions and in spite of the modest
means which were at the disposal of the prisoners, they
succeeded, as a result of their own conscious activity, in
establishing this order, which aimed to struggle against the
hard conditions of imprisonment.

—MUHAMMAD LAHAM, A FORMER PRISONER WHO SPENT
TEN AND HALF YEARS (1975–85) IN ISRAELI JAILS

TWO CHARACTERISTICS stand out in the encounter between the researcher
(or other visitor from the outside) and political prisoners in the Dheisheh
camp. The first, which was discussed extensively in Chapter 9, is the unusu-
ally high rate of imprisonment among the male population in general and
the younger generation in particular. The second characteristic, which
emerged from all my meetings with former prisoners and their families, involves the social and political significance and influence of the prison experience. In the Dheisheh that was revealed to me in the late 1980s and early
1990s, prison experience was linked to—and even identified with—the acquisition of education and the deepening of political consciousness. It would
not be an exaggeration to claim that there was a multigenerational consen-
sus of deep appreciation for the political, value-oriented, and educational
foundations that were associated with imprisonment.

"I entered prison with many emotions; I left it with knowledge and education," said a former prisoner, and dozens of other interviewees repeated
this theme in different formulations. "Prison was like a university for my
son" became a maxim among prisoners' parents, including those who do
not know how to read and write. There prevailed a discourse that under-

scored a relationship, which seemed on the face of it to be paradoxical: between prison, which more than any other institution embodies military occupation and political oppression, and the intellectual and personal development of individuals held within prison walls.

In-depth acquaintance with dozens of former prisoners from the middle and younger generations who were imprisoned for long periods (a year and more) between the years 1967 and 1987 helped to unravel the paradox. With almost no exception, their recollections of prison as a "university" were related to the role of the internal organizing by the political prisoners. Their politicization—which developed outside prison within political structures and movements and in response to various collective and personal experiences—reached a turning point, a qualitative leap, inside prison, within what I refer to as a "counterorder" that the prisoners established and sustained.[1]

A number of caveats need to be raised at this point. Unlike in other chapters, the testimonies on which I rely here are not corroborated by what is called "participant observation." I did not sit in prison with the prisoners and did not experience arrest and interrogation in the various prison installations in Israel and the Occupied Territories. My information on relations within the prison, unlike my understanding of social relations outside, rests almost solely on interviews with former prisoners. Secondly, the present discussion does not offer an institutional analysis of the prison system: its organizational structure, staff and personnel, rules and practices. Third, while I could consult a wide spectrum of literature regarding the development of the Palestinian national movement, no such corpus stood at my disposal with respect to the internal life of Palestinian prisoners in jail.[2] Nonetheless, the varied testimonies, which depict a multidimensional and complex subject, provide a certain balance to these limitations.

Arrest and Interrogation

> Sitting in jail is a situation which I could get used to and "accept," but under no circumstances can I accept the interrogation. The interrogation period was the worst time in my life. We won't forget it or forgive the Israelis for it. I can "accept" imprisonment and even deportation, but I won't accept [the interrogator's] forcing me to piss and shit in my own clothes, I won't accept his preventing me from sleeping for six continuous days, I won't accept his shitting and urinating into a sack and putting it over my head.
>
> —NASSER LAHAM, A FORMER PRISONER WHO SPENT FIVE YEARS (1985–90) IN ISRAELI JAILS

Arrest and interrogation may be a stage prior to trial and imprisonment or it may terminate with the release of the detainee, without charges. In either case, it stands as an experience in its own right, characterized by the intensive exposure of the detainee to violence and often torture, a situation wherein fear, uncertainty, and isolation prevail. In many cases, the initial arrest and interrogation are the first confrontation between the young prisoner and agents of the punitive mechanism of the military authorities.

Sometimes the Shabak interrogator is the first Israeli whom the prisoner meets face to face, as in the case of Fuad Laham, who was taken for interrogation for the first time at the age of fourteen.

There was an interrogator there called Abu Fahed who became famous in the camp as a symbol of cruelty. My cousins told me about the beatings he and his soldiers gave. His interrogation and the blows I suffered at his hands were the first time in my life that a Jew spoke to me.

Not every arrest is accompanied by interrogation; in many cases, a prisoner is held for eighteen days without questioning. Nearly every arrest, however, is followed by beating and various other methods of punishment, brutality, and physical and mental torture. In the course of one year (1983), Nasser Laham was held five times in the interrogation installation in the Farʿa detention camp:

Upon arrival at Farʿa jail, I would be ordered to undress, a stinking sack was put over my head, and soldiers would start beating me on the spot. The Shabak people would gather around me and shout like animals. One called himself Abu Khanjar, the second Abu Jabal, the third Abu Seif, and so on. Afterward they would handcuff my hands and feet. Soldiers shat and pissed in the sack and then put it over my head. Before giving me water to drink they would spit into the cup. Once they left me without sleep for six days. Anyone who hasn't gone through this can not understand what it means to stay without sleep for six days on end, to relieve oneself in the same clothes one is wearing, and all this time the blows continue to rain down without a break. You are beaten black and blue every day, you weep and cry out and hear the screams and cries of others from nearby cells.[3]

Did activists "prepare" themselves in advance for the possibility of being apprehended and interrogated? Most of my interviewees had heard a great deal from brothers, friends, and comrades who had been held under detention, and they recalled the welcoming parties for those who had been released. Everyone gathered to hear detailed reports on the interrogation, the beatings, the torture, and the new methods practiced in order to break the detainees. There were some, like ʿAdnan Ramadan, who were waiting to experience interrogation like someone anticipating a challenge or a test: "I heard a lot about detention and interrogation and I wanted to go through the experience, so I was happy when they arrested me for the first time. I went in with a happy heart."

What actually happened, however, was nothing whatsoever resembling the "fortifying" experience that they had imagined for themselves. Ibrahim Ramadan, who was arrested for the first time in 1975 at the age of fifteen, put it this way:

Without experiencing something like this, it is impossible and mistaken to believe others. You will find a hundred people, all of whom will tell you that they didn't talk and won't talk under interrogation, or won't turn anyone in, but under interrogation it doesn't work like that. We were three young guys and all of us made confessions about the others. We said what they pressed us to say because we had no prior experience, because they beat us mercilessly, because we were frightened.

ᶜAdnan Ramadan, who went into jail for the first time at the age of seventeen "with a happy heart," described what came later.

I was overwhelmed by the cruelty I found there. They wanted me to admit participating in demonstrations and stone throwing. They beat me like crazy all over my body with their hands and using a stick. All the time I thought about the possibility of becoming permanently disabled. Again and again they poured cold water over me and then left me outside in very cold weather. They stood me against a wall for hours without moving, tied me up with terribly painful knots. I was also frightened because I could never know what would come next.

Anthropologist Julie Peteet (1994) suggests that it is possible to liken the experiences of young Palestinian men under interrogation in Israeli prisons to the liminal stage in a rite of passage that confers manhood. Interrogation is presented as a "site" where the transformation takes place. In the first stage (initiation) the young man is isolated from his natural environment. In the next one (liminal) he is put into an abnormal situation of exposure to violence, where day is not day and night is not night, his body is no longer under his control, and his identity is endangered. Having endured the test, the young man, who eventually returns home, gains the respect and recognition of the community, which acknowledges that he has "moved up a stage" (aggregation). He is now in the general category of those adult males whose voice is taken into account, notwithstanding his young age and other low status attributes. Ascribing a subversive interpretation to the experience of interrogation, beating, and torture, one that is diametrically opposed to and transcends that of the occupier/interrogator, supposedly enables the young detainee—and the community of which he is a part—to convert the experience into a building block in the construction of Palestinian manhood.

The recollections of experienced "veterans" of interrogation from Dheisheh do not support such an explanation, however. If interrogation is part of a transition rite, then many, perhaps the majority, failed to pass the test. Almost all those who were eventually put in prison arrived there following their own confessions or the incriminating confessions of their comrades, extracted under interrogation. Such confessions were sufficient evidence for conviction by the Israeli judicial system in the Occupied Territories, notwithstanding the fact that they were for the most part obtained by force and torture (B'tselem, 1991a, 14–15).

A great many of those interrogated were boys in their teens, some younger than fifteen years old (see Chapter 9). For the most part they lacked experience and all lacked legal defense. Military law permitted holding a person under detention for eighteen days without a court warrant, a period that could be extended by a military judge almost automatically for up to six months at the request of the Shabak. Moreover, the military judicial system allowed delaying meetings with lawyers for thirty days, which could be extended "to the extent that this is required for the sake of interrogation" (B'tselem, 1989b, 7–8). Under these "structural" conditions, wherein the legal and judicial system worked hand in hand with the military and security services, it comes as no surprise that a large number of the arrests and interrogations culminated in the signing of confessions. Here is the testimony of Muhammad Ramadan, who as an activist in the students' committees in junior high and high school was taken no fewer than eight times to the Farʿa installation:

Each time the Mukhabarat [Israel General Security Services] tried to extract a confession using different methods. The first time they beat me all over the body, not sparing a single organ, including my head. After eighteen days I was released without charges and went directly to Makassed hospital, where I received medical treatment and stayed in bed for a week. I returned home and the same night they arrested me again. Several months later they introduced a new method. They would bind the hands with a chain tied to a hook in the wall or ceiling, and I was hung up in the air for fifteen minutes. During this time they beat me with a stick and shook me. Afterward I was left on the floor, unable to move from the spot for three days. This was the reason why many of us eventually confessed and signed whatever they wanted us to sign.

Awareness of the system and of the way it operated evoked a mature, balanced, and at times shrewd attitude to interrogation among Dheishehians, and not only among the direct victims. They did not describe interrogation in terms of a test of bravery but as a particularly horrendous confrontation that did not usually end well. This is well illustrated by the words of Nasser Laham's mother, who recalled her son's sixth experience in interrogation. It took place at the detention center in the police complex known as the Russian compound in Jerusalem and lasted twenty-seven days, during which time Nasser finally signed the confession. "One of the *shabab* mentioned his name in the interrogation, and he was left with no alternative but to confess. The Mukhabarat threatened him that they would torture him to death. I was allowed to visit him in Moscobia [the Russian compound] a whole month after the interrogation was over, and he was still unable to stand on his feet. His situation drove me out of my mind."

Nasser ʿAtallah was taken for interrogation when he was sixteen years old, and an activist in the high school committees.

They took me to the military headquarters in Bethlehem and from there transferred me to Farʿa. I was terribly scared. Because of my fright and my exhaustion, I wanted to confess but I thought of what other people would say and what my father would say. All these thoughts crossed my mind in seconds, no more. The interrogator wanted me to confess that I organized illegal demonstrations with the students' committee, and I refused. He beat me until I was unable to get up. This was repeated over and over again, and I left from there straight to Makassed hospital. There were several people from Dheisheh with me and they didn't all hold out. One of them was relatively older, twenty-five years old or so, and a person we always listened to and looked up to. He gave in after one week and signed a confession. It was hard for me to accept, but I could understand.

I even found a certain understanding, though not necessarily forgiveness, for those young men who became "collaborators" as a result of the pressures exerted on them under interrogation.[4] For years no murders of collaborators took place in Dheisheh—even though many people were suspected of having worked with the military authorities at one stage or another, and some had actually admitted having done so.

I also tend to reject the assumption that exposure of a detainee to beatings, torture, and humiliation constitutes a basis for transformation in identity and consciousness in its own right. Certainly, anyone holding out in interrogation without confessing won the admiration of others. But detention and interrogation hardly allow a person to practice self-control, neither over his body, his time, nor his actions. The issue of being more or less courageous, strong, or capable of resistance under these circumstances was likely to hold personal significance for the individual, but it did not bear conclusive consequence for the collective.

The Internal Organization of the Prisoners: Way of Total Struggle

When someone goes into prison, he loses his personal identity
and starts a search. He begins to think about his ability to
struggle with this new reality, to think how he'll cope with this,
how to defend himself in terms of his health and education.
Nobody can stand up to all these challenges alone, but only as
part of a group.
—MUHAMMAD LAHAM, IMPRISONED FOR TEN AND A HALF YEARS

CONVERTING WEAKNESS INTO STRENGTH: A COUNTERORDER

The aforementioned distinction between interrogation, during which the prisoner is denied the most basic conditions needed to grapple with his position as a detainee, and his subsequent situation in prison, is a historical and not an "essentialist" one: It relies on the cumulative achievements of the prisoners in the struggle to improve the terms of their imprisonment. Prisoners who went into jail at the beginning of the 1980s for the most part found living conditions better than did prisoners at the beginning of the 1970s. The panoramic testimony of Noah Salameh, who entered prison in 1970 at the age of seventeen and was released in 1985, provides some perspective:

The first prison to which I was confined was the Ramallah prison. About twenty of us were held in a sort of transit room, about two meters wide and three meters long. Naturally, not everyone could sit or lie down at the same time. We slept in rotation. Each sat or slept while the other stood, and then we exchanged positions. From Ramallah we were transferred to Ashkelon. We got one cup of tea a day. Breakfast consisted of half a hard-boiled egg per person. We didn't have mattresses, but each of us received blankets, which we folded on the floor during the days and used to cover ourselves up at night. Books, notebooks, and pens were forbidden, and the only newspaper we received was al-Anba [an official Arabic-language organ of the Israeli government]. They didn't even allow the Red Cross to bring us games like backgammon or chess. Cigarettes were rationed to three a day per person. The prison administration did all they could to intimidate us and break our spirit.

One can say that our struggle was conducted hour by hour and day by day around every "right" and every subject. We paid a high price for the notebook, the book, the mattress, the blanket, the shower, and for food and health care. It is important to remember that conditions differed from one prison to another and this, too, was a deliberate policy adopted by the authorities. You found that something that you had fought for in one prison for months was a recognized "right" in another prison.

Hunger strikes were the main instrument in our struggle and there were also "visit strikes," that is, the prisoners' refusing to meet their families in protest against the conditions of detention. In many cases, strikes in one prison spread to others, and often the prison strikes aroused very strong solidarity outside: demonstrations by pupils and students, leaflets expressing support, sit-in strikes by mothers opposite the Red Cross offices, and so on.

In 1972 there was an uprising of prisoners in Ashkelon prison; it started when the prisoners beat up the duty officer in the middle of the roll call. A military unit was sent to put down the revolt. It conquered the prison with tear gas and brutal beatings. One of our comrades was killed. But on the morrow we already declared a hunger strike. We passed this information from room to room and from wing to wing. The authorities erred (from their point of view) when they published [news of] the event, and from that moment the item was broadcast in every news bulletin in the Arab states, and there was a great uproar both in prison and outside. The strike continued for three weeks and ended in the wake of a visit to the jail by Minister of Police Shlomo Hillel, who met with our leaders. The result was the replacement of the officer in charge of the prison, the food rations were increased and the quality improved, the Red Cross was permitted to bring in a list of books, we were permitted to talk and to sit during the walk, and its duration was extended. Until then, they had forced us to walk around the courtyard in a circle, one after the other, in silence. One can say that the uprising of the year 1972 brought about a complete change in the conditions in Ashkelon prison.

Afterward, I was transferred to Beersheva prison because of the policy of transferring us from one jail to another so that we wouldn't get acclimatized to one place. I had to get used to different conditions and people there. The Ashkelon prison was supposedly for dangerous prisoners—those, like me, sentenced to long-term imprisonment—while in Beersheva there were also prisoners who were serving short sentences. In Beersheva we also waged ongoing struggles against the administration over our fundamental demands. There were periods when we held hunger strikes once a month. Once we conducted an extended strike for nine months, in the course of which we refused to receive family visits. The 1973 war took place precisely during that period and we were really cut off from the world. We didn't know that war had broken out, and a long time elapsed before we learned what was happening. In the end we were forced to stop the strike because at that time public interest in the prisoners' struggle was negligible.

From Beersheva they moved me in 1978 to Kfar Yonah, and from there to the old Nablus jail, then back to Ashkelon, and in 1982, with twelve years seniority, I was transferred to Tulkarem prison, which is considered particularly tough. Most of the building was below ground, the sun never reached the cells, and the damp was terrible. The Red Cross described the conditions as unfit for human habitation. Nevertheless up until now [1993], political prisoners are imprisoned there.

In the last period, before my release, I sat in Jneid prison. Every prisoner had a mattress and blankets, and we cooked our own food so that it was better suited to our taste. Many books were on the forbidden list, but we regularly got textbooks and books of fiction through the Red Cross, and through them we also received newspapers and games. Families were also permitted to bring books during visiting time, and those that were not disqualified by the censor reached us. I was the librarian of the prisoners' library.

Palestinian political prisoners were never officially recognized as political by the Israeli authorities. The official term used is *security prisoners*, referring to those who carried out an offense "against state security," and in common usage they were called "terrorists" (*mekhablim* in Hebrew). The policy of denying rights in jail can be explained as the denial of the prisoners' political status, stemming from Israeli nonrecognition of the PLO and of the Palestinian national and political institutions in the Occupied Territories.

However, in spite of official lack of recognition, within the prison walls "organization" and "membership" (*tanthim* and *intima*[2] in Arabic) were common terms not only among the prisoners but also in their constant contact with the prison authorities.[5] Veteran prisoners identified themselves with the Palestinian organizations outside, while new prisoners were "enlisted" based on their preprison political affiliations.[6] Newcomers and veterans alike participated in the structures of the internal organization that the prisoners had developed in a particular prison. These were in part affiliated with political organizations and in part common to the whole prisoner body, cutting across the political divide.

Before examining the significance of the internal organization, brief clarification is needed regarding the structural conditions under which it developed. All the prisoner's activities, apart from two daily walks of half an hour each in the prison courtyard, were conducted in a cell, room, or "hall," where he was held together with another six, eight, or twelve, or sometimes twenty or thirty inmates (the number depending on the prison and the period). Prisoners ate their meals on the floor, and within the same four walls were the toilet—a passage in the floor—and a tap or shower. They were counted three times a day, and movement between the rooms and the wings was forbidden or (in the wake of the prisoners' struggle) permitted under special restrictions. In the first decade of the Occupation, the prisoner was entitled to a monthly family visit (up to four relatives), while in the second decade one visit every two weeks was permitted. Visits took place in rooms especially assigned for this purpose and behind double bars. All written material that reached the prison, through the Red Cross or through relatives, was censored. Most publications directly related to Palestinian politics, or to subjects defined as such by the authorities, were forbidden and were confiscated if found.

Over the period of the first two decades (1967–87), the policy was to concentrate in every prison hundreds of prisoners from different age groups (in a number of prisons, but not in all, there were separate youth wings). Prisoners came from different family situations, with different social and educational backgrounds and characteristics; they of course differed in their prison seniority and history of activism and had varied ideological and political affiliations. Moreover, with the significant growth in the scope of political activity in the 1980s and the increased use of imprisonment as punishment of those involved, there was a constant rise in the ratio in jail of the very young—those fifteen to eighteen years of age—many with little experience. A deliberate policy of "planting" collaborators added to the heterogeneous composition of the prison population a constant element of suspicion and instability.

The prisoners superimposed their own agenda and timetable on the prison regulations and schedule, encompassing a number of principle areas. Cell and wing committees responsible for day-to-day affairs were set up. These dealt with matters ranging from kitchen work, apportioning food, cleanliness, and order and discipline to the regulation of hours for academic studies and political meetings to the representation of the prisoners before the authorities. Some of the tasks were allocated by a weekly or monthly rotation, while others were determined according to such criteria as seniority and experience, leadership quality, and personal proficiency.

Every prisoner was subject to a double commitment: first, to the common umbrella organization of all the prisoners, and specifically to all his comrades in the cell and the wing; and second, to the political organization to which he belonged. For example, the prisoner was likely to share his cell with another four who were affiliated with the same organization and five more belonging to another organization. He would participate in closed political meetings with the members of his organization and would study the theoretical material included in its curriculum, while parallel to this he would join a study group common to all those in the room. With the latter he also shared kitchen and cleaning tasks and other such duties. Thus, the implementation of the prisoners' internal organization along two intersupportive axes: one ideological-political, the other unionist-political. In practice, carrying out the commitment to one's political organization was conditional on the unionist commitment toward the prisoners' collective. The opposite was also true, since the prisoners' counterorder derived its legitimacy from close cooperation between the prison-based branches of the Palestinian organizations.

Imposing internal discipline was one of the outstanding foundations facilitating the maintenance of the prisoners' counterorder. For example, every cell and wing had its *shawish*, a prisoner selected to supervise the affairs of his comrades and represent their problems and demands to the prison management. Those chosen were generally people with seniority and experience who enjoyed status in the political organizations of which they were members and had held the confidence of their comrades over a long period.

Some idea of the way in which the mutual commitment to group discipline appeared to a young and "raw" prisoner can be gleaned from the testimony of Nasser ꜥAtallah, who was held under administrative detention in Jneid prison at the age of seventeen.

Only upon arriving in prison and asking the prisoners about their situation did it become clear to me that they were in administrative detention. Generally speaking, only such people as leaders of trade unions were meted out this sort of sentence, while I was accused of throwing stones. . . . In the beginning I didn't grasp my position; I was young and they were all at least ten years older than me, and I didn't know how to talk to them. But they became responsible for me and explained to me the rules and obligations.

There was a very rigorous regime over things like cleanliness and maintaining silence during study time, with everyone having to submit a monthly report on his progress and to sum up what he read during the month. If he didn't know how to write for this summing up, others would help him. At the start of every day a different person would sit and guide me. Mine was a special position. One time, I put my head out of the window and it got stuck in the bars. I couldn't withdraw it and eventually wardens had to saw through the bar. I was thoroughly ashamed of myself because it was the job of the *shawish* to look out of the window. I expected to be punished but they forgave me.

Among the characteristics of the internal order that former prisoners highlighted were the efficient and comprehensive division of time and the socialist-style social relations. Akram ʿAtallah, who was in prison in the early 1980s, noted, "This order existed well before I entered jail. Such high level of organization doesn't grow easily and it took more than a little time to achieve it. It laid down how to exploit every moment. Time for eating, time for study, time for discussions, time for cleaning up, time for rest."

Many of the interviewees noted that their attitude to the concept of time completely changed in prison, to the extent that they began to measure their sentences in terms of the reading material that they sought to finish before their release.

As regards social relations, Akram's testimony is again helpful:

In prison there are several things in private "ownership," like a towel, a cup, or a blanket. But everything else is held in common: sugar, tea, cigarettes, bread. There was neither competition nor exploitation, not only because there aren't many things there that can emphasize the differences between people, but mainly because of the importance we ascribed to this aspect. The political organizations prevented a situation in which the strong would rule over the weak. There was punishment for anyone using force, for otherwise total anarchy could have prevailed. Everything worked through committees and was coordinated. That doesn't mean that there were no manifestations of violence among the prisoners, but not as an organized system. There was also much discussion over the question of how to change the egotism that characterized relations "outside." For instance, we asked ourselves how to transfer the concern over cleanliness, which everyone was so strict about in prison, to the outside, where people don't care about a clean environment. There were other examples, such as the habit of speaking quietly, which we adopted in prison. You wouldn't hear a prisoner shouting in a discussion. Outside, we also continued to speak without raising our voices.

THE STRUGGLE TO IMPROVE CONDITIONS AND
MAINTAIN THE COUNTERORDER: INHERENT TENSION
OR COMPLEMENTARY DIALECTICAL RELATIONS?

The attempt to arrive at an overall, abstract characterization of the internal organization in prison is prone to idealization because of the difficulties in capturing the dynamics of constant fluctuations and lack of stability in the prison reality. It is therefore important to realize that neither in every prison nor over each and every time period did the prisoners succeed in organizing in a manner that guaranteed defense and support to the individual and to the group as a whole. This is understandable given the great difficulty of setting up and maintaining a structure that is in essence antithetical to the relations of power between the parties in a prison, a place where a host of violent means and the apparatus to operate them are concentrated exclusively in the hands of one side. Great importance must also be assigned to the differences in the conditions of detention in the various prisons, under changing authority or management in each, and the changing policy of prison commissioners and ministers of police. Such fluctuations often carried disruptive and at times destructive consequences for the prisoners' capacity to maintain their counterorder. The testimony of Fuad Laham, who entered Nablus prison in 1980, aged fifteen, and was held there for three years until his transfer to Hebron prison, provides some detail:

In Nablus the internal organization was very weak because of the methods practiced by the prison administration. On the one hand, most of the prisoners there were inexperienced and young, and on the other, most of the adults had a bad reputation. Among them were people who had worked with the prison authorities, who also succeeded in recruiting many collaborators from among the young prisoners. Because of this there were always disputes and tension among the prisoners. The situation was so bad that each of us suspected everyone else, even a brother and a comrade. I went around carrying a small knife. We could not organize because disturbances and irregular events were always occurring and because this prison was conducted like a Shabak laboratory. Even the doctor worked with the Shabak and tried in his dispensary to enlist people as collaborators. In spite of all this, I personally had good luck: There were several older and veteran prisoners who protected me and worried over me as if they were parents, guiding me in everything, something I won't forget as long as I live.

The situation changed at the start of 1983 when new prisoners from Ashkelon and Jneid prisons arrived in Nablus and put things in order: They punished collaborators, laid down regulations, and arranged political meetings, study sessions, lectures, rosters for work and cleaning up, and so on. It was only then that I started reading books and learning Hebrew systematically, for it had been impossible to study beforehand. The management was eventually forced to change its methods and also accepted several of the prisoners' demands.

Muhammad Laham, who was imprisoned for more than ten years (1975–85), stressed the constant tension resulting from the fact that "the relationship between prison staff and prisoner is one of hostility. The aim of the authorities is to cause the prisoner to live a life of isolation; that is, to force him to conduct the struggle for his fate alone. This punishment is outside the realm of your being a Palestinian and is directed against you as a person."

One expression of the authorities' effort to isolate the prisoners was the policy of transfers from one prison to another and of separating prisoners who had belonged to the same group prior to being tried and entering prison. One example was Muhammad Laham himself, who was incarcerated in Kfar Yonah, Ashkelon, Beersheva, Nablus, and Jneid prisons for ten and a half years without meeting the colleagues who had been involved with him originally. Commenting on this subject, Nasser Laham, who served time in Hebron, Ramallah, Jneid, Ramleh, and Kfar Yonah, invoked a book that he read in jail in Hebrew: "Everyone knows that the prisoner likes to stay in one place. In Menachem Begin's book *The Revolt* he writes of two things that particularly disturb the prisoner: searching the cell and transfer from one prison to another. The authorities were annoyed and troubled by the prisoners' internal organization and acted according to Begin's 'recommendation.'"

Naturally, the policy of transferring prisoners also influenced their families, who became acquainted with the geography of Palestine/Israel through their visits to prisons spread out over the length and breadth of the country.

It also emerges that many struggles conducted in prisons in the 1980s revolved in part around the same basic rights as struggles conducted ten and fifteen years before. The testimony of Fuad Laham, this time concerning Hebron prison where he served for about a year, is relevant here as well:

In Khalil [Hebron] the prisoners were very strongly organized. But the prison administration was particularly tough: hardly a week passed without throwing tear gas into the cells. Even the way in which one guard would relate to another was barbaric, lacking even a trace of decency, so just imagine how they treated us. Once there was a row with one of the wardens. All the prisoners began beating on the doors from inside. In reaction, they sprayed in tear gas until all of us lost consciousness. The wardens opened the windows and started to air the place before the arrival of the officer responsible for security. . . .

It was extremely crowded in the rooms, and we demanded the prison officers to improve conditions; to relieve the overcrowding, to add showers, to stop confiscating our books, to allow us newspapers; we made demands that had been accepted in South Africa years ago. Once eleven months passed without our seeing sunlight, because in protest against the conditions we carried out a strike involving a refusal to take our daily walk in the courtyard. Another time we refused to shower for four months. The prisoners' faces were yellow and they looked like ghosts, but the strike came to an end without results.

It turns out, then, that there was an internal tension between implementing a counterorder and the struggle to improve conditions. Elementary physical, material, and hygienic conditions were required to maintain the counterorder. The denial of these conditions generated struggles to attain them that were met with harsh countermeasures by the prison authorities, including the imposition of more severe regulations, thus rendering the implementation of an alternative agenda more difficult. Accordingly, when examined as isolated events, hunger strikes, visit strikes, and courtyard-walk strikes often seem to have led to a deterioration of the situation, marking a regressed starting point for coming struggles. However, a historical perspective illuminates the dialectic relation between the two dimensions of the struggle. It was the internal organization that set up committees, stimulated those who took up tasks and responsibility, and enforced discipline. In the absence of this it would have been impossible to wage the struggles over showers, food, overcrowding, books, the daily walks, and so on.

The strikes, and especially the hunger strikes, did not only entail a sense of an ultimate, nerve-wracking trial. They very often came close to actually endangering the strikers' lives, as the testimony of Nasser ʿAtallah vividly illustrates. Nasser, who it will be recalled, was held in Jneid prison as the youngest administrative detainee, participated in a hunger strike in 1986 that lasted two weeks:

In order to break the strike they transferred half of us from Jneid to Beersheva prison. It is hard to describe our feelings. They put us into a very frightening, terrorizing atmosphere, standing us up together against a wall completely naked. The Beersheva wardens didn't understand what administrative detention was, they thought that we had been brought from Lebanon. They said, "Look, terrorists have arrived," and set about beating us. All this when we were on a hunger strike and getting weaker day by day. The head of the prison treated us as if we were monsters, though something changed in his attitude after he saw that among us were people who speak French, Russian, German, and English and demand to receive books. We struck for two weeks, and I lost a kilogram every day until my weight was down to forty-nine kilograms. In the last days I got much weaker, and most of the time I was in a daze. When we stopped the strike they didn't bring us milk, as was required in such cases, but tea and spiced food. There were twenty-five of us, and we fell on the floor writhing in pain. I had terrible constipation for two weeks and awful stomach pains.

In stretching the human capacity—both physical and mental—of the individual to the edge and linking him to the organizational effort and mutual aims of the collective, the strikes were transformed into peak moments in the joint experience of the prisoners. This applies both to strikes that ended with defined achievements and to others that were forcibly put down and led to the imposition of more severe conditions. As one of the interviewees saw it, "Prisoners who don't hold a hunger strike at least once every half a year are not worthy of the title 'political prisoners.'" Conducting strikes demanded strong leadership, and leaders grew from within the accumulated experience of maintaining a counterorder and through incorporating the lessons of former strikes, unsuccessful and successful alike. The testimony of Fuad Laham provides additional illustration, this time from the last period of his imprisonment, when he was held in Jneid:

I was twenty years old and had gained rich experience during five years of organizational activity in jail. Consequently, I was given responsibility for Section 4, where 220 prisoners were held. This was a period of strikes in Jneid prison; the background was the policy of the prison commissioner to restore the prisons to their situation in 1967. A lot of new and inexperienced people from all parts of the West Bank entered the prison at that time. A vast amount of time and effort had to be invested so as to forge in their ranks the level of internal strength that would enable them to hold out during strikes. Hardly any time was left for me to read and study. We declared a hunger strike and continued with it for sixteen days. Section 4 was the only one in which not a single person was broken.

It would be erroneous to sever the prisoners' internal organization from the very specific context in which it came into being and developed. The hard conditions of imprisonment, the "divide and rule" or "transfer and rule" policy, and the use of violence in reaction to the prisoners' protest activities, all hindered the possibilities of organization, creating an unceasing oscillation between the two levels: the one representing a counterorder, the other, struggling for basic rights of survival.

Prison as a University

Before being in prison, I was connected emotionally to the national struggle, but in jail I became connected to it intellectually and ideologically. It was in prison that I read the theory. Love of the homeland became more rooted, for two reasons: my discussions with other people and my reading pamphlets and books.

—Nidal Abu–Aker, speaking about his first prolonged imprisonment

THE PLACE OF READING AND STUDY

It is rare to meet a former prisoner from Dheisheh who is not proud of his "prison studies." A great majority of the interviewees emphasized that while in prison, whenever conditions didn't prevent it, they devoted eight, ten, and even fourteen hours a day to reading and study. Some devoted most of their time to theoretical literature, such as history or political or general philosophy, while others preferred fiction. Some, particularly those who served a prolonged sentence in prison, spent a significant part of their time developing areas of personal interest. However, almost all the interviewees participated actively and continuously in the organized group studies.

On entering prison the prisoner was "registered" with a political organization on the basis of his affiliation before the prison period. If he had not been an official member of an organization but (as in very many cases) was active in one or more of its affiliate groups (student committees, volunteers' committees), he was given the possibility of joining the organization of his choice. Political affiliation obligated the prisoner, among other things, to participate in the organization's study program, to take part in its current political discussions and meetings, and to obey those representing the organization and its leadership. Hence, there was a double significance to an alternative order: on one hand, an enforced regular daily schedule or timetable, on the other, an agenda with specific content and aims.

Most interviewees described a similar daily schedule. The morning hours—after early rising, the morning head count, showers, and cleaning the rooms—were devoted to group or individual study. After the midday count and a half-hour "walk" in the prison courtyard and lunch, there was "free" time, which the prisoners spent in sleeping, reading, or sedentary games, such as backgammon or checkers. The late afternoon hours were divided between political meetings and study. After the second courtyard walk, supper, and the evening count, the rest of the hours were usually devoted to reading, either in preparation for organized study, or of the prisoner's choice. During the time allocated to reading and meetings, silence was maintained in the rooms by individuals and committees who were responsible for this; a prisoner who was not interested in reading or studying was expected not to disturb others. The majority of the organized studies took place in context of the educational programs of the organizations, in practice meaning mainly Fatah and the PFLP, with which most of the prisoners were affiliated in those years. In addition there were joint study programs that crossed the lines of organizational affiliation, on subjects such as general history, sciences, economics, and languages. The prisoner's partners in study groups were his roommates, whose numbers differed according to conditions in each prison and in different periods. So in certain cases a study group numbered three or four or six, while in others the number might reach twenty.

The important point is not the degree to which the alternative timetable governed the prisoner's life. Clearly, the path followed by one prisoner was not identical with that of his comrade; not all had intellectual inclinations, and not all exploited their time for systematic study. The significance lies in the very existence of an organized and permanent system revolving around study, education, and group discussion. The system encompassed all the prisoners, though the participation of some was more intense than that of others. However, factors such as the absence of strong leadership, periodic setbacks in the conditions of imprisonment, and prisoners' strikes and revolts and the repression they invoked, all militated against the regular implementation of the prisoners' alternative order, shifting focus again from the arena of studies to that of the struggle over rights.

GROUP STUDIES IN PRISON: LEARNING,
TEACHING, LEARNING TO TEACH

Most of the political books were forbidden. We had booklets
written by educated prisoners on every Palestinian subject:
history, economics, and politics, as well as on other liberation
movements. In the youth department I was responsible for a
very important task: copying the booklets. About every two
weeks, the authorities would confiscate them.

—AHMAD JAʿFARI, RELATING TO HIS ROLE IN THE PRISONERS'
STUDY PROGRAM

This quotation refers to a relatively late period in the history of Palestinian prisoners in Israeli prisons (1987) when, nonetheless, most of the political books were forbidden. Prisoners who were in jail in the late 1960s and in the 1970s pointed out that they couldn't be selective about reading material since the prison authorities greatly limited both the quantity and type of books. Here, for example, is the testimony of Noah Salameh, referring to the early 1970s in Ashkelon prison:

We were approximately five hundred prisoners in the prison while in the library there were fewer than three hundred books, received through the Red Cross. A large number of the books were on Islamic religion and art, with very little fiction and little translated literature and a few books on such subjects as general history and philosophy. In brief, I read whatever there was, and couldn't permit myself to be choosy.

Constant struggles went on between the prisoners and the prison administration around the problem of "permitted" books, regarding both their number and contents.

The organized studies that the political organizations conducted rested for the most part on a reservoir of educated people in the prison. Some of these had acquired their education as university students in the West Bank or abroad, while many others had become knowledgeable in the course of their stay in prison. Studies also relied upon study booklets that were written, edited, and updated by those responsible for the different courses. Distributed regularly among the prisoners in spite of systematic efforts by the prison authorities to confiscate the material, the booklets were copied in small, dense writing by the members of a prison's education committee on thin sheets of paper that could be readily folded up and hidden. They were meant to meet the great demand for basic theoretical texts explaining complicated and complex subjects in a comprehensible language suited for all. Every organization had its own booklets, which served as basic literature for members in the discussions of the study groups. The heavy censorship imposed on political literature was less strict as regards original classics and books of commentary on philosophy, general theory, political thought, and fiction. Accordingly, books on these subjects, which reached prison through the services of the Red Cross, were generally available.

The educational programs of the organizations devoted a central place to studies in the history of the Palestinian national movement, to their ideologies and to the specific development of the movement, and to discussing their positions on current political questions. Emphasis was placed upon studying the political experience of other liberation movements in modern times, particularly in Algeria, China, Cuba, and Vietnam. These studies focused on similarities and differences in the character of military versus colonial rule; the significance of conducting an armed struggle under different topographical, demographic, and political conditions; the movements' orientations toward controversy between different political blocs in the world and toward the cold war; the relationship between the headquarters in the Diaspora and the branches of the movement in the homeland, and more.

On subjects connected with social theory there were marked differences between the organizations. In Fatah, which brought together supporters with heterogeneous social outlooks, a clear overall social doctrine was lacking. On the other hand, the Fronts (PFLP and DFLP) and, naturally, the Communist Party were distinguished by their Marxist orientations. The difference was reflected in particular in the prison study programs: the left-wing organizations devoted a central place to studying the foundations of Marxist economic and political theory, especially the writings and interpretations of Marx, Engels, and Lenin. In Fatah these topics and writings were peripheral, if studied at all. However, it appears that Marxist thinking filtered down to the ranks of Fatah members in prison. Thus, for example, a former prisoner known as one of the outstanding Fatah leaders in Dheisheh stated, "The books that particularly influenced me in prison were those that had value over and above the information they supplied. That is what is special about Marxist literature, which offers a dialectical way of thinking, through which it is possible to understand many other things."

Many of the prisoners were high school pupils or graduates, and others were university students or graduates of institutions of higher learning.

However, for most, studies in prison brought the first acquaintance with varied theoretical questions and subjects previously unknown to them; they now had to grapple with a framework for study and discipline that belonged to the group and obligated the individual. The learning process is just as interesting as the content of the studies. Through the stages of this process, the interviewees testify, the prisoner was transformed from a beginner, dependent upon the help of others, to a student increasingly reliant upon his independent ability; at a certain stage he might become a teacher and guide for the incoming "generation" of prisoners. In every stage the confirmation and the test of the individual were in the hands of the group to which he belonged.

Ibrahim Abu-Ghalus, a high school graduate, entered prison for the first time in 1967 at the age of twenty-four and was released in 1971. His second prison term lasted from 1973 to 1976.

Before I entered prison for the first time, I had no theoretical education. I was not interested in literature and didn't have the reading habit; one could say that I was a tabula rasa. I am speaking about the very early days of the Occupation and the embryonic stage of organization in prison. As yet there were, for example, no booklets, and the prisoners built their library slowly from books that arrived through the Red Cross. There were quite a few educated and experienced people there, some of whom had been in prison since Jordanian times, while some had studied in Egypt and Damascus. These knew how to evaluate the books and to choose the most suitable for our needs. I started to read historical, economic, and philosophical literature. The educated among us gave lectures and general explanations on the reading material and also gave personal tutorials. There was always someone to explain things I didn't understand. Gradually, I reached the stage of being able to summarize and condense a book.

There is a wide gap between the ability to understand what is said in the book and the ability to explain what is written to other people. The latter is very hard. . . . I finally achieved that stage, but naturally this didn't happen within a year or even two, but during my second stint in prison. Altogether I sat in prison for seven years, during the first four of which I studied, while for the last three I was mainly occupied in teaching others.

Nasser ʿAtallah's first experience in prison—following his activism with the committee of high school pupils—came in 1986, almost twenty years after Abu-Ghalus's first incarceration. Despite these differences, his meeting at the age of seventeen with prison studies was very similar to that of his older comrade.

Before prison, I read a little at home, but it was in prison that I seriously studied my first book of philosophy. The subject was dialectical materialism. I devoted four hours daily to making progress in reading the book and preparing material for the meeting on the subject. Every day one of my cellmates sat with me to go over the more difficult sections. There were several people in the meeting; each would ask questions in turn and others would respond, with this continuing until the problems were overcome. In this way you learn to persuade, to discuss, and gradually you acquire tools enabling you to analyze, which you can apply to many other subjects.

Those who guided the young Nasser in his studies were the older administrative detainees with whom he shared a cell in Jneid prison. A few months after being released, he was arrested again. This time most of his partners in the room and the wing were of his age, though without prior experience in the ways of study in prison. Nasser moved forward at the age of eighteen to the status of "teacher-pupil" or "counselor-student."

In my second imprisonment [1987] most of the prisoners who were jailed with me were young. We worked out a study program that suited the different educational levels of the prisoners. The newcomers, who lacked education, mainly studied the history of the national movement, while for the most part I studied basic terms in Marxist and economic theory. Most of my time during this period was divided between my studies and meetings at which I taught for some of the time and studied the rest. In the morning hours I set aside time to prepare for the meeting at which I would teach and afterward I prepared for the second meeting, in which I participated as a student. This is how I spent about twelve hours, day by day. It is true that not everyone liked to study, and sometimes they forced someone to do so, but most of the people had the desire, and some were quite enthusiastic.

It seems that the prisoners' enthusiasm was related to the question-and-answer method of group study mentioned by Nasser. This was the popular custom in the prisons at various periods. Hussein Shaheen took part in an earlier version of it when he was in the Beersheva prison during the years 1967–71:

I remember that we once got hold of two publications, one of the Soviet Communist Party and the other of the Chinese Communist Party. In those days we were imprisoned in a large hall containing some tens of prisoners, all of whom read the material and prepared for questions and answers. I opened the discussion, which continued from four in the afternoon until eleven at night, not finishing until we were forced by the prison guard to stop. We tried to understand the party stances, who is preserving and developing the theory, and who is sinking into dogmatism.

The systematic study of abstract theoretical subjects demanded a much larger effort and intellectual investment than that required by political studies. It seems that young "rookie" prisoners grappling with difficult and complex texts relied upon interpersonal relations forged between them and the prison veterans no less than upon the common study group. Many of the interviewees attributed their intellectual development to a key figure who knew how to give them encouragement and support at the right moment.

Fuad Laham met Jasser in his third year in Nablus prison (1983). Fuad was then seventeen and Jasser thirty-five:

He was a veteran prisoner after thirteen years in jail. He sat with me for two hours every day and taught me books on political economy and on dialectics. After this I was capable of reading alone. He had many medical problems and was released in 1985 [as part of the Jibril prisoner exchange]. During the Intifada Jasser was arrested again when he was very ill and shortly afterward he died in prison. He was the person who did me the biggest favor in my whole life.

When it came to the learning process and group studies in prison, the production of study materials and their dissemination were no less important than intellectual "production." Preparing and distributing the booklets involved a range of tasks and responsibility, as demonstrated in the testimony of Ahmad Ja'fari. Upon his transfer in 1987, at the age of eighteen, from Nablus prison to the youth wing at Hebron prison, Ahmad accepted the responsibility of preparing booklets for the wing, which then housed 150 youngsters: "I handled the rewriting of the booklets from the time of my entry into the wing until I left. I probably wrote more words than the words I had spoken in my entire life. Sometimes I would write continuously for twenty-four hours."

As Ahmad explained, the regular updating of the booklets in the youth wing assisted not only in implementing the study program but also in "providing the youngsters with the regulations and the order of the internal organization." It is therefore no wonder that he sees a direct connection between his contribution to the organized study program and what he and his comrades achieved in the struggle for better conditions:

Our stand, that of the young people, in a hunger strike which went on for sixteen days, was proof that the great investment and hard work had succeeded. The prison authorities thought it would be very easy to break the strike in the youth wing, but what happened was the exact opposite: After the adults called off the strike we didn't want to stop. We went on for another day until they brought an adult prisoner to persuade us that the strike was over.

Group study also revolved around subjects that were not directly included in the educational program of the political organizations, such as languages (mainly Hebrew), the sciences, and general history. These lessons were conducted in an open forum, which included all those in a room who were interested in learning and the expert teacher. Muhammad Laham, who spoke fluent Hebrew, for which he later became renowned in Dheisheh and beyond, learned the language step by step with the help of the series of booklets called *One Thousand Words*, which is used in the Israeli *ulpan* (school for learning Hebrew) courses for new immigrants. His linguistic expertise enabled him, among other things, to become acquainted with the Zionist writings of Theodor Herzl, David Ben-Gurion, and Berl Katznelson, as well as with Hayyim Nahman Bialik's poetry and with the new Hebrew literature. Unsurprisingly, the censor did not place any special difficulty in the way of

his acquiring these books. Parallel to this, Muhammad held courses in Hebrew for beginners in all of the six prisons where he was incarcerated in the
course of his ten years of imprisonment.

Identifying with the Material: Marxist Theory
in the Worldview of the Prisoners

It is difficult, perhaps impossible, to dissociate the significance that the organized prisoners' collective accorded to the texts under study from the subjective meaning that each prisoner attributed to the written word. The individual shares his relationship with the text with others because of its place in the
collective life in prison. At the same time, the relationship is uniquely his, the
fruit of his endeavor and his understanding. This dualism emerges clearly in
the former prisoners' recollections of the learning process in prison; they underscore, along with the strong communal foundation, the development of
a personal and noninstrumental connection between the prisoner and the
world of knowledge and of thought with which he became familiar. This
connection, which as we learned, can be defined in terms of an emotional,
intellectual, and ideological identification with the content of the material
studied, was constructed mainly around the study of Marxist theory.

Hussein Shaheen was an eighteen-year-old college student when arrested at the end of the summer of 1967, only three months after the war.
Sentenced to four years of incarceration on the charge of "membership in
a hostile organization," he spent most of the time in Beersheva prison.
Some twenty-five years had passed since then until my interview with him
in the UNRWA office in the camp, where he occupied a senior post.

When I entered prison I was somewhat mature, but rather than a full ideological
maturity, mine was a very superficial awareness of the national struggle. There were
no books in Nablus prison, while there were some in Kfar Yonah, but not of a standard to satisfy a person's appetite for reading. In Beersheva there were books in various fields such as philosophy, literature, and economics, and I was motivated to devote myself to study so as to get something out of the period in jail. I hated meta-
physical concepts and wanted to know the laws of society and of nature.

I well remember the time when I studied dialectical materialism, the evolution
of society, the process of progressing from ape to man, as explained by Engels.
From Engels I learned that labor is the basis for human society and that this is what
differentiates it from animal society. At night I dreamed of the transition from ape
to man . . . I had to get up and decide whether I would live according to the old
ideas, or would realize the new ones that I had learned. It was then that I understood that I had become a scientific person.

Interestingly, other interviewees too mentioned their fascination with
Engels's *The Part Played by Labor in the Transition from Ape to Man* (1876) and

The Origin of the Family, Private Property and the State (1884), though not in the vivid language of Hussein Shaheen.

Ahmad Muhaisan had a communist outlook even before entering prison in 1974; among his relatives were leading communist activists who had been imprisoned under Jordanian rule and had contributed to his political education during his adolescence. But like others, Ahmad was only seventeen when he was sentenced to two years in prison, and in his case as well prison studies yielded broad returns in knowledge and awareness.

I'll try to speak in the name of "that Ahmad" as he learned the things in prison in those days, even if my outlook today can be discerned [after his release from prison Ahmad was an activist in the trade unions, a journalist on the paper *a-Tali°a,* and a laborer]. The Marxist idea tries to explain and answer for us why we are in the condition in which we find ourselves, to understand the wide global context. This is the difference between Marxism and that closed, limited nationalist thinking that only knows how to say: "fight the Occupation." It uses this slogan without giving an explanation for our reality and to the numerous forces at work that influence us without our recognizing them. The truth is that much of our Palestinian reality is shaped by external factors such as the U.S. political and economic interests in the region, the armament race, and the global "division of labor" between rich and poor nations, which it is our task to expose and study. Looking at our situation from this angle gives us the feeling that we are part of the wide world. Of course, this doesn't mean losing our tie to our homeland, but it takes us out of the confines of nationalism. This is something I learned from Marxism.

Marxism also differs from other schools of thought in that it searches for causes and is not satisfied solely with consequences, as in American thinking. The interest in outcomes alone is a superficial American system of thinking. Thus when I, as a Marxist, want to do something in the Dheisheh camp, I must understand all the factors influencing the reality. When I understand logically and scientifically—and I'm talking of dialectic logic and not Aristotle's formalistic logic—how things develop and change, this will help me even in relations with my wife.

°Adnan Ramadan's first prolonged imprisonment (fifteen months) was in 1985 when he was nineteen years old. He spoke of the books that most influenced him in prison:

Particularly Lenin's books, such as *The State and Revolution* (1917), *What Is to Be Done?* (pamphlet, 1902), and *"Left Wing" Communism: An Infantile Disorder* (1920), works that we studied in detail. *The State and Revolution* covered many aspects relevant to our reality. It speaks of how to organize and how to overcome problems that every organization may face. It analyzes the political significance of the state, the historical role that it played, the importance of the party, and the necessity of revolution and taking over power. For me the most important subject was the development of the party, since it can lead the people. I believed that the leaders of the party must be most outstanding from the point of readiness to sacrifice, education, discipline, morality, and so on. One can say that I thought in an idealistic way. I believed that the principle goal must be the creation of a reality that corresponds with the theoretical literature.

For Nidal Abu-ʿAker, who experienced his first prolonged imprisonment in 1987 at the age of seventeen,

The main thing in this [Marxist] theory is the struggle against exploitation and oppression in every place and on every subject: between classes, between oppressed peoples and imperialism. Since we are in a situation of Occupation and suppression and exploitation, we are connected, like it or not, with this theory. In prison you also link up with the efforts of other liberation movements and peoples in human history; in China, in Vietnam, in Algeria. Sometimes when I was depressed, I would read of the successes and victories in the struggles of others and my mood would change for the better.

For Muhammad Ramadan, who was the same age as Nidal and had undergone similar imprisonment experience, the strength of the theory was also in its application to the problems of reality.

In prison you learn not only the theory but also how to live with it, which is not the case in university. Dialectical materialism interested me very much, and especially the sources and rules of knowledge, because this enabled me to analyze things and not to cling to superficial explanations. For instance, my mother would always say that I had a "hard head" because I was born that way and it's a part of me, and she couldn't understand how the environment, education, and social situation of a person more or less determine his behavior.

My group of interviewees included a wide spectrum of former prisoners who differed from each other in political affiliation, in intellectual ability, and in personal inclinations. Not all delved deeply into studies, and of those who did, not all were devotees of Marxism. But it was rare to meet an interviewee who didn't attribute to Marxism some influence on his leanings. Ahmad Abu-Laban, who was in prison in the mid-1970s, noted:

I liked certain things in every stream of thought, and I took elements from each. I was greatly influenced by the literature of national liberation movements, and by the idea of an Arab nation and Arab unity. I was also taken by some of the Islamic literature. From Marxist literature I was convinced by the idea of political economy.

Ibrahim Ramadan, who was in prison in the years 1975–77, confessed that he did not get along with the scientific side of Marxism: "I preferred realistic fiction and existentialist philosophy related to Marxism. The economic theory was too complicated and less attractive for me. I read a lot of Russian literature, which was Marxist in spirit."

What, then, was behind the secret attraction of Marxist theory for generations of Palestinian prisoners in Israeli prisons? It appears that the explanation is not to be found in terms of "organizational (party) distribution" in prison, since Marxist theory won backing and influence over and above organizational affiliation. Moreover, as the interviews clearly show, it cannot be reduced to a question of competition over ideology between organizations. Rather, it was a matter of granting priority and higher status to a scientific and theoretical basis; in other words, attempting to embed the ideological in a world of scientific concepts. The interviews demonstrate that along with organizational affiliation, collective discipline, and the thirst for education, the prisoners were also motivated by a longing to adopt a worldview and act within it.

The source of this longing can be explained against the backdrop of the prisoners' struggle with the totality of the prison situation as part of an extreme regime of repression and denial of freedom and rights. It was the attempt to establish a comprehensive counterorder, and to maintain it under prison conditions, that necessitated an encompassing theory and world outlook, one that could provide tools for analysis, on the one hand, and a framework for belonging and solidarity, on the other. There is a totality, a holism in Marxism, and especially in its underlying attempt to connect the particular with the universal, the contemporary with the historical, the social with the economic, and of course, theory with praxis. It is this totality, as I see it, that stood at the heart of the drawing power of Marxism.

Marxism was not a substitute for national ideology and for loyalty to the Palestinian cause; rather, the latter represented a particular case in the axis of time and space and the unfolding of history, which Marxism encompassed. Thus, through the agency of theory and literature, the practice created in prison—the counterorder—joined up with processes, developments, and goals of a broader scope. Through this "mediation," the prisoners linked themselves with "partners on the path of struggle" in China, Cuba, Vietnam, and Algeria who provided support and inspiration, expanding the borders of solidarity.

The converging of the two factors—first, the experience of "total" struggle with the situation of imprisonment, and second, the "totality" of the Marxist worldview—provides an explanation for the vitality of this theory in the internal world of the prisoner-students. It would, however, be wrong to see this as an internal phenomenon of prison life, divorced from the historical connection. The "partners on the path of struggle" and the path itself, which the prisoners came to know through literature, were not imaginary or invented; they were part of the world order within which the Palestinian national movement existed in that period, namely, the years 1967–87.

The Soviet Union was then a great power and the leader of a world camp. Notwithstanding the criticism directed at its regime, it represented an opposite pole to U.S. policy in the Middle East, Southeast Asia, Latin America, Africa, and wherever revolutionary movements struggled for national independence, liberation from colonial rule, or other forms of regime change. One has of course to bear in mind the success of the United States in co-opting and winning the support of Arab regimes considered radical in the past and the expansion of American strategic pacts in the region, as well as the weakening of the PLO in the wake of the Israeli invasion of Lebanon (1982). In spite of these factors, in those years it was inconceivable that ne-gotiation of a political solution to the Palestinian problem would bypass the Soviet Union and take place outside UN auspices. In addition, the solidarity that the prisoners evinced toward other liberation movements was not new. On the contrary, it was entrenched in the well-developed contacts that the Palestinian organizations had forged since the early 1960s—separately or in the context of the PLO as an umbrella organization—with socialist and rad-ical regimes and revolutionary movements the world over. The ties were ex-pressed through political support and often also through military and mate-rial assistance provided to the Palestinians throughout the period.

The Palestinian prisoner-student did not search for an escape from reality in dialectical materialism, and in its arms he found neither consolation nor substitute. For him the strength of the theory was in its relevance to two dimensions of his existence: his struggle as part of an organized collective against the prison and his belonging to a national liberation movement steering its course in a polarized world in which socialism still constituted an alternative. We should not be surprised, therefore, if the dismantling of the regime in the Soviet Union, the decline of the Socialist bloc, and the beginning of the undisturbed hegemony of the United States exercised a profound influence, among other things, on the intellectual life of the Pales-tinian prisoners in Israeli prisons.[7]

Imprisonment and the Politicization Process

In September 1992, some five years after the eruption of the Intifada, fol-lowing a quarter of a century of Israeli Occupation of the Palestinian Ter-ritories, and approximately a year before the Oslo Accords were to appear on the horizon, more than ten thousand Palestinian political prisoners held in Israeli prisons declared a hunger strike of unlimited duration. The strike broke out over the demand of the prisoners for immediate improvements in their conditions of imprisonment, which they claimed had deteriorated. Among other demands, the strikers pressed for longer family visits and the relaxation of visiting regulations, improvements in medical care, putting an end to punishing prisoners in isolation wings, permitting the movement of prisoners between cells during the day, and immediate changes in the con-ditions under which prisoners with life sentences were held. The political background was, on the one hand, the protracted freeze in negotiations in the context of the Madrid Conference, and on the other, the entry into power three months beforehand of the Rabin government in Israel.

The hunger strike was initially met by the prison authorities' outright re-fusal to discuss the prisoners' demands, which state officials referred to as "the fruit of external incitement." The strike was maintained scrupulously and with full internal coordination in all the prisons in the areas of Israel and the Occupied Territories, and it gathered momentum as time passed. After a long period of enfeeblement and decline in Intifada activity, so-called Intifada scenes of public protest, commanding mass participation by various sectors of the Palestinian population, returned to the world's television screens. There were hunger strikes by hundreds of the prisoners' mothers in solidarity with their sons, processions and demonstrations of mass support, confrontations between school pupils and Israeli soldiers, and of course many casualties, in-cluding the killings of some protesters. Hundreds of people were arrested. All these actions linked up with the hunger strike as it entered its second week, still without results and without any real negotiations.

The reversal took place in the wake of intervention by then-Israeli minis-ter of police Moshe Shahal. Negotiations between him and the leaders of the prisoners' coordinating committee led to the granting of a large number of the strikers' demands. For fifteen days the prisoners and their demands were at the top of the agenda and of public protest activity in the Occupied Terri-tories, while in Israel a media and political storm broke out over the supposed capitulation of state officials to the strikers.

The political prisoners had succeeded in leading a move whose public and political influence and significance went far beyond prison walls. This success in the 1992 strike cannot be explained or understood without turn-ing to the internal organization in prison. The internal discipline that facili-tated the maintenance of a hunger strike by ten thousand people for fifteen days, the coordination between strikers in different prisons, the representative leadership that formulated the demands and conducted the negotiations, the detailed and well-argued demands, the link between the specific struggle and the timing in the political process, and the strong public support—these were not born in September 1992. All were the result of what had been built over years in prison.

Several conclusions follow from my findings on the prison experiences of former prisoners from Dheiseh. Imprisonment did not signify an end to po-litical participation or even a temporary distancing from it, but rather their entrance into a new and enhanced sphere of activism, the one that was de-veloped by the organized prisoners. The newcomer prisoner met face to face with the prison order, which was oppressive and violent, denying the pris-oner rights, isolating and alienating him. Countering this and struggling against it was the prisoners' order, opening up new channels before him: an intellectual world, personal responsibilities and challenges, leadership trajectories, and group life. Most of these avenues were not part of his experience, at least not in similar scope or composition, prior to the prison period. Paradoxically, it was within prison walls that Dheishehian activists gained access to long-term participation in a ramified, highly sophisticated organization and to meaningful membership in an ideological and political collective.

The ages and backgrounds of the prisoners at the time of their first prolonged imprisonment are, in themselves, evidence for this claim. The first encounter with prison life of the typical Dheishehian activist of the late 1960s and early 1970s took place at the age of seventeen, eighteen, or nineteen, usually following the exposure of the clandestine cell to which he had belonged for only several weeks or months. The typical Dheishehian activist of the 1980s was also imprisoned in his late teens, but this time in the wake of two to four years of activity in the students' committees and regular participation in demonstrations and street confrontations with army forces. Under the conditions that prevailed in the West Bank, the option of armed resistance was completely blocked, while organized political activity was continuously obstructed by clashes with the military rule and took place under the permanent shadow and threat of arrests. The prisons, where so many were to undergo their punishment, were a "sanctuary" if only because it was no longer possible to threaten their inmates with incarceration.

The uniqueness of the prisoners' internal organization lies in its development as a comprehensive means of struggling against the prison situation. The intertwined, intersupportive layers constituted axes of activity that generated relations of commitment, authority, leadership, and comradeship within the group and provided goals and meaning for its members. Moreover, the central role of studies and education in the prisoners' counterorder lent to organized prison life the dimension of a prolonged developmental process. A special merging between theory and practice and between group activity and individual progress was created through the encounter of the prisoner-student with a wide historical and social literature, through his acquisition of new theoretical tools and concepts, and concomitantly, by his gradual change in status as he passed from the stage of a beginner to taking on the responsible task of teacher and counselor. The politicization process of young men from Dheisheh thus underwent a qualitative transformation during their period of imprisonment.

CHAPTER 11

Organizing Around Political Prisoners

THE POLITICIZATION OF FAMILY LIFE

THE PRISONER IS to a large extent a "present absentee" in relation to his family. He is, of course, missing from their daily life and from the family workforce and division of labor. At the same time, his presence in an Israeli jail manifests itself in family life in several ways, particularly in changed gender and generational roles, in the concomitant changes in the interrelationships among family members, and in the forms of extrafamilial political and social contacts and activities that family members pursue. This chapter focuses on the family members who undergo politicization, tracing the attendant processes, pointing at the various resources that accrue, and evaluating the outcome of these developments in the long run, when the prison epoch is over and becomes part of the family history.

Political imprisonment, in itself, is prima facie evidence for the politicization of individuals, family, community, and society living under an occupation regime. One can therefore claim that to see imprisonment as a central factor in the politicization of family life inverts the actual chronology of development. Moreover, it is doubtful whether the effects of imprisonment can be isolated from the totality of social and economic factors giving rise to processes of change. Therefore, in examining this variable there is no avoiding generalization and simplification.

These reservations notwithstanding, I portray the confrontation of Dheishehian families with the imprisonment of their members as a structured, multistaged process. The process begins with the family's "passive participation" in the arrest and detention of a son/father/brother, continues with the involvement of family members in channels of informal organization around the prisoner and the prisoners' cause, and may reach its peak in their joining organized political frameworks.

The reconstruction of stages in the trajectories of politicization requires not only generalization but the isolation of each stage. To this end, I put aside the rather significant differences that are to be found among families in the camp. The reaction of a family whose son was imprisoned at the beginning of the 1970s was not the same as, or even similar to, that of a family whose son was imprisoned in the course of the Intifada. Similarly, members of a kinship group whose branches included many activists and political prisoners were likely to act very differently from those of a clan that was relatively uninvolved. Moreover, while my research model puts emphasis on a cumulative developmental process constructed in the course of involvement, it is doubtful if one can distinguish between what could be called the "collective means" or accumulated social experience available to a family and the personal, subjective experiences of the participants involved. Rather, these two factors are intertwined, building each other and being built by one another, and subsequently yielding the observed behavior.

The central protagonists in this chapter are women, mainly the mothers and sisters of the prisoners. One reason for this can be traced to the empirical findings of fieldwork, which show the extensive involvement of women in taking on roles demonstrating the family's concern for the prisoner's needs and maintaining continuous contact with him. The second reason is associated with my hypotheses: organization around imprisonment in general, and the prisoner, in particular, constituted a major factor in the politicization of women of different generations in Dheisheh.

The Initial Response: Shock and Helplessness

> I felt that I was defeated. A person's children help him like a
> bird's wings help it to fly, and now instead of my son's helping
> me, I had to help him.
> —ʿALI LAHAM, THE FATHER OF FORMER PRISONER NASSER LAHAM, ON
> HIS FEELING IN THE WAKE OF HIS SON'S IMPRISONMENT IN 1985

The first experience of a family with the arrest of one of its members leads to shock, uncertainty, and the paralysis of helplessness. Though neighbors and acquaintances offer help borne of prior experience, they cannot blunt the immediate impact of the blow. When first arrested, ʿAdel was not yet eighteen years old, still in his last grade of high school. He was arrested at the government high school for boys in the village of Irtas. Soldiers and agents of Shabak surrounded the schoolyard and ordered the headmaster and the janitor to go with them to the class where he was studying. From there ʿAdel was taken to the Russian compound detention center in Jerusalem. Ten years later, in 1995, his mother still found it difficult to speak of what happened to her that day: "I told you about everything you asked, about the village, about the harvest in the Jordan Valley, about working as a cleaning woman, about the family, but about this I don't want to speak. May God punish all the evildoers."

When she finally consented, she told of a boy who arrived at their house and informed her that ʿAdel had been arrested. She ran in the rain to Irtas (the school is half an hour's walk from the family home in Dheisheh) to learn details of what had happened. She rushed around, asking the headmaster, the teachers, his friends, anyone she met—but nobody had answers.

I hoped, for his and our sake, that at least they took some other lads, but then I learned that he was all by himself. They held ʿAdel for two months under interrogation, forbidding us to see him. Finally came the day when the trial was supposed to start. I traveled with my daughter to the military court in Ramallah. We sat in the courtroom and waited for them to bring him in. But he never arrived. Hours later someone told us that ʿAdel was ill and the trial was postponed. My daughter and I tore out our hair, we were almost out of our minds.

Arrests were usually made at homes, mainly at night, at a time when all family members were present. In many cases the arrests were accompanied by curses, humiliation, and brutal acts of violence, with soldiers beating family members, breaking furniture and other property, destroying foodstuffs, and appropriating personal possessions. Mahmud Ramadan, father of four sons, three of whom were arrested and imprisoned dozens of times, noted that:

My being an old man didn't stop them from beating me up. Once they tied me up and held me outside the house until they'd finished. Every time they wanted to take one of the sons, they came to this house, and every time they broke things—the outer doors and doors to the rooms, the sink, the taps, and even the toilet bowl. I don't want to replace the doors until the Occupation is over because they will break them whenever they come to my house.

Naʿim Abu-ʿAker described the first time soldiers arrested one of his twin sons, then aged fourteen: "Six soldiers came to the house. Inside, they took the boys to one room and me and their mother to another. We heard the beatings and the cries of our sons but could do nothing."

For weeks after the shock of the arrest the families would suffer from anxiety and uncertainty. As mentioned, the military law permitted holding a resident of the Occupied Territories under detention for a period of eighteen days, with automatic extension likely, without a lawyer and without bringing the detainee before a judge. As long as the interrogation continued, the individual was denied family visits and the law permitted withholding information pertaining to his whereabouts.

Withholding information sometimes continued after the prisoner was tried and transferred to one of the prisons. Jamila ʿAtallah described her search for her oldest son, Akram, who was sentenced to imprisonment in 1982:

They held him for three months of interrogation in Moscobia. After the trial they transferred him to Ramleh prison without informing us where he was being held. We started to look for him in Hebron, Beersheva, Shata, and Ashkelon prisons. Every time we would come on visiting day we were sent back. By chance a young man was released from Ramleh prison and came to tell us that Akram was there. When visitors' day came we traveled to Ramleh but in vain. The officers in charge said that he had just been transferred to another prison, without telling us which one. After a month of searching we found him in al-Khalil [Hebron] prison.

While lack of information was one source of anxiety, another was awareness of what could be expected to happen. Families knew that interrogations carried out by the Shabak (GSS) at the detention center were extremely harsh. Family members usually heard about interrogation from others: stories of beating, torture, cruelty, threats, denial of sleep, overcrowding and filth, and attempts to trick the prisoner and turn him into a collaborator. To this overall anxiety was added fear over the fate of minors, children, and youth between the ages of thirteen and sixteen, who accounted for a considerable number of the prisoners.

ʿImad Shaheen and his maternal cousin were arrested together when they were less than thirteen years old. His mother described the different fears that gripped her and her brother: "We didn't know if they were cold, if they got blankets to cover themselves, if they had food to eat. We feared the beatings, and even more than anything we were frightened that the Mukhabarat would succeed in winning them over at such a young age."

The father of Fuad Laham, who went to prison at age fifteen, said that his greatest fear in the first period was for the fate of his son thrown in suddenly among adults. Burhan ʿAtallah was taken for interrogation and arrest when he was thirteen, and his father described the desperation that took hold of him when he saw his son beaten and bruised, cleaning the soldiers' latrines in the courtyard of the military government detention center in Bethlehem: "I saw my son in the soldiers' sewerage, in their shit. I felt the pain and the humiliation all over my body. In those days I had no contacts with people who understand politics, and so I went to collaborators who had connections with the military governor and pleaded with them to help me get him out of prison."

Trials were conducted in Hebrew, with both the family members and the lawyer acting on their behalf following the proceedings with great difficulty. Accordingly, the sentence usually came as a shock to the prisoner's family. Zohara, the sister of Nasser Laham, who was sentenced on a charge of membership in a hostile organization, said that it took her father more than two years to absorb the fact that his son would spend five years in jail. Fuad Laham described his father's reaction to his sentence in 1980 to five years in prison:

Until then my father believed that there was justice in Israeli law and that since I was a minor they wouldn't sentence me to prison. He thought that at worst there would be a suspended sentence, bail, and a fine. He couldn't endure it when he heard the sentence and left without speaking to me or even looking at me. I was among the first in Dheisheh to go to prison at the age of fifteen for such a long period.

Many of the older interviewees pointed out the deterioration in the physical and mental health suffered by parents and relatives of prisoners: "The imprisonment was extremely painful. His mother fell ill because of the trial and never recovered afterward." Many felt that their sons had squandered their futures, calculating the imprisonment in terms of the number of years ·of study wasted. The third son of Abu ʿAwni was arrested for the first time in 1978 and was in prison on and off for thirteen years. During this period his two elder brothers studied at university and migrated to Saudi Arabia for work. When I asked how his son's imprisonment influenced him, Abu ʿAwni replied, "I always wanted him to study. For me that was the most important thing. Education is the most important thing. Let us assume that he becomes a political leader; even so he doesn't have a *shahada* [a certificate that attests to the completion of studies] so what future awaits him if one day a Palestinian state is established? He will be a simple worker, nothing more."[1]

Nasser, ʿAli Laham's son, was sentenced in 1985 to five years when he was a nineteen-year-old student at Bethlehem University. His older brother and his sister are graduates of that university, and another brother completed university studies in Jordan. ʿAli, who owns a small vegetable store in Dheisheh, told of his thoughts and feelings at the time: "I felt defeated in life. It was a mortal blow; first and foremost he missed out on his studies. Children are your support for the future, and now instead of his helping me I had to visit him in prison."

Imprisonment and studies, particularly higher studies, were perceived at the time by many parents as an impossible combination. And indeed, at least on the surface, daily life served to strengthen this perception: As it turned out, on the very same day that Nasser was arrested and jailed, his older brother received a scholarship to study for his degree in chemistry in the United States. In the same year that Nasser was released from prison (1990), his brother completed his doctorate.

On Visiting Day and Active Participation

It is difficult to locate the transition from the helplessness that paralyzes the family following the imprisonment to the beginning of active participation on behalf of the prisoner. However, in general the new developments began from the time when the family was permitted to be in contact with the prisoner. Family members were unable to protect him or save him from pain and gross injustice, but they could be present at the court sessions and visit him in jail. In the 1970s visits took place once a month, while in the 1980s, following the prisoners' struggles, biweekly visits were permitted. The visits, which took place on a fixed day and lasted about half an hour, constituted the main connection between the family and the prisoner. Among the four categories of relatives who received permits to visit, the prisoner's mother, and his wife if he was married, were generally regulars who did not miss an opportunity to come. Sisters came every other visit; fathers, brothers, and children every second or third visit; relatives from the extended family once every two or three months. The prisoner's colleagues and friends almost never came to visit. Military law does not allow former security prisoners to visit prison, thereby disqualifying almost all young males. Furthermore, the right to visit is preserved first and foremost for relatives.

Visiting day, which as described here focuses on the family and not on the prisoners, was an intensive, densely packed personal and collective experience. The actual meeting between family members and prisoner was the primary event, but a no less central dimension was the direct exposure of the family to the military regime's most blatant mechanisms of repression. Then there was the collective-social moment of meeting between members of the prisoner's family and hundreds of other prisoners' families from different parts of the West Bank and the Gaza Strip, all of whom were in similar circumstances. There was also the geopolitical level—journeys to prisons scattered all over Israel and Palestine. There was also the cumulative dimension of the visiting day, one link in a long chain of past and future visits.

The day would start before sunrise and end in the late afternoon or evening. Excitement and tension grew on the night before the visit, as Fauzia elucidated. A seventy-year-old widow (in 1992) whose son Youssef was sentenced in 1985 to ten years in prison, Fauzia had raised five children by herself, supporting them from cleaning work in West Jerusalem. After her son's arrest, the army sealed part of her house, and she continued to live alone in what was left of her home: one room and a kitchenette. After seven years and hundreds of visits, Fauzia still experienced anxiety the night before visiting her son:

On visiting days I wake up at one in the morning because of stomach pains and excitement. You know how a mother feels for her child? I get up, pray, and occupy myself with petty tasks. I wrap up something small to eat, and something for the grandchildren who will come with their mother. I make sure that I don't forget my identity card, heaven forbid. I kill time until four in the morning, leave the house, and walk toward the main road [a walk of at least half an hour from her house in the extreme southeast of Dheisheh, not far from the northern border of Irtas village] where I catch a service cab to Bethlehem.

Old Red Cross and Red Crescent buses, which took the prisoners' families from the region, used to leave Bethlehem at six in the morning on their way to the prisons. In the autumn of 1987, about two months before the Intifada broke out (and almost five years before my field research started), I joined families from Dheisheh on a visit to Jneid, the central West Bank prison. I documented my impressions in an article in the weekly supplement to the daily Hebrew newspaper *Davar*.

Just after six in the morning I arrived at the Red Cross quarters in Bethlehem. Had I come a few minutes later, I would have missed the last bus. Were it in their hands, the people gathered there would have set out at half past five, or perhaps even earlier. Never in my life have I encountered travelers as disciplined and restrained as this group of families on their way to their bimonthly visit to Jneid prison. My assumption that they needed time to organize themselves proved false, and less than two minutes after the doors of the bus opened it was on its way. People took their seats without superfluous talk. Most know each other from former visits or from similar occasions in the more distant past.[2]

Yusra Abu-Laban, sister of Saleh, who was in jail for fifteen years, told me that there had not always been organized visits. When her brother was imprisoned in 1970, he was held in Ashkelon prison:

The visit to Ashkelon prison was extremely difficult. Whenever the visiting day arrived [at that time visits took place only once a month] we had to get a permit from the military governor in Bethlehem. The visit depended on the good will of the governor. Now it is entirely different. In the past very few people went to visit and we all knew each other. We got used to going together to the governor to ask for the permit. Once, when it was snowing, we went by foot to Bethlehem and returned without permits.

On the way to and from prison, many friendships formed between mothers, fathers, and young people. The members of each family would compare their fate to that of others, would hear of new arrests, would be updated on news of prisoners, and would chat about the future of their sons after their release. Personal appearance was also considered important. Visitors, particularly women, were accustomed to putting on their best garments for the journey. The prisoners' mothers usually dressed in embroidered *fallaha* (peasant woman) dresses worn for special occasions, with white headscarves. Some of the visiting wives and sisters appeared in modern garb—jeans and shirt or sweater—taking care to do their hair the day before. Other, "traditional" women would wear a *jilbab* (cloak) and scarf, which covered their body and hair. The prisoner's children wore their most festive clothing and were carefully combed.

On arrival at the prison gates, the visitors had to register, line up, and wait to be called by the prisoner's name. Waiting, often under a burning sun or in rain and cold, could last hours, often ending with an announcement by the prison authorities that visits were canceled as punishment for a prisoners' strike, or without a reason being given. On the grounds near the prison the families collected new information and heard rumors about their children: the conditions under which they were held, how the prison authorities treated them, and the internal politics. There they became friends with families from villages, towns, and camps from all over the West Bank. Like the son who met fellow prisoners from Nablus, Jenin, Hebron, and the Gaza Strip, the relatives, in the course of their visits, would get to know families from some locales they had barely known of previously. They treated each other to cigarettes, sandwiches, cold drinks, or lupine seeds in salt and lemon; they exchanged addresses and got advice about trials, lawyers, and appeals.

A constant source of strength and support derived from the meeting between families who experienced a common fate and shared a joint struggle. In retrospect, family visits to prisons in the 1970s and 1980s can be identified as a significant contributor to the growth of solidarity and a shared consciousness among various sectors in the Palestinian population. These qualities found expression in the popular uprising that broke out in 1987.

The frequent transfer of prisoners from one prison to another, as well as the fact that some families had more than one family member in prison, often compelled the visitors to travel throughout Israel/Palestine. When I asked Khadija Laham about her visits to her imprisoned sons and relatives, she inquired in return: "What prison do you want to hear about? Mejiddo? Bitunia? Atlit? ʿAskelan? Khalil? A-Sabʿa? Al-Naqab? I was in all of them and they were all hard prisons. I never saw Jenin before going to Mejiddo prison, and I knew nothing of the Naqab [Negev] until I visited the Ketziot prison." Yusra Abu-Laban recounted the journeys to Ashkelon prison where her brother was held in the early 1970s: "The bus would go to Ashkelon via Beit Shemesh and Beit Jibrin. On the way we saw our village, Zakariya. Mother remembered the whole area there; she remembered the names of all the destroyed villages, the wheat and barley fields, the olive trees, and she would tell me of all this." Indeed, bus trips to prisons inside the green line very often passed near the Dheishehians' villages of origin.

The designated half-hour visit with the prisoner, the emotional summit of the day, took place in a corridor waiting room with the prisoner behind double bars. Family members thinking about what they might tell the prisoner, women asking themselves day and night before the visit whether to tell their husbands of troubles and problems, of economic difficulties, of intrigues they faced. Mothers and fathers reported on family news: who was studying, who wanted to study, who got engaged, who planned to go to the Gulf, who was building, who was arrested, what was new with a brother or friend imprisoned elsewhere. The list was long and the time short. Sisters and brothers often used the time for short talks about books they read, asking for advice or guidance. The prisoner's small children were lifted up so that he could look at them through the bars, exchanging a word or two with them and seeing how they had grown and how nicely they were dressed.

For the families, these meetings themselves were only one element in a chain of developing commitment. Prisoners from Dheisheh were often sentenced to three, five, ten, and sometimes fifteen years in jail. In the course of these years, brothers, cousins, and other relatives were most likely also imprisoned. Not a few mothers, fathers, and sisters in Dheisheh amassed hundreds of visiting days over the years and "covered" all the prisons and detention installations in the Occupied Territories and within the green line. Parents grew old, brothers and sisters matured and raised families, babies grew up, men and women found jobs or lost them. While this went on, the visits to prison remained an indivisible part of their lives and their commitments.

Yusra, who continued for fifteen years to visit her brother, described the changes in her life over the prison years:

I was in high school when my brother entered prison. I visited him when I was a pupil and then when I was in nursing school. After my marriage in 1977, and during my first pregnancy, I continued visiting him. I came with my children to visit him when I was in my second and third pregnancies. When Saleh was freed, in 1985, I was a mother of five.

Khadija, the aunt of Muhammad Laham, who was arrested in 1975 and spent more than ten years in jail, would visit him along with his mother (her sister-in-law), and was considered one of the permanent visitors. Muhammad was released in 1985 while Khadija's sons were imprisoned one after the other. During the Intifada period, three of her sons were in detention centers or prisons. When I interviewed her in 1992, one son remained in prison, having been sentenced to three years in Ketziot camp: "We have been visiting prisoners for nearly twenty years. Sometimes it is particularly difficult, when it rains, when a curfew is imposed on the camp, when we wait a long time for the bus, when soldiers beat us, but I have become accustomed to all this."

In many respects, it was the military authorities that determined the experience that the family members went through. It was they who tried the sons and imprisoned them, set the days and hours for visits, canceled visits at a moment's notice, and punished families of prisoners in different ways. Scores of family members from Dheisheh were thrown out of their jobs in government institutions such as schools and hospitals; for years others were denied travel permits; and many more were arrested in order to intimidate them. Not least among the burdens were the heavy fines imposed in addition to the prison sentence, or the bail demanded as a condition for release.

Family activism arose as a counter to these circumstances. The participation of family members in the predicament of an imprisoned son, father, or brother placed them on a different level on the axis of confrontation. The connection between prison visits and the initiation of this process is well illustrated in the case of Naᶜim Abu-ᶜAker, who recalled his first visits to his fourteen-year-old twin sons:

My wife and I arrived for the visit to the children in the detention camp of Farᶜa. We saw them through the bars. I was always more emotional than my wife; I would cry and get excited, I couldn't stand the situation. I turned to the officer who was there and begged for mercy for the children; I asked for their release; I said they were still youngsters starting out in life, and so on. Afterward I heard this officer moralizing to the prisoners. He asked them why they of all people should cause such suffering to their parents, poor and wretched residents of a refugee camp. He asked them why they didn't leave this task to rich young men. For me it was pleasing to hear the officer talking. But when the visit started, the children were angry and shouted at me. Later I understood that I was wrong, that I was naive and selfish, that I related to the officer as if he were a master whom one should flatter and appease.

On my first visits, I traveled by taxi. I wanted to get there before the others, to be the first visitor, to avoid standing in the long line. People didn't like this and said: What's the matter with you, Abu Nidal, don't go by taxi. Come with us in the Red Crescent bus. And indeed I started taking the bus and I linked up with the families of other prisoners in the camp. We would travel together to the prison and sit together in the afternoons and evenings.

In the course of the imprisonment period the visitors, and particularly the regular ones, gained expertise, including learning about certain aspects of prison politics. They learned of the special conditions in each prison, of the stubborn struggle to achieve and safeguard prisoners' rights, as well as the tactics and strategy of the prison management. Men and women alike who had never in their lives joined organized protest activities over prisoners' issues, such as sit-down strikes, demonstrations, and processions, told me how everything changed when their relatives were in prison. They gathered every crumb of information on prisoners' strikes, the methods used, and the leaders who stood at their head. Several interviewees told me that in solidarity they held a hunger strike in their homes when these were going on in prison.

The accumulation of knowledge, experience, and familiarity with the situation, making new acquaintances and contacts—all these afforded the visitors a certain control over their situation and a sense of reliance on their own strength, distancing them from the original feeling of helplessness. Family members of former prisoners described a catalyst for change being the confrontations between them and the prison authorities during their prison visits. Khalil Laham, the father of Muhammad who was in jail for ten years, described one such incident:

They once transferred him to Tulkarem and we didn't know. For three months we didn't see him. We went to Beersheva and they said he was in Ramleh. When we got there the officer told us he had been transferred half an hour ago and then my wife spat in his face, and I said, "I haven't seen my son for three months, what's going on, aren't you human beings? You think we aren't human beings?" We went home and a few days later traveled to Tulkarem; imagine how much it cost us. We got there, and they said, "There is no visit today." I said to the policeman, "Even if you shoot me five times over, I won't go before seeing my son."

Thuraia Faraj, sister of three former prisoners and of two deportees, and mother of three former prisoners, told me of an incident that occurred when she went to visit her son in the Damoun prison near Haifa:

The first time I visited him in Damoun I forgot my identity card. There were Druze policemen there, and they didn't let me in, but I started banging on the door until they opened it. The man on the other side said, "Why are you knocking?" I said that I came all the way from Bethlehem to visit my son. He said, "How will we know that you are his mother?" I said, "I am a Palestinian and my son is a Palestinian and my brother is a Palestinian and I am from this country." He wanted to search me. I said, "Why, am I carrying a bomb with me? I came to visit my son."

Whether these testimonies reflect precisely what actually happened or whether they conceal the speakers' inner desires, what stands out is the importance that these family members attribute to their own acts of resistance, however small. Conceiving imprisonment as a catastrophe, as a personal blow, an affront, gives way to conceiving it as a period which has time limits, and this also provides space for counteraction. In the words of Khadija: "The prison isn't closed with the prisoners forever; in the end, everyone who goes in also goes out."

Change in the Social Roles of Women Visitors

It may well be that the high proportion of women among the visitors was related to the traditional female role of accepting responsibility for the needs and well-being of the family, and particularly of the children. As mentioned, the composition of the family delegation resulted in part from the ban on visits by men with security records, so that many and perhaps most of the prisoners' brothers and cousins and some of their fathers were prevented from joining. While male family members may also have been concerned over loss of work, this is not a sufficient explanation of women's disproportionate involvement, if only because often they were also wage workers, some being the primary breadwinners. This was true of many of the prisoners' mothers.

Perhaps commitment to the traditional role of mother, wife, and sister, or societal imposition of this role, served as an initial motivation for the behavior of the visiting women. Nevertheless, fulfilling the role and maintaining it are to be associated with a change or expansion of its meaning. The visiting women were not solely the mothers, wives, and sisters of a certain prisoner, but also regular and active participants in a demanding situation. As noted, this involved confrontation with soldiers and police, making new acquaintances, and amassing experience. In addition, looking after the prisoner's needs usually required contact with a lawyer (at least at the time of the arrest, the trial, and to a certain extent, for the appeal against the sentence), contact with the Red Cross and Red Crescent offices, and ongoing relations with other prisoners' families. It emerged from the interviews that in many instances the mother and/or wife of the prisoner was the individual maintaining these contacts.

Men also maintained a role in the division of labor around matters concerning the prisoner, and in many instances both parents shared such obligations as attending a trial, visiting the lawyer, and biweekly prison visit journeys. But it was rare to come across instances of a prisoner's father filling more authoritative or representative roles than did the mother. And when women didn't play the leading or main role, they were not pushed to the periphery of active family participation.

None of this came easily. On the contrary, activities centered around prisoners demanded immense mental and physical exertion and imposed great responsibility and commitment. Bearing most of the burden, women acquired skills and resources that were frequently incompatible with the overall characteristics that had until then defined their social status in the family.

KHADIJA LAHAM: AUNT AND MOTHER TO PRISONERS

Khadija, who in her own words had been "going on prison visits for nearly twenty years," was fifty-six years old when I first interviewed her in 1992. She has six sons and three daughters and never had a job outside the house. Her husband worked for years as a construction worker in Israel, and after he suffered an injury at work in 1976 the sons joined the family workforce. Khadija is illiterate, and not a single one of her nine sons and daughters completed high school. The sons dropped out of school in the 1970s and 1980s and became casual laborers in chance jobs with irregular payment, leaving the family in constant financial distress. The daughters quit school a year short of graduation and did not go out to work, marrying while still young. In short, hers was a family in which education did not affect the internal division of labor or contribute to the mobility of family members; women did not take part in earning a livelihood.

With the 1975 imprisonment of Muhammad, her husband's nephew, Khadija took upon herself the role of regular visitor and would accompany her sister-in-law on nearly every visit over a period of almost ten years. Since the 1980s, when her own sons began to go in and out of prison, she has filled the parallel role as the prisoners' mother. She was still at this when we met in 1992, when her son Muᶜawiyya was held in Ketziot. Even though it was her husband who regularly had contact with the sons' lawyers, it was apparent that the mother was better versed and most experienced in matters related to prison and prisoners. She mentioned that she did not participate in the organized political activity of the prisoners' relatives, but she showed full familiarity with it and held firm opinions on subjects such as prisoners' strikes, jail conditions, and collaborators with the prison authorities. Throughout the interview, again and again, her husband dwelt on the injustice and suffering that the Occupation had caused for his sons and family, avoiding any reference to the political dimension. Unlike him, Khadija made a point of emphasizing her enthusiasm for the educational and political side of the prisoners' life in jail: "Prison also helps the young men and in the final instance it doesn't have a bad influence, but rather the opposite. The young men are getting an education, gaining wisdom, becoming people with self-respect. Prison is a school." This glance at Khadija's life directs attention to the disparity between, on the one hand, her status as a dependent without means, her lack of education, and the particularly onerous conditions in her household, and on the other hand, Khadija's independent path vis-à-vis her relatives and sons in prison. Though it did not lead to a clash with customary social relations in the family, this seeming anomaly indicates the potential inherent in the active involvement of women relatives of prisoners.

GHOZLAN RAMADAN BECOMES A HEAVY SMOKER

Ghozlan, the mother of six daughters and five sons, was sixty-three years old in 1993. She worked as an agricultural laborer and cleaning woman in Israel in the early 1970s, and after being widowed in 1981 she was for many years the main breadwinner of the family. Two of her sons became political activists in the late 1970s and a third in the 1980s. Because of frequent arrests and imprisonment, some of them protracted, the three were not part of the family workforce in the 1980s; their studies were cut off, and they did not succeed in holding fixed jobs in the intervals between successive imprisonments. Ghozlan continued to work as a cleaning woman and to support her children until they were married.

Over a period of some twelve years, she regularly visited her children in prison (other than when they were held in Ketziot in the Negev, where visits were not permitted until 1992). At the peak of the Intifada two of her sons, then on the security services' wanted list, spent most of their time in hideouts and would show up at home at irregular hours. Ghozlan recalled what happened to her on one occasion: The sons and several of their comrades, all wanted, arrived late at night; as she did many times in those days, she cooked for them all, washed their clothes, and put them up for the night. Around five in the morning the word spread that soldiers were searching the camp. The young men fled and Ghozlan remained alone. Shortly afterward, the soldiers burst into the house: "They asked me where the young men were who had been here. I said, 'Nobody was here and I'm alone.' They pointed to the ashtray, which was full of cigarette stubs and shouted, 'You whore, who smoked all those cigarettes?' I said that I am a heavy smoker." Because, unlike Khadija, Ghozlan was a working woman and the main breadwinner of the family for most of the Occupation years, the repeated imprisonments meant balancing her work with her regular activity around the jailed sons. As in other instances in Dheisheh, the imprisonments distorted the development of the generational division of labor, leaving the widowed mother as the only family member earning a livelihood, even when she was in her sixties. Imprisonment was, therefore, the factor dominating her life for twelve years.

In itself, this case does not serve as an evaluation of the influence of Ghozlan's working life on her social position or status. But, as explained in Chapter 3, the particularly high representation of women in the family workforce in Dheisheh was not a guarantee for widening their economic possibilities and social resources. This was so regardless of whether the central reason for their becoming the central breadwinners was the imprisonment of family members or other factors. As against this, the case well typifies the connection between a way of life revolving around imprisonment and Ghozlan's immediate response. Her resourcefulness was certainly not calculated or planned in advance, but to the same extent her behavior is not surprising given the background of women's activities in this sphere.

THURAIA FARAJ COMMANDS AN OBSERVATION POST AND GIVES BIRTH

Thuraia Faraj, born in Zakariya in 1946, is the oldest of her parents' nine children. The family directed its children to studies; all seven sons acquired higher education, either abroad or in the West Bank, one of them becoming a doctor and one an engineer, while Thuraia's sister graduated from a teachers' college and has been working for more than twenty years as a teacher. Thuraia is the only one who did not complete high school. She was compelled to leave school after the preparatory stage in order to help her mother with housework and rearing the children. At the age of sixteen she was married to a relative who had barely completed elementary school, had no trade, and eked out a meager living from peddling. Thuraia has never had a paid job. She and her husband have three daughters and five sons.

Thuraia's family was renowned in Dheisheh and the Bethlehem region as an "incubator" for leaders and outstanding political activists: All her brothers were in jail; one was deported to Jordan at the beginning of the Intifada, accused of membership in the Intifada leadership, one was a founder and for many years an indisputable leader of a main political faction in the camp, and two became highly influential journalists and media figures. Thuraia, who was already married with children when her brothers were jailed, consistently visited them in prison. Her husband did not participate in these journeys or in her political world. Usually she went on her visits with her mother or alone, and she closely followed the articles by her journalist brothers. According to her, at one time the partnership between her and her husband was limited mainly to bringing up the children.

Sooner or later the children each became involved in the national struggle, either through personal activism or through matrimony. Her oldest daughter, a nurse, married a well-known political figure from Jerusalem, a former prisoner released in the Jibril exchange after having spent fourteen years in jail. The second daughter also married a former prisoner, a close friend of one of Thuraia's brothers. Her oldest son was jailed for three and a half years in the 1980s and appeared on the "most wanted" list during the Intifada. Her three younger sons were also imprisoned during the Intifada; two of them were wounded by Israeli fire in the course of a demonstration in Dheisheh, one seriously.

Once the sons became prisoners, the father too joined the circle of prison visitors, taking turns with his wife, though Thuraia remained the more active of the two. She did not become an official activist in the women's organizations, but she participated regularly in sit-down strikes opposite the Red Cross offices; in processions and demonstrations in Dheisheh, Bethlehem, and Jerusalem; and in solidarity visits to families of *shuhada* (martyrs) and the wounded.[3] "There had always been many prisoners, and in the Intifada many young people were killed, wounded, and hurt. We had to support and help each other, console one another, stand by each other on occasions of grief and sorrow. Otherwise, why are we called 'the people of Palestine'?"

Thuraia told me the story of the birth of her youngest son at the peak of the Intifada: Twelve years had passed since her last pregnancy and this one came along when she was already forty-two years old and thought herself finally finished with the burden of rearing young children. During her birth pangs, her oldest son arrived in the house with a group of wanted men. Thuraia prepared them a meal, and the men ate and went to sleep on the ground floor, while she and her husband stood watch on the roof for army patrols. In spite of the pains, Thuraia remained on guard, and only when they intensified, and after detailed instructions to her husband and daughter, did she go unaided to the UNRWA clinic in the camp, from where she was taken to hospital. The son of her old age was named Yasar by his brothers, meaning "left" (in the political sense).

In spite of her participation in meetings, solidarity visits, and demonstrations in the camp and elsewhere, she took no part in discussions on the status of women, nor did she share with her coactivists her family concerns and private affairs. Her behavior reflected her perception that these were matters for the men in the family. The marriage of her second daughter did not go well, and in her resentment, the daughter sought refuge in her parents' house, where she remained for several months, za'lana. (Literally, the word za'lana means angry, annoyed, or upset. As a cultural term it refers to the status or situation of a married woman who, in the wake of abuse or misbehavior on the part of her husband, returns to her father's home, seeking support and protection. The husband is then expected to apologize, often through mediation of kin male-messengers, and beg his wife to return.) Thuraia condemned the cruel and inconsiderate behavior of her son-in-law and his kin toward her daughter, heaping insults and curses on them. She was primarily angry at their delay in coming to take the young woman back, seeing it as an expression of disrespect and an affront. In spite of her dismay over her daughter's plight, she told me that "the job of setting the problem straight is left to the men," that is, her brothers, her husband, her son-in-law, and his father and brothers.

Thuraia's duties as a sister and mother to prisoners, and as a regular participant in activities on the behalf of the national cause, posed something of a counterweight to structural factors that conditioned her social position— such as her limited formal education, her early marriage, her role as a mother of eight and a housewife, and, of course, her gender. Life under the shadow of imprisonment wove a complete social world, intertwined within the family system, the prisoner brothers and sons, and their wide network of comrades. For Thuraia this created a wide enough social context and provided a sufficient degree of "active employment" to blur the borders between the political and the private and personal. The national and political activity derived from her own positions, and she maintained them separately from her husband. At the same time, independence was apparently not extended to other matters. Thus, although the marriage of her second daughter to a former prisoner can be considered as the fruit of the political transformation of Thuraia's life and that of her family, she herself related to matrimonial life in conservative, patriarchal terms and showed a readiness to place her daughter's plight in the hands of "the men."

The connection between women's politicization and change in their social status appears to be replete with contradictions. Major, and even extreme, changes in the social experience and tasks of the mothers, wives, and sisters of political prisoners were accompanied by a change in national and political consciousness, by an increased readiness for sacrifice, and even by willingness to endanger one's self. Sometimes, as in the case of Thuraia, this reached the level of total mobilization. Yet these changes did not necessarily lead to a change in the social-gender consciousness of the main female participants or to any comprehensive change in their social status in the family. For most, change took place mainly in distinct spheres of their life.

Politicization of Interpersonal Relations and the Social Position of Women

The people of Dheisheh see the political prisoner as the embodiment of the struggle against the Occupation and for the liberation of Palestine and its people. The interviewees who spoke of imprisonment in terms of time loss, of missed years of study, economic loss, and suffering for the family knew how to differentiate between the anguish and their pride in their prisoner. As one of the fathers put it: "I am angry about the time that he is losing, the university studies that he is missing, the injustice caused to us, about our suffering. But I honor him for being in prison."

The gratitude to the prisoner was evident even before his relatives started the routine of biweekly visits. The political prisoners were respected not only in their local communities, but also by the Palestinian public as a whole. This respect was connected with a process, persisting over the years, of internal organization on the part of the prisoners, which put them at the heart of the national liberation movement in the Territories. Notwithstanding this positive overall image of the political prisoner, the concrete image of any particular prisoner unfolded over time. The regular contact between prisoner and visitors—in spite of the insufficient time and the lack of privacy during the visit—often served as a foundation for new personal relations.[4]

The following cases focus on one type of relationship, that between the prisoner and the visiting sister, and reveal these relations in terms of their influence on the sister. This was not done gratuitously. Relations between the political prisoner and his brothers outside prison were given less attention. A brother in jail indeed likely affected the political course of the brother outside; however, political movements and organizations operating outside the prison walls were perhaps even more of an influence. This leads to difficulty in isolating the influence of direct contact between a brother in jail and his brothers outside.

I also refrained from addressing relations between the prisoner and his wife and especially between the prisoner and his young wife (the situation of an older wife with a number of children is different). I was guided here by the complexity of the social position of the prisoner's wife. Whether or not she lives in his parents' home, but especially if she lives alone, her behavior will be supervised and scrutinized because of the husband's absence, thereby affecting the nature of personal relations. The great social vulnerability of the prisoner's wife, the often intrusive proximity of the husband's family, and (built-in) gossip make it difficult to isolate elements in the relationship with her husband.

There are also deep-seated social and cultural reasons for choosing to concentrate on the relations between sisters and prisoner brothers: The brother's role is to safeguard his sister's honor (the family's honor); a sister may well bring up her younger brother; they socialize one another in the process of growing up; traditionally, the brother is able to marry because of the bride price (*mahr*) given for his sister or because of an exchange *(badal)* marriage; when relations with her husband become oppressive, the wife returns to her father's or brother's house seeking intervention; the brother's gifts to his sister over the years following her marriage are a sign of ongoing support, and so on.

In addition to the above, there were two main empirical justifications for this choice. Sisters were generally numbered among the regular visitors, while on the political-social level the sister's contact with the prisoner brother serves in many cases as her first intensive exposure to political involvement.

THE WORLD OPENS UP WITH THE
HELP OF THE IMPRISONED BROTHER

Khadra was seven years old in 1975 when her brother Muhammad, eleven years her senior, was sentenced to fifteen years in jail. Their mother would often bring her along to prison visits. Apart from them, the long list of visitors included her father, her older sister, and her brothers, aunts, and uncles. But Khadra remembered her mother as the primary regular participant: "My mother went to every visit. She once told my brother that if she missed a visit, he would know that she was dead. Father went every month or two months, but she never failed to go." At the age of twelve Khadra became a "permanent visitor"; her sister married and left Dheisheh and the West Bank, one brother went to study physics in Czechoslovakia, the other brothers were still young, and Muhammad, who relished her visits, urged her to persist. The first person to introduce her to literature was the brother who studied abroad, but once she became a steady visitor her relations with Muhammad were strengthened, and he became her counselor, as she put it. He would advise her on what books to read, discuss them with her, and encourage her to take an interest in new subjects:

Under his guidance I started at the age of thirteen to read serious books. In seventh grade, when the girls from my class were still interested in children's books, I read a book by Emil Touma on the roots of the Palestinian problem. The prison visit lasted half an hour, out of which we would devote five to ten minutes to discussing books and reading. I remember that I once told him about a book by Maxim Gorky that I had read, and he was unbelievably happy about this.

Khadra mainly liked to read about the Palestinian problem and "books dealing with imperialism," as she put it. She took out a lending card at the Bethlehem public library, and reading became her central interest.

Khadra did not join any of the women's political organizations. According to her, in those days (the early 1980s) part of the camp was unsympathetic to the women's committees, and Khadra's conservative parents were concerned that their daughter might become a subject of gossip. But family imprisonment provided her with a host of opportunities for involvement. Later in the 1980s it was the turn of her paternal and maternal cousins to become active. These were the sons of the families closest to her parents, practically next-door neighbors, who supported her family in many ways, the aunts cooking for them, the uncles sitting with her father when he was depressed, and all joining in visits to Muhammad. The cousins, who had been influenced more than a little by the idea of the imprisoned cousin, themselves became activists, and later, prisoners. Khadra began to visit them in prison. In the course of time she was visiting six young cousins who had been given relatively short prison sentences. There were months when she participated in five visiting days—two to her brother, two to her paternal cousin, and one to another cousin. One of these visits almost led to her arrest: She was accused of trying to pass on a letter to her brother and of swallowing it when a guard approached. Taken for interrogation, Khadra was eventually released, but the authorities subsequently retaliated by forbidding her family to leave the Occupied Territories via the Jordan bridges for seven years.

Fuad, her paternal cousin, was sentenced to five years at the age of fifteen, and Khadra became one of his regular visitors. Two years younger than Fuad, Khadra felt that the former youthful ties of friendship between them were slowly changing into a deeper relationship, which developed into love. It is true that she did not discuss books with him, rather "ordinary matters," as she put it, but the bonds between them strengthened. Were it not for the visits, she told me, it is doubtful whether they would have chosen one another. Engaged shortly after Fuad was released from jail, they married two years later. Their apartment was attached to the house of Fuad's father and Khadra's uncle, only fifteen meters away from her parents' home.

Khadra's father, a skilled stonecutter who worked for nearly forty years, twenty of them in Israel, in quarries and construction, held a different version of his daughter's marriage. He saw it, simply enough, as a marriage between first cousins, considered to be ideal and a highly favored match in the cultural tradition, one that "strengthens the ties between our families" and allowed his daughter to continue to enjoy the proximity of parents and brothers. Muhammad, Khadra's brother, had his own opinion on the subject: When Fuad approached him with a request to give his blessing to the match, Muhammad expressed reservations, claiming that the couple was not sufficiently mature for marriage.

A significant part of Khadra's childhood, adolescence, and youth, from ages seven to eighteen, revolved around her role as the sister of a political prisoner and the cousin of a number of such prisoners. Moreover, the subsequent imprisonment of the cousins altered the way of life of the three families and the character of the transactions between them. A new quality of commitment and solidarity revolving around the political prisoners was woven into relations of kinship, neighborliness, and intimacy. Accordingly, the case constitutes an example of the politicization of family relations, not in the sense of the political use of blood ties, but rather in the sense of the prolonged joint organization of the extended family around the political imprisonment of its new generation. The source of traditional legitimization for mutual aid and support among kin resides in the blood ties themselves. However, that support and solidarity between relatives who share attention to the imprisonment situation draws its strength from a further, extrafamilial source, namely, the national and political cause.

Of particular interest are the relations that developed between Khadra and her imprisoned brother, largely due to the content of their meetings. Their discussions on literature during the visits opened a window for Khadra to the intellectual and political world outside. For the first time she saw in Muhammad not only a big brother but also a counselor and a partner in a struggle whose sources she now studied. Similarly, her brother began to direct his attention to the intellectual development of his sister. The prison visits were in themselves deeds of political significance, but discussion of books during the visits carries particular cogency. These ongoing discussions to a large extent manifested penetration of the "prisoners' university," the prisoners' culture, into the realm of interpersonal relationships within the family. Young women did not take part in the internal organization that developed inside the prisons, with all its educational and cultural ramifications, and the women's organizations and movements were relatively weak compared to those of the men. All these factors serve to emphasize the importance of direct contact as a point of departure in the building of a broader political consciousness among young women.

How did this process influence the life course of the prisoner's sister who would become the prisoners' cousin? The type and nature of a marriage is generally a practical index for examining the social situation of women (and also of men); marriages of choice are likely to indicate a tendency to greater freedom and independence, while arranged marriages point to the maintenance of tradition, with ongoing control in the hands of the patriarch. Khadra's instance is intriguing because both she and her husband-cousin,

who was interviewed separately, are convinced that they married out of love
and free choice, while her father presents himself as the architect and patron
of the match. On the formal level, Khadra and Fuad's marriage is indeed a
bint-ᶜamm marriage (of first paternal cousins), which answers the criteria of
the endogamous ideal. But on the level of interpersonal relations and subjective perceptions, it is a marriage that originated in personal acquaintance,
voluntary choice, and love. Khadra fell in love with Fuad as a young prison
visitor drawn close to the experience of political struggle and imprisonment, not out of acknowledging a paternal cousin as an ideal husband or
out of a desire to satisfy her father.

Why then did her choice fall precisely on her cousin and not on any of
the dozens of men who are not kin? It can be claimed that coincidence
reigns and that Dheisheh has a host of examples of romantic connections
leading to marriage between the sisters of prisoners and former prisoners
who are not relatives (usually friends of the brother). At the same time, however, the process of politicization of family relations fostered numerous occasions for developing romantic relations between relatives with a common
political background. These can be categorized (if to become overly formal)
as an intermediate type between free choice and family commitment. And,
of course, it can be claimed that traditional marriages are also romanticized
by the marriage partners.

Taking the pervasiveness of political imprisonment in Dheisheh into
consideration, there emerged a good likelihood that one kinship group will
"produce" a flow of prisoners. Under these conditions, the proximity between young women and men belonging to the same family or kin group-
ing is likely to take on a political dimension; a cousin held in jail is at the
same time a relative of the first or second degree, a prisoner, a friend, the
subject of admiration, and so on. Hence there is a relatively strong possibility that a woman will fall in love with a prisoner-relative and think in terms
of marriage.

Notwithstanding the ambiguity that characterizes the political-romantic
ties within the family, marriage arising out of this background reflects the
very narrow limits of personal choice. A young woman who mainly realizes
her politicization within the family setting does not enjoy a wide range of
possibilities in choice of partner. Positive attributes found in a cousin and
then love bespeaks as well the lack of opportunity for becoming acquainted
with other men. Moreover, even if the relationship between first cousins
may have an autonomous, political, romantic dimension, their married life
is, a priori, bound by structural patterns of traditional fidelity and commitment. Khadra, who went to live with her in-laws, continued to be obligated
toward them due to the expectations rooted in and justified by the blood
relationship. Fuad, meanwhile, continues to be subject to similar social de-

mands toward his wife's parents. The burden of the close physical presence of the two pairs of parents will continue to accompany them, ensuring that the needs and considerations of the couple will not impair the interests and expectations of the larger family unit.

TO LIVE LIFE AS IT MUST BE LIVED

In the twenty years before the Occupation and before ʿAli's arrest, I knew nothing apart from the usual housework. I knew nothing about prison and the prisoners and nothing about the struggle. I didn't even know why Palestine was conquered and who took it. In the last twenty-five years I got to know what is happening around me. Only then did I begin to live. Merely to eat, to drink, to clean, and to cook aren't to be considered as living. In spite of all the suffering and pain that was my lot in these years, throughout, I felt that this is life as it must be lived.

—FATMA, LEADING ACTIVIST AND FORMER PRISONER,
     RELATING TO THE TRANSFORMATION SHE UNDERWENT
     FOLLOWING THE IMPRISONMENT OF HER BROTHER

Fatma was born in the village of Dir Rafat in 1947. Her family came to Dheisheh in 1949, remained in the camp for six years, and in 1955 went to live in ʿAqabat Jaber camp, near Jericho. Fatma never went to school nor did she learn to read and write; her older sister was married at a very early age, and Fatma was left at home to help her mother in the house and in rearing her brothers. Subsisting mainly from casual labor by two of Fatma's brothers, the family later moved to Amman, where the two found work in a restaurant. In 1961, when she was fourteen years old, Fatma was married to her paternal cousin, who lived in Dheisheh. Living conditions were very difficult; Fatma, her husband, his mother, and his divorced sister lived in one room, without an indoor toilet, shower, or kitchen, subsisting from the husband's work in a small factory making mementos for tourists. Her first daughter was born in 1968 and immediately afterward she became pregnant again.

ʿAli, Fatma's oldest brother, joined the ranks of Fatah before the 1967 war ("in Shuqeiri's time," as she puts it) and underwent training in Iraq. After the war he participated in a number of guerrilla operations in the Jordan Valley, of which Fatma knew nothing at the time. In 1968 ʿAli was taken prisoner in the course of an operation aimed, as his sister explained to me, at transferring arms to a hideout on the Israeli side of the Jordan Valley area. Israeli forces encountered the twelve-man group, and in the exchange of fire a senior Israeli officer and two members of the group were killed. Five, including ʿAli, were wounded and taken prisoner, while another five escaped. ʿAli's family was mistakenly informed that he had died, and only six months later were they notified that he was being held in an Israeli prison.

Fatma, a young woman who previously had never been without "supervision," the mother of a baby and pregnant, now linked her life to that of her brother. ʿAli was given six life sentences and jailed in the Ramleh prison. Fatma began to visit him regularly. She remembers that from the very start most of the visiting time was devoted to discussions on national and political subjects. Her brother explained to her the basics about Palestinian politics, the organizations and the differences between them, and the struggle against Occupation. Family affairs were hardly raised.

In 1970 her family in Jordan suffered a series of disasters. Her younger brother, who had joined the *fidaʾiyyun* was killed in an action while trying to cross the border into the West Bank. "The 'terrorist cemetery' that Israel set up near Jericho started with my brother's body . . . they never even put markers with the names of those buried there, only serial numbers." Another brother committed suicide after his parents prevented him from practicing with the gun of the dead brother. The Jordanian army killed two of her cousins during the events of Black September.

In 1972 Fatma's husband was arrested and sentenced to thirty months in prison for membership in Fatah. Looking after a four-year-old girl and two babies, she continued with her regular visits to her brother, and now to her husband as well. Soon after her husband's arrest, the Israeli security services interrogated her for nine days.

The interrogators once told me to undress in a dark room. ʿAli had spoken with me before about what happens in interrogation, so I said I was ready. My answer drove them crazy. They called me *kahbah* and *sharmuta* [whore] and said they'd bring me seven men. I replied that I didn't consider that there were any men in the room. For me you are the enemies of my homeland and my dignity, so in my eyes you aren't men, I told them.

At about the same time another prisoner, whom Fatma called "the Iraqi," entered her life. The Iraqi had been ʿAli's comrade when they trained together in the ranks of Fatah in the 1960s. He was taken prisoner several years after ʿAli and was eventually put in the same jail. Since the Iraqi had no family, ʿAli asked her to visit him:

The Mukhabarat knew that I was visiting him and began interrogating me. They asked me what was behind my visiting him. I said he was my cousin. The interrogator yelled, "That's impossible," and I said that my aunt had married a young man from Iraq when I was a little girl. They told me, "You are a whore. He is not a relative of yours at all." Afterward they separated the two men. ʿAli was held in Ramleh and the Iraqi in Ashkelon. I could only visit one of them and ʿAli suggested that I continue visiting the Iraqi. For some months I didn't see ʿAli.

On one of her visits the commander of the Ramleh prison met her. She recalled, "He saw the way I was limping and in pain, but determined to manage three visits. He said to me, 'You are going to visit ʿAli in Ramleh prison and Ahmad (the Iraqi) in Ashkelon prison and your husband's also in prison; you'll soon be an invalid. After you become an invalid, we'll see what the revolution will do for you.'" Fatma continued to visit the Iraqi for seven years, until his release in a prisoner exchange.

Fatma noted how not only she had changed in the wake of her visits to ʿAli; he also had become a different person. "He changed for the better, she explained. "He had been a fighter without knowing the roots of the Palestinian problem. In jail he read a lot of books on all subjects: the history of Palestine, revolutionary movements in the world. He read Lenin, though this was not part of the organization's study program."

Even though she did not become literate, probably because of a form of dyslexia, Fatma values education and is surprisingly knowledgeable. She also intimated that ʿAli, who in their youth opposed her going to school and even forbade her to leave the house, apologized for his past behavior and implored her to study. According to Fatma, the new relationship compensated for the wrongs of the past. She began to participate in demonstrations, sit-down strikes, and public gatherings and events at the university, recounting everything in detail to her brother.

The visits to ʿAli lasted thirteen years. He died in the course of a hunger strike by political prisoners in 1981. He and another prisoner fell victim to an attempt by prison officials to force-feed the strikers. But Fatma had already become a wholehearted political activist. She was arrested following an event in which she was only indirectly involved and sentenced to eight months in prison on a charge of concealing information. It was painful for her, mainly because of the children she left at home with their father and eighty-year-old grandmother, but she acclimated quickly. Though reading still remained Fatma's chief problem, her cellmates extended their help, "reading thirteen books out loud to me."

After her release in 1982, Fatma was among the founders of the women's committee of Fatah in Dheisheh, and as part of her activity she started a kindergarten in the camp, where she continued to work until 1991. In 1984 she renewed the round of bimonthly prison visits, this time in the wake of her son's four-year sentence. Shortly after the Intifada erupted, the authorities put Fatma on the wanted list, forcing her to leave home in order to avoid arrest. Her son Ahmad was arrested again, and Fatma disguised herself in an attempt to attend his trial in Ramallah. She was identified there by collaborators and taken for interrogation that ended in a three-month jail sentence and a fine of one thousand shekels. According to Fatma, "This second imprisonment was more difficult because all the action was taking place outside and not much could be achieved inside prison. I felt I was missing a lot now that the Intifada was at its height."

There are, of course, other sides to Fatma's life. She and her husband had two sons and three daughters. Not one of them completed secondary school, and the daughters entered early traditional marriages. While her son Ahmad was in prison, Fatma set out to find him a wife. She chose a fifteen-year-old girl, the daughter of a refugee family living in Irtas village. A web of marriage ties connected the prospective bride's family with Fatma's: The girl's brother had married Fatma's oldest daughter, and her sister married Fatma's nephew. Years later Fatma would justify her behavior in 1987 as stemming from her desire to "make her son happy" and choose "the very best" for him.

Fatma's imprisoned son was not yet eighteen years old, and his intended wife was still in junior high school. Fatma held a symbolic engagement ceremony in her home, with Ahmad's brother putting the ring on the fiancée's finger. On her next prison visit, Fatma came accompanied by the fiancée, and Ahmad put the ring on her finger. Following the ceremony, the girl left school, and in the remaining year before Ahmad's release she regularly visited him in prison along with the persevering Fatma.

I met and interviewed Ahmad and his wife in 1992 in his parents' house, where the couple was living in a room of their own. Each of them explained separately that their marriage hadn't gone well. Ahmad, who didn't settle down after his release, expressed open anger with his mother, who was responsible for his marriage. He stressed that he and his mother were extraordinarily close and that he always consulted her on political matters and saw her as his full partner. However, he could not forgive her for denying him the right to choose a wife on his own. He also regretted that his wife's studies had been terminated. Ahmad's wife was not happy living in shared rooms with her mother-in-law and complained of her husband's authoritarian and alienated attitude. For example, he compelled her to wear a headscarf though he himself is not religious and she prefers to go uncovered.

Fatma's starting point is worth repeating: an illiterate housewife whose life course—from her childhood chores, minimal schooling, and marriage at the age of fourteen, continuing with life as a married woman—was largely conducted within the family and determined by others. Fatma's high point, meanwhile, was that of an activist in her own right, aware of her strength, taking part in shaping social and political action frameworks. The transitional stages from the start to the peak were, at the least, stimulated by her ongoing visits to her brother ʿAli.

It is difficult to identify any particular factor that facilitated such a deep transformation in Fatma's life. It may be related to her brother's history as a guerilla fighter, which is exceptional when compared with the great majority of Dheisheh prisoners. ʿAli's personality probably played a decisive part, and undoubtedly central importance should be attributed to the extremely violent circumstances under which his life ended and to his particularly symbolic death. But apart from the uniqueness of the case and of the personalities—for it was revealed again and again that Fatma's strong character, her courage, and her adventurousness were indispensable factors—the critical component was the dynamic between ʿAli and his sister. What was structurally and emotionally built into the comradeship between the two went far beyond the boundaries of the interpersonal.

Four years separated ʿAli's imprisonment in 1968 from that of Fatma's husband in 1972, in the course of which time Fatma acquired a new awareness and a changed perception of herself, clearly discernible in her description of her interrogation by the Shabak. Realizing that her interrogators sought to exploit her weakness and vulnerability as a female and as a married woman, she struggled with her fears of sexual assault by turning to her interrogators in words that demeaned their macho identity, while reducing the situation to its political essence. The years of prison visits made Fatma conscious of the confrontation between conqueror and conquered and between warder and prisoner. In her own way she managed to transform what aroused distress, fear, and helplessness into a focus of strength. She knew that her obstinate presence on visiting days with "her" three prisoners was stronger than all the shameful words, threats, humiliations, and other forms of maltreatment that had been her lot.

Fatma's visits to the Iraqi over the course of seven years were in themselves a unique phenomenon. I did not encounter a similar situation among any of the other interviewees. One can relate to the Iraqi's adoption as an extension of her great devotion and loyalty toward her brother, but this would be too limited a view of the matter. After all, at stake were dozens, if not hundreds, of visits by a woman, married and with children, to a bachelor prisoner who was not a relative, a spectacle that was likely to be considered irregular and threatening not only by the prison authorities but also, and perhaps mainly, within her own society. It appears that Fatma conceived of these visits in terms of political commitment (in which a spirit of adventure mixed with a spirit of defiance). Thus, they were among her first independent political steps.

The years after ʿAli's death brought this process to complete fulfillment. Fatma turned to political activity that revolved not around "private" prisoners from her kin group but around organizational goals. The protracted imprisonment of her son forced her back to family visits, but this time as a side activity, taking place parallel to her main political involvement.

Fatma's politicization and her entry into activism did not involve the acquisition of academic knowledge in a way similar to what we have encountered among activists and former prisoners from Dheisheh. In spite of all her efforts, in spite of the thirst for knowledge, in spite of her rubbing shoulders with educated men and women, her illiteracy remained a constant reminder of the education that had been denied to her as a child. This did not prevent her from extracting the maximum from verbal exchange and from discussion and listening, nor from ascribing importance to the value of a wide political education. Her remark about ʿAli's joining the struggle before he understood "the roots of the Palestinian problem" indicates that despite her limitations she was not without critical capacity.

The essence of the change that Fatma underwent is in the awareness, first, of the way in which her brother was transformed in prison, and second, of the double task that she fulfilled in relation to him. At the beginning ʿAli was the teacher, and she learned to see the world through his eyes. However, in the course of time she understood that the teacher, too, is educated in prison, and she realized that he also learned to see certain things through her—not only because she brought him closer to events outside the walls, but also because he finally learned to recognize her as an equal.

In light of this life story, Fatma's behavior pertaining to the marriages of her daughters and her son comes as utter dissonance. How is it possible that a woman broke through the bounds that circumscribed her life only to force her children into traditional marriages? How, after all she had undergone, could Fatma impose on her son, a seventeen-year-old prisoner, something reminiscent of what her parents imposed on her when she was fourteen?

One might answer these questions by presenting the developments in terms of seemingly naked power struggles: It could be claimed that Fatma converted the political power that she had accumulated in years of public political activity into social power, generally recognized to be an exclusive (Arab) male patrimony. She then realized her strength in the accepted way—that is, as does a male enjoying his position in a patriarchal society. Her use of her ticket of entrance into the world of male dominance mimicked rather than challenged it.

I am not inclined to accept such an explanation, mainly because it diminishes the importance of the profound change in her consciousness and ignores the radical content of her political activity. The very emergence of the disparity between her long-term struggle to free herself from restrictive social fetters and her own willingness to impose similar restraints on her children can be attributed, I believe, to a deeper structural contradiction. Fatma lived in two subworlds founded on different, often contradictory sets of values and norms, social resources, and avenues of upward mobility: the realm of national-political activism and that of peasantlike family and kinship relations.

Under what circumstances, then, does the tension between these subworlds develop into an open collision or conflict? It seems that such a conflict only breaks out when the political body or organization produces a real alternative that can compete successfully with traditional kin values and the security they provide for the individual. Though Fatma had to make her way past numerous obstacles in order to establish her position in the realm of political activism, this did not yield her sufficient means and tools to challenge prevalent traditional preferences pertaining to gender relationships and matrimonial arrangements. Fatma married off her teenage son not because she aspired to force her authority on him (though that was the unavoidable consequence), but because she wanted to assure for him and for herself a "successful" and recognized marriage. Politics apparently didn't offer her a commensurable alternative.

Social Networks of Prisoners' Families in Dheisheh

Prior case studies showed how a kinship group comprising a number of prisoners served as a source of group identification and of opportunities for active participation of its cohort. The networks discussed in this section illustrate another tendency: how connections between prisoners' families develop into an extrafamilial support group. In both cases, active participation linked the personal to the national, public, and political aspects. However, it may well be that the network offered its participants a further means of transcending the boundaries of familism.

Visiting days in prison led to new social connections between families from the length and breadth of the West Bank. In Dheisheh—at least throughout the period when I was doing my fieldwork—one could trace interfamily networks of mutual support for, and identification with, political prisoners. Their members maintained strong contact on a regular basis, sometimes even day to day. When visiting days corresponded, they traveled together to prison, and when a son was added to the list of detainees, they provided his family with material assistance and moral support: offering good advice, raising funds in order to finance a lawyer, or taking turns in paying home visits to the parents. Once the prisoner's sentence had been set, the appeal rejected, or his arrest extended, the members gathered to soften the blow. On ordinary days, the members of the network would spend time with one another, often entire afternoons and evenings; when a prisoner was released and for the entire following week, they would be the first to visit for the family celebrations.

Close communication on a basis other than kinship, including close relations of friendship and mutual aid, was always part of life in Dheisheh, where families originating in dozens of different villages live as neighbors in immediate proximity. Many of the manifestations of cooperation and solidarity found among "mere neighbors" are indeed similar in appearance to those that characterize the networks of prisoners' families. Nevertheless, the latter networks are unique. Their difference lies in the very reason that brought them into being and in part in their social characteristics.

The first network structures appeared at the beginning of the Occupation period. Prisoners' parents and siblings remember well the relatives of prisoners jailed during the same period as their sons and brothers, and they continue to maintain ties with many of them. They recall the assistance of "veteran" relatives of prisoners who advised them on which lawyers to trust and which to avoid, where to look for a son transferred from prison to prison, and what to expect from a military trial. But fear and anxiety in the Palestinian public also characterized the first period (the late 1960s and early 1970s)—the organizations were secret and the suppression and punishment by imprisonment were harsh. Many people chose to keep their distance from any collective identified with the prisoners, fearing it would be to their detriment.

The appearance of new networks and the expansion of existing ones were hastened as the avenues of political action broadened, starting in the late 1970s, with steady growth in the number of detained and imprisoned people from Dheisheh. Some of the networks developed around prisoners who were arrested, sentenced, and imprisoned under the same circumstances. Other networks came together around prisoners belonging to a common organization, such as faction-based students' committees, even though sons might have been arrested and imprisoned under different circumstances and at different times.

The connection between the sons' organizational affiliations and the families' support groups was not always maintained. In many instances the political affiliation of the activists, male and female, "divided" families when some of the sons and daughters were close to one organization and others were identified with a second or even a third. Imprisonment in families with such divided loyalties generally drew the parents close to more than one support group.

The network "resides" in the area between the family unit and the institutionalized political groupings such as parties, women's organizations, and political committees. Its members were made more amenable to mobilization for organized political activity by the social tasks they shared and by their common political and social way of life. This did not usually lead to full membership in a political organization but to less demanding affiliation with regional or local popular committees and to participation in protest activities. Many protest activities revolved directly around the subject of prisoners, some of the demonstrations taking place in parallel to hunger strikes inside the prisons or as part of a public campaign for improving conditions of imprisonment.

In many instances women took a more active part in sustaining the network. It was women who in effect implemented most of the activities and the mutual aid: It was they who cooked for the family of the wounded and for the distressed relatives of the prisoner, they who helped the sick mother of a prisoner in her housework. The way of life of the women of the network revolved, therefore, to a large extent around the practical assistance that they provided one another. The activity of the male members of the network included less actual labor, tending to consist of leisure hours spent together.

In the arena of organized activities as well, the presence of the women was conspicuous; it was rare to meet a male who had sat opposite the Red Cross offices on a hunger strike, as against the many women who amassed dozens of such strike days and who also had behind them dozens of organized solidarity visits to the families of prisoners, the bereaved, and the wounded, throughout the West Bank. This can perhaps be explained by gender differential, women being less threatened by detention, imprisonment, and physical injury. While demonstrative gatherings of men or mixed gatherings were in many instances dispersed by the use of live ammunition, tear gas, beatings, and arrests, the measures taken against a gathering of women were usually, though not always, less violent.

TO BE SUPPORTED, TO SUPPORT, AND TO ACT: THE PARENTS OF THE 'SHAHEED' MUHAMMAD

Every child in Dheisheh in the 1990s knew how to take a visitor to the house of Muhammad Abu-ʿAker, perhaps the best-known *shaheed* of the Intifada in the camp. For thousands of Dheishehians, including many who did not know him personally, the fatal injury sustained by Muhammad in the summer of 1988, his stubborn struggle for life, and his death in the autumn of 1990, symbolize the essence of the popular uprising. I would always get a warm welcome at this house, constantly bustling with activity and crowded with people for most of the day, and over a long period of time it served as the home base for my fieldwork.

The parents, Malika and Naʿim, are cousins whose origins were in the village of Raʾs Abu ʿAmar in the Judean Mountains. Both were in their midforties when I first became acquainted with them in 1992. Naʿim is a house painter by trade but worked for many years as an attendant at a Bethlehem gas station. Neither has much education; he completed the ninth grade and she finished primary school. The couple had four sons and two daughters: the twins Nidal and Raʾfat were twenty-three in 1992; Muhammad was born in 1972; and Hazem, Nida, and Hala were in their teens. Since 1967 Malika's brothers and sisters have been living outside the West Bank, while Naʿim's brothers and sisters live in Doha, a neighborhood built opposite Dheisheh and outside the camp area.

Until the 1980s, Malika and Naʿim were distant from all political activity and from any involvement in the political life of Dheisheh. Naʿim even told me of a stone fence that he built around his house in the hope that it would prevent his children from "going into the street" and endangering them-selves. The picture changed in 1983 when the twins became activists and the arrests began. At the age of thirteen, the two joined the youth and student movement of Jabhat al-ʿAmal ("the Action Front," identified with the PFLP), and they continued their involvement in high school. In the pre-Intifada years, each of them was held under detention or in prison some ten times. Their young brother Muhammad managed to be detained three times before reaching the age of sixteen.

Nighttime incursions into their house and searches by the Israeli army, confrontations with soldiers, recurring detentions, prison visits, the twins' expulsion from school on Shabak orders, these events now regulated the course of everyday life in the Abu-ʿAkers' home. Eventually, Malika and Naʿim joined a network that included parents, brothers, and sisters of young prisoners—youngsters of the same age as their sons and their immediate partners in activity and imprisonment—as well as more veteran families who had been involved since the 1970s. The group, which was diverse in age, education, work, and political background, gradually replaced the cou-ple's former social circle. They themselves did not become formal members of an organization but intensively lived the political experience of their sons, not to speak of a cross-section of a young generation that moved freely in their home.

In August 1988, at the height of the Intifada, Muhammad, then aged six-teen, was injured in the course of a demonstration that took place in one of the streets of Dheisheh not far from his parents' house. A high-velocity (dum-dum) bullet shattered his intestines. Considered by the doctors to be a hope-less case, he was hospitalized at Makassed hospital in East Jerusalem, where he remained without improvement for nearly two months. At the time, the twins were held under administrative detention in the Ketziot camp in the Negev. Hazem, the younger brother, was injured by a rubber bullet during a protest demonstration following Muhammad's injury and lost the sight in an eye. The parents sat in Makassed hospital for weeks surrounded by dozens of Dheishe-hians. Women from the network, mothers of prisoners, cooked for the family and their visitors every day, and the prisoners' fathers took turns sleeping in the hospital alongside Muhammad's parents, while the young people orga-nized constant shifts of visitors and arranged transportation.

With further deterioration in Muhammad's condition, the doctors at Makassed recommended an operation and treatment by a specialist in the United States. The Israeli authorities were in no hurry to permit the pa-tient's exit from the country, and members of the network rallied their con-tacts and acquaintances among human rights activists, journalists, and pub-lic figures in Israel and throughout the world. Finally, their intervention and lobbying facilitated Muhammad's trip to a Boston hospital, accompanied by his father. The intestines were excised and an intravenous device inserted.

His return to Dheisheh was heralded by the residents of the camp as "the return of the living martyr." The ceremonial reception lasted for days, immortalized on film and video. In spite of his disability, Muhammad attempted a return to "normal" life and managed to complete his studies and to acquire a driving license. Some two years after his injury, however, complications arose, causing his death.

Muhammad's death widened his parents' support circle. The network of prisoners' parents remained at the core, with new groups and individuals joining the periphery: youngsters of both sexes from all political streams who frequented their house; other networks of prisoners' families; representatives of the sons' political organization; public personalities from the West Bank; delegations of support from pro-Palestinian organizations in Europe; representatives of the Quakers, human rights activists, and journalists. That was also the period when I got to know the family and in a certain sense became part of its wider network.

The parents did not revert to passivity. Rather, they extended their activity. Naᶜim began to participate in local popular committees, which were now active in Dheisheh, while Malika missed no opportunity to join in demonstrations, solidarity visits, and gatherings in the refugee camp, in Bethlehem, and in more distant venues. Hosting dozens of visitors in their home every day also added for both of them, and particularly for Malika, endless obligations and work, while at the same time helping them to make new contacts and to maintain their political commitment.

I spent a lot of time in the company of the family in the summer of 1992, about two years after their son's death. The twins were then twenty-three, released prisoners and unemployed, the young son, though he hadn't been in prison, was also unemployed, while the girls were at school. The family maintained itself from the father's work at the gas station and in house painting. This was a period of decline in the uprising and many Intifada prisoners from Dheisheh were released and returned home. Yet the social life of Malika and Naᶜim continued to revolve around the network of prisoners' families.

Most of the twins' friends at that time were released prisoners in their early twenties and, like them, unemployed. They were accustomed to visiting the house of the Abu-ᶜAker family at different times of the day, separately or in a group, where they were tended to by the mother. On more than one occasion, I heard her admonish them, encouraging them to visit a neglected or wounded comrade or to participate in this or another voluntary committee. She also liked to recount to them events of the Intifada years: how with her own body she repelled soldiers who beat her sons, how she ridiculed the soldiers during their search for her wanted son when he came home to shower, how she sat on a military jeep and refused to move until they released a child they had arrested, how she caused a commotion so as to distract them from escaping persons on the wanted list.

Some of the veterans of the network became close friends with Malika and regularly visited her home, even after their prisoner sons had been released. New daily problems were now their main concern: What can the released prisoners do if they cannot find work? Is it too risky to enter Israel without a permit? Who is building? Who is about to marry? In other words, with the decline of the phenomenon of imprisonment, the mutual relations forged around the common cause took on the character of regular friendships. But even when the political focus of the friendship tended to become obscure, camaraderie was strong and it remained possible to rally the concerned. This was evident during the strike of the political prisoners in October 1992, when Malika and the members of the network joined a series of protest activities at a time when their own family members were no longer prisoners.

Malika never failed to fulfill her obligations to the network families. Even when the ranks of Dheisheh prisoners diminished greatly, she continued to strengthen the parents of those in jail and did not miss a reception for those released. I saw her prepare herself for these events. In order to look her best, she would wear an embroidered *fallaha* dress, one of the three choice ones she owned, carrying a gift on her head for the family of the released: drinking glasses, a set of coffee cups, or some small present. And she fulfilled a variety of attendant obligations outside a direct political context, such as participation in the mourning rituals of whomever had been a member of the prisoners' family network.

During that period most of the daily contacts of the Abu-ʿAker family did not include its more extended kin group. In practice, the relations with Naʿim's brothers and cousins and with the branches of the family in Jordan were more formal than those with the network members. Family gatherings revolved mainly around holidays or invitations extended in the context of mutual obligation. Although when the twins wanted to marry girlfriends met during shared activities, their parents preferred that they marry cousins; in the end neither they nor the uncles imposed their will.

CHAPTER 12

Prisoners Return Home

IMPRISONMENT continued to have a long-term influence on family life even after the prisoner's release and return to the family. At the center of this chapter stands the reconstruction of the family life of Lila and Ibrahim—both former political prisoners from the intermediate generation—which covers a twenty-five-year period. It is based on close acquaintance with the couple and their nine children (aged nine to twenty-seven in 1999) that began at a very early stage of my fieldwork (1992) and continues today. The difficulties of generalizing from this case study—which stem primarily from the fact that long-term imprisonment of women was and remains a rarity in Dheisheh, and also from the fact that both spouses were imprisoned during a relatively early period—are counterbalanced by general trends in the lives of former prisoners from the younger generation.

The story of my introduction to Lila and Ibrahim's family is worth appending, if only for the important lessons it taught me at the time: I met Ibrahim by chance during the spring of 1992, when I was carrying out my first interviews with former prisoners in the camp. I arranged to meet the director of Dheisheh camp on behalf of UNRWA, himself a former prisoner, at his office. Frustrated after more than an hour of waiting, I approached the watchman who was sitting under a mulberry tree outside the building, wondering if he knew anything about the whereabouts of the director. No sooner did Ibrahim, the watchman, learn about the intention of my visit, than he offered himself as a substitute for the interviewee, arguing that I would find his seven-year-long prison experience no less rewarding. I spent the next three hours under the mulberry tree, listening to Ibrahim's prison memories and life story. When he mentioned that he was married to a former prisoner, I felt that I was the most fortunate of researchers and immediately expressed my enthusiasm about speaking with her. Ibrahim's reaction surprised me somewhat. His wife would surely be very happy to receive me at their home, he said, but it was very unlikely that the conversation with her would add much to what I heard from him because, as he put it, "We see things eye to eye."

The next day I went to visit Lila. A smiling, noticeably overweight woman in her early forties, she greeted me at the gate with a few words of courtesy in Hebrew, which, as she explained to me later, she had picked up from the exchange between the Israeli women guards during her prison term. It was early afternoon; everybody was at home and Lila's youngest children, twin boys, then less than three years old, competed with me for the attention of their mother. But once she managed to close the bedroom door behind us, Lila was quick to open up. As I listened to her, it struck me how almost none of what she was describing resembled what I had heard from Ibrahim the day before. Moreover, the gaps appeared to become wider the more she moved from recollections of the distant days of imprisonment to the recounting of her married life and to evaluations of the present and the recent past. In contrast to her husband's brief assessment that the two saw "eye to eye," Lila spoke at length about deprivation and alienation.

The first interviews with Ibrahim and Lila opened the door to what proved to be a long-lasting friendship. Alongside my frequent visits to their home, during which I spent time together with both spouses and their children, however, I also maintained "separate tracks" to Lila and Ibrahim. If Lila's vantage point appears to predominate in the presentation here, this is not accidental. It was mainly through her that the contradictions between the convictions and aspirations of the past and the realities of the present were revealed.

Camaraderie Turns to Estrangement

The beginning looked promising. Ibrahim and Lila, both newly released from prison, decided to marry. Lila, then aged twenty-one, had been an administrative detainee (imprisoned without trial) from 1969 to 1971—among the first women political prisoners in the Bethlehem area. Ibrahim, then aged twenty-eight, spent four years in prison for membership in an outlawed organization. They first met when Lila came to welcome Ibrahim and his family on his release from prison. They had not been acquainted before, but Lila felt that she "must marry a former prisoner, a political person, and not a man lacking awareness and understanding." Ibrahim was interested, as he put it, in "someone with a background of political activity." Their families did not favor the idea. Lila's father thought marriage to a former prisoner to be a less desirable match, while Ibrahim's parents wanted him to marry a relative, as had his brother and sister. In spite of the opposition, however, the two were married only two months after Ibrahim's release and three months after that of Lila.

Lila has warm memories of the first period. They held interests in common and discussed books they bought and read: an encyclopedia of Palestinian history, novels by Maxim Gorky, and Arabic literature. But their material situation could not have been worse. Ibrahim, with a high school education but without a trade or a diploma, was a construction worker; they lived in a single room within his parents' house. Their first daughter was soon born, and Lila quickly became pregnant once again. Problems between mother-in-law and daughter-in-law surfaced early in the marriage, Ibrahim's mother openly bewailing her son's choice.

Ibrahim went to prison for the second time in 1973 with a three-year sentence. Lila continued to live in her in-law's home with her daughter and the baby son born after his father's imprisonment, with the tensions ever increasing. At the beginning they traveled together for prison visits, but Ibrahim's mother used the visiting time to disparage her daughter-in-law. Lila, in dire economic straits, started work, picking fruit in Israel, with her mother-in-law spreading rumors that she was consorting with her Jewish employer and workmates, making sure this reached her son's attention. He sent a message to his wife that she should cease her prison visits as long as she continued to work. In reaction, Lila stopped working and stopped visiting her husband.

Penniless and with two children to care for, she returned to her father's house. She won no sympathy and support there. Her two brothers had left the West Bank in the 1960s, one for Saudi Arabia, the other for Libya, and her sister had also emigrated. Only her father and sick mother, who died in 1974, were left in Dheisheh. The father, who from the beginning had opposed the marriage tie with Ibrahim's family, saw his daughter's situation as justification of his opinion. For a long time Lila did not visit her imprisoned husband: "I stopped going but they [his parents] continued to visit and to tell incredible lies about me. Undoubtedly, Ibrahim was undergoing a difficult internal conflict. For two years I didn't see him at all. He sent letters and wrote terrible things. At that time I had two children and we lived at the expense of my father. My husband's family didn't give me a *kirsh* [penny]." The turnabout occurred when Ibrahim's friends in prison told him that they wanted to meet his wife: "I went with the children to meet him and his friends. The impression made on his friends was very good and he began to regret what had taken place." It was Ibrahim Youssef, the veteran Communist activist—who was imprisoned along with Ibrahim and was accorded a special status among the prisoners and the activists—who stood by Lila all along, she recalled.

When Ibrahim was about to be released, her father conditioned her return to her husband on an apology from him. Lila, however, decided to return without conditions and waited for him at his parents' house when the day came. She regarded her decision to marry five years earlier as a commitment, while obeying her father would have been considered admission of an error. In the wake of this, her father terminated relations with his daughter.

Ibrahim was released from prison in poor physical condition. According to Lila, "he was athletic before entering jail," but after seven years encompassing two periods of imprisonment, "he was a partial wreck." After a period without work, he got a job in an Israeli towel factory in Talpiot (Jerusalem). The wages were low, and the family grew. In four years they had three more children; seven souls now crowded together in one room.

Lila paints a grim picture. Her husband indeed regretted his behavior during his imprisonment, but in effect he was "hand in glove with his mother." Lila explains: "Before getting married I was free and went where I wished, I had tens of friends. Afterward, his family wanted to imprison me at home. My husband beat me whenever his mother was angry with me. He interrogated me like the Mukhabarat interrogated him. His old mother didn't want me."

Finally, Ibrahim, Lila, and the children moved to a separate room elsewhere in Dheisheh. Only in the late 1980s, when the family numbered nine persons, did they build their present home—a bedroom serving Lila, the daughters and the younger sons, a guest room where Ibrahim and the older sons sleep, and a kitchen, bathroom, and hall. Even though the house is little more than makeshift and the rooms too small for its occupants, its construction left them heavily in debt, which still plagued them when we first met in 1992. The furniture consisted of a bed, a couch, a dozen foam mattresses, a few ancient armchairs, an old refrigerator, an ancient washing machine, and a closet.

Until the Intifada Ibrahim continued working in the factory, and for several years he took on a second job as a driver taking workers to Israel. He did not cease his political activity, and the Israeli Shabak continued to harass him with detentions and interrogations. However, his chief concern was to provide for his family, which by 1989 numbered eleven. Lila claims that she tried to use contraceptives but was forced to stop taking pills for medical reasons. Her daily life revolved around her housework and the children, an endless routine of washing, cleaning, baking, cooking, going to market, and infant care.

Unlike Ibrahim, who kept his organizational connections intact, became a member of various action committees in Dheisheh, and was elected several times to head the *shabab* club in the camp, Lila lacked a support system. When she came out of prison the Palestinian women's committees did not yet exist, and when Ibrahim was imprisoned for the second time, the camp-based networks of prisoners' relatives were still in an embryonic stage. At the same time, her connections with the few members of her family living in Dheisheh remained tenuous. After her mother died, her father, who had not forgiven her for defying him, married a woman some thirty years younger than himself, with whom he had two children. He was reluctant to reestablish regular contact with Lila and her family until shortly before his death. Neither did the death of Ibrahim's mother dispel the difficulties between his family and his wife. The widower in his seventies remarried, this time to a woman forty years younger than himself, had children, and maintained the hostile attitude toward his daughter-in-law.[1]

This background and what she described as a growing sense of isolation drew Lila closer to religion. Gradually, she became an orthodox Muslim; she prayed five times a day, often read the Quran and books of religious commentary, would not shake hands with a man, and on leaving the house took care that she was covered from head to foot. At the same time, Lila is among the few housewives in Dheisheh who regularly read a daily newspaper and keep track of the detailed unfolding of political events. The people she most admires in the camp are secular political activists, particularly those from her own generation, many of whom had spent time in jail during the 1970s. A thoroughly secular outlook informs her evaluation of political developments.

The main influences upon her religious revival were apparently the moral demands she imposed on herself and her own rigid behavior. She tried to spread the faith among her female neighbors. More than once I found her engrossed in reading a section of the Quran to the illiterate among them while they were taking a break between household tasks. Within her family her religiosity had considerable influence. Her husband remained secular ("He doesn't interfere in my personal affairs"), but her two oldest daughters followed in their mother's footsteps. The younger of the two was the first to be drawn to religion and to wear a *jilbab*, when she was a fifteen-year-old pupil in the ninth grade; the older daughter adopted the *jilbab* before her marriage while a student at Bethlehem University. The two explained, on more than one occasion, that the *jilbab* gives them a feeling of protection against the imposing eyes of men, while faith in God distances evil.

The Intifada was a blow to the family economy. Ibrahim stopped working as a driver at the beginning of 1988 in compliance with the one-time call of the Intifada leadership for workers to sever ties with Israeli employers.[2] Shortly after, in the wake of "downsizing," he lost his job at the factory in Jerusalem. After spending some time without employment or income, he got a job as a watchman with UNRWA. The work in seven-hour shifts was indeed easy, but the pay was poor. Because of building debts, as well as the need to feed eleven on a meager wage, the family suffered repeated bouts of economic hardship.

Lila and Ibrahim's oldest son, Kifah, was imprisoned twice during the Intifada. The first time, in 1989, at the age of sixteen, he was sentenced to seven months in prison, and approximately one year later he received a year's sentence and was sent to Ketziot prison in the Negev desert. Kifah was a well-known activist in his own right, and his imprisonment was regarded by his parents as more or less expected. Their home became a frequent target for army raids, during one of which Lila, then five months pregnant, fell and lost the baby.

Kifah was released from prison in 1991, made up the studies he had missed, and two years later passed his matriculation exams. He subsequently began to study at Bethlehem University, the expenses being largely covered by a special scholarship granted to former prisoners. During this period Kifah worked as a watchman and a laborer in two separate places. He and his father divided the two part-time jobs between them. For a brief two-year period they enjoyed a certain income, allowing them to pay off the debts the family had accumulated and finance the university studies of the oldest daughter.

Following the loss of one workplace in 1995, the family returned to subsisting on a single salary covering less than half their expenses. The relations between Ibrahim and Lila deteriorated further, at least from Lila's standpoint. Ibrahim spent less time at home, and she was left with the burden of tending to an impoverished household. Nevertheless, both were determined to provide high school education for their children. Lila, who rarely left the house, except for classes that she attended at the camp mosque and for her own missionary duties, created an atmosphere encouraging study and learning. She made sure that her children went to school properly dressed and clean. She placed the guest room at the disposal of her high school children while they prepared for matriculation exams, crowding the rest of the family into the other room. She was careful to divide the housework as equally as possible among the children, so that while the girls did the heavier work (washing floors, cooking), the boys washed their own clothes, served at meals, cleared the table afterward, and more. The importance attributed to acquiring an education and succeeding in studies also contributed to uniting the family. I was always touched by the devotion, cooperation, mutual respect, and warmth with which the children related to each other and to their parents.

Nonetheless the family failed to give daughters and sons equal support or show equal cognizance of their needs. Ibrahim and Lila sought to marry their oldest daughter, Mona, while she was still in high school, though ultimately the engagement was broken. Mona worked for a time at the center for deaf and mute children in Dheisheh and subsequently registered for university studies. She was accepted for a two-year program leading to a certificate in education. Meanwhile, a young man from the camp asked to marry her, and both the family and Mona accepted. The agreement obligated the husband to enable her to complete her studies. However, along with receiving her certificate, Mona gave birth to her first child, and soon after she was pregnant again. Her aspirations to take up professional work were delayed, along with the hope for continuing studies. The relationship between the couple turned problematic, and Mona was in need of repeated intervention by her father in order to improve her position in her husband's house.

Iman, who is five years younger than her sister, completed high school in 1995. Her matriculation exam score was second in her class, and she intended to register for Bethlehem University. During the examination period, the family of a young Dheisheh man approached her parents and asked for her in marriage. The parents approved, asked Iman for her opinion, which was to first get acquainted with the man, and they met a number of times in her parent's house before she consented. Iman held to her wish to continue studies at the university, and her father concluded an agreement with her future husband stipulating that he would permit her to do so.

The future bridegroom worked as a gardener for an institution in Beit Jala, and from the start it was clear that he would have very limited means. The wedding took place in autumn 1995, a few months after the couple had become acquainted. Iman canceled her registration for studies, in the hope that she would be accepted as a student the following year. Neither sister's marriage included the payment of a *mahr* (bride price). The prevalent custom in Dheisheh today is for the groom to furnish the apartment (in many cases, bedroom furniture is considered sufficient) and purchase gold jewelry and wedding clothes for his bride. In both the above instances, the wives went to live in apartments that their future husbands had constructed on the roofs of their parents' homes.

Iman's father tried to justify her early marriage with the claim that his daughter was not "truly" convinced of her desire to continue her studies, while her mother explained that this was a "good" marriage to a sensitive and understanding person. Iman did not give up her plans altogether, and one year after she gave birth to her first child she registered for the Open University, opting for a part-time program to which she adhered very seriously even after becoming a mother of two.

Kifah remained a bachelor throughout his undergraduate studies at Bethlehem University, where he also became a popular student leader and head of the student council. Graduating with distinction in 1997, he was granted a full scholarship to complete a master's degree in business administration in the United States.

Had Ibrahim and Lila not joined the ranks of the Palestinian national movement in the 1960s and spent time in jail as political prisoners, their paths would have probably never crossed. Yet the trajectory of their family life over twenty-five years raises questions as to the relative import of political imprisonment among other determinant factors. In what manner was Ibrahim and Lila's family history different from that of other families, equally poor and with numerous children, established by men and women of their generation who did not become political activists? Weighty structural factors played a central role in the story presented here. Among these we can find the application of traditional control on the part of Ibrahim and Lila's families of origin, Ibrahim's lowly and unstable position in the labor market, Lila's not joining the waged work force, and the size of the family that the two set up. These factors largely derived from their situation within an existing system but also, in part, from their own personal conduct. Against these stood the resources and outlook that each acquired through their experience of political activity and imprisonment, thus introducing a constant source of strain and tension.

Ibrahim and Lila's marriage was their sole great joint act of defiance against "society" and the institution of traditional marriage. Much of what occurred later can be understood as a counterresponse to, or a chain of acts of self-defense against, society's reaction to that "original sin." The marriage expressed the need and will of each to realize in their personal lives a partnership that embodied continuity of their political life. Accepting the potential consequences, they each rejected the attempts of their families to arrange their marriages. It is in this light that one should also understand the "institutionalization" of the relations between them so soon after their release from prison. Each had to act rapidly in order to resist the family's intentions, since it is usual for parents of former prisoners to have their sons, and particularly their daughters, marry quickly, so as to distance them from the danger of further militant activity. It is important to remember that Ibrahim and Lila's rebellion was extraordinary for the Dheisheh of the early 1970s. Arranged marriage was the norm even for men and women with higher education and those with professions.

But the act of exercising personal choice in marriage is in itself, unless accompanied by a system of support for each of the partners, likely within a short time to lose its significance as an expression of independence and resistance. The factors feeding and accelerating this process of retreat are not necessarily due to the character of the personal relations between the couple, though these were quickly affected by the dynamics of the situation. More important here (and in similar instances) were the social and material dependence of the young couple on the wider family, and particularly on the husband's side, and their protracted inability to provide the means to secure a family unit.

The two were entrapped; their existence as a family came to be dependent upon those very parents who had opposed the marriage. Even after

Ibrahim started to work, his earnings as a part-time laborer did not enable the couple to move from the parents' house. But the drawback of living under a single roof was not endured equally. Lila remained the unwanted "stranger," while Ibrahim remained his parents' beloved offspring. Compared to the imprisonment of the two, which created a basic camaraderie and desire for partnership while they were single, Ibrahim's second imprisonment only underscored the oppressive nature of the family relations that now confined them. Lila chose to marry Ibrahim out of a desire to realize her freedom and independence, but in order to maintain normal married family life in Dheisheh she was in need of those support systems that every woman—with or without political consciousness—requires. Lacking her own source of income (or property), and without support from her father, brothers, or other relatives, Lila's life became unbearable.

The "test" that Ibrahim's prison friends arranged for Lila illuminates the existence and the limitations of alternative solutions. Their arbitration (to the benefit of Lila) caused Ibrahim to recognize and retract his error, which perhaps shows that extrafamilial organized group activity can be a counterweight to family-imposed pressures. But the inadequacy of this intervention stemmed from its temporary character. Strengthened by the prisoners' stand, Lila decided to return to her husband's house, but her move was not accompanied by further support. Thus, Lila's small victory failed to bring about a practical improvement of her situation.

Many links in the chain of events of their family life after Ibrahim's release from prison in 1976 can be explained without resorting to the couple's political background: the dependence upon the very low income of one unskilled breadwinner, the absence of additional resources such as the material support of kin, and of course the size of the family—nine children are more than the average for second-generation families in Dheisheh. All greatly restricted the possibilities for maneuver.

Lila did not lose her need and desire for self-expression, for belonging to something beyond housework and child-rearing and the struggle for survival under conditions of poverty. True, the early hope of realizing solid relations with her husband diminished, as did the zeal of the strong social ties that marked her youth. She had gained a political education, but the channels for acquiring systematic academic skills were blocked, and her daily life distanced her from tackling intellectual challenges. Some inferences are in place here: The return to religion offered her a double defense. It became part of an order of reference with its own commitment, at the same time that it provided protection from society by concealing her behind a *mandil* (head scarf) and a *jilbab*. No one can castigate a God-fearing woman, meticulous in her religious duties, for being rebellious or a threat to the social order. Indeed, she constitutes no such threat.

Thus consciously or unconsciously, Lila imposed upon herself the conformity and obedience demanded by domineering, intractable fathers and husbands in the name of modesty and humility. Nevertheless, what stands out are the dichotomies that inhere in Lila's internal world: her secular approach to the political sphere versus her conservative religious approach to the emotional and personal realm; her continued interest in political affairs versus her detachment from organized participation; and the commitment to the national cause, which she passed on to her children, versus her aspiration to bring her daughters and neighbors closer to religion. Such disparities prevented her new penitence from being total and devoid of contradiction.

It is interesting to note that her daughters' turn toward religion took place quickly and lacked any element of revision and/or conflict. Unlike their mother, they did not reach religion after participating in organized political activity; they had no such experience. It is clear that Lila, who encouraged the religious course, strove to defend and distance her daughters from exposure to experiences like hers. This was so even at the expense of their freedom and independence, values so dear to her in the past. Neither is it a coincidence that Ibrahim and Lila's son became a central political activist while the daughters became religious. Lila fostered political and national consciousness among all her children, daughters and sons alike, but preferred that her daughters stay away from organized political activity. Her son's activism aroused no opposition in her because, as she saw it, it would not diminish his social status but rather enhance it.

It is possible to find the traces of Ibrahim and Lila's politicization in their attitude to their children's education. But their commitment had a "red line," which was not crossed, as manifested in the arrangement of marriages for the two girls before they had completed higher education and professional training. I do not think that Ibrahim and Lila deliberately discriminated against their daughters' education. After all, it was the parents who encouraged the girls to study and paid for the university education of the oldest one, despite the not-uncommon practice of withdrawing the oldest daughter from high school. Yet it seems that pragmatic economic consideration and social pressure exceeded concern for the daughters' enlightenment and readiness to uphold their rights.

It is easier to support babies and small children than university students and schoolchildren. While in principle it is possible to defer a daughter's marriage, completion of a higher education and acquisition of a salaried position may take time; such a delay is not economical unless the family intends to use the daughter's wages to augment the family income. There is also a great demand among young men for particularly young women to marry (under age twenty).

In these circumstances, marrying the daughters was a relief for Lila and Ibrahim, especially since they succeeded in assuring improvement over the girls' material conditions at home. This was one of the main reasons for the daughters' agreeing to the marriages. That the opportunity for their own homes arose through arbitration by parents and others may well have assumed less importance. However, in many cases great pressure is exerted on the young bride to have children immediately; pregnancy, childbirth, and rearing children then present an obstacle to any return to studies. An advance agreement between the couple on family planning may overcome this problem, and many women in Dheisheh have continued studies after marriage and children. But without common understanding there is no guarantee for this in arranged marriages, and the woman's economic and social dependence on her husband is a strong factor in determining her future.

In examining the impact of the acquisition of higher education by women on family patterns in Dheisheh, I focused on cases wherein families delayed marriages of their educated daughters in order to prolong command of income from salaried work. Delaying marriages and arranging early marriages are both manifestations of the control that families exert over their daughters. One evil is not to be preferred over the other, but it appears to me that at least in some of the cases, early marriage leaves the young woman in a more vulnerable situation.

Former Prisoners from the Younger Generation: Characteristics and Trends

Lila and Ibrahim belong to the intermediate generation in Dheisheh and to the first generation of activists and prisoners after the 1967 war. Most of the former prisoners in Dheisheh are younger and belong to a later generation of activists, the majority of whom went to prison between the years 1975 and 1992. In the years separating the two generations, a number of changes of central importance took place in the social and political way of life in the camp. Noteworthy among these are the significant growth in the number of people with higher education, and especially women; the increase in the number of educated women employed in professional branches; the increase (until the early 1980s) in the number of men and women emigrating in order to take up professional or skilled employment in the Gulf; the appearance of popular political organizations; and the unprecedented spread of imprisonment.

Men who were imprisoned in the 1980s and early 1990s came back to different circumstances than those prevailing in the early 1970s, a fact that also found expression in their family life after their release. A number of trends and developments worthy of further research can be identified.

"POLITICAL" AND ARRANGED MARRIAGES: OPPOSING TRENDS

The 1980s and early 1990s saw increasing numbers of "political friendships" in Dheisheh, that is, friendships between young men and women based on common political affiliation. In some cases these also led to marriage. The proliferation of activists who went to jail in those years implied also instances of meaningful friendship, or even formal engagement, between prisoners and young women who waited years for their release.

In the course of these decades there emerged a trend toward decreased opposition by families to "political marriages." One of the reasons is latent in the strengthening of informal networks of prisoners' families and the intergenerational rapport that was created through them between younger activists and the parental generation. Political activists in key positions also won admiration and prestige among older members of the network and some of them acquired the status of mediators and arbitrators in family affairs. On occasion these would assist in arranging marriages to the partner of choice for their coactivists. I was personally acquainted with several instances of marriage that came about with the help of a sponsor of this sort, one accepted both by the young couple (the man a former prisoner) and by the parents (members of the network). There is no doubt that this sort of intervention could have helped Ibrahim and Lila.

Most of the prisoners, however, did not have the opportunity to form close friendships before their imprisonment. The majority were very young and, in general, the youth and action committees operated on a single-sex basis. Further, in their conservative society, young people were strongly inhibited concerning intimate relations outside marriage. Personal relations grew out of visits to prison by young women, but for most of the bachelor prisoners there was no girlfriend waiting upon their release.

Even though political education was likely to give rise to expectations regarding life after release from jail, realization of these hopes was often problematic. Thus, for example, long-term prisoners, freed at a relatively adult age, found it difficult to meet suitable candidates for marriage on their own. They quickly learned that most women their age were married or obliged to a cousin marriage, that much younger women did not necessarily comprehend their prison experience, that parents sought established men with trades, and, foremost, that their own families had made arrangements for them in advance.

Nor was the path of prisoners released at a relatively young age greatly different from that of young men who had not been in prison. Those who went to university had greater prospects for a partner of choice; for laborers, independent opportunities to meet women were limited and the dependence upon family arbitration greater.

MARRIAGE TO EDUCATED AND GAINFULLY EMPLOYED WOMEN

Parallel to the significant growth in the number of women with secondary and higher education and with salaried employment was the great increase in the number of young men who, because of prolonged imprisonment and/or repeated arrests, had lost years of study. These men were in their late twenties and early thirties, without diploma, trade, or employment. This difference between men and women of the younger generation found expression in the significant incidence (the obstacles mentioned above notwithstanding) of marriages between reasonably secure women from the point of view of employment and income and men living in uncertainty concerning their economic future.

The difficulty of finding work in Israel, the high unemployment rates in the West Bank, and the length of time necessary to acquire a higher education and to find a suitable job have had inevitable consequences for former prisoners. Differences in the earning capacity of spouses and in their status in the labor market have often persisted. Thus, one finds an increase in the number of households where the main breadwinner is the young woman in her twenties or thirties with fixed work in her profession, while the former prisoner is a part-time earner.

Division of labor of such kind often promoted further change: The salaries of women employed in various public institutions, though not high, were reliable and steady, allowing the family to maintain a reasonable standard of living. Women's "respectable" work, along with their position as primary providers, enhanced their situation with regard to decision making and allocation of resources. Their regular, uninterrupted employment has generally led to a decrease in childbearing. The number of children prevalent in this type of family is three or four, much smaller than the number among the intermediate generations. However, the prolonged asymmetry between the occupational status of former prisoners and that of their wives has contributed to tensions in family life. The elevated social status of a former prisoner generally compensates for, and can mask, his low economic state initially, but deferred entry into the labor market over time undermines the earlier prestige.

Nonetheless, in more than a few cases, over time the asymmetry "evened out," mainly due to efforts made by former prisoners to complete their education. A definite trend could be seen in Dheisheh during the 1990s wherein former prisoners returned to systematic academic studies; not bachelors in their early twenties, but rather older men in their late twenties and thirties with families. Some worked at part-time (and often extremely casual) odd jobs during their studies, while their wives were the primary earners. The shared division of labor enabled the former prisoner to complete his degree, thereby increasing his prospects for salaried employment. Choosing this path demands joint planning, defining long-term common goals, a more egalitarian division of child care, and smaller family size.

EMPLOYMENT IN THE SECURITY FORCES AND ADMINISTRATION OF THE PALESTINIAN NATIONAL AUTHORITY

With the redeployment of 1995—the retreat of Israeli forces from the major Palestinian towns and the consolidation of the PNA there and in the nearby refugee camps—significant changes took place in the employment possibilities of activists and former political prisoners in Dheisheh. Statistical data on the scope of the phenomenon in the camp is lacking, but my follow-up research in 1996–98 indicated that many of the activists in the political organizations, and particularly prisoners who had served long prison sentences, were integrated into the security apparatuses of the PNA (intelligence, preventive security, and police), as well as into various government offices and associated institutions. In addition, the PNA rescinded the dismissal of teachers of both sexes who had lost their positions in government schools due to the intervention of the Israeli security services. Many activists and former prisoners who were affiliated with factions and movements opposed to the by and large Fatah-based PNA were excluded from government and security jobs. Yet this should not be taken as a sweeping generalization since there existed notable exceptions and, as well, signs of a reversal to this tendency were apparent in the late 1990s.

Undoubtedly, significant improvement was felt in the standard of living of families of the newly employed, many of whom had known not only imprisonment in the past, but also years of continuous or intermittent unemployment. However, the capacity of the PNA to enhance the position of employees in its protostate organs (especially in terms of salaries and work-related benefits) was greatly undermined by the multitude of obstacles that stood in its way throughout the Oslo years. First and foremost among these were limited sovereignty, ongoing political uncertainty, scarcity of resources and revenues, and the very large number of those seeking work. These observations notwithstanding, an evaluation of the impact of employment in the apparatus of the PNA on family patterns of former prisoners in Dheisheh deserves and awaits systematic research.

A Retrospective Overview

PARTS I AND II OF this book followed Dheishehians in various arenas of action, among them day wage work in the Israeli or local labor markets, the multiple stages leading to acquisition of an education and a profession, the West Bank-based professional and semiprofessional employment market, and the migrant labor-based job market in the Gulf. All arenas brought Dheishehian refugees of both sexes and all three generations to confront various facets of the extremely unequal power relations that underlie the system of Israeli Occupation. All gave rise to familial patterns of organization in the form of generation- and gender-based divisions of labor and responsibilities, which utilized the limited resources generated by few family members to sustain large, multigenerational, and extended family households. Moreover, in the long run, patterns of organization that developed around the educational achievements and professional employment of family members—unlike those that depended entirely on their day wage labor—further enabled families to transcend the survival level, improve their standards of living, and advance the opportunities of their younger members vis-à-vis Occupation-imposed limitations and constraints. Finally, heavy reliance on the wage-generated income of unmarried family members, as well as that of married female family members, characterized family patterns of organization in all spheres of action. This introduced changes, tensions, and conflicts into the social and economic relationships within families and in the Dheishehian community, a factor that challenged—to varying extents—the perpetuation of patriarchal control.

Political activism—the arena of action discussed in Part III—brought the confrontation of individuals and families with political imprisonment to the forefront. In the context of their engagement with this arena, Dheishehian families were exposed to the most violent manifestations of Israeli military control, repression, and punishment. Given the suffering and anguish caused by the policy of imprisonment, as well as the denial of formal or legal means of fighting it, the patterns of organization sustained by family members of the imprisoned loom large in their impact on the lives of individuals, families, and the refugee community. Nonetheless, there is considerable difficulty in assessing the outcomes of this process—which I call *politicization*—in rigid, quantifiable terms. Politicization—unlike day wage labor, education, and professional employment—does not bring the individual an income, a diploma, a trade, or a defined position in a given market. In order to evaluate the achievements that politicization bestows, as well as its weaknesses and failures, there is a need for largely creative and experimental criteria and systems of evaluation.

One of the most outstanding characteristics of the politicization processes was the speed and intensity of the transformation in Dheishehians' ways of acting and thinking. Another outstanding characteristic was the capacity to assimilate men and women—mainly the latter—whose economic, educational, or professional resources were either meager or lacking. The decades-long work experiences of male and female day wage laborers placed at their disposal few means and produced no assets or durable funds that could be passed on to the younger generations. Acquiring high school and higher education and professional training demanded a prolonged effort and overcoming numerous obstacles. The near absence of new openings in the impoverished local public sector left many men and women who did acquire professional qualifications unemployed, and forced many others to emigrate. In contrast, the activity around imprisonment brought many Dheisheh residents close to the focus of the national-political struggle and endowed them within a short time with ability, skills, awareness, and social legitimation. Whereas educational resources primarily characterized men and women of the younger generation, and while official membership in political organizations hardly included the older generation and accounted for many more men than women, the activism into which family members of the prisoners were incorporated affected all age groups and both sexes, but primarily women. Change was particularly blatant for those women who, until they experienced the imprisonment of a family member, had no contact with channels of action likely to confer resources and social power.

The explanation for both the rapidity and intensity of politicization, and for its wide social incidence, is to be found mainly in the coming together of a number of factors pertaining to imprisonment. The fact that almost every family in Dheisheh felt the scourge of arrest and imprisonment bound the personal experience to the collective one. Thus, the cumulative social experience of "veterans," foremost among them relatives of many hundreds of activists who were imprisoned in the distant or recent past, was placed at the disposal of the newcomers. At the same time, the special standing that the organized political prisoners achieved within the national movement—that of being one of the pillars of resistance to the Occupation—was a key (perhaps the key) factor in facilitating and enhancing the politicization of family members of the imprisoned. Thus, maintaining contact with one's "own" prisoner through participation in the visiting days implied also bonding, and at times completely identifying oneself with a powerful and highly esteemed group.

It should be emphasized that this access by family members to an organized group to which imprisoned sons, brothers, and husbands belonged was unique to the political arena. Dheishehian day wage laborers who were employed in Israel (or for that matter on the local labor market) were not organized in trade unions, and educated and professionally skilled Dheishehians were forced to compete with each other over scarce job opportunities in the local public sector or to migrate and resign themselves to the strict labor laws of the Gulf states. This implied that the patterns of organization that developed around day wage labor and around professional employment remained an internal family affair, never binding the participants to an extrafamilial collective based on class, professional, or national affiliation.

Notwithstanding the empowerment derived from affiliation with the organized collective of political prisoners and from drawing on the experience of another collective, that of the prisoners' relatives, the intensity and rapidity of politicization were, at one and the same time, products of the nonmediated, personal involvement, and commitment that active participation demanded. This (third) factor found expression in the direct confrontation of participants, especially female relatives of the imprisoned, with agents of the regime: soldiers and officers, prison guards and other personnel, and the military court system. Their ongoing exposure to violence, and at times the endangering of their lives, entailed situations that hinged upon the individual's ability to rely on her or his own inner strength. Alongside this were the interpersonal relations that developed between visitors and their imprisoned relatives as sources of the individualization of the tie with the contents of the political struggle.

This by no means suggests that patterns of family organization in other arenas of action relied to a lesser degree on the personal commitment of individuals. Indeed, family members possessed a willingness, especially unmarried women, to endure enormous hardship, to sacrifice for the sake of others, and to deny their own needs and aspirations, a willingness indispensable to the "work chains" (the divisions of labor) that developed around day wage labor and the acquisition of education. The difference lay, however, not in the scope of personal investment but in the (nonmaterial) "returns" it yielded. Years of self-sacrifice on the part of a young, unmarried female schoolteacher for the sake of educating her younger siblings were unlikely to win her an improved social status in her parents' home.

The fourth (and not unrelated) factor encouraging the speedy and comprehensive instilling of politicization is the absence of the "appropriating-inhibiting" dimension of family intervention found in other arenas of action and confrontation. In the first and second parts of the book we saw how the economic, educational, and professional resources of young people, women, and especially unmarried women were appropriated for family benefit, denying them economic and social independence or delaying it and producing a source of conflict, open or concealed. In contrast, family organization around imprisonment, which rested in many cases on women, both single and married, young and old, did not prevent them from enjoying various social advantages achieved through active participation. Their familiarity with prison ways, their political grasp, their experience and skill in contact with soldiers and warders, and the new social contacts they acquired became recognized and valued assets in family and community, though there were restrictions and limitations. Moreover, family organization on behalf of the prisoner drew fathers and mothers to the national struggle, which, for the most part, was led and fought by the generation of the sons and daughters. As demonstrated by the recollections of fathers from visits to their imprisoned sons and by the networks of prisoners' relatives, this factor contributed to the erosion of traditional aged-based hierarchy and the redefinition of intergenerational relations.

Strong as the upheaval was that active political participation wrought in the lives of its Dheishehian subjects, however, it did not carry with it the same degree of influence on the different layers or dimensions of social relations and family life. The extent to which politicization penetrated unevenly into social relations found ample expression in the ambiguities and contradictions that marked the lives of most of the female protagonists found in Part III. This is particularly true regarding perceptions of gender relations and patterns of behavior based on these perceptions. Marriage patterns served as convenient and accessible indicators for examining the manifestations of such contradictions. The enlightening, emancipating, and rebellious elements, so central to the politicization process, were liable to be halted at the threshold by arranged marriages. Thus, to cite two key examples, exposure to intensive political socialization over years of ongoing, regular visits to prison did not stop an adolescent girl from "choosing" her paternal cousin as husband, nor did the unbelievable hardships a married (and exceptionally courageous) woman surmounted on her road to becoming an activist in her own right prevent her from forcing a traditional match upon her son. And Chapter 12 demonstrates that even when the decision to marry was an outcome of voluntary personal choice on the part of both spouses and directly inspired by political radicalization, the couple's subsequent relationship as well as various aspects of their matrimonial and family life could well fall victim to intrusive, prejudiced, "traditional" intervention by members of the wider kinship groups.

The quest for an explanation of the unequal penetration of politicization's influences is likely to engage a number of levels of consideration. It might be argued that family organization around arrests and imprisonment, like other forms of mobilization in times of emergency, took shape in "suspended time," as it were, outside the usual, normal social time. As such, it granted recognition and legitimation to independent and even anomalous conduct on the part of women in the public-political sphere. Such conduct did not threaten the family, but rather, in many cases, it assisted it to sustain itself in hard times. Yet the new resources that women acquire become a threat in the transition to more normal times, if and when women want to realize them for their own personal benefit.

Appealing in its simplicity, this explanation nevertheless does not stand the test of the empiric reality of Dheisheh. When emergency situations are stretched out over a period of nearly three decades, as occurred in Dheisheh, "suspended time" loses its distinctness and cannot be isolated. Moreover, the closed circuits of functionalist explanation fail to consider those changes that did take place, among them the widening incidence of marriage on grounds of political partnership or affiliation; the emergence of extrafamilial, cross-generational support "networks"; and even the phenomenon of split consciousness or double standards found in women.

An alternative explanation rests upon the multigenerational perspective. As in other areas, the long-term influence of politicization should not be examined through a lens focused on the individual, or even on a single generation. Political radicalization indeed took place more rapidly than did acquisition of education or professional job security. Yet, its realization in the area of gender relations was conditioned by far slower processes, as well as by the synchronization of resources generated through political activism with the availability of other resources. Hence, for example, marriage stemming from political partnership, which met with opposition in the early 1970s, gained much wider recognition during the 1980s with the gradual institutionalization of the networks of prisoners' families in Dheisheh. To cite an even more central example, the increase in the rate of professional and semiprofessional employment among Dheishehian women during the 1970s and 1980s provided a material setting more conducive to the realization of more egalitarian relations within matrimonial life—a development that bore crucial significance in the case of former prisoners and their (politicized/former activist) wives.

Nonetheless, changes in behavior, outlook, and awareness resulting from (prisoner-centered, grassroots-level) activism were, in themselves, insufficient to challenge patriarchal control and transform gender relations. However, the explanation for this observed limitation of the politicization process is not found in the specific case of Dheisheh camp but in the macrostructure level discussed at the beginning of this investigation. In the final analysis, the weaknesses (and strengths) of politicization should be evaluated in the light of the power relations between the system of Israeli Occupation and the Palestinian national movement that waged resistance against it.

In the introduction to the third part of the book it was suggested that the absence of a military option (in the face of Israel's ultimate military superiority) distanced the national movement in the Occupied Territories from armed struggle and led it to prioritize the public–civilian channel of resistance. In the subsequent examination of the history of political activists and activism in Dheisheh I underscored the transition from clandestine cells to popular committees, which began in the mid-1970s and culminated in the Intifada, as the heart and substance of the path that was embarked upon. While popular organizations with an ever-growing capacity for mass mobilization became the backbone of the national movement in the Occupied Territories, this civilian infrastructure of resistance nonetheless did not and could not compensate for the vulnerability that stemmed from its lack of military power. As the case of Dheishehian political prisoners and their families demonstrated, this vulnerability found utmost expression in the inability of the national movement to protect its constituency—leaders, activists, supporters, and sympathizers—from the repressive, violent measures directed against them by the Occupation regime, first and foremost the ongoing policy of mass imprisonment. Neither was the movement capable of offsetting the discrimination, exploitation, deprivation, and injustice that were the lot of Palestinian day laborers, salaried employees, students, professionals, and indeed, the population as a whole, under the Israeli Occupation. Under these extremely unequal power relations, the "remuneration" for political activism, especially (but not only) at the grassroots level, was confined to politicization: the empowerment achieved through resistance as a national collective and the transformation in outlook, consciousness, and behavior that this entailed for participants. In a sense, one may say that politicization was an end in itself, rather than becoming a means by which participants could secure other gains for themselves. Remuneration in the form of access by activists/participants to much-needed material resources, social services, and legal rights was bound to be deferred until the achievement of full independence from the Occupation. This structural weakness of the Palestinian national movement in the Occupied Territories was the main obstacle inhibiting the extension of the radical mores of politicization to the sphere of gender relations.

Reference Matter

Notes

INTRODUCTION

1. The literature referring to different aspects of the social, economic, and political transformation of the Palestinians since 1948 is discussed throughout the text. I will therefore confine myself here to a short list of sources with direct bearing on the topics mentioned above. On the situation of Palestinian communities in exile vis-à-vis the state policies of the Arab regimes, see Rosemary Sayigh 1979, 1994; Aruri 1972; Aruri and Farsoun 1980; and Brand 1988; see also Kimmerling and Migdal 1993; and Farsoun and Zacharia 1997. On the process of proletarianization and class transformation, see Henry Rosenfeld 1978; and Carmi and Rosenfeld 1974 (for Palestinians in Mandatory Palestine and Palestinian citizens of Israel); and Hilal 1976; Tamari 1980, 1981; and Hiltermann 1991a (for Palestinians of the Occupied Territories). On the acquisition of education in the Diaspora, see Shaath 1972; Ibrahim Abu-Lughod 1973; and Tahir 1985. On the political economy of labor migration to the Gulf, see Owen 1985; Ibrahim 1982; Hiro 1982; and Birks, Seccombe, and Sinclair 1988; for an analysis of the consequences of the "exportation" of Palestinian high-level manpower, see Zahlan and Zahlan 1977.

Studies on the development of the Palestinian national movement in exile and in the Occupied Territories are numerous, and they all pertain, in one way or another (though not always explicitly), to the problem of building and sustaining a liberation movement in the context of an extremely unequal balance of powers—that is, against the backdrop of Israeli military and political aggression and superiority, a consistent pro-Israeli U.S. policy, and the conflicting interests and the attempts of tutelage and patronage on part of the Arab regimes. Of special interest here are studies on the Palestine Liberation Organization (PLO) during and shortly after the Lebanon era (1969–82), for example, Cobban 1984; Gresh 1985; Rubenberg 1983; and Yezid Sayigh 1997. For an overview and analysis of the political situation (crisis) of the PLO in the early 1990s, in the aftermath of the Gulf War and the collapse of the Soviet Union, see Hilal 1993.

2. According to annually adjusted figures from the United Nations Relief and Works Agency for Palestine Refugees in the Near East (UNRWA), by December 2002 the population of refugees registered with the agency reached 4,025,694 persons, of which 1,282,472 (32 percent) lived in camps. The percentage of refugees

living in camps (versus noncamp refugees) varies greatly and is highest in Lebanon (56 percent in camps) and the Gaza Strip (53 percent in camps), and lowest in Jordan (17 percent in camps). Some 27 percent of the registered refugees in the West Bank live in camps (see http://www.UNRWA.org).

3. The majority of these villages were located within the confines of a relatively small area in the eastern part of central Palestine. One group of villages, among them Ra᾿s Abu ʿAmar, ʿAlar, Qabu, Walaje, Beit ʿItab, and Jarash, were located on the western slopes of the Judean Mountains, within distances that do not exceed fifteen kilometers from the site where the Dheisheh camp was set up. Another concentration of villages, among them Beit Natif, Zakariya, ʿAjur, Mughalis, Beit Jibrin, Dir Aban, Sarʿa, and ʿArtuf, from where a significant number of Dheishehians originated, were located in the valley that stretches to the northwest of the Hebron mountain range and to the west of the Judean Mountains.

4. In the immediate wake of their uprooting, that is, in the summer and autumn of 1948, the peasant refugees sought temporary refuge in the towns and villages of the Bethlehem and Hebron areas. The more fortunate among them either stayed with relatives or rented rooms from homeowners in exchange for livestock and grain they had brought along with them. Many others, however, stayed in the open, in caves and improvised shelters, as well as in the yards of schools, mosques, and churches. By the winter and spring of 1949, the majority of the "Dheishehians-to-be" had gathered in the Nuʿeima, ʿEin al-Sultan, and ʿAqabat Jaber refugee camps that were set up in the vicinity of Jericho. Particularly harsh physical conditions prevailed in the Jordan Valley–based camps, and this, together with the gradual institutionalization of the camps that UNRWA came to administer on the outskirts of all West Bank towns, resulted in a high rate of turnover, especially during the first five years. The majority of my elderly interviewees reported arriving in Dheisheh after having spent months to years in Nuʿeima camp.

5. The establishment of the UNRWA was approved by the UN General Assembly in December 1949, following the report of the UN economic survey mission (otherwise known as the Clapp Commission) on the situation of the Palestinian refugees in the lands of their dispersal. For a discussion and evaluation of UNRWA's operations since their inception in 1950 with a focus on the sphere of education, see Chapter 4. For more detail, see Buehrig 1971; Viorst 1989; Schiff 1995; and UNRWA 1986.

6. This is, of course, a highly simplified version of the thesis (primarily associated with the earlier [1960s and early 1970s] works of <u>Andre Gunder Frank</u>), and its treatment of key concepts such as capitalist world system, colonial expansion, core/center, dependency, and underdevelopment. I am highlighting the basic argument and the interrelated concepts employed in its articulation, rather than elaborating on either the origin of the theoretical approach(es) or the ongoing internal debates, controversies, and lines of convergence that marked the paths followed by the early proponents. For these, consult, for example, the two volumes coauthored by Amin, Arrighi, Wallerstein, and Frank, *Dynamics of Global Crisis* (1982) and *Transforming the Revolution* (1990). Especially worth noting are the later works of Frank, such as *Re-Orient* (1998), which completely diverge from and even discard the (hitherto central) theme of *capitalist* world system. While zealously holding to the world system as the fundamental holistic unit of analysis, Frank argues against placing the starting

point of the system in the late fifteenth or early sixteenth century and against attributing major significance to the rise of modern capitalism in Western Europe, rejecting such analysis (including that of Marx himself, and that of Wallerstein) as partial and Eurocentric. Indeed, according to the "revisionist" Frank, capitalist development is no longer a sine qua non for the explanation of worldwide division of labor. The question of how this revised interpretation impinges upon such issues as class structure, class struggle, dependency, and prospects for revolution remains basically open.

Nor can I address within this framework the enormous body of critique to which modern world system and dependency theories gave rise. For a sense of the wealth of this literature, see Frank's "Answer to Critics," pp. 245–278, in Frank 1984.

7. In two detailed studies, Shulamit Carmi and Henry Rosenfeld (1989, 1992) have shown how, especially since the 1960s, foreign aid, specifically U.S. aid in the form of huge, annual unilateral grants and low interest loans, became a—perhaps the—significant factor that enabled Israel to maintain what they refer to as a (booming) welfare and warfare economy. In their analysis of the transformation of the political economy of Israel since the early 1950s through the 1980s, they have argued that from a relatively early stage (the 1950s) successive Israeli governments have opted for militarism as a major axis of state conduct and as a preferable political orientation. This path was extremely beneficial, in fact, for the (young) state's economic development: Israel's military performance attracted U.S. support, political and financial, of an unprecedented and unparalleled scope (an annual transfer of three billion dollars in the form of military and nonmilitary aid is a salient example, but far from being the only one). Israel's "very special status" as client and as provider of services spared it from the fate that was generally the lot of developing nation-states across the globe—spirally growing debts—and instead enabled it to climb from the list of the developing states to that of the developed, affluent states. The gain entailed, and was manifested in, an ongoing, state-sponsored investment in infrastructure, in several leading industries, and in welfare provisions that for a long time remained at a comparatively high level. The spoils of militarism were, of course, not evenly distributed among the different class and national constituencies of the Israeli society, but this is another issue. As for the Occupation, the authors do not deny that the prolonged Israeli economic control over the Palestinian Territories and the aggressive policy of Jewish settlements in their midst provided immense opportunities for profit making and upper mobility on the part of various social strata, including the Jewish settlers themselves. However, according to their analysis this was a "link," albeit a significant one and central in terms of political consequences, in the Israeli political economy, but not the heart of it, so to say.

8. Examples include the reports of the research department of the Bank of Israel, for example, Bregman 1974; Meron 1982; Zakai 1988; and Arnon and Gottlieb 1993. The reports addressed the perceived "accelerated economic growth" in the Occupied Territories during the first six to seven years of Israeli control (1967–74) and the subsequent "attenuated growth" in later years, as measured through such indicators as GNP, GDP, GNP per capita, changing (increasingly "modernized") patterns of consumption, etc. The economic relationships between Israel and the Occupied Territories is described in terms of "integration" without exploration of the structure of the Occupation regime's political economy and/or the underlying policies

of (military) control. The movement of goods and labor through what was once the "green line" (the 1949 armistice lines) is perceived in terms of "lifting of economic barriers" (Meron 1982, 3), "lifting of state boundaries" (Zakai 1988, 14), or "interaction between two very different economies *which met at the market place*" (Arnon and Gottlieb 1993, 3; emphasis mine). "Attenuation of growth" is attributed primarily to the fluctuations in the "neighboring economies," that is, Israel, Jordan, and the more distant Gulf states, rather than to the prolonged underdevelopment of the local economies in the West Bank and the Gaza Strip, and the exploitative terms of employment of Palestinian workers in the Israeli labor market. Nonetheless, without searching for the roots and causes, these reports deal with symptoms or features of dependence and underdevelopment, for example, heavy reliance on the structure of employment opportunities outside the Territories, lack of investment in local industry, and increasing unemployment among the ranks of the educated. See, for example, Zakai 1988, 13, 19.

Another account by a state official, though of a very different kind, is authored by former Israeli general Shlomo Gazit, who was appointed the first coordinator of the Occupied Territories in 1967 and remained in that position for seven years. Following his discharge from the army, Gazit was to become president of Ben-Gurion University of the Negev and director-general of the Jewish Agency. In his book *Trapped* (1999), Gazit attempts a critical account of thirty years of Israeli policy in the Territories, sparing no effort to explain the protracted shortsightedness of Israeli policy makers and policy making with regard to ruling the Palestinians. Surprisingly, however, apart from very general reference to the "open bridges policy" (the controlled movement of people and goods across the bridges that connect west and east banks of the Jordan River associated with former Israeli minister of defense Moshe Dayan) and further brief reference to the "integration of economies and infrastructures" that he maintains acted to the benefit and interests of both sides (1999, 270–71), there is no treatment of the political economy of the Israeli Occupation.

9. The numerous scholarly assessments of the prospects for economic and social development in the West Bank and Gaza Strip during this time period were of course related to the establishment of the PNA and the backing of the interim agreements between Israel and the Palestine Liberation Organization (PLO) with guarantees by donor states to extend economic aid to the PNA. Within the Palestinian Territories, we find a proliferation of both PNA-administered and supported research institutions—the most prominent of which is the Palestinian Central Bureau of Statistics (PCBS)—and nonstate, NGO-sponsored research institutes. The research conducted by these bodies is geared toward fact finding—the creation of long-needed, reliable databases—as well as toward policy making, with prolonged underdevelopment being a built-in premise. Two examples of such studies (among a multitude) are the PCBS publication *Women and Men in Palestine* (1998) and a publication of the Palestine Economic Research Institute (MAS) entitled *Towards a Social Security System in the West Bank and Gaza* (Hilal et al. 1998). On another level, that of international financing institutions, the six-volume publication of the World Bank, *Developing the Occupied Territories—An Investment in Peace* (1993), is worth noting as an example of a fairly extensive and detailed study that (unsurprisingly)

adopts a "constructivist" approach and bypasses in-depth analysis of the political economy of the Occupation.

10. Underdevelopment in the West Bank during Jordanian rule (1950–67) will be further discussed in Chapter 1. On the impact of the 1948 war and the inflow of hundreds of thousands of refugees to Jordan, see Aruri 1972; Plascov 1981; Mazur 1979; Mishal 1978; and Brand 1988. On underdevelopment in the Gaza Strip in the years 1948–67, see Roy 1995a; and Abu-Amr 1988.

11. For a detailed discussion of these pillars, see Chapter 1.

12. An illustrative example is found in *Intifada: Palestine at the Crossroads* (Nassar and Heacock 1991), a collection of essays by (mostly) Palestinian academics on the origins and central facets of the Palestinian uprising: In the essay "The Sociology of the Intifada," Farsoun and Landis discuss the uprising in terms of a collective political response to prolonged political, institutional, and economic repression without providing an account of the social processes that gave rise to it. Similarly, Taraki's analysis of the development of political consciousness in the Occupied Territories focuses on institutions and frameworks of action without systematically relating their emergence and spread to social and class transformation.

A notable exception to this trend, and indeed pathbreaking in its attempt to fuse an analysis of mass-based popular organizations and of political mobilization with an analysis of long-term socioeconomic processes, is Hiltermann 1991a.

13. I refrain from extending this line of criticism beyond applications of the theory to the case of the Palestinians and the Occupied Territories. For a penetrating and comprehensive theoretical critique of the weakness of Frank's and Wallerstein's thesis of development of underdevelopment and Wallerstein's analyses of class struggle and of (capitalist) relations of production in the periphery, see Brenner 1977.

It should be stressed that in its original phase, if not for many years later, the theme of the development of underdevelopment was part of an emphatically revolutionary outlook that aimed to change the world, not only to interpret it. As is well known, and as Frank himself noted over and over again (see, for example, Frank 1984), it came into being not merely as an intellectual response and challenge to modernization theory but also, and perhaps more importantly, against the backdrop of Latin America of the 1960s with its revolutionary upsurges and prospects (especially in the wake of the success of the Cuban revolution). A factor no less significant was what Frank and his contemporaries conceived as the shortcomings of revolutionary movements, first and foremost the "traditional" Latin American Communist Parties. Unlike the latter, the theory discarded the strategy that necessitated a (temporary) alliance of revolutionary movements with the national bourgeoisie, portraying that class as dependent and fundamentally reactionary, while seeking to provide an alternative path and strategy for the oppressed peoples of the underdeveloped world.

The theory and analyses of modern world system and development versus underdevelopment found wide support among diverse circles of readers, including leaders and supporters of revolutionary movements and radical academics. There is no better example of the latter than Eric Wolf's introduction to his *Europe and the People without History* (1982).

14. Among the forerunners of this (then) emergent direction Ortner notes the works of Bourdieu (1977) and Sahlins (1981) in anthropology, Giddens (1979) in sociology, Raymond Williams (1977) in literary criticism, and E. P. Thompson (1978) in social history.

15. In the introduction to his *Genealogies of Religion* (1993, 1–24), Talal Asad attacks the free-floating, supposedly agent-centered notions of "history making" and "real people" invoked by Ortner in her review article, which he associates with a leading fashion among anthropologists ("the anthropological chorus of protest," in Sahlins's words) to dismiss the political economy/world system approach, whose most influential proponent was Eric Wolf (1982). Asad takes issue with Marshal Sahlins—who attributes to the people of the periphery a kind of "cultural logic" that informs and shapes the structure and content of their encounter with colonialism (for example, Sahlins 1994)—claiming that Sahlins's is a theory of adjustment or adaptation, rather than one that illuminates the role of people as the "authors of their own history." Yet, the alternative perspective that Asad adopts relocates the focus of theoretical concern from "history making" and the material and political conditions within which it takes place, to the *concept* of history-making, that is, the *idea* or *project* of history-making, as the latter was conceived and consolidated in Western thought since the Enlightenment and as it influenced and shaped the anthropological discipline. Hence Asad's concern is with the trajectory of a Western concept and its transmission/translation in a non-Western world, rather than history-making itself.

16. "Failing to grasp their own situation as one aspect of a whole system, the subproletarians cannot link the betterment of their condition to a radical transformation of the system: their aspirations, their demands, and even their revolt are expressed within the logic the system imposes on them" (Bourdieu 1979, 61).

17. Writing at the height of the Algerian Revolution, Frantz Fanon noted in his *A Dying Colonialism* (1965) that the "surface level" could easily mislead the "experts" (indeed, it is hard to read this passage without bearing Bourdieu's *Algeria 1960* in mind): "The deep hold taken by colonial society, its frenzy to transform itself into necessity, the wretchedness on which it was built, gave to life that familiar tinge of resignation that specialists in underdeveloped countries describe under the heading of fatalism." But, he immediately continues: "And it was in these inauspicious circumstances that the first salvos of November 1954 burst forth" (Fanon 1965, 102). Fanon subsequently explains how the revolutionary consciousness, by now embedded in the outlook and conduct of sons, affects and transforms their relationships with fathers, whose initial positions with respect to the revolution was ambiguous or confused: "The militant would replace the son and undertake to indoctrinate his father. The father no longer knew how to keep his balance. He would then discover that the only way to do it was to join his son" (103). Where Bourdieu found circular reproduction of system and people, fed by the "fatalist" acceptance by the Algerian of his position, Fanon found that "there is a new kind of Algerian man, a new dimension to his existence. The thesis that men change at the same time that they change the world has never been so manifest as it is now (1959) in Algeria. . . . We witness in Algeria man's reassertion of his capacity to progress" (30).

18. See also Alex Callinicos's evaluation that although "Pierre Bourdieu's sympathies are plainly with the 'dominated' . . . he does not offer those at the bottom of

society any prospect of a collective escape from the structures of class domination and cultural distinction" (Callinicos 1999, 294–95).

19. The "ideal" Muslim Arab family is described as patriarchal in the sense of the control exercised by men over women, by older adults over younger ones, and by the head of the family over the household economy, and in the sense that the greater privileges of men are anchored in and justified by means of the values and ideas of kinship (Joseph 1993, 459–60). Additional central features that are connected to, interwoven with, and that reinforce patriarchy through a complex of institutionalized practices are patrilocality, patrlineality, endogamy, and the "extended family" setting.

Whether studied as part of and in relation to the sociopolitical-economic system or separately from it, these patriarchal elements have constituted the point of departure for an explanation of observed phenomena in various dimensions of family and social life, such as the custom of family-arranged marriages and the use of marriage ties to keep property within the family and/or to create interfamilial alliances; practices of inheritance that exclude women from property rights; patterns of socialization that produce and preserve control over women, block their access to the public sphere, and channel their activity into the "private sphere"; adherence to systems of values and norms that put "family honor" at the center; identification of the preservation of "honor" with the sexual chastity of the women of the family; and reproduction of the patriarchal hierarchy in the domains of the economy and the government (Barakat 1993; Sharabi 1985; Joseph 1993). Although these characteristics acquire particular and local forms and while some have undergone significant changes in the wake of processes of urbanization, "modernization," expanded acquisition of an education, migration, and state intervention, the existence of historical continuity despite all of the above emphasizes their centrality.

The literature (mainly anthropological) dealing with family and kinship in the "Arab world" and Middle East is very extensive. For an overview of the field see Eickelman 1981; for a critical review article of the literature, see Lila Abu-Lughod 1989. For a discussion of the patriarchal system of norms, values, and practices of the Arab family and their consequences for gender relationship in particular and for societal relations in general, see Saadawi 1980; Mernissi 1987; Tucker 1993; Sharabi 1985; Barakat 1993; and Joseph 1993, 1994a, 1994b. For an analysis of the barriers to change of patriarchal family relations in the wake of (restricted) socioeconomic transformation, see Henry Rosenfeld 1968.

20. Some two years into the Intifada, and approximately three years before the imposition of the general closure on the Occupied Territories (March 1993), the military government began to issue green-colored identity cards to a target population of former political prisoners and administrative detainees. These periodically renewable identity cards replaced the usual orange-colored ones for residents of the Occupied Territories, preventing their holders from entering and working in Israel (not yet sealed off) and subjecting them to strict surveillance.

21. CAMPUS, an acronym in Hebrew for a student group for political and social action, was active on the campuses of the Hebrew University, Tel Aviv University, and the University of Haifa during the 1970s, 1980s, and part of the 1990s, and unique in its binational composition, support of a two-state solution, and emphasis

on Arab-Jewish solidarity. In the early 1980s many of CAMPUS's activities were launched in protest of the occasional closure of Palestinian universities by the military government.

CHAPTER 1

1. For a discussion of the Gaza Strip economy under Egyptian military administration, see Roy 1995a, ch. 3.

2. For estimates of the refugee population according to areas of arrival (1948–49), see Zureik 1996, 17.

3. On the adjustment of judicial procedures for the purpose of land confiscation, see Benvenisti 1984, 30–36. On the stages of legislation adopted in order to render the status of Jewish settlements in the Occupied Territories equal to that of localities inside Israel proper and the status of settlers identical to that of other Israeli citizens (and distinct, of course from that of "native" Palestinians), see Shehadeh 1993, 103–22.

4. Whereas, as we shall see, Israeli policies ensured the perpetuation of a "supply" of Palestinian labor, the initial "reservoir" was already there at the onset of the occupation, particularly among the peasant and refugee populations. According to Tamari (1981), more than 70 percent of the West Bankers who were employed in Israel during the first decade of the Occupation were villagers. Seasonal nonmechanized agriculture, and the absence of primogeniture, were the main (internal) factors that gave rise to a large surplus of working hands among the peasantry and subsequently accounted for the high response among their ranks to wage work opportunities—a phenomenon that had been recorded (though in smaller magnitude) since the time of the British Mandate.

5. The manifestations, implications, and long-term consequences of the Israeli policy of nondevelopment and neglect of the public sector in the Occupied Territories are covered extensively in my discussion of the education system and professional employment in the West Bank (see Chapters 4 and 6).

6. Under curfew, Palestinians from the Occupied Territories were prohibited from leaving their homes for however long the order was in force. During the first years of the Intifada (1988–89), extended curfews, at times for as long as ten or even fourteen straight days, were commonly imposed by the military, and more often on refugee camps than on other localities.

7. Closure, as distinct from curfew, prohibits Palestinian residents of the Occupied Territories from crossing the green line and entering Israel, while it does not impose restrictions on movement inside the Territories. However, on numerous occasions "internal" closures were enforced, wherein Palestinians' movement was confined to their residential districts. Moreover, since the early 1990s movement from the West Bank to the Gaza Strip and vice versa has been subjected to extreme restrictions.

8. The detrimental consequences of this policy and regulations for workers from the Occupied Territories were documented in the 1993 report of the International Labor Office (1993, 25–26), and described in full detail in Kav La'Oved newsletters

(July 1993, Feb. 1994, May 1994). For the impact of the closure policy on the Gaza Strip, see Roy 1994a and 1994b.

CHAPTER 2

1. The eighty men in the larger sample are the fathers of the eighty interviewees from the younger generations who were included in the core sample. Each of these interviewees was asked to report about the (former) employment of her/his father in terms of location of workplaces and type of work. Although this data was collected indirectly (that is, it is "secondhand" information), and should therefore be regarded with some caution, it appears to corroborate the findings obtained through the interviews.

2. According to the evaluation of the World Bank, Palestinian wages in Israel were about $450 per month (1993), with earnings varying from one-third what Israelis were paid in industry and construction to more than 40 percent in agriculture (World Bank 1993, vol. 2: 26). As noted, however, the per-month calculation is misleading, since the wage basis was daily, or rather hourly.

3. It goes without saying that "illegally" employed (nonregistered) workers were denied the right to unemployment benefits, as well as to any other entitlement.

4. The reference is to Rabbi Moshe Levinger, an ultrarightist settler who (together with a small group of families, later joined by a yeshiva [religious seminary]) made his home in Hebron, in the middle of a Palestinian neighborhood. Levinger was convicted of manslaughter after having killed a Palestinian merchant but was subsequently sentenced to only a short (one-year) term in prison.

5. Thirteen of the thirty-nine interviewees (33 percent) in the core sample had worked in Israel and/or the West Bank for periods that ranged from three to twenty-four years. Of the fifty-three women older than fifty-five who were included in the survey on women and employment, nineteen had worked in Israel for periods ranging from one to twenty years, seven had worked in the West Bank for periods ranging from one to twenty-seven years, and eight had worked in family-owned shops in Dheisheh.

6. I found this inclusive definition—a more flexible one by far than the formal definitions employed by the International Labour Office (ILO) and the Israeli Central Bureau of Statistics (CBS)—much more fruitful for my research purposes, that is, the tracing of the labor histories of Dheishehian women over a twenty-five-year period.

7. The data with respect to the forty interviewees in the core sample population should probably be regarded with caution, since the category of manual wage laborers was conspicuously absent; fourteen of the interviewees were salaried employees in semiprofessional and professional jobs (nurses, teachers, secretaries, and journalists) against only one woman who reported having been a factory worker prior to her marriage.

8. The low rate of Palestinian women's participation in the waged labor force is generally comparable with the rates in most Arab countries. Although on the increase in the last decades, the relative share of women in the Middle Eastern and

North African labor force (19 percent in 1994 according to the UNDP Development Report) is by far smaller than in all other parts of the globe (Moghadam 1995, 19). Even when factoring in the large disparities in the scope of female employment between states of this region (for example, rates of 18 percent and 4.4 percent in Egypt [1989] and Algeria [1987], respectively), the recent trend of a general increase in women's employment, the substantial number of unpaid female family workers, the women in the "informal sector" and the numerous flaws in data collection, the regional average rate remains low (Hijab 1996, 41–43).

Whereas features of Arab male participation in the regional labor force are usually discussed in terms of supply and demand and attributed to determinants of the political economy of the region, the discussion of female employment has tended to revolve around the impact of tradition, religion, and the "value system." The low rate of Arab women's participation in the waged labor force has often been explained as emanating from the cultural-religious attributes of the region, particularly the perception of women and of family honor in Islam and tradition and its effect on social norms and practices—specifically the exclusion of women from the "public sphere" and the strict control over their movement. Exclusion and control are reflected in the commonplace pattern of arranged, early marriages; the encouragement of high fertility; the discrimination against women's education; and the reliance on the *shariʿa* as a basis for personal status law—all of which are noted to have had a quintessentially negative effect (direct and indirect) on women's participation in the labor force (Azzam, Abu-Nasr, and Lorfing 1985). In the absence of an alternative explanation, it seems that the cultural-religious factor gained the status of an overarching cause.

The writings of Nadia Hijab (1988, 1996) and Valentine Moghadam (1993, 1995) on gender and work in the Arab world (and Middle East in general) represent a significant break from the socioreligious-cultural line of argument. Hijab called for a framework of analysis that examines three interlinked factors: "The need for women's work, whether as a result of national economic development or the need for more family income; the opportunities for women's work that are created through legislation and the removal of socio-cultural barriers; and the investment in women's abilities through education and training" (1996, 46).

Moghadam introduced a comprehensive paradigm for her analysis of women's status in the context of economic development in the Middle East and North Africa, wherein she endeavored to give full weight to "world-system" determinants, the political economy of each regime, state policy, class structure, and gender relations. Accordingly, interregional resemblance in the patterns of women's labor force participation is explained against the background of the major function of the Middle East in the world economy as supplier of oil, whereas significant dissimilarities in rate and types of women's participation are attributed to the highly unequal distribution of the oil resources, concomitant disparities in wealth, and the impact of these latter factors on specific patterns of industrialization and on economic policies of various regimes (Moghadam 1995, 6–33; 1993, chs. 1, 2, 4).

My study of women and wage labor in Dheisheh incorporated the above general premises of the "political economy" approach as a point of departure, though the units of analysis are of course different, given the nature, scope, and purpose of the research, and the focus is on the analysis of labor histories as *processes,* that is, beyond the prevalence of women's waged labor as such.

CHAPTER 3

1. On February 24, 1994, Baruch Goldstein—a physician, Israeli army reserve officer, and settler from Kiryat Arba—murdered twenty-nine Palestinians inside the Haram al-Ibrahimiya mosque in Hebron, shooting them down while they were attending the morning prayer. The intervention of the army in the immediate aftermath of the massacre cost the lives of another thirteen Palestinians. Shortly after these events, in a move that further punished the victim, the army imposed a curfew on the city of Hebron and tightened the closure that had been imposed upon the entire Occupied Territories in March 1993.

2. Clearly, the "cultural" block continues for women in the patriarchal households of their husbands as well. And women, necessarily, are carriers of their culture; indeed, they are locked-in to it, since they are denied freedom of movement, are (made) dependent on males, etc. The point here is that the imposition of the "block" leading to the contradiction is greatest during the time period that the daughter is unmarried. No less clear is that the block is not impregnable; often enough both men and women see into, and go beyond, it.

CHAPTER 4

1. A refugee was initially defined by UNRWA as "a person who, as a result of the Palestine conflict, had lost his home and his means of livelihood." This definition was later progressively refined, and today the accepted UNRWA definition of a refugee is "a person whose normal residence had been Palestine for a minimum of two years preceding the 1948 conflict and who, as a result, lost both his home and his means of livelihood and took refuge in 1948 in one of the countries where UNRWA provides relief." According to this definition, such refugees and their direct descendants are eligible for agency assistance "if they are registered with UNRWA, living in the area of UNRWA's operations, and in need" (UNRWA 1986, 66; Schiff 1995, 24, 54). The figure of 960,000 refugees for 1950 is based on the records of the United Nations Relief for Palestine Refugees (UNRWA's predecessor) (UNRWA 1986, 4).

2. In 1991–92 some 18,699 Palestinian refugees were on UNRWA's payroll, more than half of whom (10,888) were employed in the education system. In that year the number of refugees registered with UNRWA was 2,648,707 (UNRWA 1992, 43, 56). In 1998–99 the total Palestinian staff numbered 21,521, of whom 15,286 were employed in the education system, whereas the number of registered refugees was 3,625,592 (UNRWA 1999, 41, 50). Less than 1 percent of the registered refugees (precisely 0.59 percent) are therefore currently employed by UNRWA. Though the figures would appear to speak for themselves, some scholars went as far as accusing the agency of keeping an inflated "army" of employees in an attempt to perpetuate its own institutional existence in the Middle East, which critics charged had become less and less necessary (see Marx 1992, 290–91).

3. The overwhelming majority among the interviewees in the core sample (forty-one men aged forty-five to fifty-five and forty-one women aged forty-one to fifty-four) were of school age during the decades under concern (the 1950s and 1960s). The findings pertaining to the male core sample were supported by the results of a survey I conducted among 232 additional male respondents, showing that only about a quarter (25.8 percent) have an education of six years or less. However, the findings pertaining to the female core sample were not fully supported by those for a larger population. For example, as many as sixty respondents (80 percent), in a survey I conducted among seventy-five women aged forty to fifty-four, reported acquiring no more than six years of education. This result points to an even larger gap between the educational attainments of men and women from the intermediate generation than reported above.

4. The annual statistics of UNRWA did not provide information on either the dropout rate or the percentages enrolled in the relevant age groups. I therefore suggest an alternative indicator: a calculated ratio of the pupils enrolled on the preparatory level to those enrolled in elementary school, for specific years in each of the agency's five fields of operation (Gaza, West Bank, Jordan, Syria, and Lebanon). This indicator enables us to assess the percentage of students who continued from elementary to preparatory level. In the optimal scenario with an almost zero dropout rate, the number of those at the preparatory level (three grades) should be approximately one half those in the elementary six grades. That this method of calculation is imprecise is indisputable, but nonetheless it allows for general estimation; and indeed it enabled me to trace the incremental changes over time, which is the most important result. The rates of "continuees" mentioned in the text are the weighted averages for all five fields. Once we look into the breakdown, significant gaps/variations between the regions can be discerned, but the analysis of this is left outside our discussion.

5. The data for the core sample of forty male and forty women interviewees from the young generation are supported by my findings for much larger population samples. In a survey that encompassed 277 men from the young generation, 221 respondents (79.8 percent) reported to have attended the preparatory level, as did 232 of the 284 women surveyed (82 percent). It should be noted, however, that these figures include all those who had entered the preparatory stage, including those who did not complete the full, three-year-long cycle.

6. Based on A. B. Zahlan's findings and projections from 1976, Don Peretz (1977) gives a higher estimate for the rate of Palestinian students in the population in the mid-1970s than that provided by Tahir. Zahlan (summer 1977) estimated the rate in 1974 at twenty-one students for every thousand Palestinians, which approached the rate in Israel. Zahlan also demonstrated that in the mid-1970s Palestinian students constituted one-tenth of all students in the Arab world, whereas the relative share of Palestinians in the Arab population was only 2.2 percent (Peretz 1977, 66). Muhsin Yusuf (1979) estimated the number of Palestinian students in 1977–78 at eighty thousand, again higher than Tahir's estimate for that year, which stood at sixty thousand.

7. Some caveats are nevertheless in order here. It was Ibrahim Abu-Lughod who, in 1973, pointed out the weaknesses of the Arab university system in general, and that of the natural sciences faculties in particular. Abu-Lughod argued that the entire Arab

student population suffered from a relative scarcity of opportunities to enroll in science faculties and from the low academic standards in both these and in the humanities. The insufficient capacity of the science faculties, which at some stage led to the enforcement of admission quotas that favored local citizens, greatly restricted the options opened to Palestinian students, and channeled the majority into the humanities (Ibrahim Abu-Lughod 1973, 110). Yusuf's study, however, focusing on the mid-1970s, points to the significant percentage of medical and engineering students among Palestinians who studied abroad. According to the data he provides, 19.2 percent of the Jordanian students of Palestinian origin who were enrolled in universities in 1975–76 specialized in medicine, one of the highest rates worldwide (Yusuf 1979, 84).

8. In the early 1980s women constituted approximately 39 percent of the total student body in the five major Palestinian universities. Women were more highly represented at Bethlehem and Hebron Universities (45 and 55 percent of all students, respectively), while their share at Birzeit, Al-Najah, and Gaza Islamic Universities was lower (36, 37, and 38 percent, respectively) (Graham-Brown 1984a, 84). In 1996–97, women comprised 45.1 and 38.9 percent of all students in West Bank- and Gaza Strip-based universities and colleges, respectively (PCBS 1998, 58).

9. These findings are based on interviews I conducted with participants in the core sample of forty men, as well as on the results of a survey I conducted among an additional 277 men from the young generation.

10. These findings are based on the interviews I conducted with the core sample of forty women, as well as on the results of my survey on women and employment, which encompassed an additional 318 women from the young generation.

11. It should be stressed, nevertheless, that my definition of postsecondary education is probably more liberal than that adopted in most formal surveys. In addition to those with university or college education, I have included in the category all those who were enrolled in training centers offering a certificate. Some of the latter did not complete high school successfully; that is, they failed to pass the matriculation examination, a disadvantage that rendered them unqualified for admission to university or to UNRWA's college, but did not prevent enrollment in some of the nurses' training centers. Therefore, the "Dheishehian advantage" may indeed be somewhat exaggerated, or at least bent upward once we employ stricter criteria.

CHAPTER 5

1. The case study examined in detail by Wahlin was the rural district of Al'an in the northwestern part of Jordan, encompassing some twenty small villages. The first three government primary schools in the region, all for boys, started to function in 1948, serving a population within a three-kilometer radius. The first regional primary school for girls was established in 1954, when the number of female pupils was fifty-five (as compared to 428 males). In 1965, 142 girls studied in government primary schools, as against 536 boys in primary schools and seventy on the preparatory level. The great leap forward came only in the 1970s. In 1977 there were thirty government schools in the region: seven for boys, seven for girls, and sixteen joint

schools. In 1979–80 the number of girls enrolled in government primary schools reached 46 percent of the total number of pupils (Wahlin 1987, 152–64).

2. It is again worth comparing the data from Dheisheh with the rural region of Al⁽an in Jordan. There a preparatory school for girls was established only in 1968 and the rate of female enrollment in the 1970s was 40 percent lower than that for males (Wahlin 1987, 162).

CHAPTER 6

1. Reliance on an especially large migrant labor force in all sectors of production, as well as in the services and administration, has characterized the economies of the Gulf states since the inception of oil production on a commercial scale shortly after the end of World War II. This trend was amplified with the expansion of the operations of Arabian American Oil Company (ARAMCO) in Saudi Arabia in the 1950s, the growth of the Kuwaiti Oil Company (KOC), and the intensification of oil extraction in Abu Dhabi and Bahrain in the 1960s. Thus, for example, the 6.5–fold population increase in Kuwait between 1944 and 1965, from 70,000 to 467,339, can be almost solely attributed to the constant inflow of migrant laborers (single or with families), many of them Palestinians (Owen 1985).

2. There is a severe shortage of data on the breakdown along nationality and occupation of migrant laborers who worked in the Gulf during the 1960s. Nonetheless, official Kuwaiti figures for 1975 provide some idea of the general attributes of Palestinian labor migration in the preceding decade. In that year around half of the Palestinian migrants in Kuwait were employed in professions that demanded either university or other postsecondary degrees. The prevalence of Palestinians in positions that require high skills and/or higher education is evident, especially in comparison with migrants of other nationalities (Birks and Sinclair 1980, 53).

3. For an insightful analysis of the political considerations and goals that led Israel to set up the Civil Administration in 1981, and a critical evaluation of its policies during the early years of its operation, see Benvenisti 1984, 43–47.

4. These figures do not include employees of the armed forces and police.

5. The most important among these in terms of employment opportunities for Dheishehian women were Caritas Baby Hospital and the Holy Family Hospital (al-Françawi) in Bethlehem and Jabal Daoud Hospital in Beit Sahour.

6. Owens's figures draw heavily on the research estimates of Birks and Sinclair from the early 1980s that refer to migrant laborers in the six Gulf states of Kuwait, Saudi Arabia, Qatar, Bahrain, Oman, and the United Arab Emirates (which in 1981 formed the Gulf Cooperation Council). Thus, data on labor migration to Iraq (which in the mid-1980s had become the second-largest importer of migrant labor among the oil-producing states in the Gulf) is not included. The figure for 1975 (of 1,250,000 migrant laborers in the six Gulf states) was disputed by other studies as far too low (see Kanovsky 1989, 7).

7. The distribution of noncitizen employees along the various sectors of the economy was quite similar in all six GCC countries (Birks, Seccombe, and Sinclair 1988, 268, 275).

8. For a review of the policies adopted by the GCC states vis-à-vis the migrant labor force with a focus on the post–Gulf War era, see also Winckler 1997.

9. The most salient example is that of Jordan; it was estimated that in 1987, 90 percent of all unemployed persons in the country were university or college graduates. The majority of the three hundred thousand Jordanian migrants in the Gulf were professionals (Kanovsky 1989, 61–62).

10. Small wonder that in this context and under these circumstances, the labor-exporting Arab regimes were not willing to intervene on behalf of their migrant citizens through monitoring their citizens' conditions of employment.

11. Nine out of twelve with secondary education (ten to twelve years) were laborers, against two who worked in journalism and one who was a clerk with UN-RWA. Of the thirteen interviewees with postsecondary education (fourteen to sixteen years) seven were laborers in Israel and the West Bank, three were teachers with UNRWA, one taught in a government school, one worked as an engineer, and one worked at an insurance company.

12. Twenty-eight of the forty women in this sample acquired secondary or post-secondary education; sixteen completed ten to twelve years of schooling, eleven are college graduates (fourteen years of schooling) and one is a university graduate (sixteen years). All of the fifteen women who were in the labor force came from this category of the educated and, as mentioned, all but one of the fifteen were professionally or semiprofessionally employed.

13. This sample encompassed all women of the relevant age group who live in one of Dheisheh's "neighborhoods." Unlike the sample of males, however, this one did not include migrants.

14. As indicated before, I do not have quantitative data pertaining to the rate of labor migration among females of the young generation. Qualitative findings suggest that the phenomenon was relatively widespread, especially during the late 1970s and early 1980s, that is, the height of the "oil-boom" period. As well, labor migration of women with postsecondary education from among the intermediate generation was by no means a rare occurrence. Again, quantitative data on the scope of the phenomenon is lacking.

CHAPTER 7

1. I carried out my interviews with members of the Abu-Laban family in 1992 and continued with follow-up meetings into early 1995. Therefore, most developments that took place after that date are not recorded here. The life stories and ages were updated as of the mid-1990s. Sheikh Abu-Ibrahim died in April 2002 during the Israeli invasion and reoccupation of Bethlehem and all other major cities in the West Bank. For more than a month a curfew regime was strictly imposed in the Bethlehem urban area, including Dheisheh and the adjacent Doha municipality, where the sheikh was staying before his death with one of his sons. The military authorities prevented the Abu-Laban family from conducting a funeral ceremony and burying the sheikh in the local cemetery. Eventually, after keeping the body at home for several days, the family decided to bury him in the backyard garden.

2. I was acquainted with a number of women and men from Dheisheh who studied in the Soviet Union, Czechoslovakia, and Yugoslavia and did not make use of their newfound freedom; others, almost all men, met and married "foreigners" and became citizens of the countries where they had studied. The divorce rate among these couples seems to be very high, but in those cases where marriages did not end in divorce, gradual economic and social separation from the family of origin in the camp became inevitable.

PART III INTRODUCTION

1. Imprisonment without trial, on the basis of the Israeli emergency regulations (adopted from the emergency regulations of the British Mandate in 1945).

2. Students of the Palestinian national movement in the Occupied Territories did not accord this question sufficient attention until fairly recently. The Intifada has given rise, among other things, to a rather extensive literature on women's political activism and its short- and long-term consequences. Research, commentators, and women activists underscored the central role of women in sustaining the uprising (especially during its first year in 1988) as regular participants in demonstrations and in confrontations with the Israeli military, and as members of popular committees and of the various women's committees (affiliated with the Palestinian organizations). At the same time they pointed out the incompatibility between the proven capacity of political organizations to mobilize women and their by far lesser contribution to the enhancement of women's social status (excluding the salient transformation that took place in the private lives and social standings of leading activists).

For research on and analysis of the development, performance, and various political and social implications of the Palestinian women's movement under Israeli Occupation and during the Intifada, see, for example, Hiltermann 1990, 1991a; Geadeh 1992; Jad 1991; Kuttab 1993; Hammami 1990; Abdo 1991; Strum 1992; Warnock 1990; and Augustine 1993. For retrospective evaluation of women's political activism and the Palestinian women's movement, see, for example, the contributions by Kamal, Strum, Sabbagh, Giacaman and Johnson, and Hiltermann to the collection *Palestinian Women of Gaza and the West Bank* (Sabbagh 1998). For a comprehensive study of the long-term implications of participation in the resistance to the Israeli Occupation on the lives of Palestinian women of different social origin, background, and socialization, see Rubenberg 2001. For an autobiography of a leading activist of the first decade of the Occupation, see Tawil 1979. For fiction focusing on the life situation and problems of Palestinian women of different social classes in a society under military occupation, see Khalifeh 1978, 1987.

CHAPTER 8

1. On Palestinian leaders and activists in the Arab Nationalists Movement, see Walid Kazziha's detailed analysis of the ANM's emergence, history, and decline (Kazziha 1975). On Palestinians in the opposition parties to the Hashemite monarchy, and

particularly in the Jordanian Communist Party during the 1950s and 1960s, see Aruri 1972; and Cohen 1980. This topic receives detailed elaboration in Chapter 9.

2. For a detailed study of the major Palestinian guerrilla organizations in the wake of the 1967 war and into the beginning of the 1970s, see Chaliand 1972. See also Quandt 1971. Both these studies provide an elaborate picture of the ideologies and political orientations of the various factions as well as evaluations of their capacities to wage armed resistance/guerrilla warfare.

3. On the reorganization of the PLO institutions in the late 1960s, see Quandt 1971; and Cobban 1984. On the structure and composition of PLO institutions and on decision making within them, see Rubenberg 1983; Cobban 1984; and Yezid Sayigh 1997. For a critical discussion of the quota representation system, see Hilal 1993; and Yezid Sayigh 1997.

4. On the attempt to set up a network of underground resistance cells in the West Bank during the early period of Israeli Occupation, see Yezid Sayigh 1997, 155–73; Abu-Iyad 1979, 92–94; Cobban 1984, 37–39. On armed and civilian resistance in the Gaza Strip from 1967 through 1971, see Lesch 1989a, 229–30.

5. At the time, these organizations maintained the position that the liberation of Palestine could only be achieved through joint Arab effort and mobilization—a precondition for which was overthrowing the reactionary Arab dictatorial regimes, first and foremost Jordan, via mass-supported, revolutionary struggles. The regimes were to be replaced by popular democratic governments. Analysis of the political situation in Jordan, and of the weaknesses of the palace vis-à-vis other sectors of the society and state, led DFLP and PFLP leaders to believe that such a goal of revolutionary transformation was within reach. This conviction found special expression in the political work (education, consciousness raising) among Jordanian peasantry by cadres from both organizations.

6. On the Palestinian resistance infrastructure in Jordan during the years 1967–71 and on Black September and its aftermath, see Abu-Iyad 1979, 116–45; Cobban 1984, 48–57; and Sayigh 1997, 243–81.

7. On the harsh conditions experienced by the Palestinian refugees in Lebanon during the 1950s and 1960s, see Rosemary Sayigh 1979, 98–143; for an analysis of their legal, political, and social status, see Aruri and Farsoun 1980; Said 2001; Hudson 1997. On the ascendance of the Palestinian resistance movement and the consequences for the refugee community, see Rosemary Sayigh 1979, 144–87; see also Shiblak 1997. For an outstanding anthropological study of women and the Palestinian resistance, see Peteet 1991. On the PLO civilian and military infrastructure in Lebanon, see Rubenberg 1983; and Brynen 1990. On the Lebanese civil war and its impact on the Palestinians, see Abu-Iyad 1979, 225–78; Cobban 1984, 58–80; Brynen 1990, 79–106; and Yezid Sayigh 1997, 358–423. On the Israeli invasion of Lebanon and its aftermath, see Rashid Khalidi 1986; Brynen 1990, 179–200; Rosemary Sayigh 1994; and Yezid Sayigh 1997, 523–44.

8. For a detailed and most enlightening discussion of the internal debate inside the PLO that preceded the adoption of the Ten-Point Program, as well as of the role of the Soviet Union in promoting the strategic shift, see Alain Gresh 1985.

9. For more on the PNF, see Dakkak 1983, 75–80; Taraki 1991, 57–58; and Sahliyeh 1988, 51–55.

CHAPTER 9

1. Doubtless, were I to research the years prior to the 1948 war, when the Dheishe-hians were still living in their villages of origin, earlier layers of political activity could be exposed.

2. It is not easy to give a satisfactory justification for this exclusion. Whereas women were undoubtedly underrepresented in the sphere of political activism in the Dheisheh of the 1950s and early 1960s, and while their participation in the clan-destine formations that underscored the resistance to the Occupation from 1967 to the mid-1970s was negligible, the picture changed during the second decade of Is-raeli rule. Though to a much lesser extent than their male counterparts, a significant number of young Dheishehian women were active members of high school and university student committees, and many joined the various women's committees and organizations that operated in the camp. Some became official members in one or another of the political factions within the national movement. My choice not to cover the course of this development stemmed from two main considerations. The first has to do with the central thesis that underlies the entire chapter: the cor-relation between activism and imprisonment. Whereas the path of male activists led almost invariably to prison, women were underrepresented (though of course not absent) among the ranks of the incarcerated. The second consideration involves the limits I set for my examination: bringing in women's political participation as an added variable would have demanded a review and analysis of the status of women in the Palestinian national movement, a topic of merit in its own right, but one from which I chose to refrain.

3. It should be stressed again that this section only briefly highlights aspects of political activism in Dheisheh during the Jordanian period, a topic that deserves sep-arate research. Unlike in the sections that follow, I confronted a major problem in the collection of primary material/empirical data on the activists of the 1950s; the lion's share of the relevant persons from this generation were no longer around— many died in the course of the decade that preceded my fieldwork, while many others left Dheisheh in the aftermath of the 1967 war and were not allowed to re-turn. Among the ranks of younger people who became politically active during the 1960s, too, I found out that the rate of migration was especially high. Consequently, I could not substantiate evidence by comparing material from interviews and was forced to rely mainly on one key interviewee and on secondary sources.

4. As Cohen (1980) and Sela (1984) specify explicitly, a substantial part of the empirical data that served them in their research on political parties in the West Bank was drawn from the archives of the Jordanian intelligence services, which fell, in complete form, into the hands of the Israeli forces during the 1967 war. Among other information, these documents included lists of the names and full personal de-tails of hundreds of activists, supporters, and leaders of the various opposition par-ties, as well as reports on their whereabouts. The researchers used this once-classi-

fied material to reconstruct the sociodemographic profiles of the parties and their members.

5. Hundreds of thousands of inhabitants fled the areas that Israel occupied during the 1967 war, to Jordan, Syria, and Egypt. According to UNRWA, the total number of war refugees was 350,000; some 200,000 of them from the West Bank, among them approximately 100,000 refugees of the 1948 war (UNRWA 1968; Zureik 1996, 20–23). Israel prevented the return of these refugees in spite of UN Resolutions 242 (1967) and 338 (1973), with the minor exception of "family reunification" quotas. This policy determined the fate of close to one-fourth of the West Bank population. The policy of nonreturn of refugees was extended as well to West Bank and Gaza Strip residents who were outside these areas at the time of the September 1967 census conducted by Israel (Zureik 1996, 22). Israeli military rule also denied residence rights (that is, refused return and did not issue identity cards) to every resident of the Occupied Territories who was outside the territorial boundaries and had not renewed exit permits for three years from the time of departure (a procedure possible to expedite only within the Occupied Territories). The number of those whose return was denied, termed "latecomers" in Israeli jargon, was estimated at one hundred thousand. Jordanian and Palestinian sources estimate the number of those uprooted, expelled, denied return, plus their offspring, to be between eight hundred thousand and one million (Zureik 1996, 22–23).

6. The decline in the influence of the Communists in Dheisheh in the postwar period is related not only to the changed political circumstances but also to the physical exodus of many longtime Communist activists from the camp. Substantial numbers of them were among the many camp residents who fled Dheisheh to the East Bank during the war and were not allowed to return. Still others were caught, at the outbreak of the war, in Kuwait, Saudi Arabia, and other Gulf states where they worked as migrant teachers and professionals, and they were subsequently denied residency by the Israeli authorities.

7. Rosemary Sayigh reconstructs the advent of al-Thawra, the revolution, in the camps in Lebanon in 1969 (Rosemary Sayigh 1979, ch. 4). The Cairo Agreement, which was signed in November 1969 (see previous chapter), signaled the initiation of a rather free Palestinian political organization (confined to specific zones and abiding by the terms of the agreement). The various factions/organizations began to set up institutions and frameworks for action; thousands of youths joined the youth movements of the organizations and enrolled in paramilitary training; and the PLO and the component organizations set up hospitals and clinics and provided a range of other social services. Sayigh argues that the "social revolution" lagged far behind the political one, but she does not play down the impact of the former altogether. Her documentation gives central emphasis to the enthusiasm and hope that were triggered by the political revolution and swept through all generations in the camps, particularly the younger one. Within the older generation, "the generation of Palestine" in her terminology, Sayigh found some ambivalence, related to the not uncommon inclination among them to support the preservation of patterns of domination and leadership of the past. Among the intermediate generation, "the generation of al-Nakba" who were children when the 1948 war broke out, she found

many who had become ardent supporters of the radical pan-Arabism that was endorsed by various political parties in the early 1960s, but who were later to join the ranks of the Palestinian organizations. It is clear that the development of Palestinian organizations in Lebanon in the late 1960s had a much more profound impact on the refugee population than the process that was taking place in the West Bank during those years.

8. Chaliand accompanied Palestinian guerrilla fighters for several months in their training camps in Jordan as well as "in the field." Unlike Sayigh, he focuses on guerrilla life rather than on Palestinian communities and populations. Yet, through his writing, which covers a diverse range of topics, such as the daily schedule in the training camps, the political and ideological orientations of the various organizations, and the corresponding educational training programs, he exposes the individuals themselves. Alongside social profiles of the fighters, most refugees and sons of refugees from 1948 and 1967, Chaliand brings to the forefront the significance for these people of joining the ranks of the revolution. Recruitment to an organization entailed a total transformation of former ways of life, including complete separation from home and a civilian environment. Again, this is in contradistinction to the process that took place in the West Bank at the time. It is nonetheless important to mention that many of Chaliand's interviewees came from the West Bank, most being first- or second-time refugees who arrived in the East Bank in the aftermath of the 1967 war.

9. Muhammad's release was conditioned upon his exile to Jordan, where he subsequently became a PLO official. Noah and Saleh were to restart their lives in Dheisheh. They both chose to complete their formal education; each earned a bachelor's degree from Bethlehem University in his late thirties and went on to gain a master's degree abroad. After the establishment of the PNA they were both appointed to high posts.

10. As specified earlier, the core sample pertains to forty-one male interviewees of the intermediate generation (aged forty-four to fifty-five at the time of the survey), with whom in-depth interviews were carried out. The larger sample included all male siblings of these interviewees, as well as all male siblings of their spouses, who belong to the relevant age group.

11. The duration of imprisonment was calculated as the sum total of years/months a person spent in prison.

12. The Israeli authorities systematically employed arrests, interrogations, and harassment of family members of activists. The purposes were many: to spread fear among people, to punish and threaten, to exert pressure on the activists themselves. In fact, my data shows that among former prisoners belonging to the older generation (older than sixty at the time of the research), the majority were held in connection with the imprisonment or activism of their sons, rather than being charged with offenses themselves. It was a commonplace procedure to arrest the father of a suspect and keep him as a hostage while the son was being interrogated, so that the latter would give in and "talk." A typical example is the case of Abu 'Adel, summoned to the military headquarters in 1970 upon the arrest of his oldest son who had just returned from an extended stay in Jordan. During interrogation the father,

who was then in his fifties, was beaten so badly that his two front teeth were broken. He was kept in jail for two weeks longer to pressure his son to confess. As several of my interviewees disclosed, it was also common for the Shabak to pressure parents of prisoners to persuade their sons to collaborate with the Israeli authorities in turn for their early release.

13. Generally speaking, those Dheishehians who were convicted on the grounds of membership in an illegal organization, but were not charged with participation in planning a specific offense against the state's security, were sentenced to one to five years in prison. Those convicted of membership in an armed group, but not on grounds of a specific offense, were imprisoned for terms ranging between five to ten years. Those convicted of membership and a failed attempt at an armed assault were sentenced to ten to twenty years. The majority among Dheishehians who were imprisoned for long terms fall into the first and second categories.

14. The seventy-eight families are families of the forty-one male and thirty-seven female interviewees (their spouses) of the intermediate generation. Four of the female spouses were not brought up in Dheisheh camp, and therefore their families of origin were not included.

15. The first voluntary committees appeared on the scene in 1972–73, in parallel with the emergence of the Palestinian National Front (PNF) as a guiding public political body. They were first formed in the Ramallah and Jerusalem districts and later spread to other regions of the West Bank. Most founders of the committees were intellectuals—primarily students and lecturers from the recently established Birzeit University who were drawn to the Left and to Marxist thought; some were affiliated with the Communist Party. Although most founders came from rather well-to-do or economically established strata and from an urban background, the committees marked the inception of the trend that was to gain impetus at the end of the 1970s and in the decade that followed: the inclination to open, popular, mass-supported frameworks of political action. The committees initiated and implemented voluntary works, especially in rural areas, such as road paving, land reclamation for agriculture, assistance to farmers during picking seasons, and literacy classes—activities that were later adopted by the youth movements of most Palestinian organizations as well as by the women's movements. Another significant feature of the committees was bringing young women and men together (see Taraki 1991). It is also important to mention that Birzeit University adopted volunteer work as part of its official obligatory curriculum (see Sullivan 1988).

16. In terms of timing, the establishment of the NGC in 1978 should be viewed as a direct response to the signing of the Camp David Accords and to the plan for Palestinian autonomy that was a part of the Israeli-Egyptian agreement. The committee called for—and led—public gatherings, demonstrations, and processions to protest the American policy in the Middle East; what was perceived as a U.S., Israeli, and Egyptian attempt to liquidate the Palestinian cause; and the massive land confiscation and settlement schemes, which received a boost under the then-recently elected Likud government. The NGC publicly supported the PLO, though it was distinguished by its explicit position in favor of a two-state solution, a position that would be formally adopted by the PLO only in 1988. It included representatives of

all factions of the national movement, yet its orientation was known as relatively more left-wing than that of Fatah, the dominant organization in the PLO (as was expressed in the NGC's critical assessment of the signs of rapprochement between the PLO and Jordan in the late 1970s) (Sahliyeh 1988; Hiltermann 1991a; Dakkak 1983).

17. In the particular case of Bethlehem University, the main competition for the hearts of students was between the left-wing, Marxist-oriented student committees identified with the PFLP, DFLP, and the Communists, and the "center," affiliated with Fatah; the Islamists were weak.

18. As specified, the core sample included forty men of the young generation, with whom in-depth interviews were carried out. The second sample encompassed all the male siblings of the latter interviewees and of their female spouses, and the third one included all the sons of thirty-nine couples of the older generation. The data in these two latter cases was not based on personal interviews, but rather supplied by either siblings or parents.

19. The majority of activists whose age in 1997 was between twenty-seven and forty were sent more than once during the 1980s to the Farʿa prison interrogation installation near Nablus. They claim that at the beginning of that decade Farʿa installation was "readjusted" by the Shabak to become the number-one interrogation center for particularly young activists, in an attempt to break down the youngsters and run them as informers. (For more on interrogation in Farʿa and elsewhere, see Chapter 10.)

CHAPTER 10

1. The term *counterorder*—denoting the manifold aspects of the internal organization of Palestinian political prisoners in Israeli jails—is mine. My interviewees often used the expressions "internal organization" (*tanthim dakhili*) or "internal order/regime" (*nitham dakhili*).

2. This caveat concerning the absence of literature on the subject is nevertheless a generalization. While it is true, as far as I know, that there is no published academic research on the internal organization of Palestinian political prisoners in Israeli jails, the abundant literary output of the political prisoners (fiction, prose, poetry, critiques, and the like), while in jail and after their release, are an invaluable resource. Some works have been published in a book form, examples being *Point of Departure–Letters from Prison* (1993) by ʿIzzat Ghazzawi (in Arabic and English); *Three Minus One* (1990), short stories by Sami Kilani (in Arabic); and *A Road to Life* (1999), short stories by Elias Jeraiseh (in Arabic). While others have been published for limited circulation, the majority of literary pieces, notes, and recollections probably remain unpublished. Many of my interviewees kept some notes concerning their prison experiences, though not necessarily related to the topic under review here (internal organization).

Another mitigating factor is the immense value of comparison with other cases, particularly that of political prisoners from South Africa under apartheid. Prisoners of the African National Congress and the South African Communist Party succeeded in setting up a very strong internal organization while held in the central prison at Robben Island, placing strong emphasis on the spread of education—political, historical, and social. This was at times carried out through study groups very similar to those discussed in this chapter.

Last, but certainly not least, there is a wealth of reports and documentation produced by various human rights organizations, among them the Israeli B'tselem, the Palestinian Human Rights Information Center (PHRIC), and Al-Haq (International Commission of Jurists and Law in the Service of Man), on the conditions of imprisonment in detention centers, and especially on the use of torture and violence against Palestinian detainees under interrogation and detention. These materials include very detailed testimonies by former prisoners, as well as analysis, reference to international law, and more. Again, however, since my main focus is on the attempt of prisoners to build a counterorder to that imposed by the prison authorities, my reference to these sources is limited. Moreover, most of the documentation produced by human rights organizations focuses on the initial stage of detention and interrogation that antedates trial and imprisonment, whereas I concentrate on life inside jail, once prisoners begin to serve their sentences.

3. Testimonies of youth about physical and mental torture, beatings, and humiliation during their interrogation at the Farʿa detention compound served as a basis for one of the earliest detailed reports on this issue, published in 1984 by al-Haq: *Torture and Intimidation in the West Bank: The Case of Al-Farʿa Prison*.

4. Interrogations were regularly exploited by the Shabak to recruit collaborators from among the detainees. Indeed, many of the interviewees expressed the opinion that the Farʿa detention compound was initially designed for this purpose ("to bring about our downfall," in their words). The method and the "logic" behind it were simple: to frighten (terrorize) and torture a detainee, and then to threaten him with a very harsh sentence (for example, ten years inside) unless he was willing to work with/for the Shabak. When detainees succumbed they were usually kept in detention for a while, so as not to arouse suspicion, and then released without charges. Such "recruitment" should not be confused with squeezing a confession from a detainee—bringing him to admit to having done this or that in the company of X and Y in return for nothing (apart from the interrogation being brought to a halt). It is important to note in this context, however, that the terms *collaboration* and *collaborator* may denote a range of "services" provided to the Shabak, as well as different intensities and lengths of contact between the Shabak and the collaborator. Thus, "collaborator" (ʿameel [agent] or jusus [spy] in Arabic) may refer to a person who provided a one-time "service" to the Shabak in return for a one-time "favor" (for example, information about the whereabouts of a local political leader/activist in return for a travel permit, or even in return for the Shabak withholding some sensitive information about the person at stake). The same term may be also employed, however, to describe someone who provides Shabak agents with information on a regular basis, in return for a regular income and additional provisions in the form of licenses, permits, etc.

5. Daily contact between the prison's authorities and the body of prisoners did not take place randomly. Rather, the prisoners nominated their representatives,

who were the only ones "authorized" to deal with the authorities. Thus, despite the fact that the prisoners were not officially recognized as political, the authorities were "forced," in a sense, to approach them through representatives of their internal organization.

6. Naturally, many prisoners, especially the younger ones, were not yet affiliated politically, at least not as official members of an organization, prior to their imprisonment. In such cases, they would usually join the prison-based branch of the organization with which they identified most, or the organization within the youth or student movement of which they were active prior to their imprisonment. This "arrangement" implied a degree of flexibility, in the sense that a prisoner could switch affiliation during the term of imprisonment, even though this was not very common.

7. An examination of this question, which should also take into account the central events and developments that have shaken the Palestinian-Israeli arena—primarily the Intifada, the signing of the Oslo Accords, and the establishment of the PNA—remains outside the scope of the present research.

CHAPTER 11

1. Abu ʿAwni's dark prophecy went unrealized. While a Palestinian state was not established, his son was appointed to a senior position in the PNA in 1995.

2. *Davar*, Dec. 1987.

3. *Shuhada* is the plural form of *shaheed,* denoting those who sacrificed their lives for the sake of the Palestinian cause; in this case, those who were killed by the Israeli army.

4. Still, not all remembered the meetings as causing a change in their perception of their prisoner. When I asked the father of Muhammad, who remained in jail for more than ten continuous years, what he learned of his son and how the relations between them changed during the prison period, again and again he emphasized the harsh conditions that affected his son's health: "He went into prison as a big healthy young man and came out as thin as a rake; he went in at the age of seventeen strong and powerful and came out at the age of twenty-eight with the illnesses of a sixty-year-old . . . he got an ulcer and all his teeth rotted." He refused to relate to other developments or changes in his son: "At my age, what new things can I learn of him?"

In another context he told me that his son and those imprisoned with him "were not politicians or anything like that . . . they were youths and did what they did and it was only afterward, in prison, that they became politicians." He denied the possibility that the process influenced the relations between father and son, which he took care to define only in family and emotional terms. Yet in most cases the relatives of the former prisoner testified about changes in the attitude toward him while in prison. Thus, for example, older parents spoke with admiration of the education that the son acquired, of the number of books he read, of his becoming a leader, and even of the development of his political awareness. This was so even though the parents did not know what he studied or which books he read and even though often enough they themselves were illiterate.

CHAPTER 12

1. The phenomenon of aged widowers remarrying, often to women several decades younger than themselves, though not very common in Dheisheh, is by no means rare. In contrast, I have never come across a case of a Dheishehian widow over the age of forty who remarried, and in fact, even marriages of younger widows with children are rare. The gender-differentiated norms that apply to rights and behavior account also for the huge age gaps one encounters between female and male spouses in cases of remarriage by the elderly. Unlike women, men (old and young alike) are not used to tending to their own basic needs, that is, cooking, washing, cleaning for themselves, and they are not normatively expected to. If and when they are widowed, the responsibility for catering to their needs usually falls on their sons, and in practice, on the shoulders of their daughters-in-law. Remarrying requires that the widower have certain means, and therefore it is not very common among elderly camp widowers, who more often than not continue to live in an extended household together with their sons and the sons' families. Sons of previous marriages often frown upon the remarriages of elderly fathers, which are commonly followed by additional children. This attitude can be traced, at least partially, to the detrimental economic consequences that a father's remarriage carried for his sons in the bygone village days, when inheritance was measured in land and equally divided among all male offspring. With no land to divide and with the property at the disposal of most individuals being meager, the significance of inheritance in the context of camp life has been greatly reduced. Still, (male) children of a second marriage are entitled to shares, for example, of their father's house and the land on which it is built.

2. This call came out at the very beginning of the Intifada, when the Unified National Leadership of the Uprising (UNLU) sought to include all Palestinian laborers who were employed in Israel in the campaign of civil disobedience and thereby strike a severe blow to the Israeli economy (at least to the construction branch). However, in the wake of the continuation of the Intifada, and since the UNL could not provide the more than one hundred thousand workers with substitute employment or income, the call for workers to boycott working places in Israel was subsequently dropped. It was replaced with the demand that workers comply with the organized "general strike days" that the UNL scheduled on a regular basis.

Bibliography

Abdo, Nahla. 1991. "Women of the Intifada: Gender, Class and National Liberation." *Race and Class* 32, no. 4: 19–34.

Abed, George, ed. 1988. *The Palestinian Economy: Studies in Development Under Prolonged Occupation*. London and New York: Routledge.

___. 1990. "The Economic Viability of a Palestinian State." *Journal of Palestine Studies*
19, no. 2: 3–38.

Abu-Amr, Ziad. 1988. "The Gaza Economy: 1948–1984." In *The Palestinian Economy: Studies in Development Under Prolonged Occupation*, ed. George Abed, 101–38.
London and New York: Routledge.

Abu-Helwa, Mussallam, and Brian Birch. 1994. "The Demography and Housing
Conditions of Palestinian Refugees in and Around the Camps in Amman, Jordan." *Journal of Refugee Studies* 6, no. 4: 403–13.

Abu-Iyad (Salah Khalaf). 1979. *Palestinian Without a Homeland*. Conversations with
Eric Rolo (Hebrew translation). Tel Aviv: Mifras.

Abu-Kishk, Bakir. 1988. "Industrial Development and Policies in the West Bank and
Gaza." In *The Palestinian Economy: Studies in Development Under Prolonged Occupation*, ed George Abed, 165–98. London: Routledge.

Abu-Lughod, Ibrahim. 1973. "Educating a Community in Exile: The Palestinian
Experience." *Journal of Palestine Studies* 2, no. 3: 94–111.

___, ed. 1987. *The Transformation of Palestine: Essays on the Origin and Development of
the Arab-Israeli Conflict*. 2d ed. Evanston, Ill.: Northwestern University Press.

Abu-Lughod, Janet. 1984. "The Demographic Consequences of the Occupation."
In *Occupation: Israel Over Palestine*, ed. Naseer Aruri, 255–68. London: Zed Books.

Abu-Lughod, Lila. 1989. "Zones of Theory in the Anthropology of the Arab
World." *Annual Reviews in Anthropology* 18: 267–306.

Adda, Itshak. 1993. "The Palestinian Labor Force: Survey of Existing Conditions
and Prospects for the Future." Paper presented at the conference on Sustaining
Middle Eastern Peace Through Regional Cooperation, Brussels (Oct.).

Amin, Samir. 1974. *Accumulation on a World Scale: A Critique of the Theory of Underdevelopment*. New York: Monthly Review Press.

___. 1976. *Unequal Development: An Essay on the Social Formations of Peripheral Capi-
talism*. New York: Monthly Review Press.

___. 1994. "After Gaza and Jericho: The New Palestinian-Middle Eastern Problem." *The Beirut Review*, no. 8 (fall): 113–20.

Amin, Samir, Giovanni Arrighi, Andre Gunder Frank, and Immanuel Wallerstein. 1982. *Dynamics of Global Crisis*. New York: Monthly Review Press.

___. 1990. *Transforming the Revolution*. New York: Monthly Review Press.

Anabtawi, Samir. 1986. *Palestinian Higher Education in the West Bank and Gaza: A Critical Assessment*. London: Kegan Paul.

Arnon, Arie, and Daniel Gottlieb. 1993. *An Economic Analysis of the Palestinian Economy: The West Bank and Gaza, 1968-1992*. Jerusalem: Bank of Israel, the Research Department.

Arnon, Arie, Israel Luski, Avia Spivak, and Jimmy Weinblatt. 1997. *The Palestinian Economy: Between Imposed Integration and Voluntary Separation*: Leiden, New York, and Koln: E. J. Brill.

Aronson, Geoffrey. 1996. *Settlements and the Israeli-Palestinian Negotiations: An Overview*. Final Status Issues, paper no. 3. Washington D.C.: Institute for Palestine Studies.

Aruri, Naseer. 1972. *Jordan: A Study in Political Development 1921–1965*. The Hague: Martinus Nijhoff.

___. ed. 1984a. *Occupation: Israel Over Palestine*. London: Zed Books.

___. 1984b. "Universities Under Occupation: Another Front in the War Against Palestine." In *Occupation: Israel Over Palestine*, ed. Naseer Aruri, 319–36. London: Zed Books.

Aruri, Naseer, ed. 2001. *Palestinian Refugees and the Right of Return*. London and Sterling, Va.: Pluto Press.

Aruri, Naseer, and Samih Farsoun. 1980. "Palestinian Communities and Arab Host Countries." In *The Sociology of the Palestinians*, eds. Elia Zureik and Khalil Nakhleh, 267–306. London: Croom Helm.

Asad, Talal. 1976. "Class Transformation Under the Mandate." *Middle East Research and Information Project*, no. 53 (Dec.): 3–8.

___. 1993. *Genealogies of Religion*. Baltimore and London: Johns Hopkins University Press.

Ashmore, Robert. 1986. "Palestinian Universities Under Israeli Occupation—A Human Rights Analysis." *American-Arab Affairs*, no. 16 (spring): 79–92.

___. 1990. "Nonviolence as an Intifada Strategy." *American-Arab Affairs*, no. 32: 92–104.

Augustine, Ebba, ed. 1993. *Palestinian Women: Identity and Experience*. London: Zed Books.

Awartani, Hisham. 1979. *A Survey of Industries in the West Bank and Gaza Strip*. Birzeit: Birzeit University.

___. 1988. "Agricultural Development and Policies in the West Bank and Gaza" In *The Palestinian Economy: Studies in Development Under Prolonged Occupation*, ed. George Abed, 139–64. London: Routledge.

___. 1993. "Palestinian Israeli Economic Relations: Is Cooperation Possible?" In *The Economics of Middle East Peace*, eds. Stanley Fischer, Dany Rodrik, and Elias Tuma, 281–304. Cambridge, Mass.: MIT Press.

Azzam, Henry, Julinda Abu-Nasr, and I. Lorfing. 1985. "An Overview of Arab Women in Population, Employment and Economic Development." *Women, Employment and Development in the Arab World*, eds. Julinda Abu-Nasr, Nabil F. Khoury, and Henry T. Azzam. Berlin and New York: Mouton Publishers.

Bahiri, Simcha. 1987. *Industrialization in the West Bank and Gaza*. Jerusalem: The West Bank Data Project.

Barakat, Halim. 1985. "The Arab Family and the Challenge of Social Transformation." In *Women and the Family in the Middle East: New Voices of Change*, ed. Elizabeth Fernea, 26–48. Austin: University of Texas Press.

___. 1993. *The Arab World: Society, Culture, and State*. Berkeley: University of California Press.

Baramki, Gabi. 1992. "Aspects of Palestinian Life Under Military Occupation." *British Journal of Middle Eastern Studies* 19, no. 2: 125–32.

___. 1996. "Palestinian University Education Under Occupation: Palestinian Higher Education Sets Out to Reverse the Brain Drain." *Palestine Israel Journal of Politics, Economics and Culture* 3, no. 1: 37–43.

Barghuthi, Mustafa, and Rita Giacaman. 1991. "The Emergence of an Infrastructure of Resistance: The Case of Health." In *Intifada: Palestine at the Crossroads*, eds. Jamal R. Nassar and Roger Heacock, 73–87. New York: Birzeit University and Praeger Publishers.

Baron, Beth, and Nikki Keddie, eds. 1991. *Women in Middle Eastern History: Shifting Boundaries in Sex and Gender*. New Haven and London: Yale University Press.

Beck, Lois, and Nikki Keddie, eds. 1978. *Women in the Muslim World*. Cambridge, Mass.: Harvard University Press.

Benvenisti, Meron. 1984. *The West Bank Data Project: A Survey of Israel's Policies*. Washington, D.C., and London: American Enterprise Institute for Public Policy Research.

___. 1987. *West Bank Data Base Project 1987 Report: Demographic, Economic, Legal, Social and Political Developments in the West Bank*. Jerusalem: The Jerusalem Post.

Besson, Yves. 1997. "UNRWA and Its Role in Lebanon." *Journal of Refugee Studies* 10, no. 3: 335–48.

Birks, J. S., Ian J. Seccombe, and C. A. Sinclair. 1986. "Migrant Workers in the Arab Gulf: The Impact of Declining Revenues." *International Migration Review* 20, no. 4: 799–814.

___. 1988. "Labour Migration in the Arab Gulf States: Patterns, Trends and Prospects." *International Migration Review* 26, no. 3: 267–85.

Birks, J. S., and C. A. Sinclair. 1980. *Arab Manpower: The Crisis of Development*. New York: St. Martin Press.

Bourdieu, Pierre. 1977. *Outline of a Theory of Practice*. Cambridge: Cambridge University Press.

___. 1979. *Algeria 1960*. Trans. R. Nice. Cambridge: Cambridge University Press.

___. 1998. *Practical Reason: On the Theory of Action*. Stanford: Stanford University Press.

Bourdieu, Pierre, and Jean-Claude Passeron. 1977. *Reproduction in Education, Society and Culture*. London and Beverley Hills: Sage Publications.

Brand, Laurie. 1988. *Palestinians in the Arab World*. New York: Columbia University Press.

Bregman, Arie. 1974. *Economic Growth in the Administered Areas, 1968–1973.* Jerusalem: Bank of Israel.

Brenner, Robert. 1977. "The Origins of Capitalist Development: A Critique of Neo-Smithian Marxism." *New Left Review* 104: 25–92.

Brynen, Rex. 1990. *Sanctuary and Survival: The PLO in Lebanon.* Boulder, Colo.: Westview Press.

———. 2000. *A Very Political Economy: Peace Building and Foreign Aid in the West Bank and Gaza.* Washington, D.C.: United States Institute of Peace Press.

B'tselem (The Israeli Information Center for Human Rights in the Occupied Territories). 1989a. *Annual Report 1989—Violations of Human Rights in the Occupied Territories.* Jerusalem: B'tselem.

———. 1989b. *The Military Judicial System in the West Bank.* Jerusalem: B'tselem.

———. 1990a. *Collective Punishment in the West Bank and the Gaza Strip,* by Carmel Shalev. Jerusalem: B'tselem.

———. 1990b. *The Use of Firearms by the Security Forces in the Occupied Territories.* Jerusalem: B'tselem.

———. 1991a. *The Interrogation of Palestinians During the Intifada: Ill Treatment, "Moderate Physical Pressure," or Torture?* by Stanley Cohen and Daphna Golan. Jerusalem: B'tselem.

———. 1991b. *Violations of Human Rights in the Occupied Territories 1990–1991.* Jerusalem: B'tselem.

———. 1992a. *Activity of the Undercover Units in the Occupied Territories,* by Naama Yeshuvi. Jerusalem: B'tselem.

———. 1992b. *Detained Without Trial: Administrative Detention in the Occupied Territories,* by Daphna Golan. Jerusalem: B'tselem.

———. 1992c. *The Interrogation of Palestinians During the Intifada: A Follow-up Report.* Jerusalem: B'tselem.

———. 1998. *Routine Torture: Interrogation Methods of the General Security Service,* by Yuval Ginbar. Jerusalem: B'tselem.

———. 2000. *Legislation Allowing the Use of Physical Force and Mental Coercion in the Interrogation by the General Security Service.* Jerusalem: B'tselem.

———. 2002. *Land Grab: Israel's Settlement Policy in the West Bank.* Jerusalem: B'tselem.

Budeiri, Musa K. 1982. "Changes in the Economic Structure of the West Bank and Gaza Strip under Israeli Occupation." *Labour Capital and Society* 15, no. 1: 46–63.

Buehrig, Edward. 1971. *The UN and the Palestinian Refugees: A Study in Nonterritorial Administration.* Bloomington: Indiana University Press.

Bull, Vivian. 1975. *The West Bank—Is It Viable?* Lexington, Mass.: D. C. Heath and Company.

Callinicos, Alex. 1987. *Making History.* Cambridge: Polity Press.

———. 1999. *Social Theory: A Historical Introduction.* Cambridge: Polity Press.

Carmi, Shulamit, and Henry Rosenfeld. 1974. "The Origins of the Process of Proletarianization and Urbanization of Arab Peasants in Palestine." *Annals of the New York Academy of Sciences* 220: 470–85.

———. 1989. "The Emergence of Militaristic Nationalism in Israel." *Politics Culture and Society* 3, no. 1: 5–49.

___. 1992. "Israel's Political Economy and the Widening Class Gap Between Its Two National Groups." *Asian and African Studies* 26, no. 1: 15–61.

CBS (Central Bureau of Statistics). 1968. *Statistical Abstract of Israel 1968*, no. 19. Jerusalem: CBS.

___. 1980. *Statistical Abstract of Israel 1980*, no. 31. Jerusalem: CBS.

___. 1985. *Statistical Abstract of Israel 1985*, no. 36. Jerusalem: CBS.

___. 1988. *Statistical Abstract of Israel 1988*, no. 39. Jerusalem: CBS.

___. 1993. *Statistical Abstract of Israel 1993*, no. 44. Jerusalem: CBS.

___. 1994. *Statistical Abstract of Israel 1994*, no. 45. Jerusalem: CBS.

Center for Policy Analysis on Palestine. 1995. *Settlements and Peace: The Problem of Jewish Colonization in Palestine.* Washington, D.C.: The Center for Policy Analysis on Palestine.

Chaliand, Gerard. 1972. *The Palestinian Resistance.* Middlesex, England: Penguin Books.

Cobban, Helena. 1984. *The PLO: People, Power and Politics.* London: Cambridge University Press.

Cohen, Amnon. 1980. *Political Parties in the West Bank Under the Hashemite Regime (1948–1967)* (in Hebrew). Jerusalem: The Magnes Press, Hebrew University of Jerusalem.

Cook, Robert. 1992. "The Evolution of the Food and Nutrition Problems of the Palestine Refugees." *Journal of Refugee Studies* 5, nos. 3–4: 271–88.

Dajani, Suad. 1993. "Palestinian Women Under Israeli Occupation." In *Arab Women: Old Boundaries, New Frontiers,* ed. Judith Tucker. Bloomington: Indiana University Press.

Dakkak, Ibrahim. 1983. "Back to Square One." In *Palestinians Over the Green Line,* ed. Alexander Scholch, 64–101. London: Ithaca Press, 1983.

___. 1988. "Development from Within: A Strategy for Survival." In *The Palestinian Economy: Studies in Development Under Prolonged Occupation,* ed. George Abed, 287–310. London and New York: Routledge.

Darwish, Marwan. 1989. "The Intifada: Social Change." *Race and Class* 31, no. 2: 47–61.

Davies, Philip. 1979. "The Educated West Bank Palestinians." *Journal of Palestine Studies* 8, no. 3: 65–80.

Durkheim, Emil. [1895] 1958. *The Rules of Sociological Method.* Reprint, Glencoe, Ill.: The Free Press.

___. [1893] 1964. *The Division of Labour in Society.* Reprint, New York: The Free Press.

Eades, Jeremy, ed. 1987. *Migrants, Workers, and the Social Order.* London and New York: Tavistock Publications.

Educational Network. 1990–97. *Educational Network,* nos. 1–25. Ramallah: Educational Network.

Eickelman, Dale. 1981. *The Middle East: An Anthropological Approach.* Princeton, N.J.: Prentice-Hall Inc.

Elmusa, Sharif S. 1993. "Dividing the Common Palestinian-Israeli Waters: An International Water Law Approach." *Journal of Palestine Studies* 22, no. 3: 57–77.

____. 1994. "The Israeli-Palestinian Water Dispute Can Be Solved." *Palestine-Israel Journal of Politics, Economics and Culture* 1, no. 3: 18–24.

Elmusa, Sharif, and Mahmud El-Jaafari. 1995. "Power and Trade: The Israeli Palestinian Economic Protocol." *Journal of Palestine Studies* 24, no. 2: 14–32.

El-Sarraj, Eyad. 1992. *Mental Health of the Palestinians Under Occupation*. Gaza: Gaza Community Mental Health Programme.

____. 1993. *Peace and Children of the Stone*. Gaza: Gaza Community Mental Health Programme.

Emmanuel, Arghiri. 1972. *Unequal Exchange: A Study of the Imperialism of Trade*. London: Monthly Review Press.

Fanon, Frantz. 1963. *The Wretched of the Earth*. Middlesex, England: Penguin Books.

____. 1965. *A Dying Colonialism*. New York: Grove Press.

Farsoun, Samih, ed. 1985. *Arab Society*. London: Croom Helm.

____. 1988. "Oil, State, and Social Structure in the Middle East." *Arab Studies Quarterly* 10, no. 2: 155–75.

Farsoun, Samih, and Jean Landis. 1991. "The Sociology of the Uprising: The Roots of the Intifada." *Intifada: Palestine at the Crossroads*, eds. Jamal R. Nassar and Roger Heacock, 15–36. New York: Birzeit University and Praeger Publishers.

Farsoun, Samih, with Christina E. Zacharia. 1997. *Palestine and the Palestinians*. Boulder, Colo.: Westview Press.

Fasheh, Munir. 1984. "Impact on Education." In *Occupation: Israel Over Palestine*, ed. Naseer Aruri, 295–318. London: Zed Books.

Feiler, Gil. 1993. "Palestinian Employment Prospects." *Middle East Journal* 47 (fall): 633–51.

Frank, Andre Gunder. 1969. *Capitalism and Underdevelopment in Latin America: Historical Studies of Chile and Brazil*. New York: Monthly Review Press.

____. 1971. *Sociology of Development and Underdevelopment of Sociology*. London: Pluto Press.

____. 1975. *On Capitalist Underdevelopment*. Bombay: Oxford University Press.

____. 1984. *Critique and Anticritique: Essays on Dependence and Reformism*. London and Basingstoke: Macmillan Press.

____. 1998. *ReOrient: Global Economy in the Asian Age*. Berkeley: University of California Press.

Freedman, Robert O., ed. 1991. *The Intifada*. Miami: Florida International University Press.

Frisch, Hillel. 1983. *Stagnation and Frontier: Arab and Jewish Industry in the West Bank*. Jerusalem: The West Bank Data Project.

____. 1989. *Institution-Building in the Territories, 1967–1985*. Ph.D. diss., Hebrew University.

____. 1990. "From Armed Struggle Over State Borders to Political Mobilization and Intifada Within It." *Plural Societies* 19, nos. 2–3: 92–115.

Gazit, Shlomo. 1999. *Trapped* (in Hebrew). Tel-Aviv: Zmora-Bitan Publishers.

Geadah, Yolande. 1992. "Palestinian Women in View of Gender and Development." In *Women and Development in the Middle East and North Africa*, eds. Joseph Jabra and Nancy Jabra, 43–55. International Studies in Sociology and Social Anthropology, vol. 59. Leiden and New York: E. J. Brill.

Geertz, Clifford. 1973a. "Deep Play: Notes on the Balinese Cockfight." In *The Interpretation of Cultures: Selected Essays by Clifford Geertz*, 412–53. New York: Basic Books.

——. 1973b. "Thick Description: Toward an Interpretive Theory of Culture." In *The Interpretation of Cultures: Selected Essays by Clifford Geertz*, 3–32. New York: Basic Books.

Gerner, Deborah. 1989. "Israeli Restrictions on the Palestinian Universities in the Occupied West Bank and Gaza." *Journal of Arab Affairs* 8, no. 1: 74–123.

Gharaibeh, Fawzi. 1985. *The Economies of the West Bank and Gaza Strip*. Boulder, Colo., and London: Westview Press.

Ghazzawi, Izzat. 1993. *Point of Departure: Letters from Prison*. Jerusalem: Arab Center for Contemporary Studies.

Giacaman, Rita. 1984. "Palestinian Women and Development in the Occupied West Bank." *Birzeit University Research Review.*

——. 1997. *Population and Fertility: Population Policies, Women's Rights and Sustainable Development*. Palestinian Women: A Status Report, no. 2. Birzeit: Women's Studies Program, Birzeit University.

Giacaman, Rita, and Penny Johnson. 1998. "Intifada Year Four: Notes on the Women's Movement." In *Palestinian Women of Gaza and the West Bank*, ed. Suha Sabbagh, 216–32. Bloomington: Indiana University Press.

Giddens, Anthony. 1976. *New Rules of Sociological Method*. London: Hutchinson.

——. 1979. *Central Problems in Social Theory*. London: The Macmillan Press.

——. 1989. "Reply to My Critics." In *Social Theory of Modern Societies: Anthony Giddens and His Critics*, eds. David Held and John B. Thompson, 249–301. Cambridge: Cambridge University Press.

Gowers, Andrew, and Tony Walker. 1991. *Behind the Myth: Yasser Arafat and the Palestinian Revolution*. New York: Olive Branch Press.

Graham-Brown, Sarah. 1984a. *Education, Repression and Liberation: Palestinians*. London: World University Service Press.

——. 1984b. "Impact on the Social Structure of Palestinian Society." In *Occupation: Israel Over Palestine*, ed. Naseer Aruri, 223–54. London: Zed Books.

Gresh, Alain. 1985. *The PLO: The Struggle Within: Towards an Independent Palestinian State*. London: Zed Books.

al-Haj, Majid. 1987. *Social Change and Family Processes: Arab Communities in Shefar-Am*. Boulder, Colo.: Westview Press.

——. 1995. *Education, Empowerment and Control: The Case of the Arabs in Israel*. Albany: State University of New York Press.

Hallaj, Mouhammad. 1980. "Mission of Palestinian Higher Education." In *A Palestinian Agenda for the West Bank and Gaza*, ed. Emile Nakhle. Washington, D.C.: American Enterprise Institute.

Halliday, Fred. 1982. " Labour Migration in the Arab World: The Ugly Face of the New Economic Order." *Labour Capital and Society* 15, no. 1: 8–22.

Hammami, Rema. 1990. "Women, the Hijab, and the Intifada." *Middle East Report* 20, nos. 3–4: 24–28.

_____. 1997. *Labor and Economy: Gender Segmentation in Palestinian Economic Life*. Palestinian Women: A Status Report, no. 4. Birzeit: Women's Study Program, Birzeit University.

al-Haq/Law in the Service of Man. 1984. *Torture and Intimidation in the West Bank: The Case of Al-Farʿa Prison*. Ramallah: al-Haq/Law in the Service of Man.

_____. 1988a. *Israel's War Against Education in the Occupied West Bank: A Penalty for the Future*. Ramallah: al-Haq/Law in the Service of Man.

_____. 1988b. *Punishing a Nation: Human Rights Violations During the Palestinian Uprising, December 1987 to December 1988*. Ramallah: al-Haq/Law in the Service of Man.

_____. 1989. *A Nation Under Siege: al-Haq Annual Report on Human Rights in the Occupied Palestinian Territories*. Ramallah: al-Haq/Law in the Service of Man.

Heiberg, Marianne, and Geir Ovensen et al. 1993. *Palestinian Society in Gaza, West Bank, and Arab Jerusalem: A Survey of Living Conditions*. Fafo Report no. 151. Oslo: Fafo (Norwegian Institute for Applied Social Sciences).

Hijab, Nadia. 1988. *Womanpower: The Arab Debate on Women at Work*. New York: Cambridge University Press.

_____. 1996. "Women and Work in the Arab World." In *Arab Women: Between Defiance and Restraint*, ed. Suha Sabbagh, 41–53. New York: Olive Branch Press.

Hilal, Jamil. 1976. "Class Transformation in the West Bank and Gaza." *Middle East Research and Information Project*, no. 53 (Dec.): 9–15.

_____. 1993. "PLO Institutions: The Challenge Ahead." *Journal of Palestine Studies* 23, no. 1: 46–60.

_____. 1998. *Al-nitham al-siasi al-falastini baʿd Oslo: dirasa tahliliya naqdiya* (The Palestinian Political System After Oslo: A Critical Assessment). Ramallah, Muwati: the Palestinian Institute for the Study of Democracy.

_____. 1999. *Al-mujtamaʿ al-falastini wa ishkaliyat al-dimuqratiya (Palestinian Society and the Problems of Democracy)*. Nablus: The Center for Palestinian Researches and Studies.

Hilal, Jamil, Yasser Shalabi, Majdi Malki, and Hasan Ladadweh. 1998. *Towards a Social Security System in the West Bank and Gaza Strip*. Ramallah: Palestine Economic Policy Research Institute (MAS).

Hiltermann, Joost. 1990. "Sustaining Movement, Creating Space: Trade Unions and Women's Committees." *Middle East Report*, nos. 164–65: 32–36.

_____. 1991a. *Behind the Intifada*. Princeton, N.J.: Princeton University Press.

_____. 1991b. "Work and Action: the Role of the Working Class in the Uprising." In *Intifada: Palestine at the Crossroads*, eds. Jamal R. Nassar and Roger Heacock, 144–58. New York: Birzeit University and Praeger Publishers.

_____. 1998. "The Women's Movement during the Uprising." In *Palestinian Women of Gaza and the West Bank*, ed. Suha Sabbagh, 41–52. Bloomington and Indianapolis: Indiana University Press.

Hiro, Dilip. 1982. *Inside the Middle East*. London and Henley: Routledge and Kegan Paul.

Hudson, Michael. 1997. "Palestinians in Lebanon: The Common Story." *Journal of Refugee Studies* 10, no. 3: 243–60.

Hunter, Robert F. 1991. *The Palestinian Uprising.* Berkeley: University of California Press.

Ibrahim, Saad Eddin. 1982. *The New Arab Social Order: A Study of the Social Impact of Oil Wealth.* Boulder, Colo.: Westview Press.

International Bank for Reconstruction and Development. 1957. *The Economic Development of Jordan.* Baltimore: Johns Hopkins University Press.

International Labour Office. 1993. *Report of the Director General on the Situation of Workers of the Occupied Territories.* Appendix 2. Geneva: ILO.

Jaber, Nadim. 1987. "The Gulf States and the Palestinians—A Changing Relationship?" *Middle East International* (April 17): 13–15.

Jabra, Nancy W., and Joseph G. Jabra. 1992. "Introduction: Women and Development in the Middle East and North Africa." In *Women and Development in the Middle East and North Africa* (International Studies in Sociology and Social Anthropology), eds. Joseph Jabra and Nancy Jabra, 1–10. Leiden and New York: E. J. Brill.

Jad, Islah. 1991. "From Salons to the Popular Committees: Palestinian Women 1919–1989." In *Intifada: Palestine at the Crossroads,* eds. Jamal R. Nassar and Roger Heacock, 125–52. New York: Birzeit University and Praeger Publishers.

Jenkins, Richard. 1982. "Pierre Bourdieu and the Reproduction of Determinism." *Sociology* 16: 270–81.

———. 1992. *Pierre Bourdieu.* London: Routledge.

JMCC (Jerusalem Media and Communication Centre). 1994a. *Israeli Obstacles to Economic Development in the Occupied Palestinian Territories.* 2d ed. East Jerusalem: JMCC.

———. 1994b. *Water: The Red Line.* East Jerusalem: JMCC.

———. 1997. *Signed, Sealed, Delivered: Israeli Settlements and the Peace Process.* East Jerusalem: JMCC.

———. 1999. *Foreign Aid and Development in Palestine,* by ʿAdel Zagha. Jerusalem: JMCC.

Johnson, Penny. 1986. "Palestinian Universities Under Occupation." *Journal of Palestine Studies* 15, no. 4: 127–33.

———. 1987a. "Palestinian Universities Under Occupation." *Journal of Palestine Studies* 17, no. 1: 129–35.

———. 1987b. "Palestinian Universities Under Occupation." *Journal of Palestine Studies* 17, no. 2: 143–50.

———. 1988a. "Palestinian Universities Under Occupation." *Journal of Palestine Studies* 17, no. 3: 100–105.

———. 1988b. "Palestinian Universities Under Occupation." *Journal of Palestine Studies* 17, no. 4: 116–22.

———. 1989. "Palestinian Universities Under Occupation." *Journal of Palestine Studies* 18, no. 2: 92–100.

Joseph, Suad. 1993. "Connectivity and Patriarchy Among Urban Working Class Arab Families in Lebanon." *Ethos* 21, no. 4: 452–84.

———. 1994a. "Brother/Sister Relationships; Connectivity, Love and Power in the Reproduction of Patriarchy in Lebanon." *American Ethnologist* 21, no. 1: 50–73.

___. 1994b. *Gender and Family in the Arab World*. Women in the Middle East, no. 4. Washington, D.C.: Middle East Research and Information Project (MERIP).

Kamal, Zahira. 1998. "The Development of the Palestinian Women's Movement in the Occupied Territories: Twenty Years After the Israeli Occupation." In *Palestinian Women of Gaza and the West Bank*, ed. Suha Sabbagh, 78–88. Bloomington and Indianapolis: Indiana University Press.

Kanafani, Ghassan. 1997. *Men in the Sun and Other Palestinian Stories*. Trans. from the Arabic by Hilary Kilpatrick. Boulder, Colo.: Lynne Rienner Publishers.

Kandiyoti, Deniz, ed. 1991. *Women, Islam and the State*. London and Hong Kong: Macmillan Academic and Professional.

___. 1996. "Contemporary Feminist Scholarship and Middle East Studies." In *Gendering the Middle East*, ed. Deniz Kandiyoti, 1–28. New York: Syracuse University Press.

Kanovsky, Eliyahu. 1976. *Economic Development of Jordan*. Tel Aviv: University Publishing Project.

___. 1985. "The Rise and Fall of Arab Oil Power." *Middle East Review* 18, no. 1: 5–10.

___. 1989. *Jordan's Economy: From Prosperity to Crisis*. Tel Aviv: The Shiloah Institute.

Kav La'Oved. 1992a. "Layoffs and Payoffs." *Kav La'Oved Newsletter* (Feb.).

___. 1992b. "The Histadrut and the Workers from the Territories." *Kav La'Oved Newsletter* (June).

___. 1992c. *Kav La'Oved Newsletter* (Sept.).

___. 1993a. "Labor Bureau's Payments Division." *Kav La'Oved Newsletter* (Mar.).

___. 1993b. "Kav La'Oved Activities Following the Closure Imposed on the Occupied Territories." *Kav La'Oved Newsletter* (July).

___. 1994. "Employment of Workers from the Occupied Territories in Israel." *Kav La'Oved Newsletter* (May).

___. 1995. "Employment of Workers from the Occupied Territories in Israel: Processes and Trends." *Kav La'Oved Newsletter* (Jan.).

___. 1997. "The Closure, Contractors and the Histadrut." *Kav La'Oved Newsletter* (Sept.).

___. 1998. "Palestinian Workers." *Kav La'Oved Newsletter* (Dec.).

Kawar, Amal. 1996. *Daughters of Palestine: Leading Women of the Palestinian National Movement*. Albany: State University of New York Press.

Kazziha, Walid. 1975. *Revolutionary Transformation in the Arab World*. London: Croom Helm.

Khalidi, Rashid. 1986. *Under Siege: PLO Decision-making in the 1982 War*. New York: Columbia University Press.

Khalidi, Walid, ed. 1992. *All That Remains*. Washington, D.C.: Institute of Palestine Studies.

Khalifeh, Sahar. 1978. *Wild Thorns* (al-Sabar, Hebrew translation by Salman Masalha). Jerusalem: Galileo.

___. 1987. *The Sun-Flower* ('Ibad a-Shams, Hebrew translation by Rachel Halvah). Tel-Aviv: Mifras.

Khuri, Nabil, and Valentine Moghadam, eds. 1995. *Gender and Development in the Arab World*. London: Zed Books and United Nations University Press.

al-Kilani, Sami. 1989. *Qabbala al-Ard Wa'istaraha* (in Arabic). Jerusalem: The Union of Palestinian Writers in the West Bank and Gaza.

Kimmerling, Baruch, and Joel Migdal. 1993. *Palestinians: The Making of a People.* New York: Free Press.

Kleiman, Ephraim. 1993. "Some Basic Problems of the Economic Relationships between Israel, the West Bank and Gaza." In *The Economies of Middle East Peace*, eds. Stanley Fischer, Dany Rodrik, and Elias Tuma, 305–33. Cambridge, Mass.: MIT Press.

Kossaifi, George. 1980. "Demographic Characteristics of the Arab Palestinian People." In *The Sociology of the Palestinians*, eds. Elia Zureik and Khalil Nakhleh, 13–45. London: Croom Helm.

Kuttab, Eileen. 1993. "Palestinian Women in the Intifada: Fighting on Two Fronts." *Arab Studies Quarterly* 15, no. 2: 69–86.

Le Troquer, Yann, and R. H. al-Qudat. 1999. "From Kuwait to Jordan: The Palestinians' Third Exodus." *Journal of Palestine Studies* 28, no. 3: 37–51.

Lesch, Ann Mosely. 1989a. "Gaza: History and Politics." In *Israel, Egypt, and the Palestinians: From Camp David to Intifada*, eds. Ann Mosely Lesch and Mark Tessler, 223–37. Bloomington and Indianapolis: Indiana University Press.

———. 1989b. "Gaza: Life Under Occupation." In *Israel, Egypt, and the Palestinians: From Camp David to Intifada*, eds. Ann Mosely Lesch and Mark Tessler, 238–54. Bloomington and Indianapolis: Indiana University Press.

———. 1991. "Palestinians in Kuwait." *Journal of Palestine Studies* 20, no. 4: 42–54.

Lesch, Ann Mosely, and Mark Tessler, eds. 1989. *Israel, Egypt, and the Palestinians: From Camp David to Intifada*. Bloomington and Indianapolis: Indiana University Press.

Lockman, Zachary, and Joel Beinin, eds. 1989. *Intifada*. Toronto: MERIP.

Lustick, Ian S. 1993. *Unsettled States, Disputed Lands*. Ithaca and London: Cornell University Press.

Lutffiya, Abdulla. 1966. *Baytin: A Jordanian Village*. The Hague: Mouton and Co.

Mahshi, Khalil, and Kate Bush. 1989. "The Palestinian Intifada and Education for the Future." *Harvard Educational Review* 59, no. 4:470–83.

Mahshi, Khalil, and Ramzi Rihan. 1980. "Education: Elementary and Secondary." In *A Palestinian Agenda for the West Bank and Gaza*, ed. Emile Nakhle, 29–57. Washington, D.C.: American Enterprise Institute.

Mansour, Antoine. 1988. "The West Bank Economy 1948–1984." In *The Palestinian Economy: Studies in Development Under Prolonged Occupation*, ed. George Abed, 71–100. London: Routledge.

Marx, Emanuel. 1990. "The Social World of Refugees: A Conceptual Framework." *Journal of Refugee Studies* 3, no. 3: 189–203.

———. 1992. "Palestinian Refugee Camps in the West Bank and the Gaza Strip." *Middle Eastern Studies* 28, no. 2: 281–94.

Mazur, Michael. 1979. *Economic Growth and Development in Jordan*. London: Croom Helm.

Mbeki, Govan. 1991. *Learning from Robben Island: The Prison Writings of Goven Mbeki*. London: J. Currey.

Mernissi, Fatima. 1987. *Beyond the Veil: Male Female Dynamics in Modern Muslim Society*. Bloomington: Indiana University Press.

Meron, Raphael. 1982. *Economic Growth and Structural Changes: Economic Development in Judea-Samaria and the Gaza District, 1970–80* (in Hebrew). Jerusalem: Bank of Israel Research Department.

Migdal, Joel, ed. 1980. *Palestinian Society and Politics.* Princeton, N.J.: Princeton University Press.

Mishal, Shaul. 1978. *West Bank/East Bank: The Palestinians in Jordan, 1949–67.* New Haven and London: Yale University Press.

Mishal, Shaul, with Reuben Aharoni. 1989. *Speaking Stones: The Words Behind the Palestinian Intifada* (in Hebrew). Tel-Aviv: Hakibutz Hameuchad.

Moghadam, Valentine. 1993. *Modernizing Women: Gender and Social Change in the Middle East.* Boulder and London: Lynne Rienner Publishers.

———. 1995. "The Political Economy of Female Employment in the Arab Region." In *Gender and Development in the Arab World*, eds. Nabil Khoury and Valentine Moghadam, 6–35. London: Zed Books and United Nations University Press.

Morris, Benny. 1987. *The Birth of the Palestinian Refugee Problem, 1947–1949.* Cambridge: Cambridge University Press.

Muslih, Muhammad. 1988. *The Origins of Palestinian Nationalism.* New York: Columbia University Press.

Nassar, Jamal R., and Roger Heacock, eds. 1991. *Intifada: Palestine at the Crossroads.* New York: Birzeit University and Praeger Publishers.

Nixon, Ann Elizabeth. 1990. *The Status of Palestinian Children During the Uprising in the Occupied Territories (Part I: Child Death and Injury: A Chronology).* Jerusalem: Radda Barnen, Swedish Save the Children.

Ortner, Sherry. 1984. "Theory in Anthropology Since the Sixties." *Society for Comparative Study of Society and History* 26: 126–66.

Ovensen, Geir. 1994. *Responding to Change: Trends in Palestinian Household Economy.* FAFO Report no. 166. Oslo: FAFO.

Owen, Roger. 1985. *Migrant Workers in the Gulf.* The Minority Rights Group, Report no. 68. London: MRG.

———. 1988. "Economic Development in Mandatory Palestine: 1918–1948." In *The Palestinian Economy: Studies in Development Under Prolonged Occupation*, ed. George Abed, 13–36. London: Routledge Chapman and Hall.

———. 1993. *State, Power and Politics in the Making of the Modern Middle East.* London and New York: Routledge.

———. 1994. "Establishing a Viable Palestinian Economy." *Beirut Review*, no. 8 (fall): 45–57.

PCBS (Palestinian Central Bureau of Statistics). 1995. *Labor Force Survey: Main Findings* (Sept.–Oct. 1995 Round). Ramallah: PCBS.

———. 1996. *Labor Force Survey: Main Findings* (July–Oct. 1996 Round). Ramallah: PCBS.

———. 1997a. *Labor Force Survey: Main Findings* (Feb.–Mar. 1997 Round). Ramallah: PCBS.

———. 1997b. *Labor Force Survey: Main Findings* (July–Sept. 1997 Round). Ramallah: PCBS.

———. 1998. *Women and Men in Palestine: Trends and Statistics.* Ramallah: PCBS.

Peretz, Don. 1977. "Palestinian Social Stratification: The Political Implications." *Journal of Palestine Studies* 7, no. 1: 48–74.

____. 1990. *Intifada*. Boulder, Colo., and London: Westview Press.

Peristiany, J. G., ed. 1976. *Mediterranean Family Structures*. London: Cambridge University Press.

Peteet, Julie. 1991. *Gender in Crisis: Women and the Palestinian Resistance Movement*. New York: Columbia University Press.

____. 1994. "Male Gender and Rituals of Resistance in the Palestinian Intifada: A Cultural Politics of Violence." *American Ethnologist* 21, no. 1: 31–49.

Plascov, Avi. 1981. *The Palestinian Refugees in Jordan, 1948–1957*. London: Frank Cass.

PLO, Economic Department: Central Bureau of Statistics. 1988. *Educational Statistical Bulletin for the West Bank and Gaza Strip and Pre-1967 Occupied Palestine, 1985–86*. Damascus: PLO.

Quandt, William B. 1971. *Palestinian Nationalism: Its Political and Military Dimensions*. Santa Monica, Calif.: Rand Corporation.

____, ed. 1988. *The Middle East Ten Years After Camp David*. Washington, D.C.: Brookings Institution.

Quota, Samir, and Eyad El-Sarraj. 1993. "Collective Punishment and the Mental Health of Children: A Study on the Children of Gaza." Gaza: Gaza Community Mental Health Programme.

Rigby, Andrew. 1989. *The Intifada: The Struggle Over Education*. Jerusalem: Palestinian Academic Society for the Study of International Affairs.

____. 1991. "Coping with the Epidemic of Violence: The Struggle over Health Care in the Intifada." *Journal of Palestine Studies* 20, no. 4: 86–98.

Rigsbee, Lynn, and Joseph Biblic. 1995. "Israelis, Palestinians and the Politics of Higher Education Under Occupation." *Journal of South Asian and Middle Eastern Studies* 18, no. 3: 41–54.

Robinson, Glenn. 1997. *Building a Palestinian State: The Incomplete Revolution*. Bloomington and Indianapolis: Indiana University Press.

Rosenfeld, Henry. 1964. "From Peasantry to Wage Labour and Residual Peasantry: The Transformation of an Arab Village." In *Process and Pattern in Culture: Essays in Honor of Julian Steward*, ed. R. A. Manners, 211–34. Chicago: Aldine.

____. 1968. "Change Barriers to Change, and Contradictions in the Arab Village Family." *American Anthropologist* 70, no. 4: 732–52.

____. 1976. "Social and Economic Factors in the Explanation of the Increased Rate of Patrilineal Endogamy in the Arab Village in Israel." In *Mediterranean Family Structures*, ed. J. G. Peristiany, 115–36. London: Cambridge University Press.

____. 1978. "The Class Situation of the Arab National Minority in Israel." *Comparative Studies in Society and History* 20, no. 3: 374–407.

Rosenfeld, Maya. 1997. *Ways of Life, Division of Labor and Social Roles of Palestinian Refugee Families: The Case of Dheisheh Camp* (in Hebrew). Ph.D. diss. Hebrew University.

____. 2002. "Power Structure, Agency and Family in a Palestinian Refugee Camp." *International Journal of Middle East Studies* 34, no. 3: 519–51.

Roy, Sara. 1986. *The Gaza Strip Survey*. The West Bank Data Project. Jerusalem: The Jerusalem Post.

____. 1990. "From Hardship to Hunger: The Economic Impact of the Intifada on the Gaza Strip." *American-Arab Affairs*, no. 34 (fall): 109–34.

_____. 1991. "Development Under Occupation? The Political Economy of U.S. Aid to the West Bank and Gaza Strip." *Arab Studies Quarterly* 13, nos. 3–4: 65–89.

_____. 1994a. "Development or Dependency? The Gaza Strip Economy Under Limited Self-Rule." *Beirut Review*, no. 8: 59–79.

_____. 1994b. "Separation or Integration: Closure and the Economic Future of the Gaza Strip Revisited." *Middle East Journal* 48, no. 1: 11–21.

_____. 1995a. *Gaza Strip: The Political Economy of De-Development*. Washington, D.C.: Institute for Palestine Studies.

_____. 1995b. "Alienation or Accommodation?" *Journal of Palestine Studies* 24, no. 4: 73–82.

_____. 1999. "De-development Re-visited: Palestinian Economy and Society Since Oslo." *Journal of Palestine Studies* 28, no. 3: 64–82.

Rubenberg, Cheryl. 1983. *The Palestine Liberation Organization: Its Institutional Infrastructure*. Belmont, Mass.: Institute of Arab Studies.

_____. 1989. "Twenty Years of Israeli Economic Policies in the West Bank and Gaza: Prologue to the Intifada." *Journal of Arab Affairs* 8, no. 1: 28–73.

_____. 2001. *Palestinian Women: Patriarchy and Resistance in the West Bank*. Boulder, Colo.: Lynne Rienner Publishers.

Rugh, Andrea. 1985. "Women and Work: Strategies and Choices in a Lower Class Quarter in Cairo." In *Women and the Family in the Middle East: New Voices of Change*, ed. Elizabeth Fernea, 273–88. Austin: University of Texas Press.

Saadawi, Nawal. 1980. *The Hidden Face of Eve: Women in the Arab World*. London: Zed Books.

Sabatello, Eitan. 1983. *The Population of the Administered Territories: Some Demographic Trends and Implications*. Jerusalem: The West Bank Data Project.

_____. 1984. "The Missing Age Group: Demography." In *The West Bank Data Project: A Survey of Israeli's Policies*, ed. Meron Benvenisti, 1–7. Washington, D.C., and London: American Enterprise Institute for Public Policy Research.

Sabbagh, Suha, ed. 1996. *Arab Women Between Defiance and Restraint*. New York: Olive Branch Press.

_____. 1998. *Palestinian Women of Gaza and the West Bank*. Bloomington and Indianapolis: Indiana University Press.

Sahlins, Marshal. 1981. *Historical Metaphors and Mythical Realities: Structure in the Early History of the Sandwich Islands Kingdom*. Ann Arbor: University of Michigan Press.

_____. 1994. "Goodbye to Tristes Tropes: Ethnography in the Context of Modern World History." In *Assessing Cultural Anthropology*, ed. Robert Borofsky, 377–94. New York: McGraw-Hill.

Sahliyeh, Emile. 1988. *In Search of Leadership: West Bank Politics Since 1967*. Washington, D.C.: Brookings Institution.

Said, Wadie. 2001. "The Obligations of Host Countries to Refugees Under International Law: The Case of Lebanon." In *Palestinian Refugees: The Right of Return*, ed. Naseer Aruri, 123–51. London and Sterling, Va.: Pluto Press.

Samara, Adel. 1992. *Industrialisation in the West Bank*. Jerusalem: Al-Mashariq Publications for Economic and Development Studies.

Sanabary, Nagat. 1985. "Continuity and Change in Women's Education in the Arab States." In *Women and the Family in the Middle East: New Voices of Change*, ed. Elizabeth Fernea, 93–110. Austin: University of Texas Press.

Sayigh, Rosemary. 1979. *Palestinians: From Peasants to Revolutionaries*. London: Zed Press.

___. 1988. "Palestinians in Lebanon: Status Ambiguity, Insecurity and Flux." *Race and Class* 30, no. 1: 13–32.

___. 1994. *Too Many Enemies*. London: Zed Press.

___. 1995. "Palestinians in Lebanon: Harsh Present, Uncertain Future." *Journal of Palestine Studies* 25, no. 1: 37–53.

Sayigh, Yezid. 1989. "The Intifada Continues: Legacy, Dynamics and Challenges," *Third World Quarterly* 11, no. 3: 20–49.

___. 1997. *Armed Struggle and the Search for State: The Palestinian National Movement, 1949–1993*. Oxford and Washington, D.C.: Oxford University Press and Institute for Palestine Studies.

Sayigh, Yusif. 1988. "Dispossession and Pauperisation: The Palestinian Economy Under Occupation." In *The Palestinian Economy: Studies in Development Under Prolonged Occupation*, ed. George Abed, 259–65. London: Routledge.

Schiff, Benjamin. 1989. "Between Occupier and Occupied: UNRWA in the West Bank and Gaza." *Journal of Palestine Studies* 18, no. 3: 60–75.

___. 1995. *Refugees unto the Third Generation: UN Aid to the Palestinians*. Syracuse: Syracuse University Press.

Seccombe, Ian. 1985. "International Labor Migration in the Middle East: A Review of Literature and Research, 1974–84." *International Migration Review* 19, no. 2: 335–52.

___. 1986. "Immigrant Workers in an Emigrant Economy: An Examination of the Replacement Migration in the Middle East." *International Migration* 24, no. 2: 378–89.

___. 1987a. "Labour Emigration Policies and Economic Development in Jordan: From Unemployment to Labour Shortage." In *The Economic Development of Jordan*, eds. Adnan Badran and Bichara Khader, 118–32. Beckenham, Kent: Croom Helm.

___. 1987b. "Labour Migration and the Transformation of a Village Economy: A Case from North-West Jordan." In *The Middle Eastern Village*, ed. Richard Lawless, 115–44. London: Croom Helm.

Sela, Avraham. 1984. *The Palestinian Baʿth*. Jerusalem: The Magnes Press, Hebrew University.

Shaaban, Bouthaina. 1991. *Both Right Handed and Left Handed: Palestinian Women Talk About Their Lives*. Bloomington: Indiana University Press.

Shaath, Nabil. 1972. "High Level Palestinian Manpower" *Journal of Palestine Studies* 1, no. 2: 80–95.

Shadid, Mohammed. 1988. "Israeli Policy Toward Economic Development in the West Bank and Gaza" In *The Palestinian Economy: Studies in Development Under Prolonged Occupation*, ed. George Abed, 121–38. London and New York: Routledge.

Shakhatreh, Hussein. 1995. "Determinants of Female Labour-Force Participation in Jordan." In *Gender and Development in the Arab World*, eds. Nabil Khoury and Valentine Moghadam, 125–47. London: Zed Books and United Nations University Press.

Sharabi, Hisham. 1985. "The Dialectics of Patriarchy in Arab Society." In *Arab Society*, ed. Samih Farsoun, 83–104. London: Croom Helm.

Share, M. A. J. 1987. "The Use of Jordanian Workers' Remittances." In *The Economic Development of Jordan*, ed. Adnan Badran and Bichara Khader, 32–44. Beckenham, Kent: Croom Helm.

Sharp, Gene. 1990. "The Intifada and Nonviolent Struggle." *Journal of Palestine Studies* 19, no. 1: 3–13.

Shehadeh, Raja. 1980. *The West Bank and the Rule of Law*. Ramallah: The International Commission of Jurists and Law in the Service of Man.

———. 1984. "The Changing Juridical Status of Palestinian Areas Under Occupation." In *Occupation: Israel over Palestine*, ed. Naseer Aruri, 97–116. London: Zed Books.

———. 1993. "The Legislative Stages of the Israeli Military Occupation." In *The Law and the Land*, ed. Raja Shehadeh. Jerusalem: Palestinian Academic Society for the Study of International Affairs.

Shehadeh, Raja, and Jonathan Kuttab. 1980. *The West Bank and the Rule of Law*. Geneva: International Commission of Jurists and Law in the Service of Man.

Shiblak, Abbas. 1997. "Palestinians in Lebanon and the PLO." *Journal of Refugee Studies* 10, no. 3: 261–74.

Siniora, Randa. 1989. *Palestinian Labor in a Dependent Economy: Women Workers in the West Bank Clothing Industry*. Cairo Papers in Social Science, vol. 12, monograph 3. Cairo: American University in Cairo Press.

Smith, Pamela Ann. *Palestine and the Palestinians: 1876–1983*. New York: St. Martin Press, 1984.

Sosebee, Stephen. 1991. "The Palestinian Women's Movement and the Intifada: A Historical and Current Analysis." *American-Arab Affairs*, no. 32 (spring): 81–91.

Stork, Joe. 1988. "The Significance of Stones: Notes from the Seventh Month," *Middle East Report* (Sept.–Oct.): 4–11.

Strum, Philippa. 1992. *The Women Are Marching: The Second Sex and the Palestinian Revolution*. New York: Lawrence Hill Books.

———. 1998. "West Bank Women and the Intifada: Revolution Within the Revolution." In *Palestinian Women of Gaza and the West Bank*, ed. Suha Sabbagh, 63–77. Bloomington and Indianapolis: Indiana University Press.

Sullivan, Anthony. 1988. *Universities Under Occupation*. Cairo Papers in Social Science, vol. 11, monograph 2. Cairo: American University in Cairo Press.

———. 1989. "Politics and Relevance in Palestinian Higher Education: The Case of Birzeit University." *American-Arab Affairs*, no. 27 (winter): 58–69.

———. 1994. "Palestinian Universities in the West Bank and Gaza Strip," *The Muslim World* 84, nos. 1–2: 168–88.

Taha, Almutawakel. 1988. *Zaman Al Su'ud: Poetry of Taha Almutawakel* (in Arabic). Jerusalem: Union of Palestinian Writers in the Occupied Territories.

Tahir, Jamil. 1985. "An Assessment of Palestinian Human Resources: Higher Education and Manpower." *Journal of Palestine Studies* 14, no. 3: 32–53.

Tamari, Salim. 1980. "The Palestinians in the West Bank and Gaza: The Sociology of Dependency." In *The Sociology of the Palestinians*, eds. Khalil Nakhleh and Elia Zureik, 84–111. London: Croom Helm.

———. 1981. "Building Other People's Homes: The Palestinian Peasant's Household and Work in Israel." *Journal of Palestine Studies* 11, no. 1: 31–66.

___. 1984. "Israel's Search for a Native Pillar: The Village Leagues." In *Occupation: Israel over Palestine*, ed. Naseer Aruri, 377–90. London: Zed Books.

___. 1988. "What the Uprising Means." *Middle East Report*, no. 152 (May–June): 24–30.

___. 1990. "The Uprising's Dilemma." *Middle East Report*, nos. 164–65 (May–Aug.): 4–8.

___. 1991. "The Palestinian Movement in Transition: Historical Reversals and the Uprising." *Journal of Palestine Studies* 20, no. 2: 57–70.

Taraki, Lisa. 1991. "The Development of Political Consciousness Among Palestinians in the West Bank and Gaza Strip, 1967–87." In *Intifada: Palestine at the Crossroads*, eds. Jamal Nassar and Roger Heacock, 53–72. New York: Birzeit University and Praeger Publishers.

Tawil, Raymonda. 1979. *My Home, My Prison*. New York: Holt, Reinhart, and Winston.

Thompson, E. P. 1978. *The Poverty of Theory and Other Essays*. New York and London: Monthly Review Press.

Thompson, John B. 1989. "The Theory of Structuration." In *Social Theory of Modern Societies: Anthony Giddens and His Critics*, eds. David Held and John B. Thompson, 56–76. Cambridge: Cambridge University Press.

Tilly, Charles. 1978. *From Mobilization to Revolution*. Reading, Mass.: Addison-Wesley.

Tucker, Judith. 1993. "The Arab Family in History: 'Otherness' and the Study of the Family." In *Old Boundaries, New Frontiers*, ed. Judith Tucker, 195–207. Bloomington: Indiana University Press.

UNCTAD (United Nations Conference on Trade and Development). 1993. *Prospects for Sustained Development of the Palestinian Economy in the West Bank and Gaza Strip*. Report of a Meeting of Experts, convened by the UNCTAD secretariat, 19–22 May 1992 at the Palais des Nations, Geneva. UNCTAD/DSD/SEU/2 (Sept.).

___. 1996. *Prospects for Sustained Development of the Palestinian Economy: Strategies and Policies for Reconstruction and Development*. UNCTAD/ECDU/SEU/12 (Aug.).

UNESCO (United Nations Educational, Scientific, and Cultural Organization). 1970. *Statistical Yearbook*. Paris: UNESCO.

___. 1981. *Statistical Yearbook*. Paris: UNESCO.

___. 1994. *Statistical Yearbook*. Paris: UNESCO.

UNRWA (United Nations *Relief and Works Agency for Palestine Refugees in the Near East*). 1951. *Report of the Commissioner General (1 July 1950–30 June 1951)*. General Assembly, Official Records, Sixth Session, Supplement nos. 16 and 16A (A/1905 and Add. 1).

___. 1955. *Report of the Commissioner (1 July 1954–30 June 1955)*. General Assembly, Official Records, Tenth Session, Supplements nos. 15 and 15A (A/2978 and Add. 1).

___. 1958. *Report of the Commissioner General (1 July 1957–30 June 1958)*. General Assembly, Official Records, Thirteenth Session, Supplement no. 14 (A/3931 and A/3948).

___. 1964. *Report of the Commissioner General (1 July 1963–30 June 1964)*. General Assembly, Official Records, Nineteenth Session, Supplement no. 13 (A/5813).

___. 1966. *Report of the Commissioner General (1 July 1965–30 June 1966)*. General Assembly, Official Records, Twenty-first Session, Supplement no. 13 (A/7213).

———. 1968. *Report of the Commissioner General (1 July 1967–30 June 1968)*. General Assembly, Official Records, Twenty-third Session, Supplement no. 13 (A/7213).

———. 1971. *Report of the Commissioner General (1 July 1970–30 June 1971)*. General Assembly, Official Records, Twenty-sixth Session, Supplement No. 13 (A/8413).

———. 1975. *Report of the Commissioner General (1 July 1974–30 June 1975)*. General Assembly, Official Records, Thirtieth Session, Supplement no. 13 (A/10013).

———. 1980. *Report of the Commissioner General (1 July 1979–30 June 1980)*. General Assembly, Official Records, Thirty-fifth Session, Supplement no. 13 (A/35/13).

———. 1985. *Report of the Commissioner General (1 July 1984–30 June 1985)*. General Assembly, Official Records, Fortieth Session, Supplement No. 13 (A/40/13).

———. 1986. *UNRWA: A Brief History, 1950–1982*. Vienna: UNRWA.

———. 1989. *Report of the Commissioner General (1 July 1988–30 June 1989)*. General Assembly, Official Records, Forty-fourth Session, Supplement no. 13 (A/44/13).

———. 1992. *Report of the Commissioner General (1 July 1991–30 June 1992)*. General Assembly, Official Records, Forty-seventh Session, Supplement no. 13 (A/47/13).

———. 1997. *Report of the Commissioner General (1 July 1996–30 June 1997)*. General Assembly, Official Records, Fifty-second Session, Supplement No. 13 (A/52/13).

———. 1999. *Report of the Commissioner General (1 July 1998–30 June 1999*. General Assembly, Official Records, Fifty-fourth Session, Supplement No. 13 (A/54/13).

Usher, Graham. 1991. "Children of Palestine." *Race and Class* 32, no. 4: 1–18.

———. 1995. *Palestine in Crisis*. London: Pluto Press.

Van Arkadie, Brian. 1977. *Benefits and Burdens: A Report on the West Bank and the Gaza Strip Economies Since 1967*. New York and Washington, D.C.: Carnegie Endowment for International Peace.

Viorst, Milton. 1989. *Reaching for the Olive Branch: UNRWA and Peace in the Middle East*. Washington, D.C.: The Middle East Institute.

Wahlin, Lars. 1987. "Diffusion and Acceptance of Modern Schooling in Rural Jordan." In *The Middle Eastern Village*, ed. Richard Lawless, 145–75. London: Croom Helm.

Wallerstein, Immanuel. 1974. *The Modern World System*. New York: Academic Press.

Warnock, Kitty. 1990. *Land Before Honor: Palestinian Women in the Occupied Territories*. New York: Monthly Review Press.

Williams, Raymond. 1977. *Marxism and Literature*. Oxford: Oxford University Press.

Winckler, Onn. 1997. "The Immigration Policy of the Gulf Cooperation Council (GCC) States." *Middle Eastern Studies* 33, no. 3: 480–93.

Winternitz, Helen. 1991. *A Season of Stones*. New York: Atlantic Monthly Press.

Wolf, Eric. 1982. *Europe and the People Without History*. Berkeley: University of California Press.

Wolpe, Harold. 1975. "The Theory of Internal Colonialism: The South African Case." In *Beyond the Sociology of Development*, ed. Ivar Oxaal, Tony Barnet, and David Booth. London: Routledge and Kegan Paul.

The World Bank. 1993a. *Developing the Occupied Territories: An Investment in Peace*. Vol. 1. Overview. Washington, D.C.: World Bank.

———. 1993b. *Developing the Occupied Territories: An Investment in Peace*. Vol. 2. The Economy. Washington, D.C.: World Bank.

____. 1993c. *Developing the Occupied Territories: An Investment in Peace.* Vol. 3. Private Sector Development. Washington, D. C.: World Bank.

____. 1993d. *Developing the Occupied Territories: An Investment in Peace.* Vol. 4. Agriculture. Washington, D.C.: World Bank.

____. 1993e. *Developing the Occupied Territories: An Investment in Peace.* Vol. 5. Infrastructure. Washington, D.C.: World Bank.

____. 1993f. *Developing the Occupied Territories: An Investment in Peace.* Vol. 6. Human Resources and Social Policy. Washington, D.C.: World Bank.

Yusuf, Muhsin D. 1979. "The Potential Impact of Palestinian Education on a Palestinian State." *Journal of Palestine Studies* 8, no. 4: 70–93.

Zahlan, Antoine B., and Rosemary Zahlan. 1977. "The Palestinian Future: Education and Manpower." *Journal of Palestine Studies* 6, no. 4: 103–12.

Zakai, Dan. 1988. *Economic Development in Judea-Samaria and the Gaza District, 1985–88* (in Hebrew). Jerusalem: Bank of Israel, Research Department.

Zureik, Elia. 1977. "Toward a Sociology of the Palestinians." *Journal of Palestine Studies* 6, no. 6: 3–16.

____. 1979. *The Palestinians in Israel: A Study in Internal Colonialism.* London: Routledge and Kegan Paul.

____. 1996. *Palestinian Refugees and the Peace Process.* Washington, D.C.: Institute for Palestine Studies.

Index

In names beginning with "Al-", that prefix is ignored for alphabetization purposes.